THE GHOST IN THE SHELL

STAND ALONE COMPLEX

EPISODE1:SECTION9

001

Yu Kinutani

Translation by
Andria Cheng

Adaptation by
Michael Braff

Lettered by
North Market Street Graphics

KC

KODANSHA
COMICS

A Kodansha Comics Trade Paperback Original.

Published in the United States by Kodansha Comics, an imprint of Kodansha USA Publishing, LLC., New York.

Publication rights for this English edition arranged through Kodansha Ltd., Tokyo.

First published in Japan in 2010 by Kodansha Ltd., Tokyo.

ISBN 978-1-935-42985-2

Printed in the United States of America.

www.kodanshacomics.com

9 8 7 6 5 4 3

Translator: Andria Cheng
Adapter: Michael Braff
Lettering: North Market Street Graphics

CONTENTS

HONORIFICS EXPLAINED

Throughout the Kodansha Comics books, you will find Japanese honorifics left intact in the translations. For those not familiar with how the Japanese use honorifics and, more important, how they differ from American honorifics, we present this brief overview.

Politeness has always been a critical facet of Japanese culture. Ever since the feudal era, when Japan was a highly stratified society, use of honorifics—which can be defined as polite speech that indicates relationship or status—has played an essential role in the Japanese language. When addressing someone in Japanese, an honorific usually takes the form of a suffix attached to one's name (example: "Asuna-san"), is used as a title at the end of one's name, or appears in place of the name itself (example: "Negi-sensei," or simply "Sensei!").

Honorifics can be expressions of respect or endearment. In the context of manga and anime, honorifics give insight into the nature of the relationship between characters. Many English translations leave out these important honorifics and therefore distort the feel of the original Japanese. Because Japanese honorifics contain nuances that English honorifics lack, it is our policy at Kodansha Comics not to translate them. Here, instead, is a guide to some of the honorifics you may encounter in Kodansha Comics books.

-san: This is the most common honorific and is equivalent to Mr., Miss, Ms., or Mrs. It is the all-purpose honorific and can be used in any situation where politeness is required.

-sama: This is one level higher than "-san" and is used to confer great respect.

-dono: This comes from the word "tono," which means "lord." It is an even higher level than "-sama" and confers utmost respect.

-kun: This suffix is used at the end of boys' names to express familiarity or endearment. It is also sometimes used by men among friends, or when addressing someone younger or of a lower station.

-chan: This is used to express endearment, mostly toward girls. It is also used for little boys, pets, and even among lovers. It gives a sense of childish cuteness.

Bozu: This is an informal way to refer to a boy, similar to the English terms "kid" and "squirt."

Sempai/
Senpai: This title suggests that the addressee is one's senior in a group or organization. It is most often used in a school setting, where underclassmen refer to their upperclassmen as "sempai." It can also be used in the workplace, such as when a newer employee addresses an employee who has seniority in the company.

Kohai: This is the opposite of "sempai" and is used toward underclassmen in school or newcomers in the workplace. It connotes that the addressee is of a lower station.

Sensei: Literally meaning "one who has come before," this title is used for teachers, doctors, or masters of any profession or art.

-[blank]: This is usually forgotten in these lists, but it is perhaps the most significant difference between Japanese and English. The lack of honorific means that the speaker has permission to address the person in a very intimate way. Usually, only family, spouses, or very close friends have this kind of permission. Known as yobisute, it can be gratifying when someone who has earned the intimacy starts to call one by one's name without an honorific. But when that intimacy hasn't been earned, it can be very insulting.

Ghost in the Shell
Stand Alone Complex
Episode 1: Section 9

Yu Kinutani

001

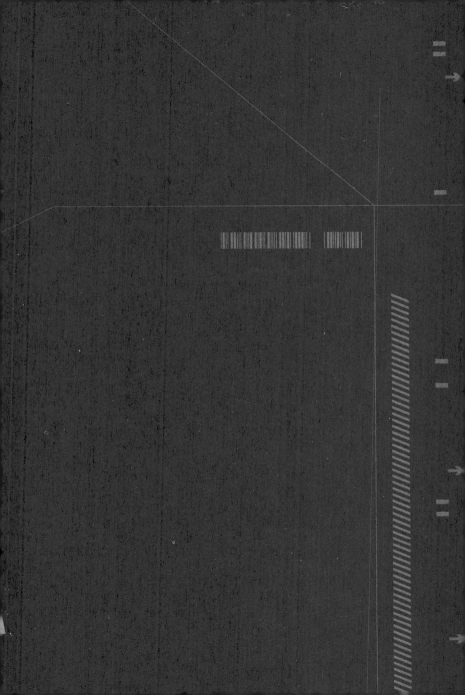

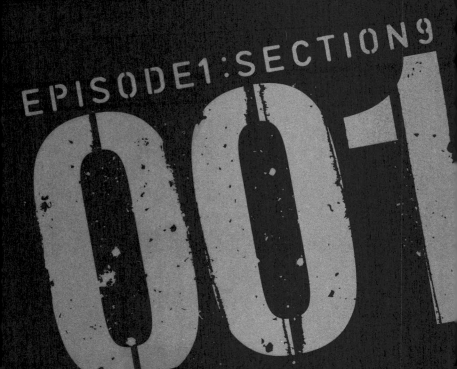

THE GHOST IN THE SHELL
STAND ALONE COMPLEX

EPISODE1 : SECTION9

00-1

CONTENTS

IN A TIME WHEN CONSCIOUSNESS
CAN BE DIGITIZED AND UPLOADED TO THE
NETWORK, ONLY THE "STANDALONES" REMAIN
OUTSIDE THE SYSTEM.

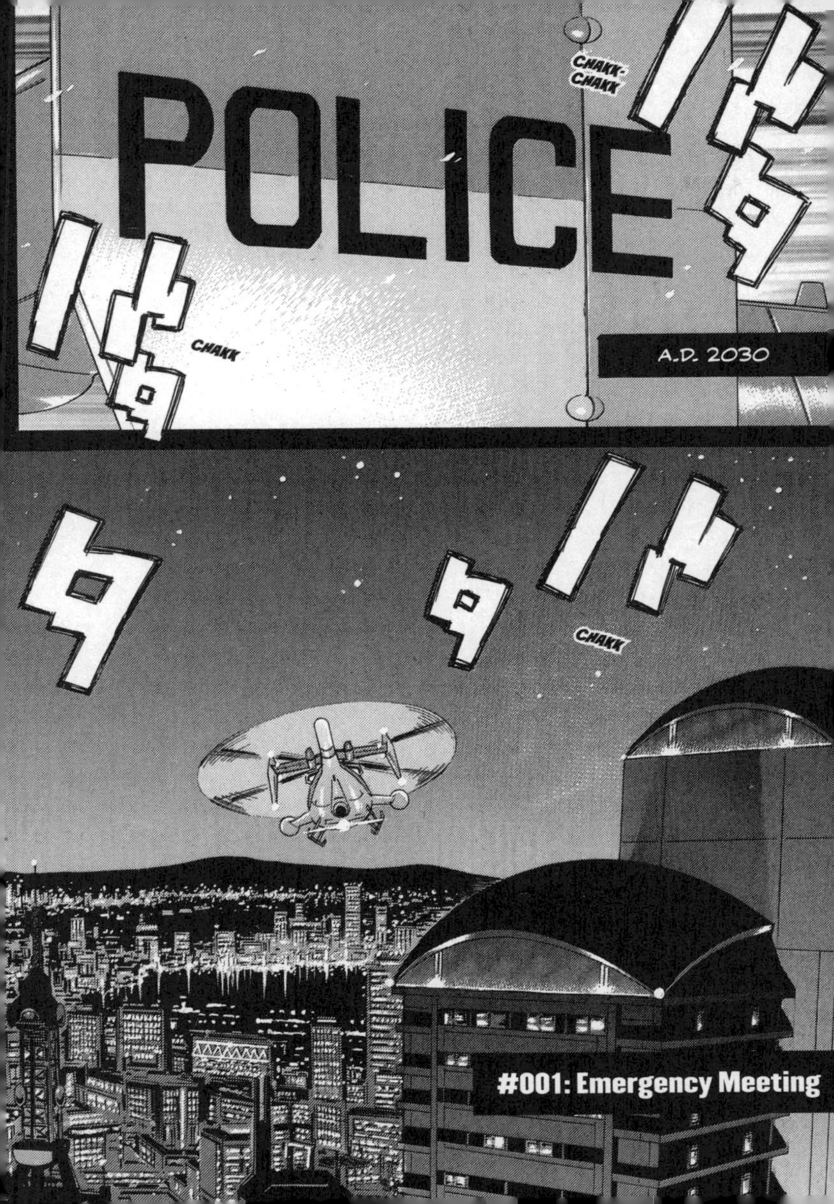
POLICE
CHAKK-
CHAKK
CHAKK
A.D. 2030
CHAKK
#001: Emergency Meeting

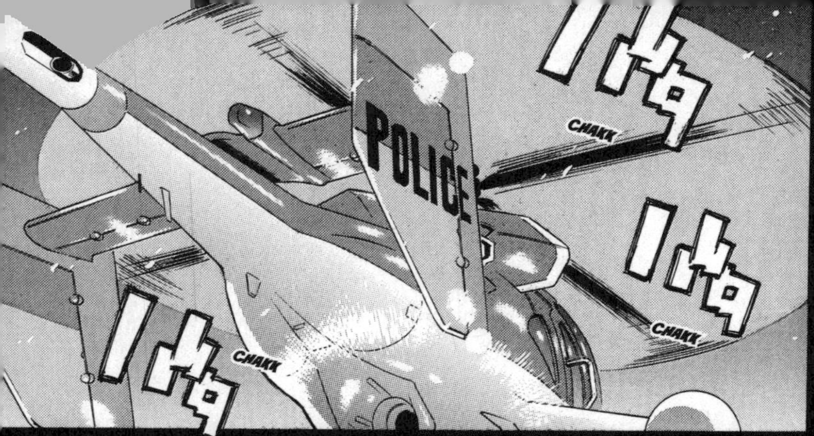
CHAKK
CHAKK
CHAKK

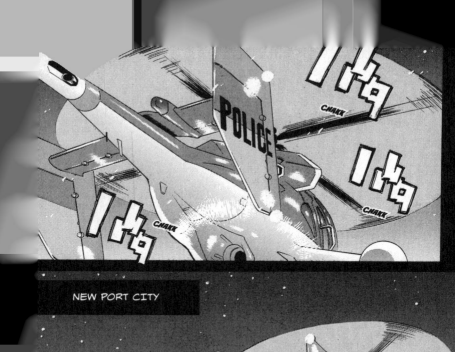

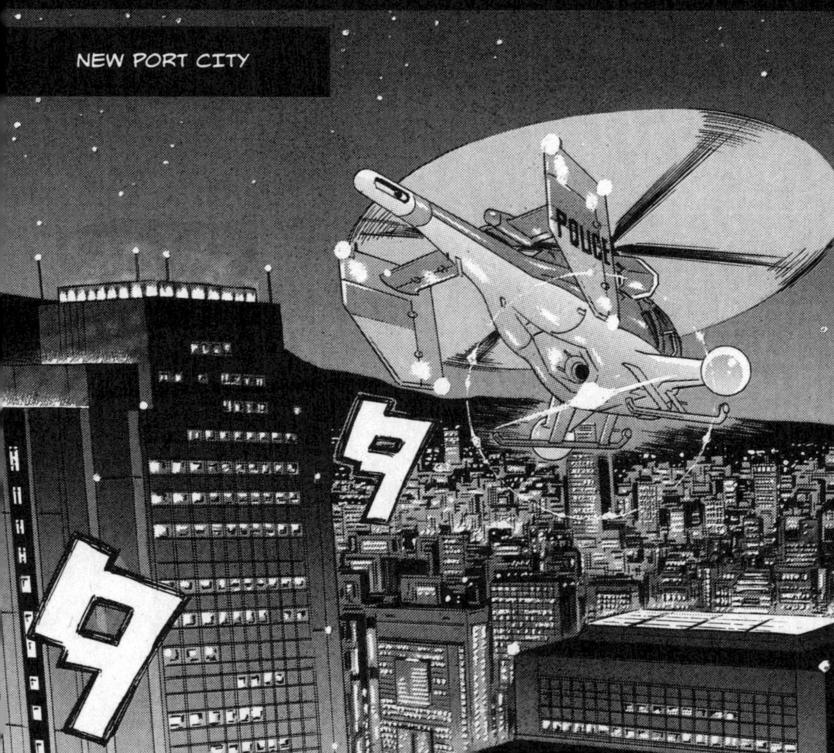
NEW PORT CITY

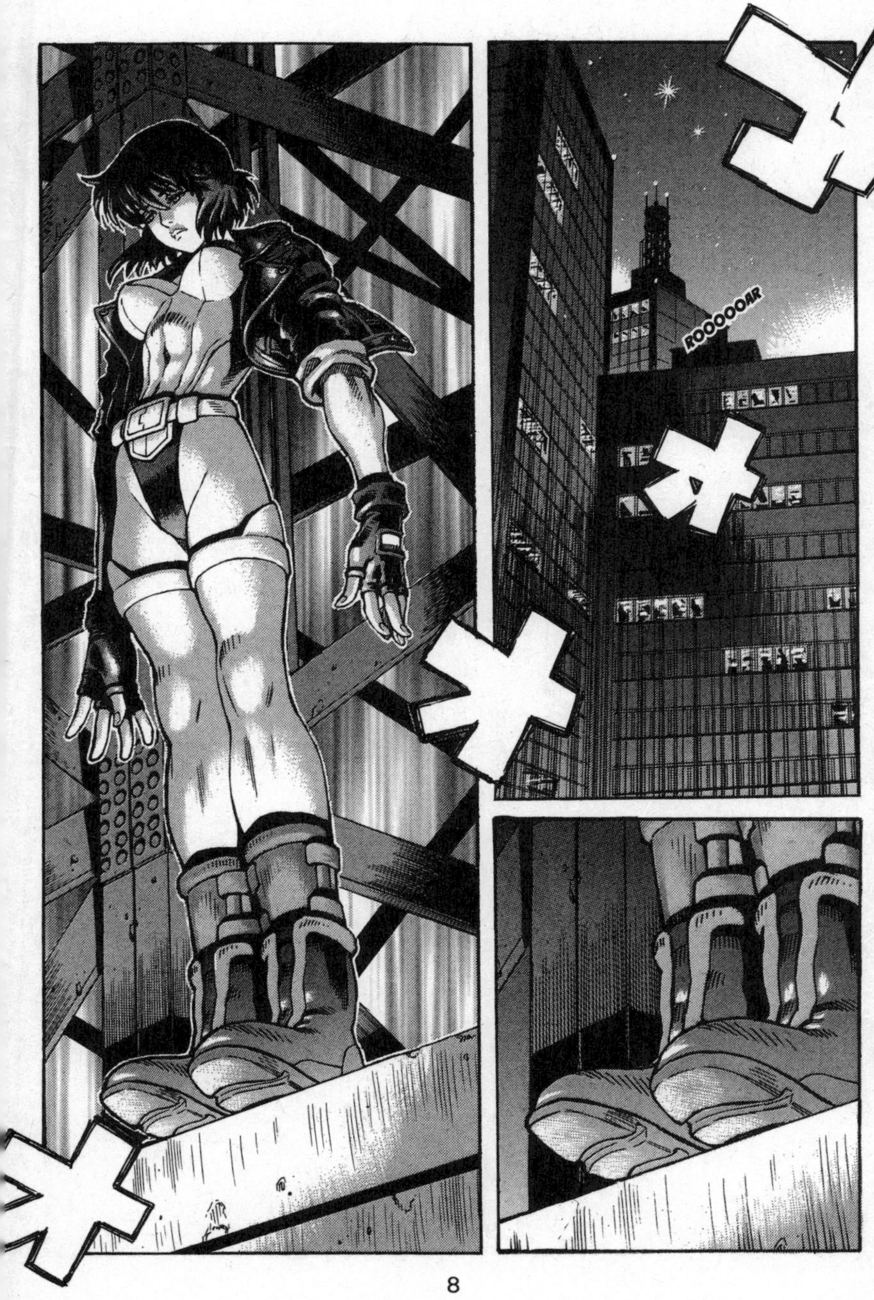
ROOOOOAR

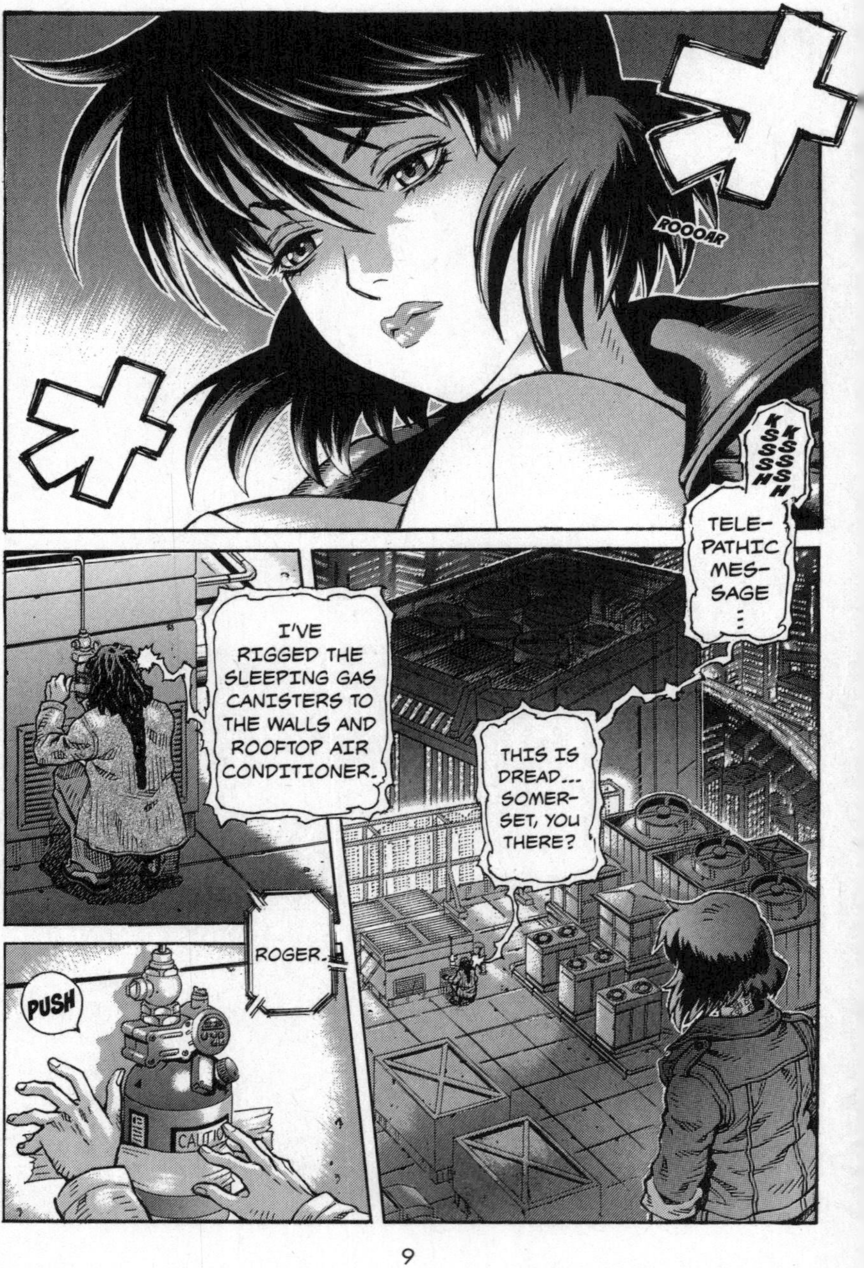
ROOOAR
KSSSH KSSSH
TELE-PATHIC MES-SAGE ...
THIS IS DREAD... SOMER-SET, YOU THERE?
I'VE RIGGED THE SLEEPING GAS CANISTERS TO THE WALLS AND ROOFTOP AIR CONDITIONER.
ROGER.
PUSH
CAUTIO

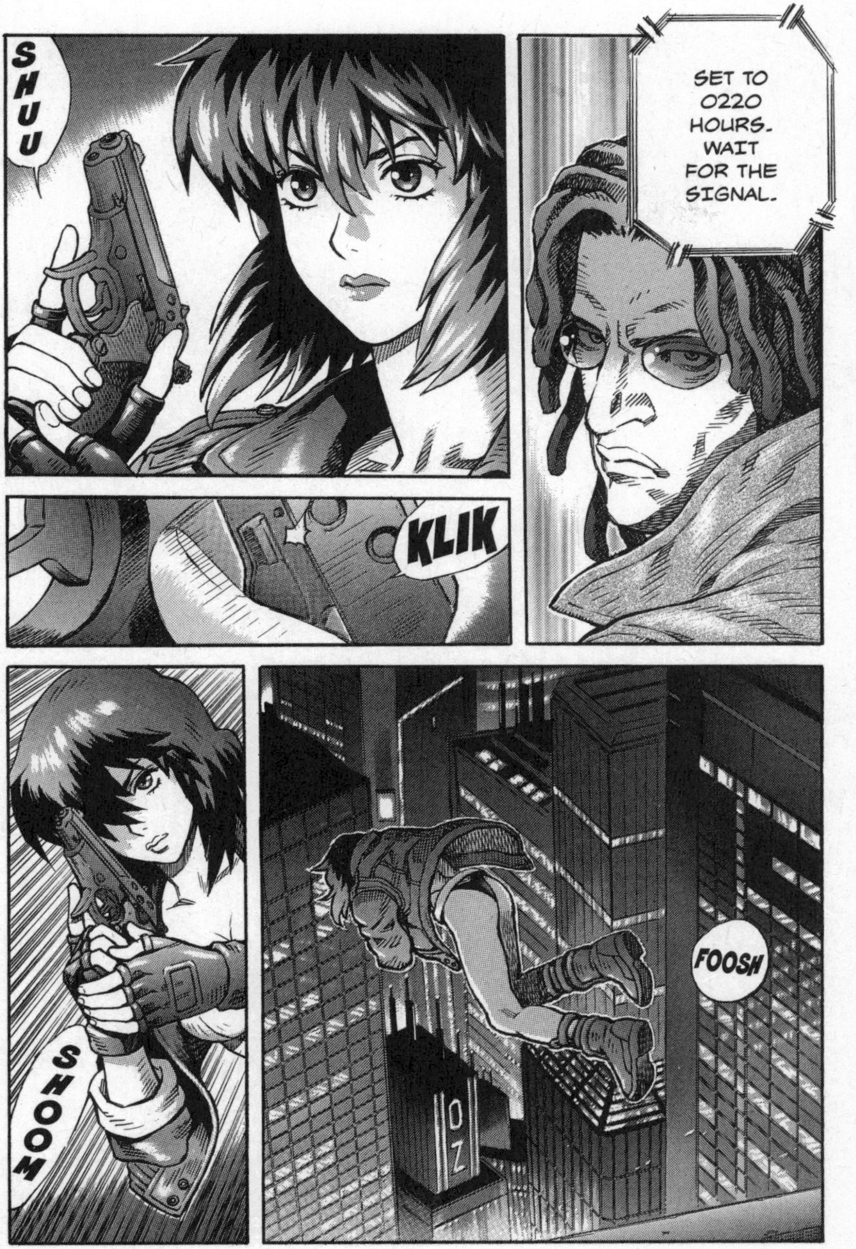
SET TO 0220 HOURS. WAIT FOR THE SIGNAL.
SHUUU
KLIK
FOOSH
SHOOM

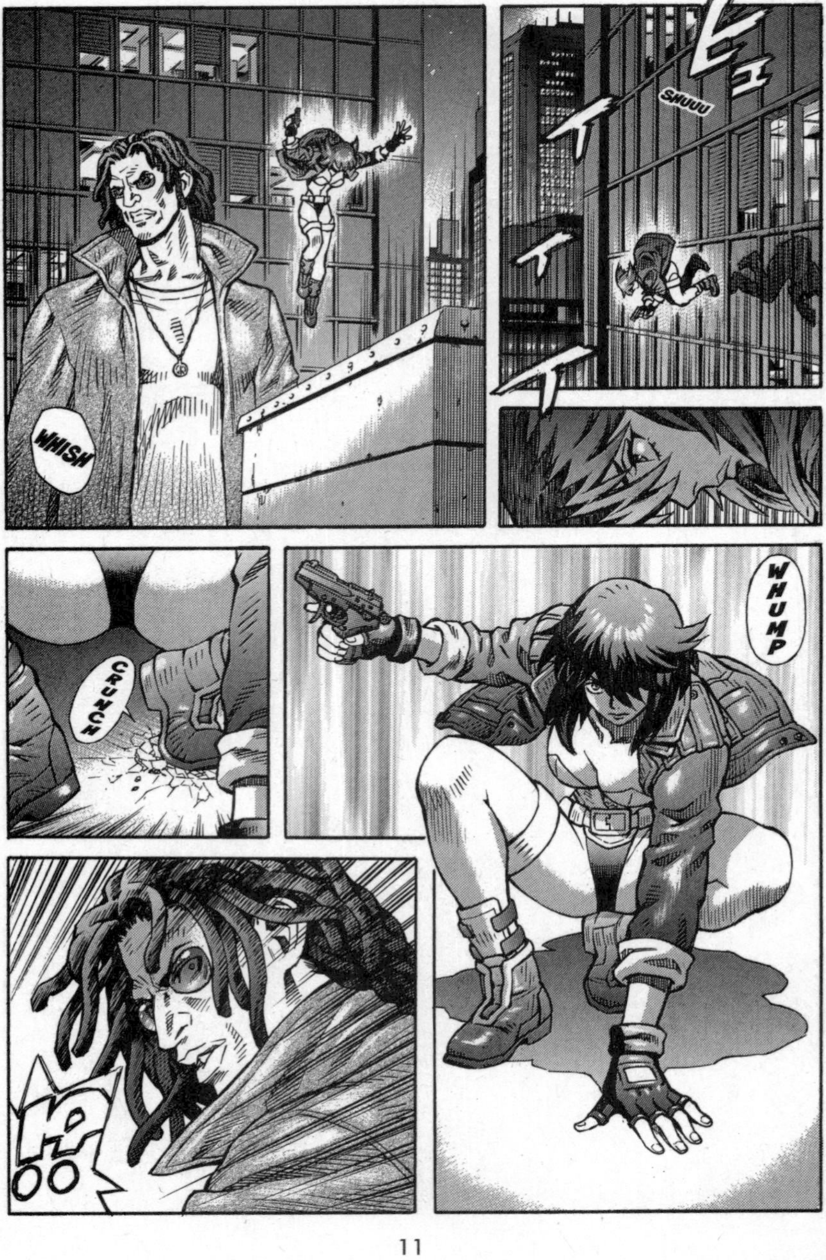
ヒュイイイ
SHUUU
WHISH
WHUMP
CRUNCH

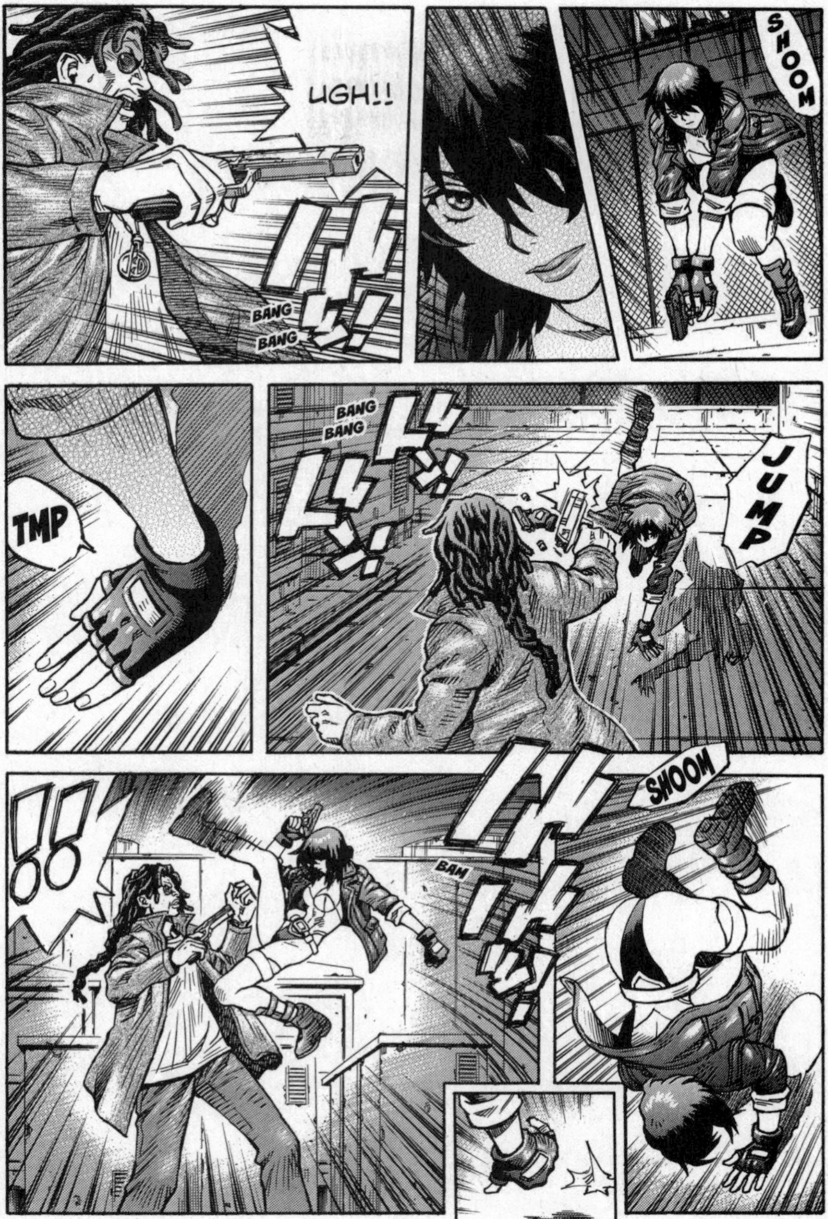
SHOOM
UGH!!
BANG
BANG
BANG
BANG
JUMP
TMP
SHOOM
BAM
!!

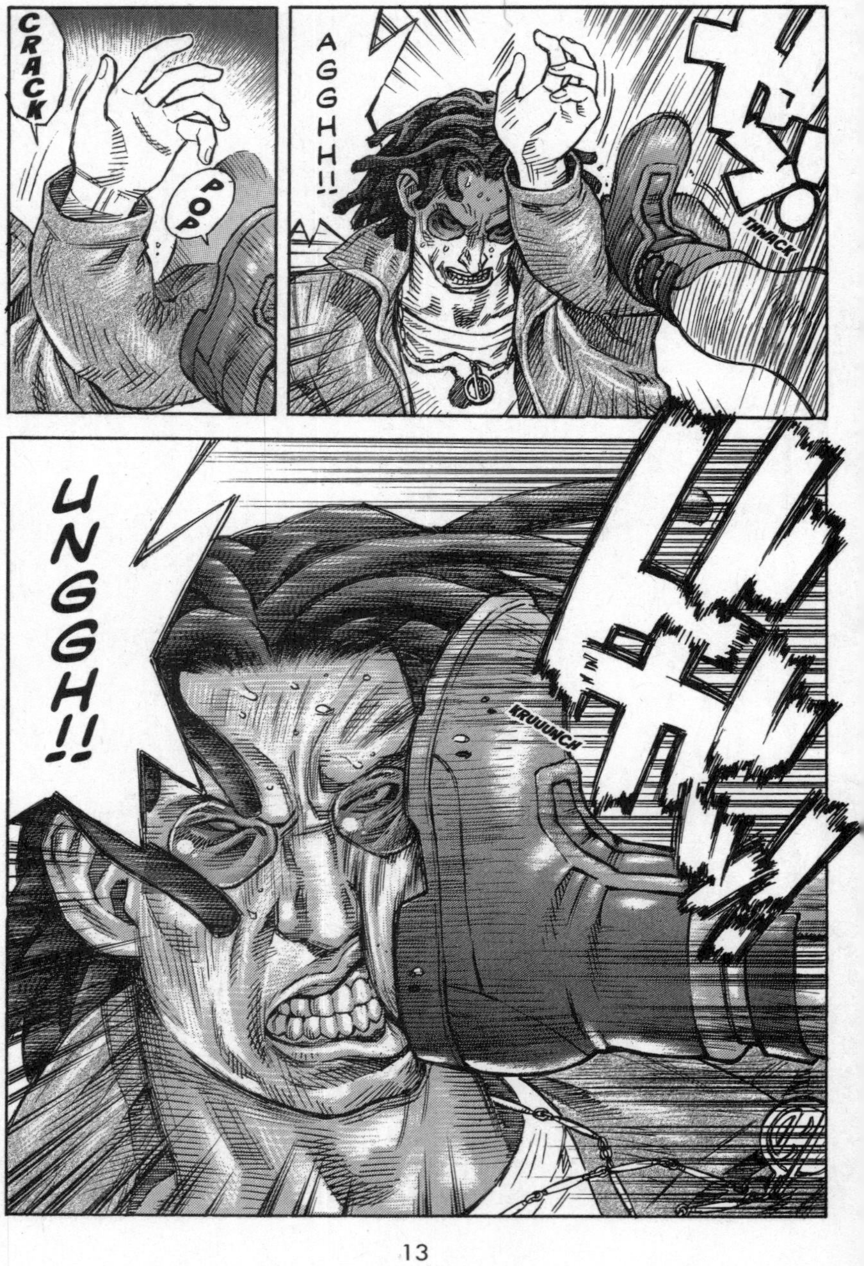
AGGHH!!
THWACK
CRACK
POP
UNGGGH!!
KRUUUNCH

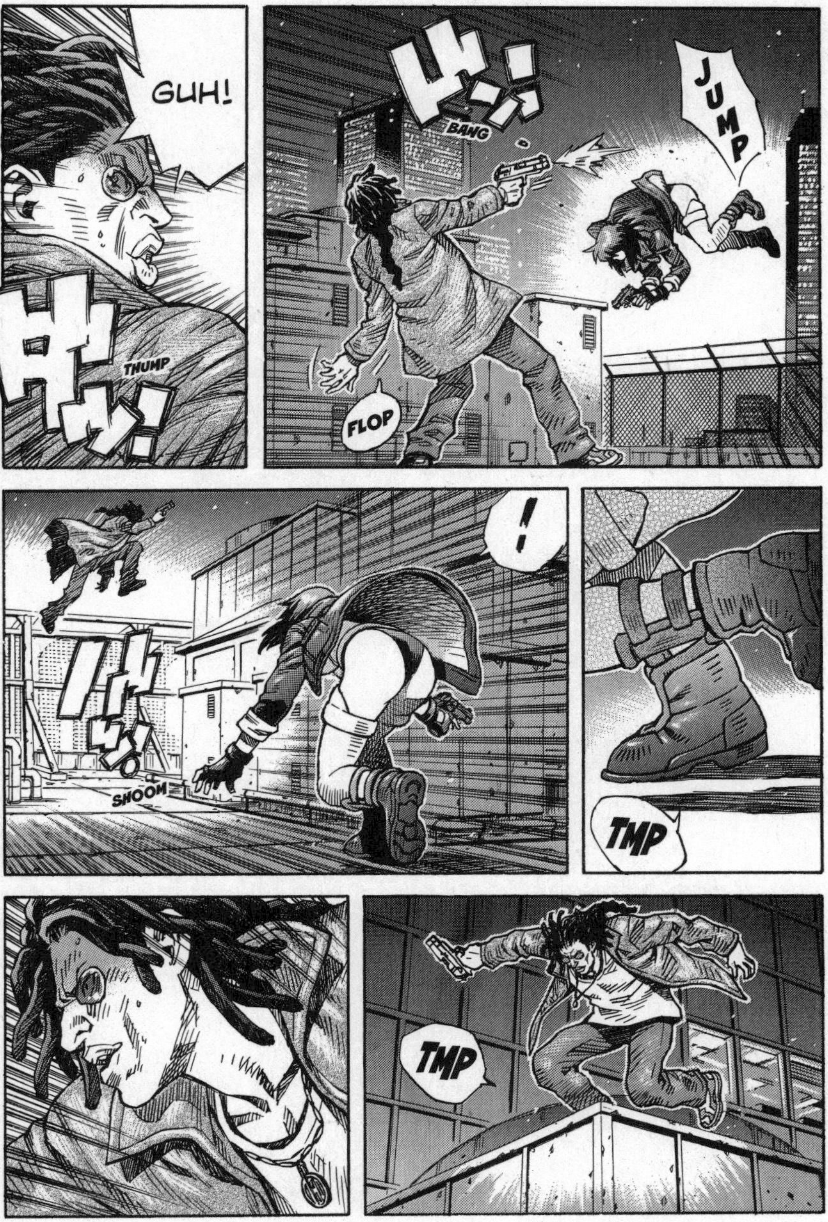
JUMP
BANG
FLOP
GUH!
THUMP
TMP
!
SHOOM
TMP

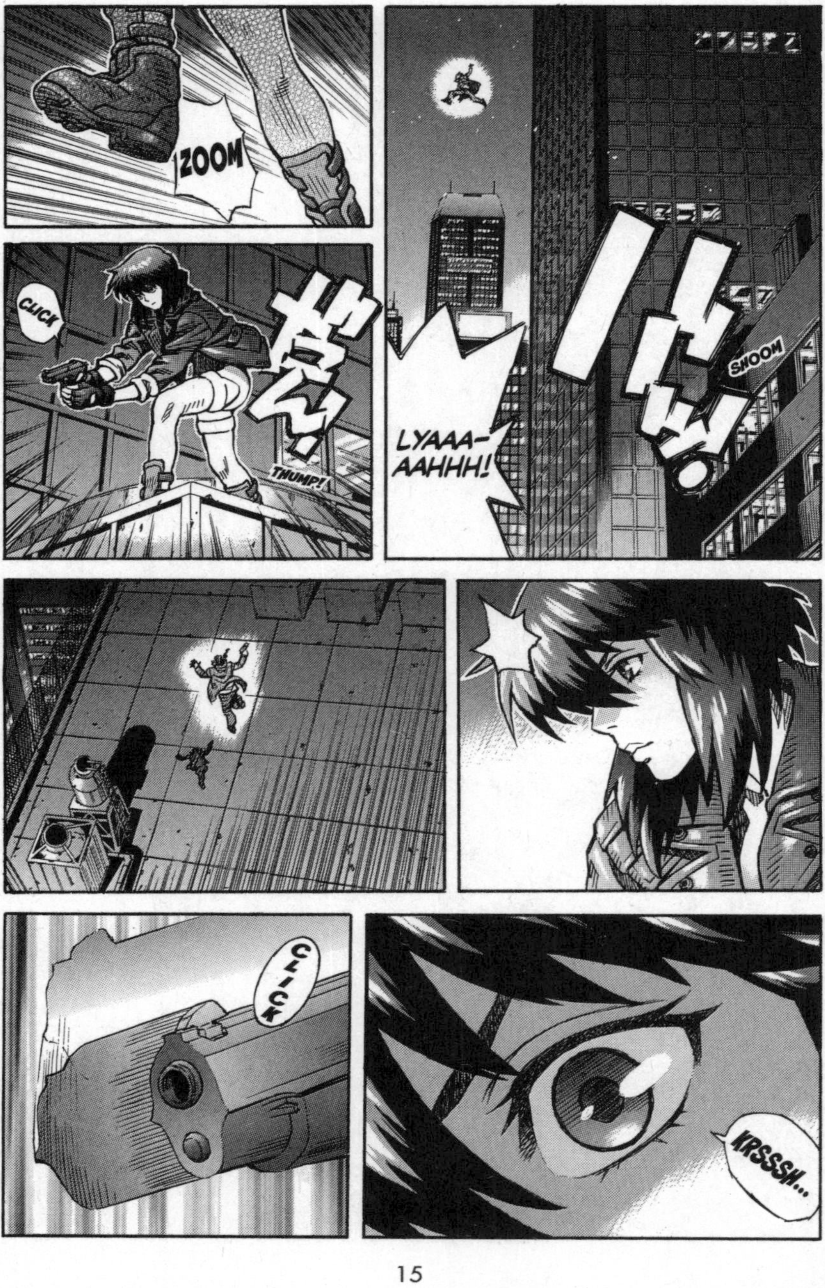
LYAAA-AAHHH!
SHOOM
ZOOM
CLICK
THUMP!
KRSSSH...
CLICK

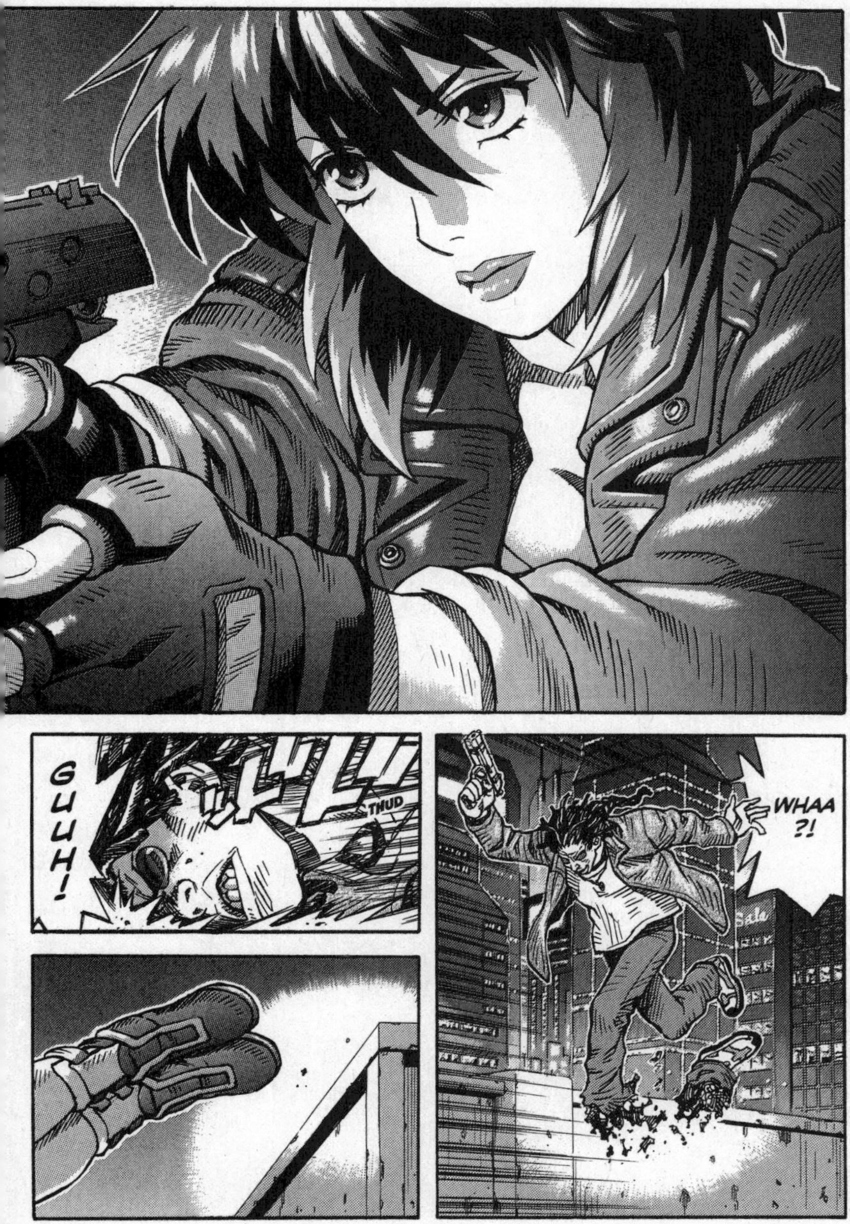
WHAA ?!
THUD
GUUH!

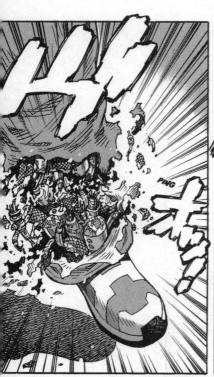

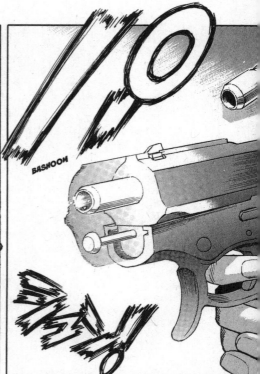

BASHOOM

PING

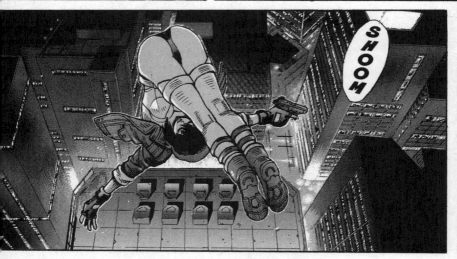

SHOOM

17

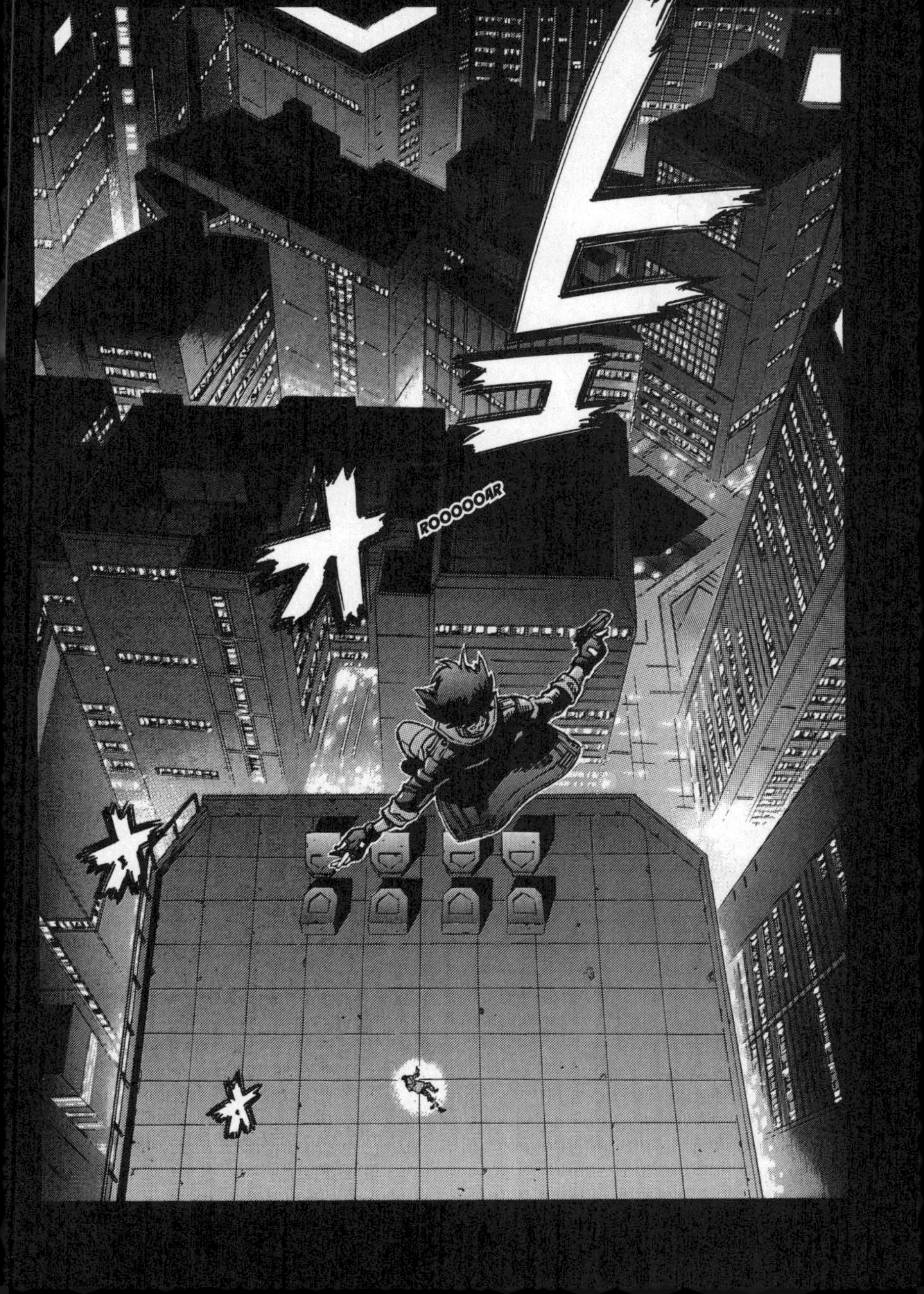
ROOOOOAR

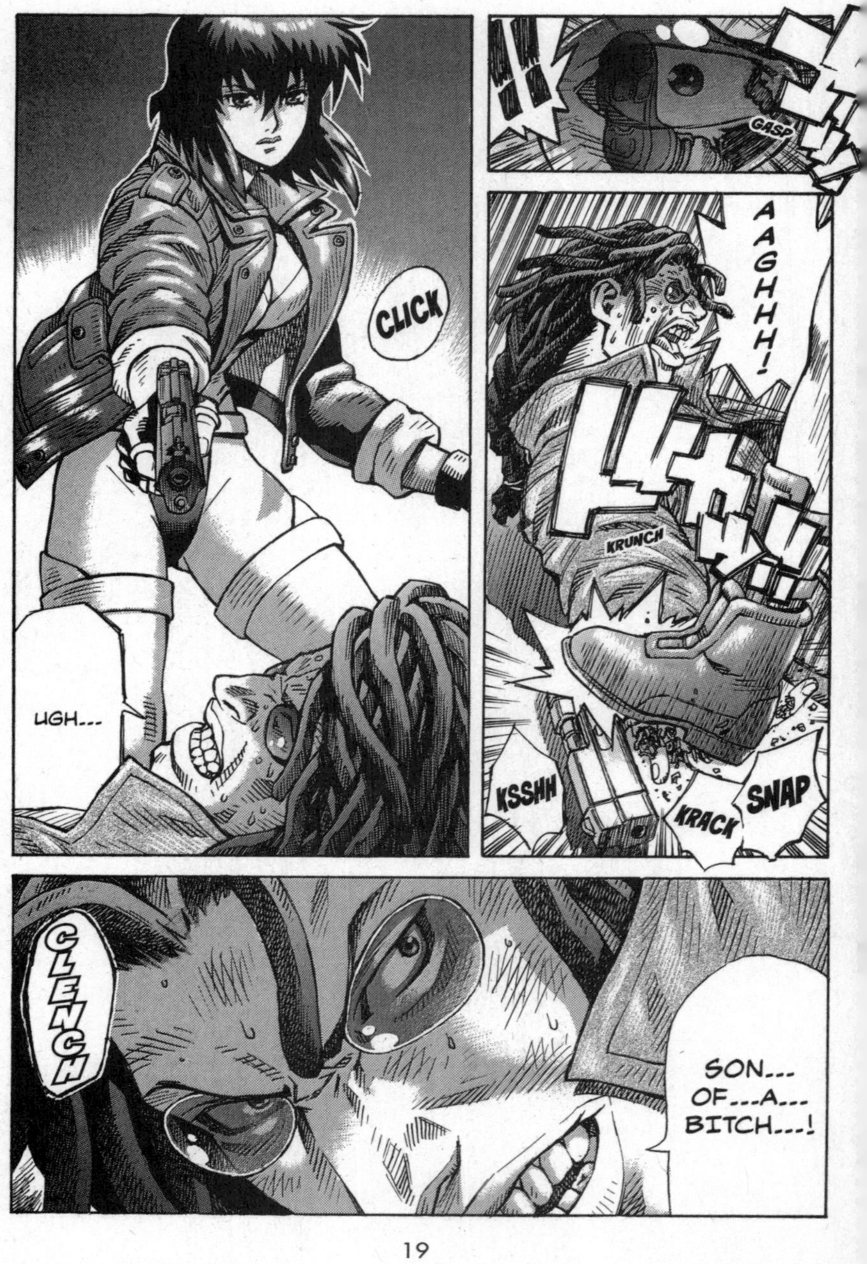
GASP
AAGHHHH!
KRUNCH
KSSHH
KRACK
SNAP
CLICK
UGH...
CLENCH
SON...
OF...A...
BITCH...!

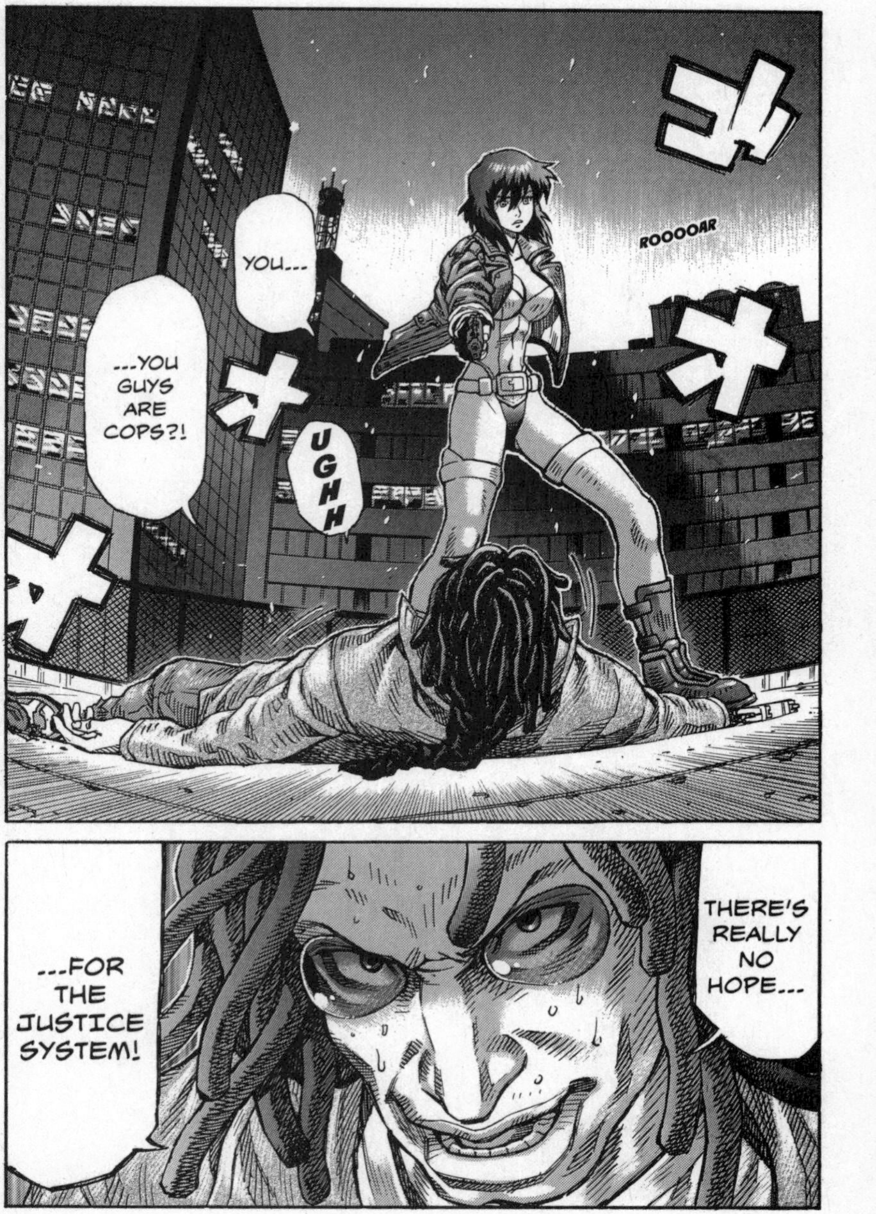
ROOOOAR
YOU...
...YOU GUYS ARE COPS?!
UGHH
THERE'S REALLY NO HOPE...
...FOR THE JUSTICE SYSTEM!

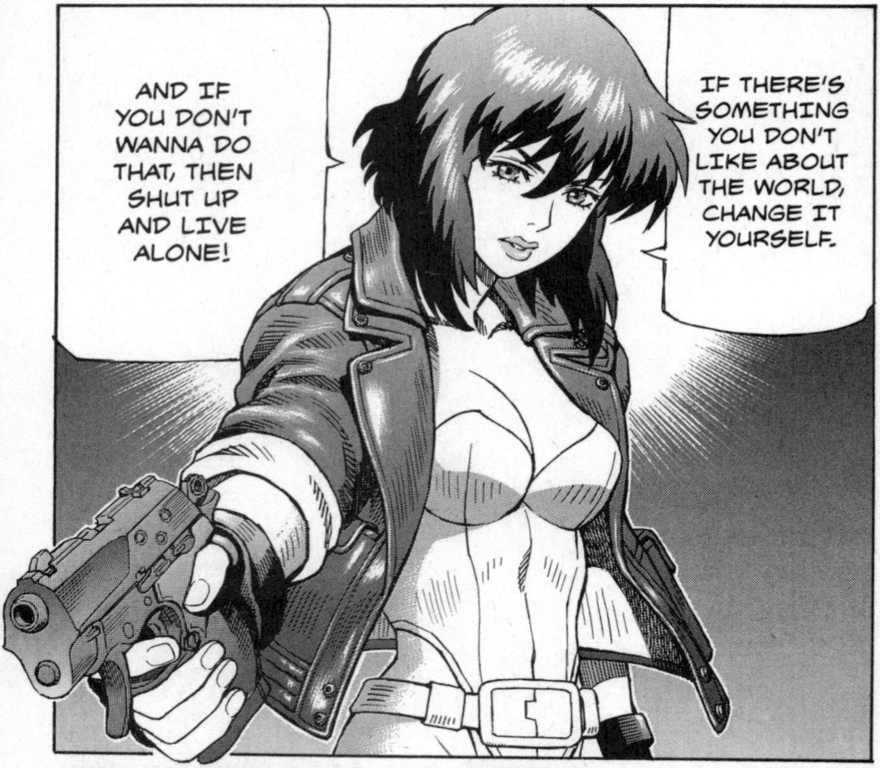
IF THERE'S SOMETHING YOU DON'T LIKE ABOUT THE WORLD, CHANGE IT YOURSELF.
AND IF YOU DON'T WANNA DO THAT, THEN SHUT UP AND LIVE ALONE!

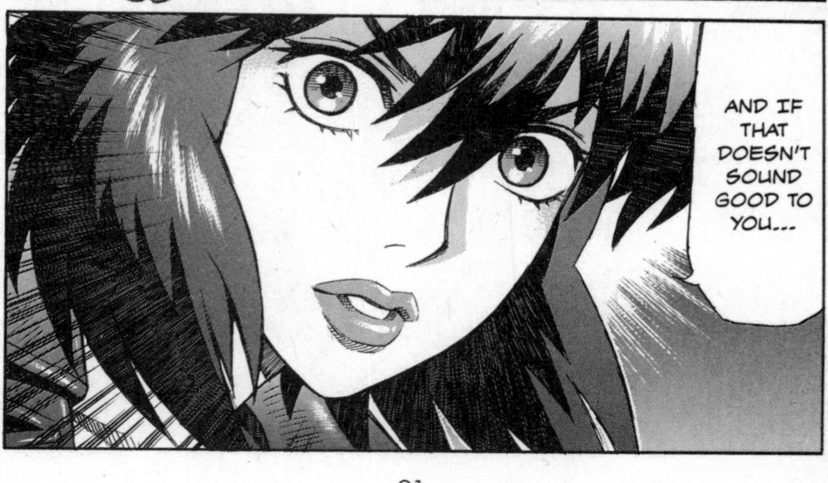
AND IF THAT DOESN'T SOUND GOOD TO YOU...

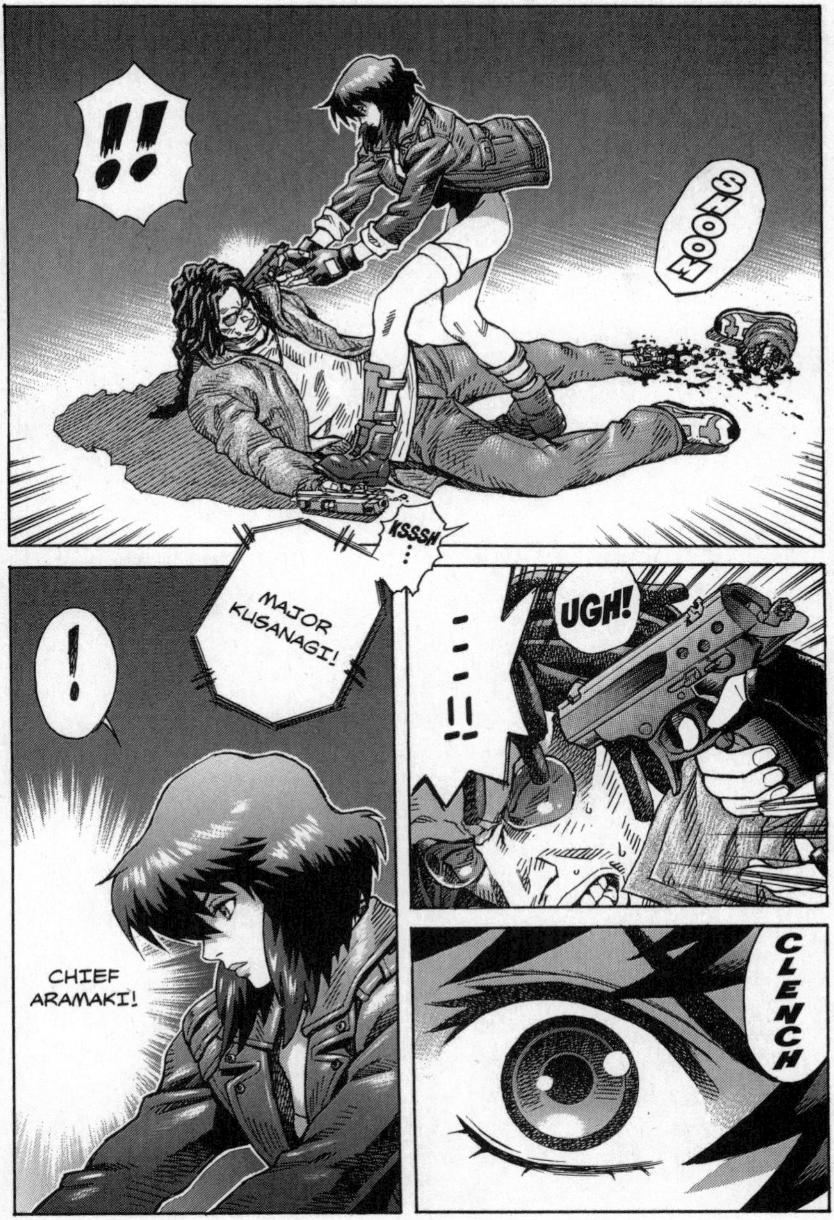
SHOOM
!!
KSSSH...
UGH!
...!!
CLENCH
MAJOR KUSANAGI!
!
CHIEF ARAMAKI!

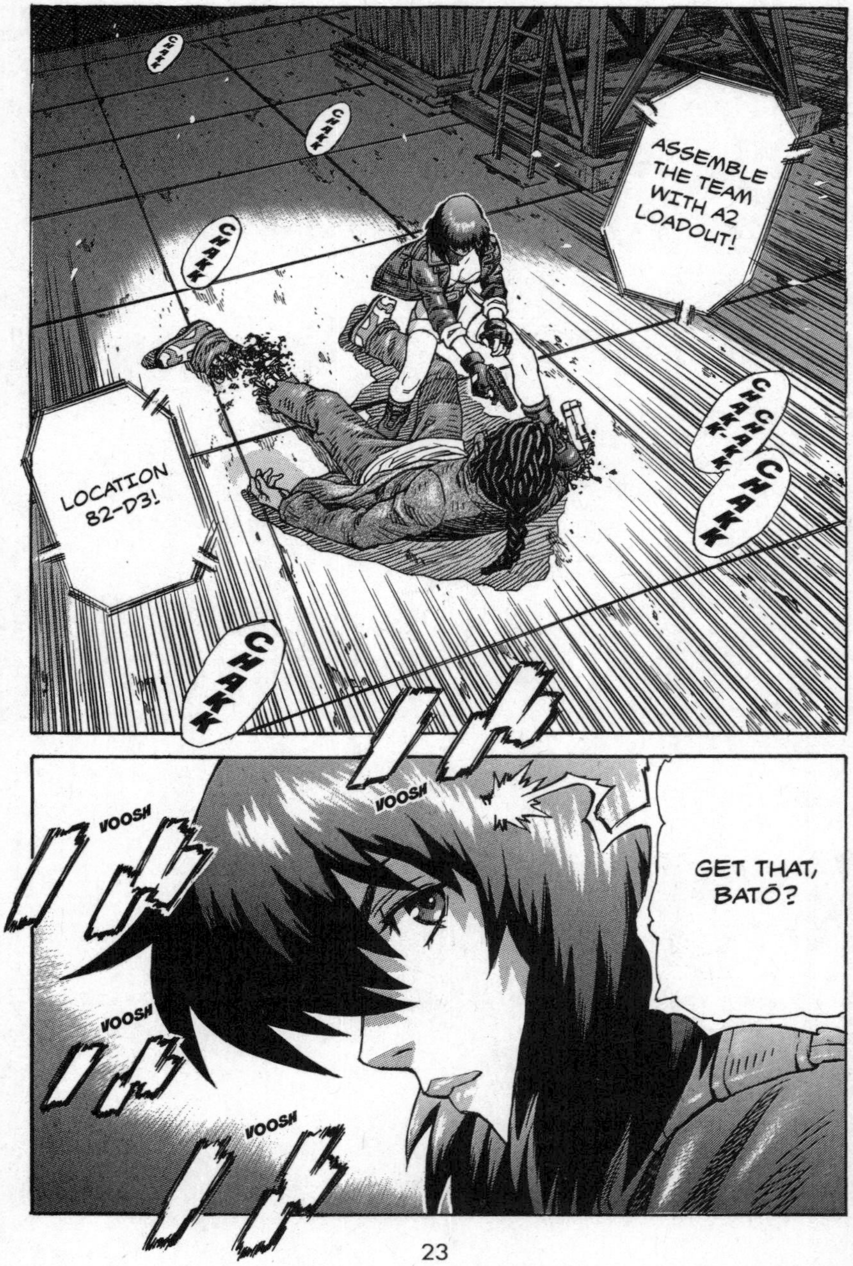
ASSEMBLE THE TEAM WITH A2 LOADOUT!
CHAKK
CHAKK
CHAKK
CHAKK
CHAKK
LOCATION 82-D3!
CHAKK
GET THAT, BATŌ?
VOOSH
VOOSH
VOOSH
VOOSH

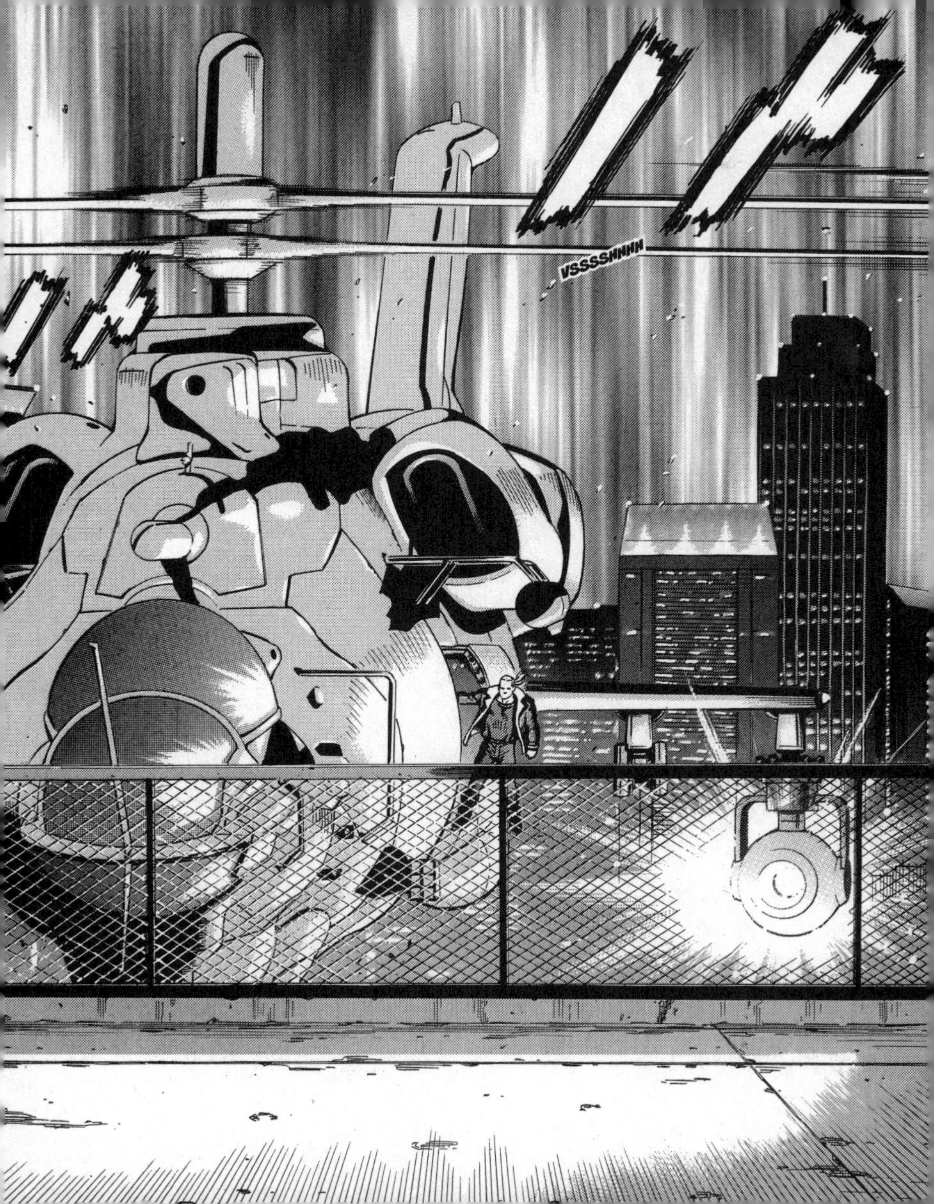
VSSSSHHHH

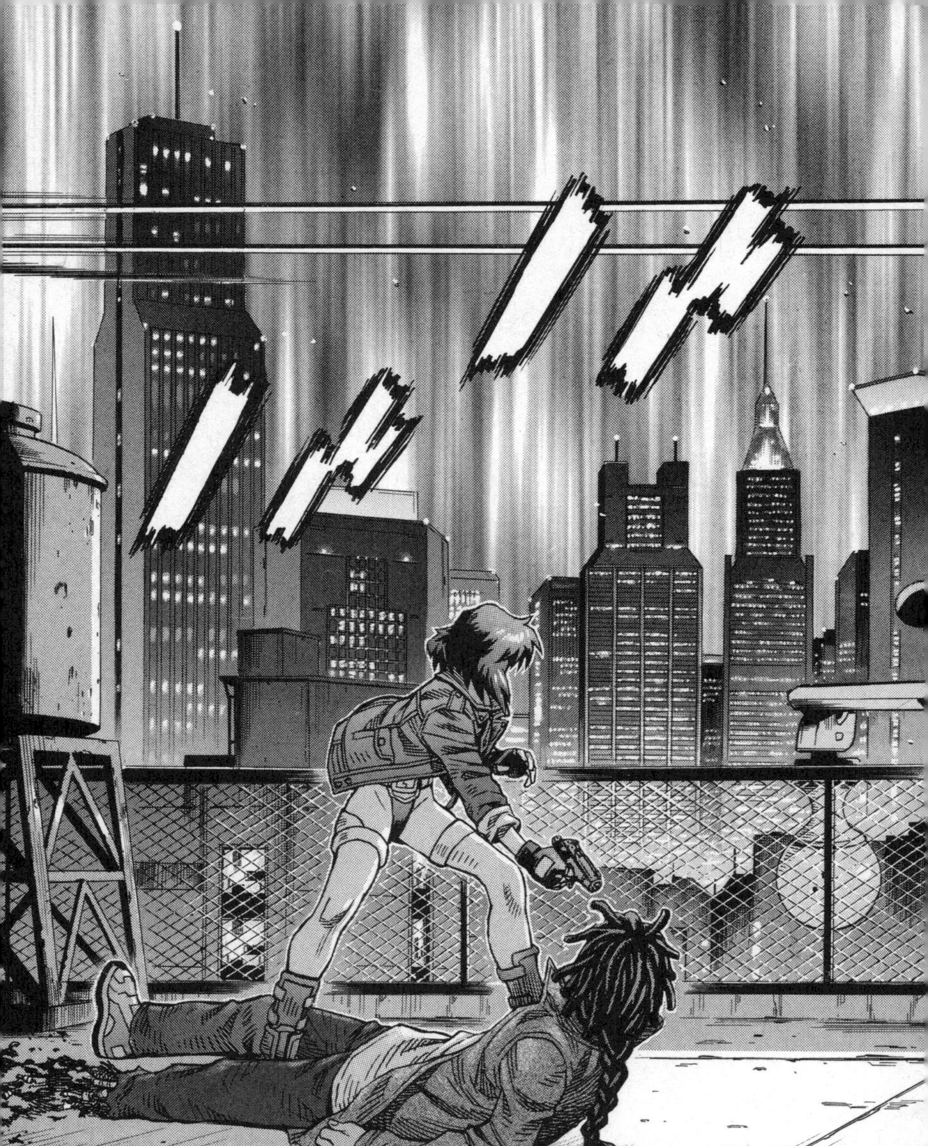

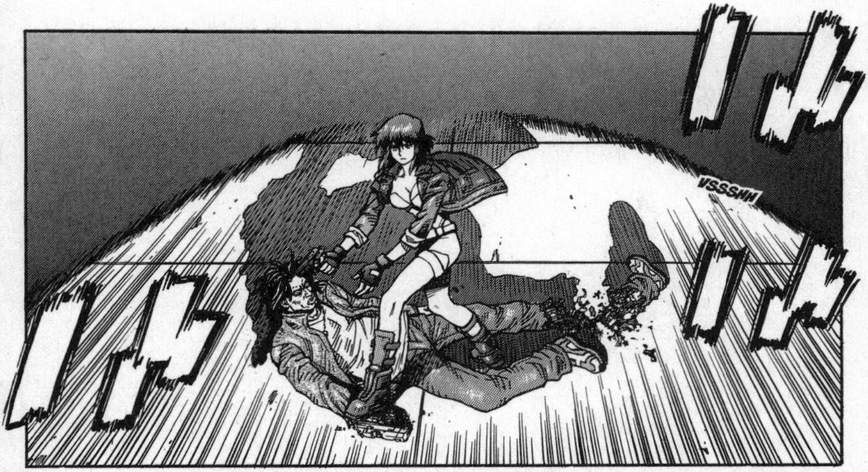
VSSSHH
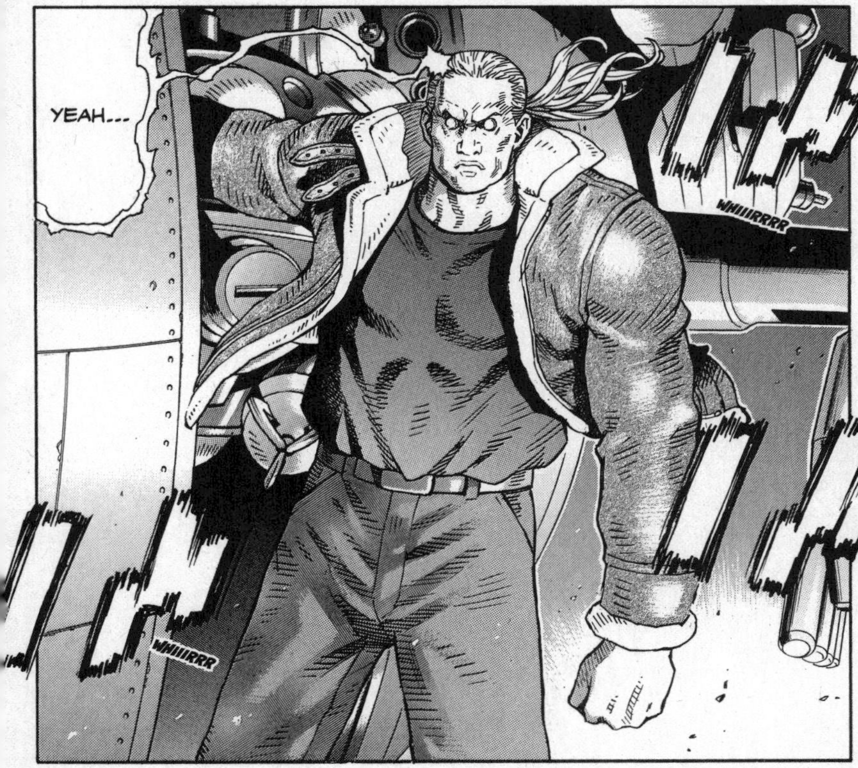
WHIIIRRRR
YEAH...
WHIIIRRR

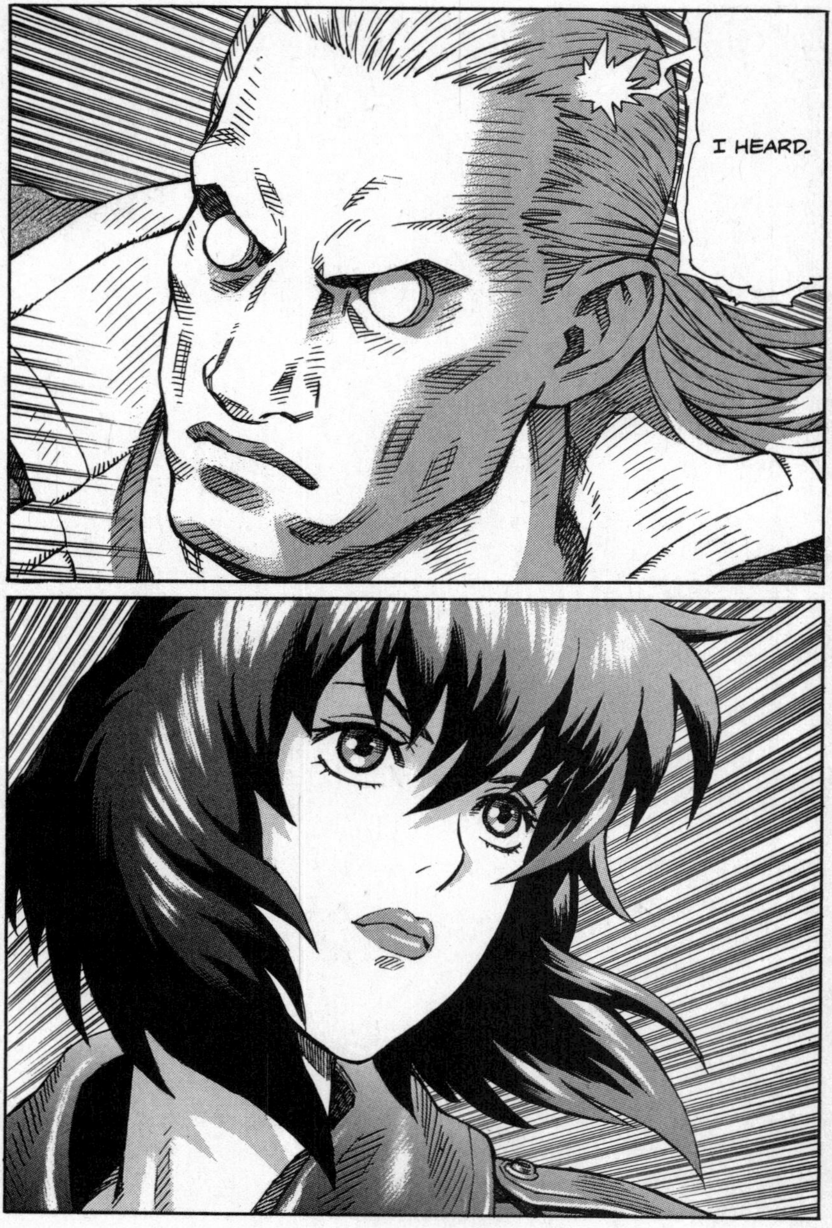
I HEARD.

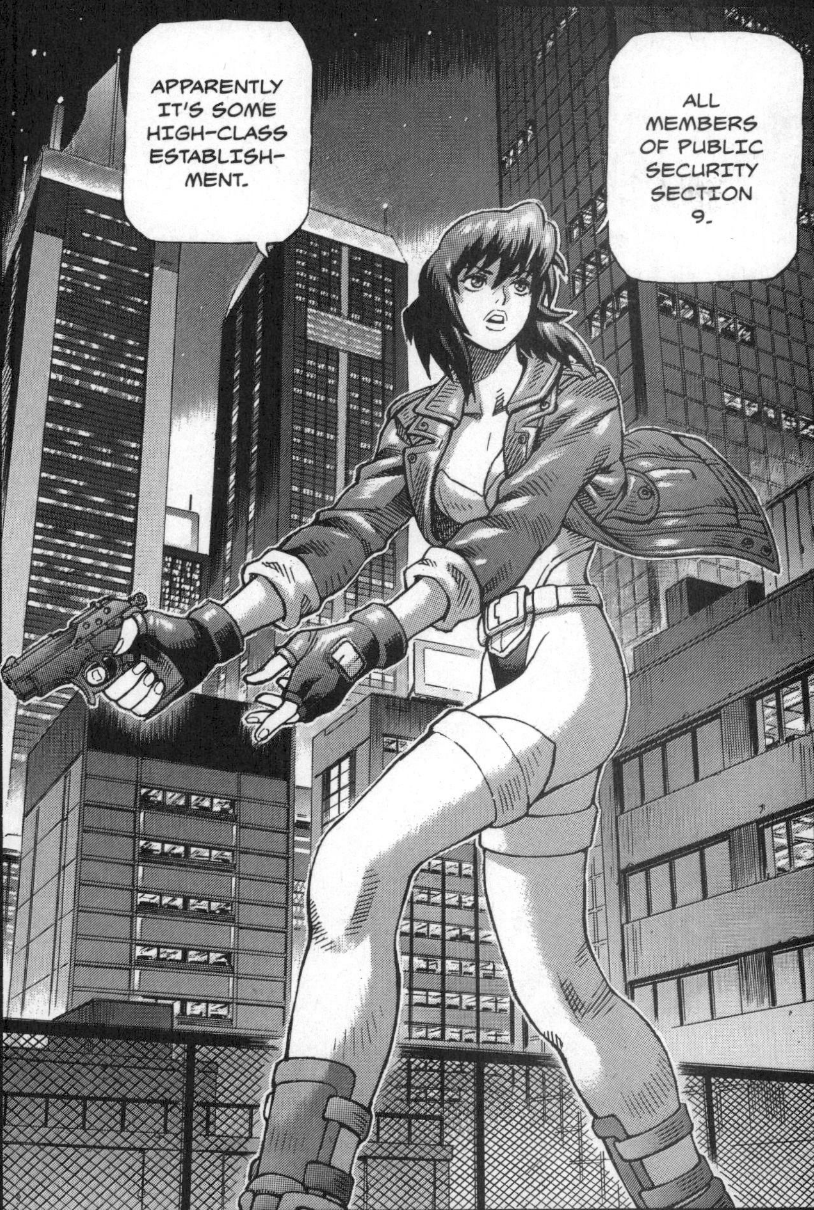
ALL MEMBERS OF PUBLIC SECURITY SECTION 9.
APPARENTLY IT'S SOME HIGH-CLASS ESTABLISHMENT.

WEEOOO
WEEOOO
WEEOOO
WUMP
WUMP
WUMP
WUMP
POL
CHIKAFUMI
WUMP

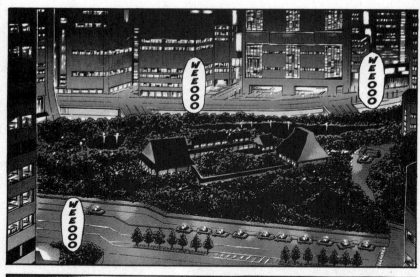

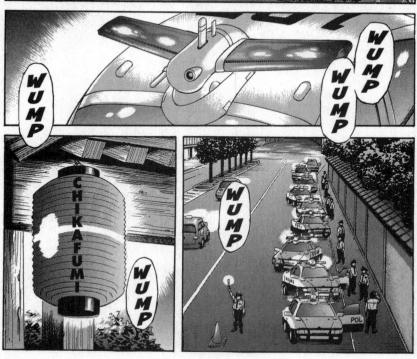

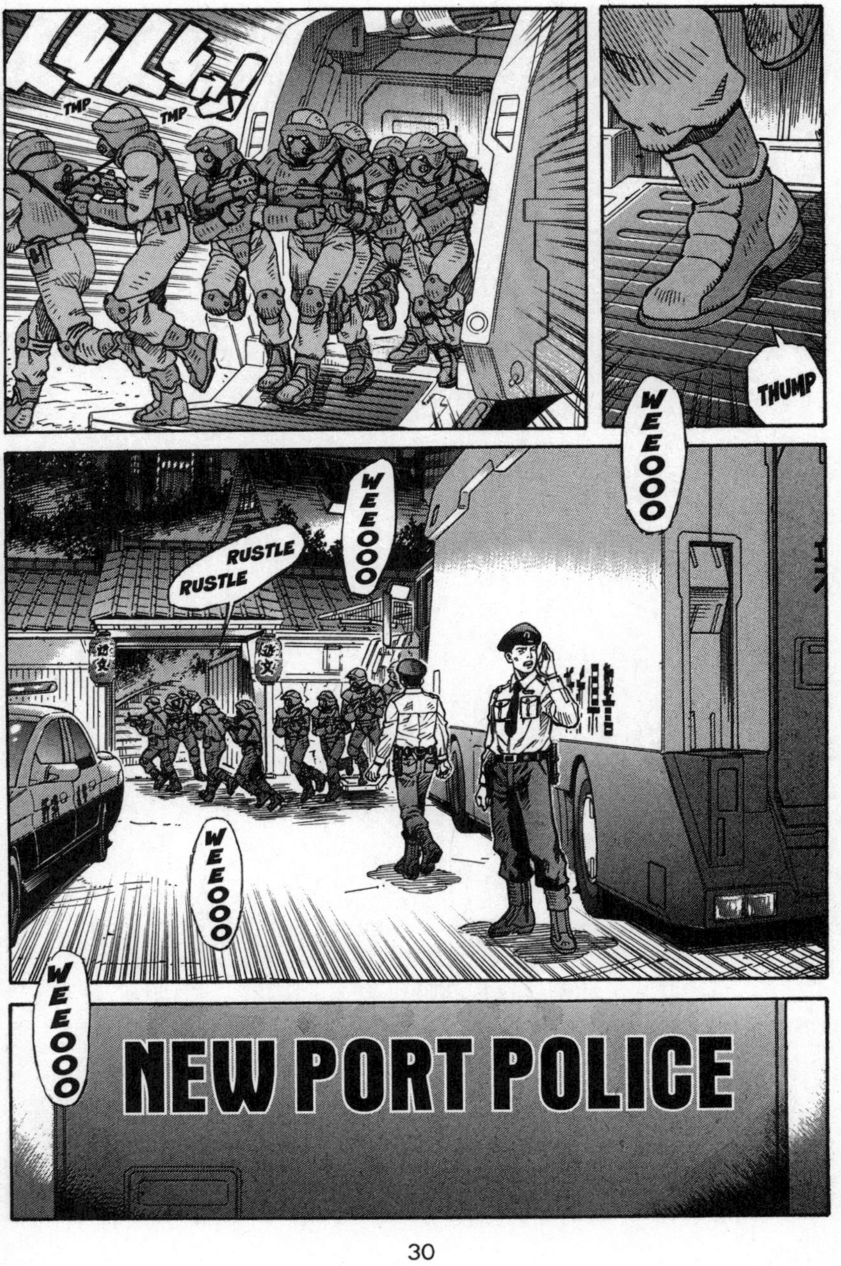
THUMP
TMP
TMP
WEEOOO
WEEOOO
RUSTLE
RUSTLE
WEEOOO
WEEOOO
NEW PORT POLICE

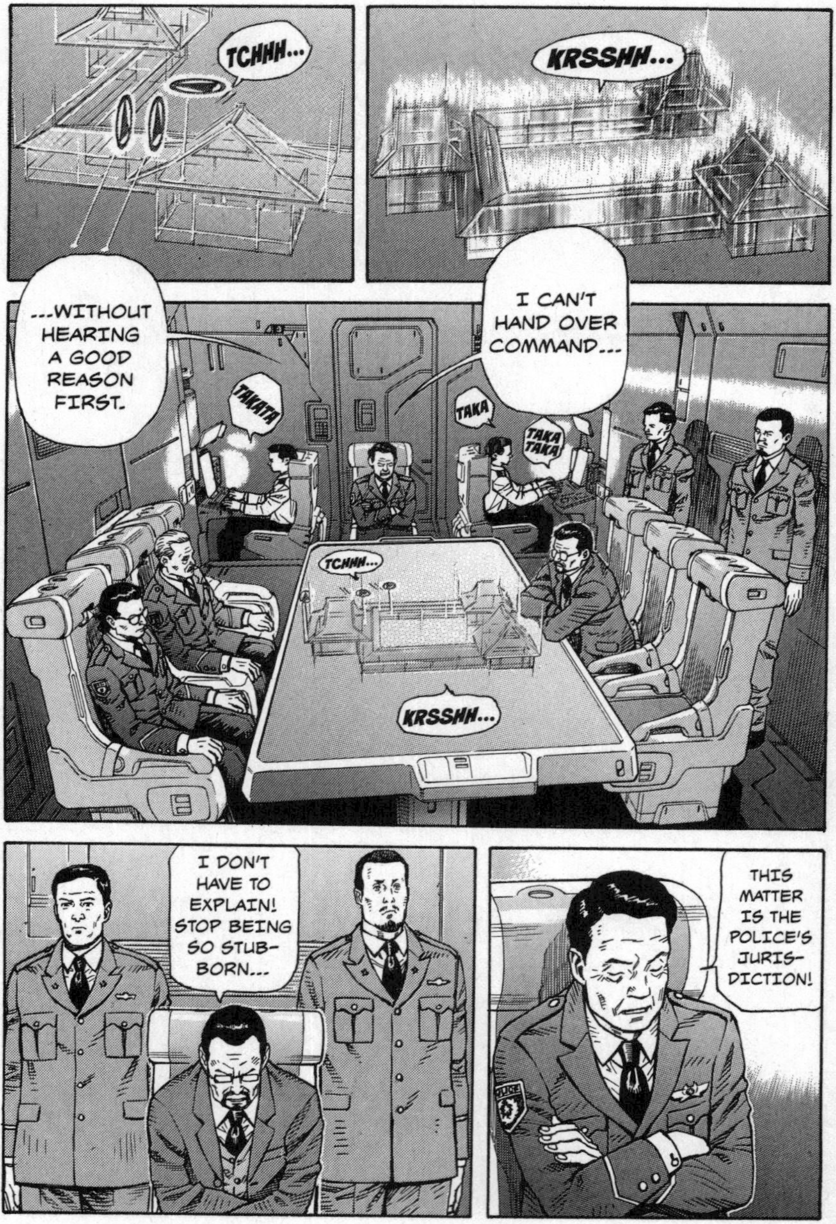
KRSSHH...
TCHHH...
I CAN'T HAND OVER COMMAND...
TAKA TAKA
TAKA
...WITHOUT HEARING A GOOD REASON FIRST.
TAKATA
TCHHH...
KRSSHH...
THIS MATTER IS THE POLICE'S JURIS-DICTION!
I DON'T HAVE TO EXPLAIN! STOP BEING SO STUB-BORN...

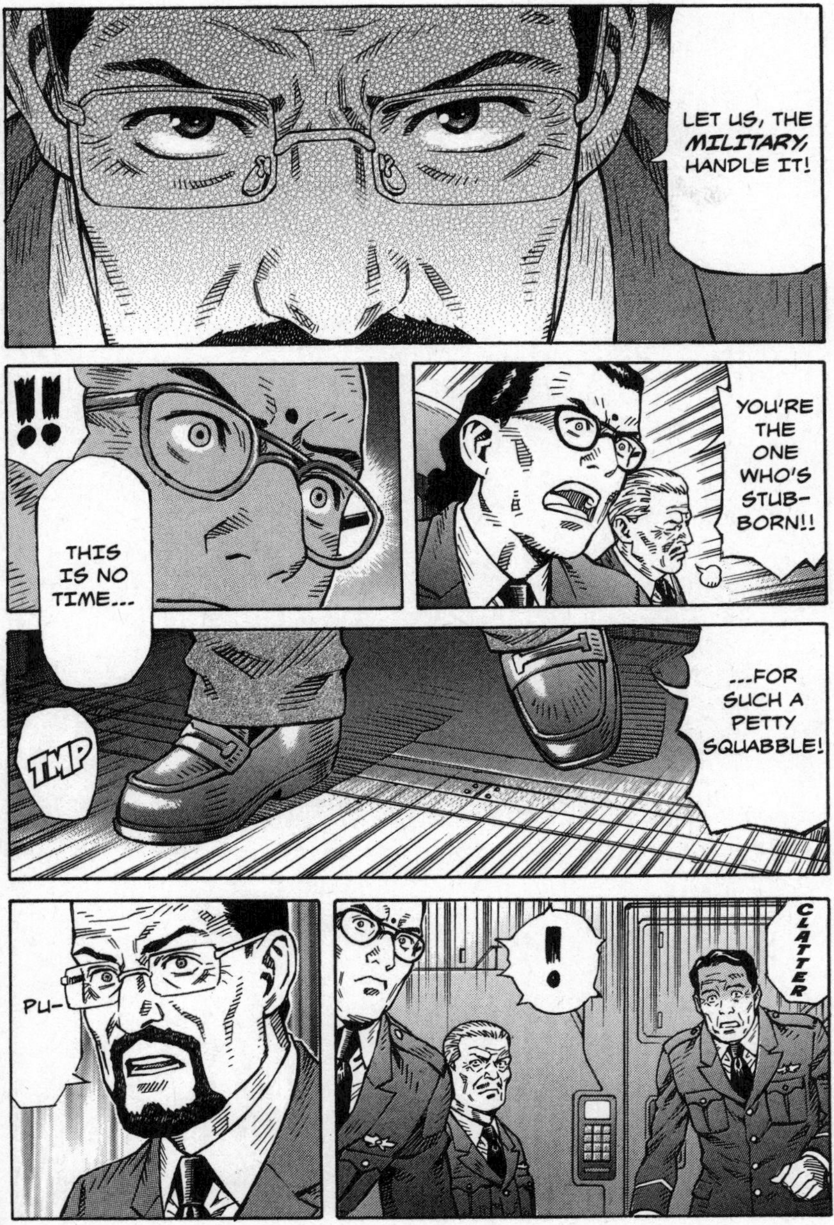
LET US, THE *MILITARY,* HANDLE IT!
YOU'RE THE ONE WHO'S STUB-BORN!!
!!
THIS IS NO TIME...
...FOR SUCH A PETTY SQUABBLE!
TMP
CLATTER
!
PU-

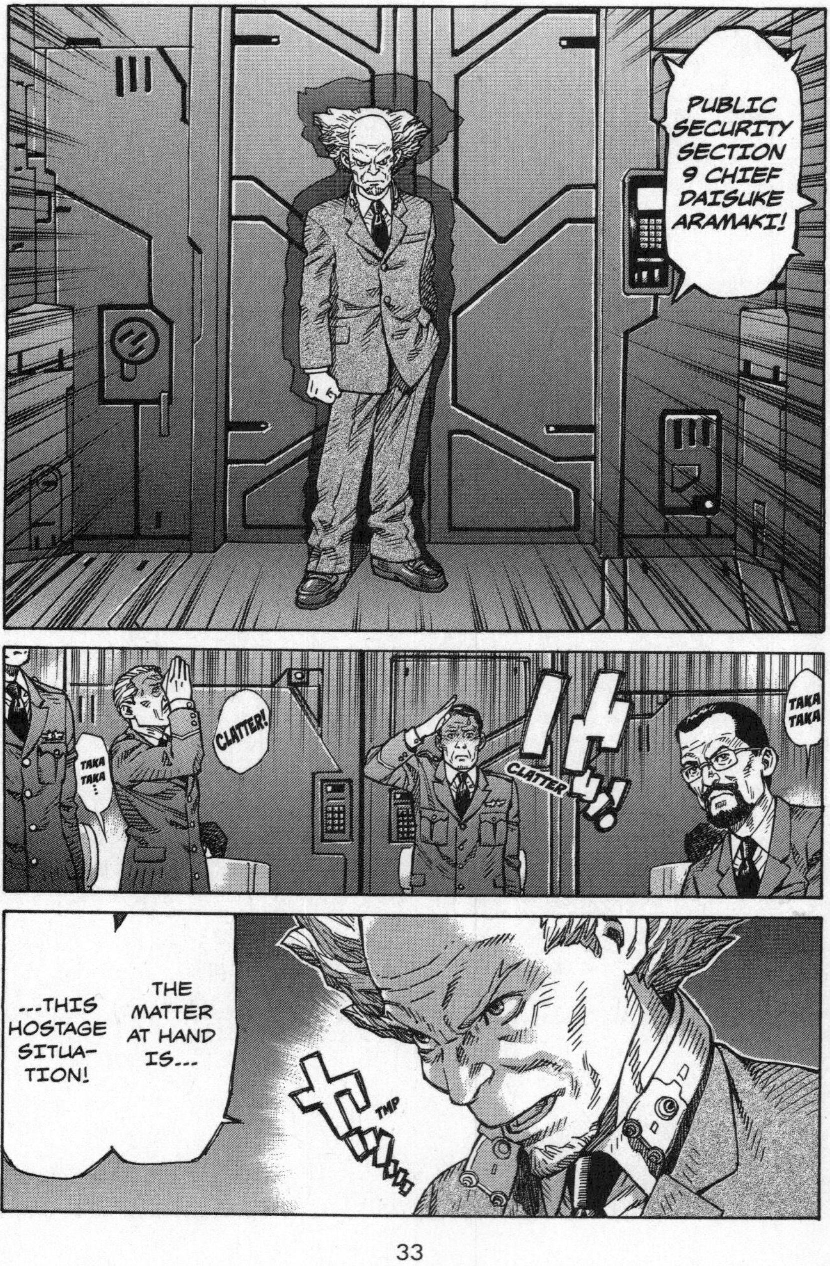
PUBLIC SECURITY SECTION 9 CHIEF DAISUKE ARAMAKI!
TAKA TAKA
CLATTER
CLATTER!
TAKA TAKA...
THE MATTER AT HAND IS...
...THIS HOSTAGE SITUATION!
TMP

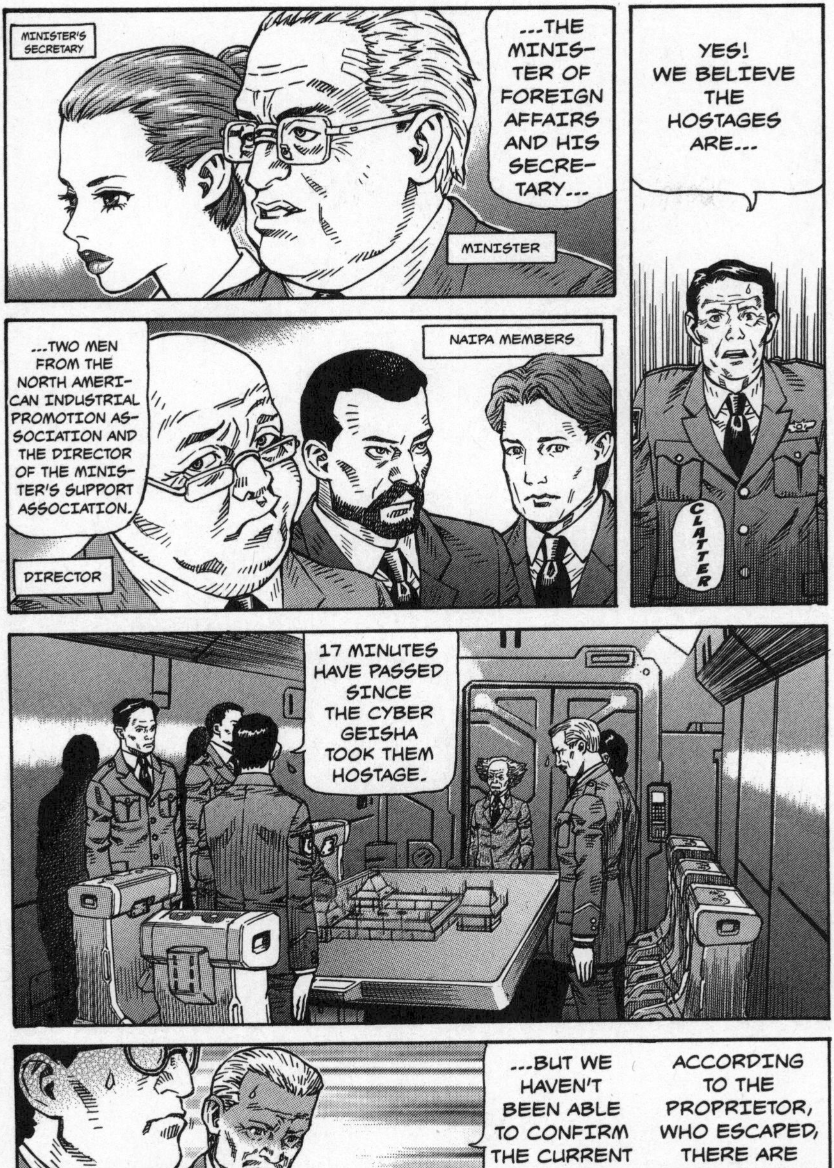
YES! WE BELIEVE THE HOSTAGES ARE...
CLATTER
...THE MINISTER OF FOREIGN AFFAIRS AND HIS SECRETARY...
MINISTER'S SECRETARY
MINISTER
NAIPA MEMBERS
...TWO MEN FROM THE NORTH AMERICAN INDUSTRIAL PROMOTION ASSOCIATION AND THE DIRECTOR OF THE MINISTER'S SUPPORT ASSOCIATION.
DIRECTOR
17 MINUTES HAVE PASSED SINCE THE CYBER GEISHA TOOK THEM HOSTAGE.
ACCORDING TO THE PROPRIETOR, WHO ESCAPED, THERE ARE TWO POSSIBLE CASUALTIES...
...BUT WE HAVEN'T BEEN ABLE TO CONFIRM THE CURRENT SITUATION YET.

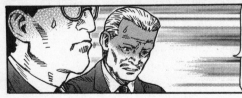

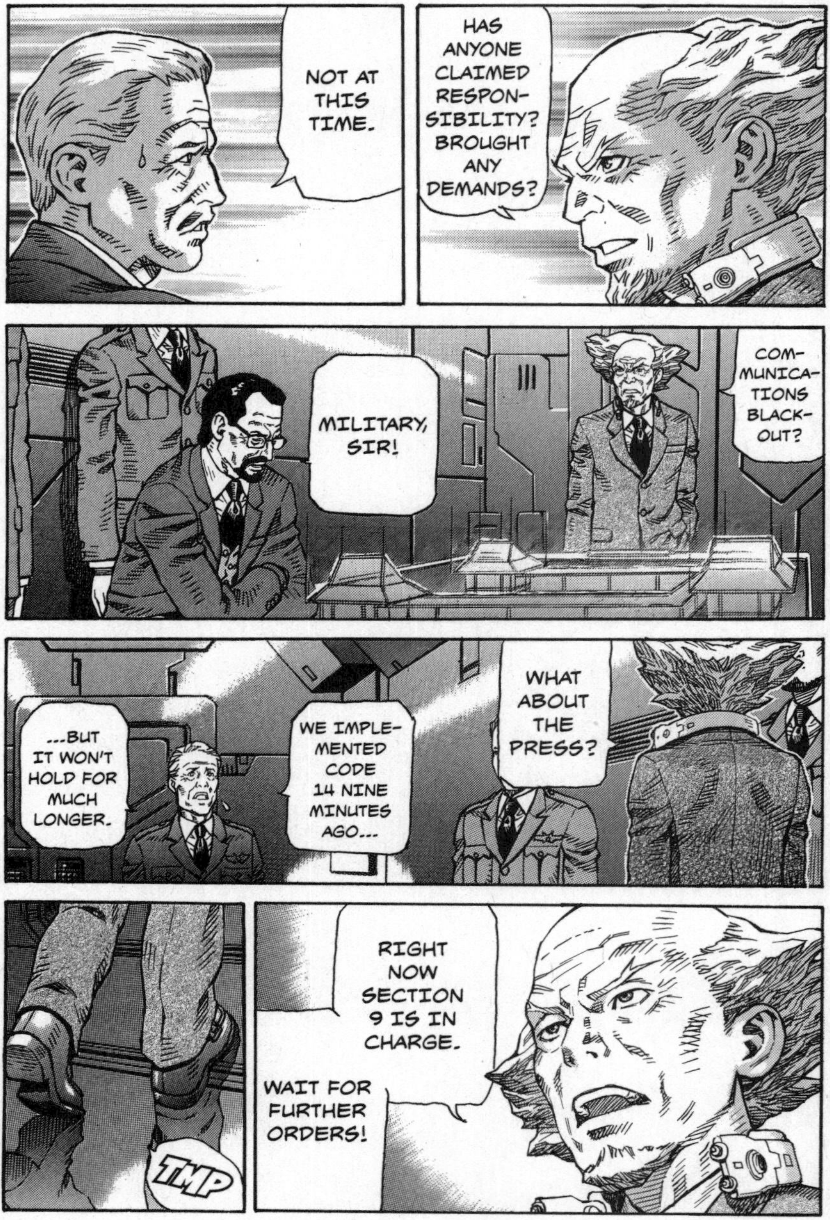

HAS ANYONE CLAIMED RESPON-SIBILITY? BROUGHT ANY DEMANDS?
NOT AT THIS TIME.
COM-MUNICA-TIONS BLACK-OUT?
MILITARY, SIR!
WHAT ABOUT THE PRESS?
WE IMPLE-MENTED CODE 14 NINE MINUTES AGO...
...BUT IT WON'T HOLD FOR MUCH LONGER.
RIGHT NOW SECTION 9 IS IN CHARGE.
WAIT FOR FURTHER ORDERS!
TMP

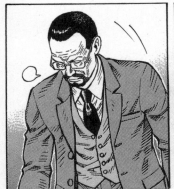

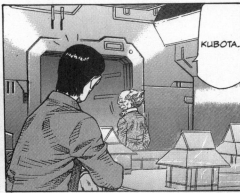

KUBOTA.

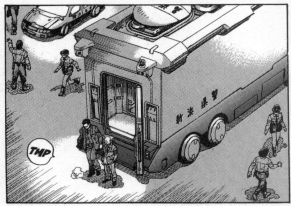

TMP

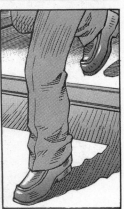

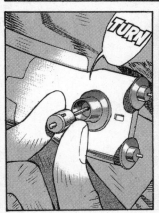

TURN

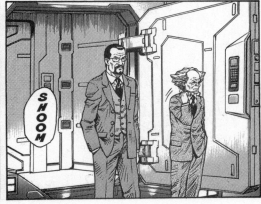

SHOOM

36

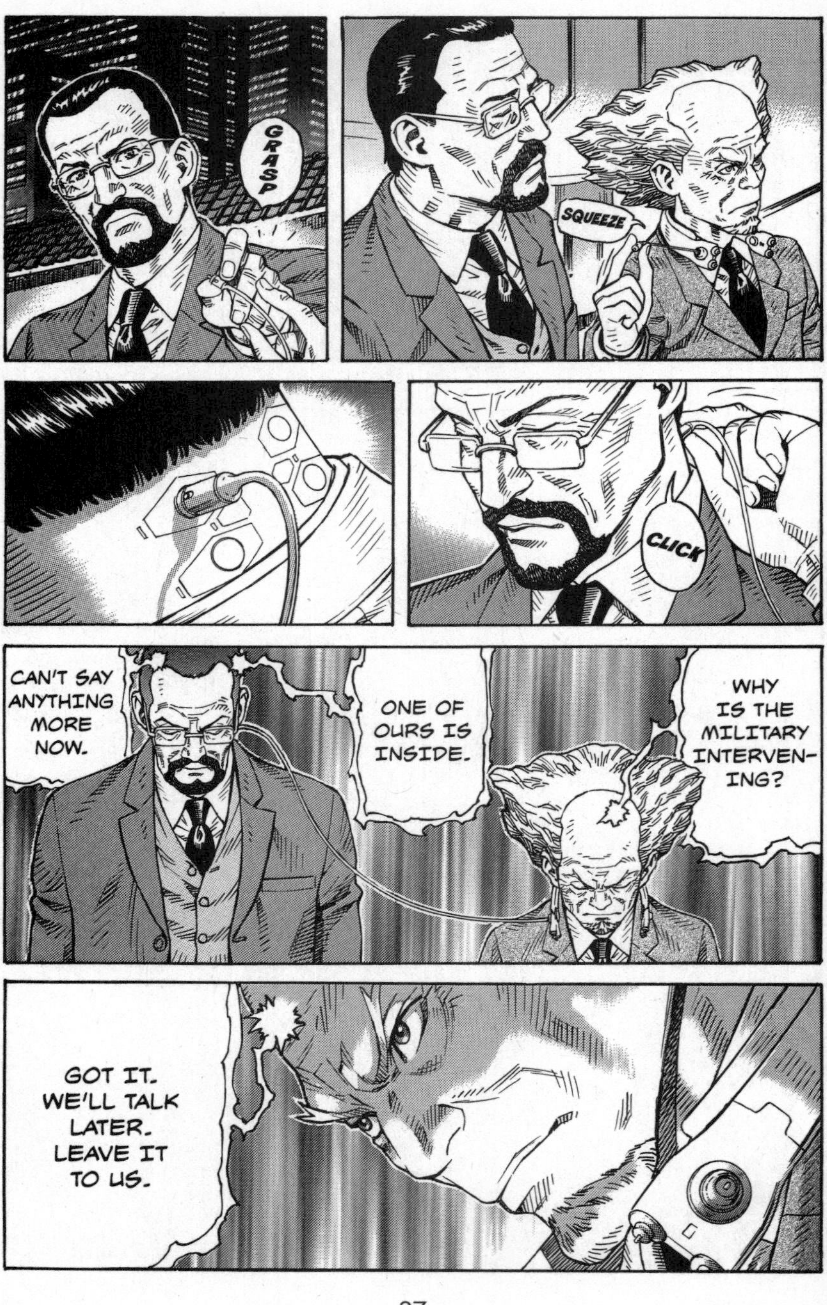
SQUEEZE
GRASP
CLICK
WHY IS THE MILITARY INTERVEN-ING?
ONE OF OURS IS INSIDE.
CAN'T SAY ANYTHING MORE NOW.
GOT IT. WE'LL TALK LATER. LEAVE IT TO US.

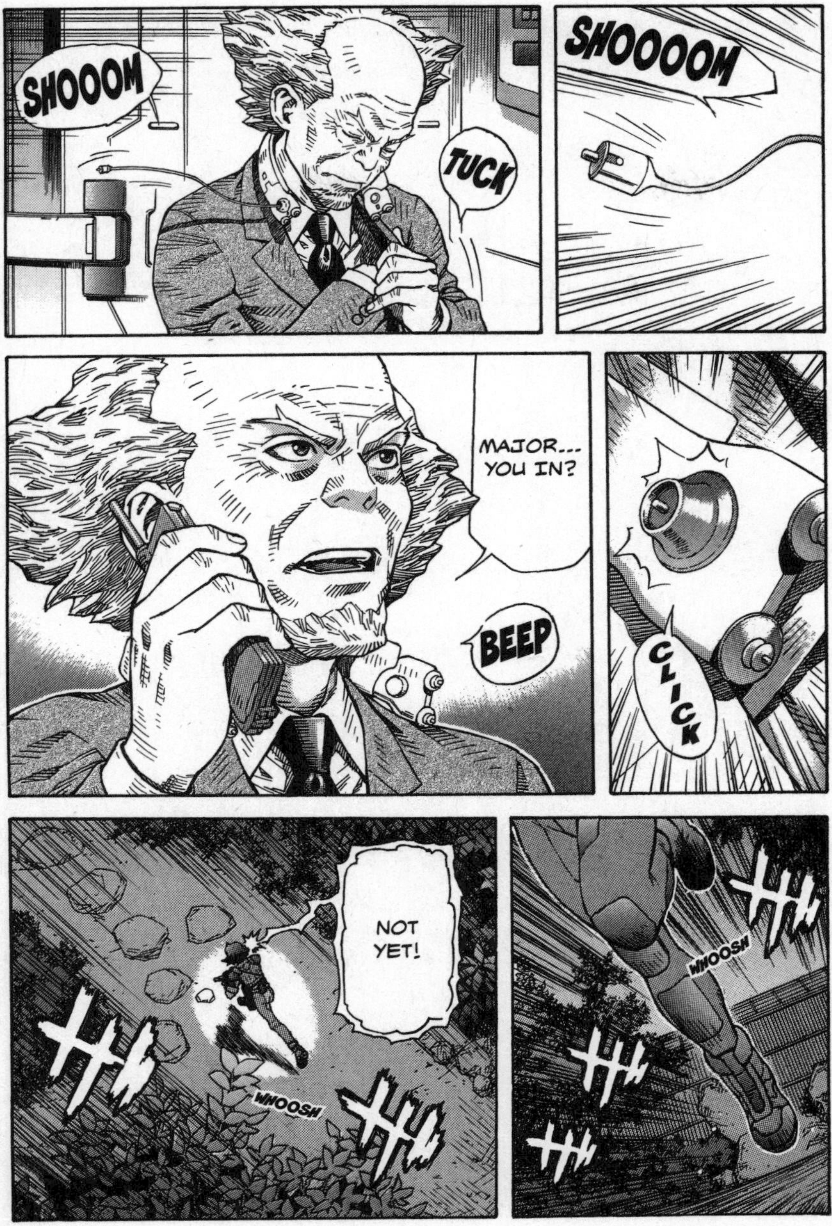
SHOOOOM
SHOOOM
TUCK
CLICK
MAJOR... YOU IN?
BEEP
WHOOSH
NOT YET!
WHOOSH

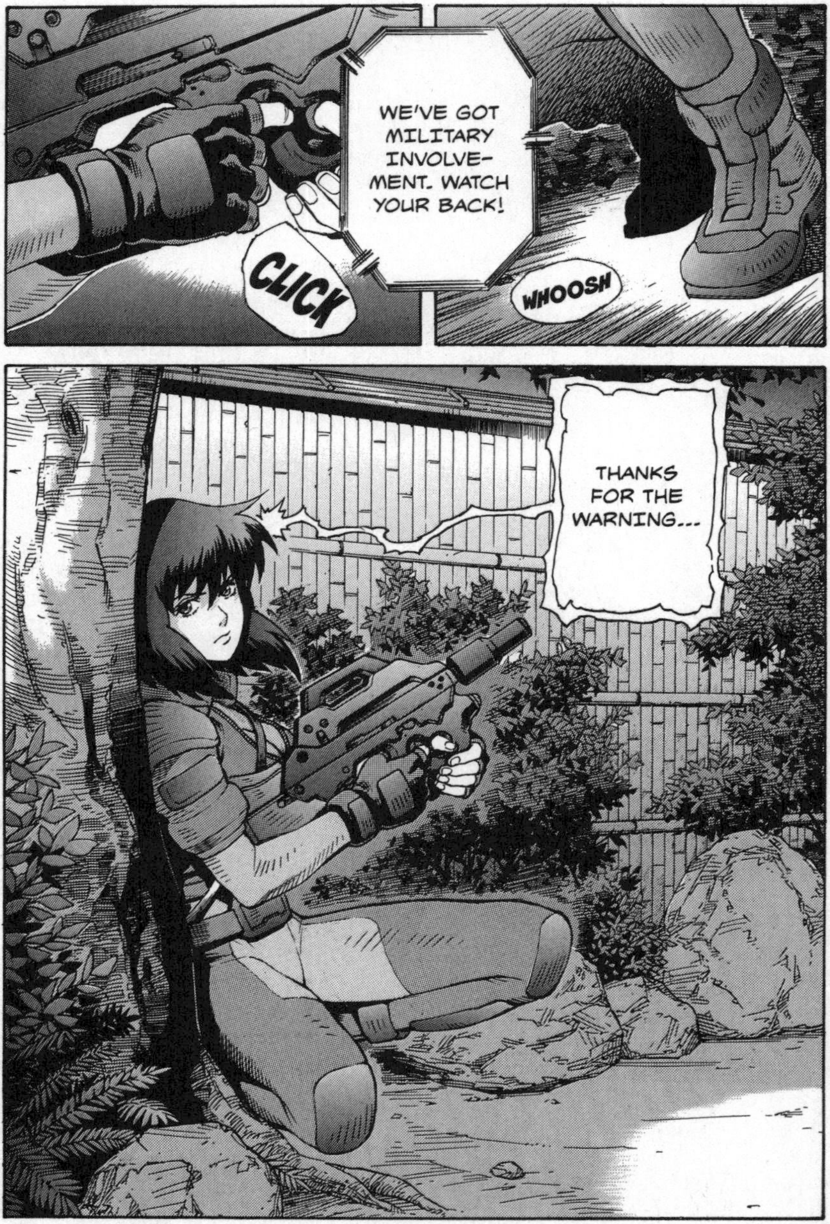
WHOOSH
WE'VE GOT MILITARY INVOLVE- MENT. WATCH YOUR BACK!
CLICK
THANKS FOR THE WARNING...

#001 / End

#002: Surrounded

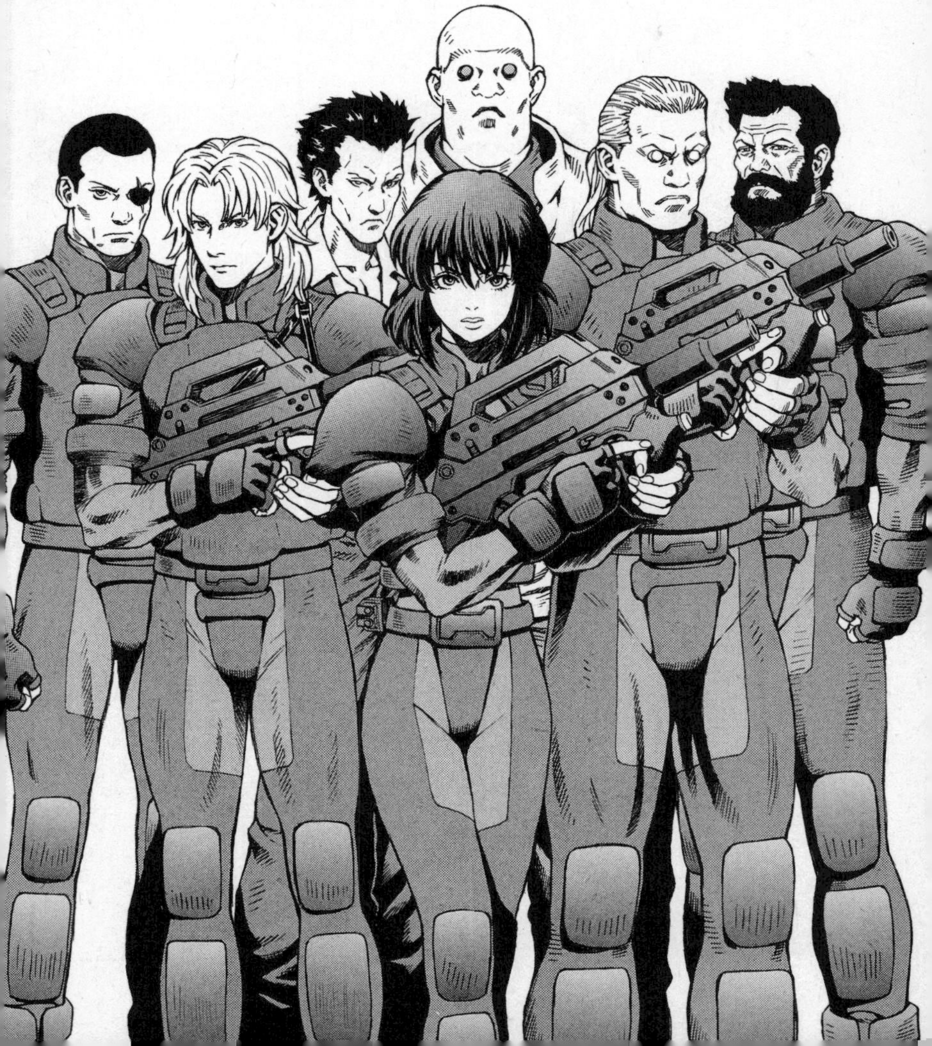

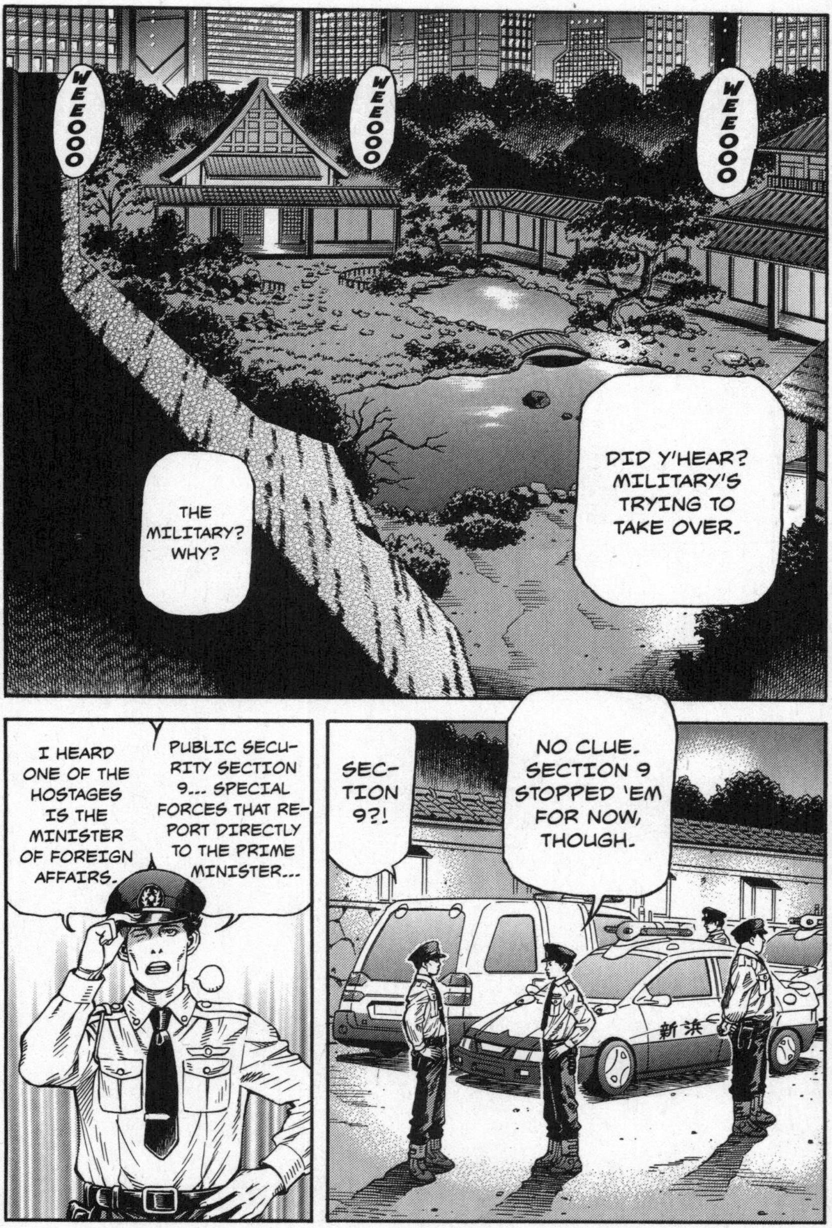
WEEOOO
WEEOOO
WEEOOO
DID Y'HEAR? MILITARY'S TRYING TO TAKE OVER.
THE MILITARY? WHY?
NO CLUE. SECTION 9 STOPPED 'EM FOR NOW, THOUGH.
SEC-TION 9?!
新浜
PUBLIC SECU-RITY SECTION 9... SPECIAL FORCES THAT RE-PORT DIRECTLY TO THE PRIME MINISTER...
I HEARD ONE OF THE HOSTAGES IS THE MINISTER OF FOREIGN AFFAIRS.

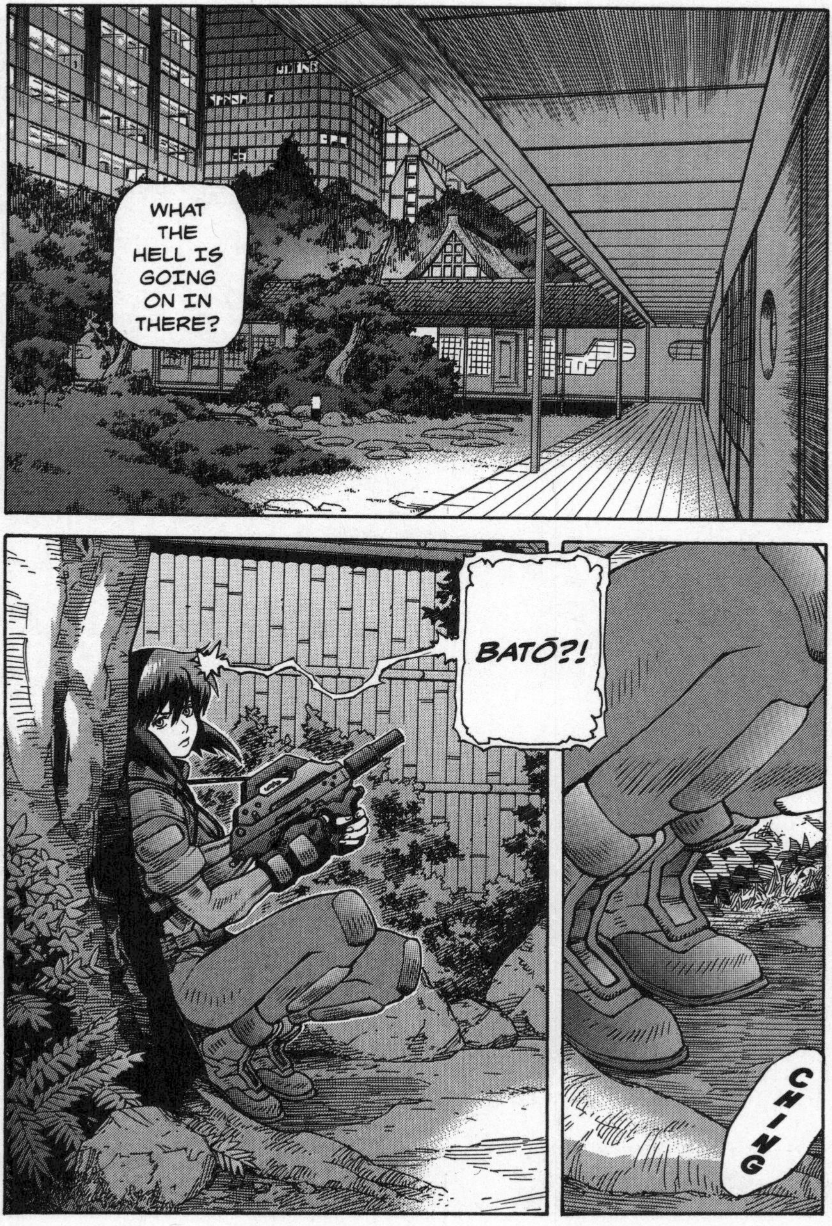
WHAT THE HELL IS GOING ON IN THERE?
CHING
BATŌ?!

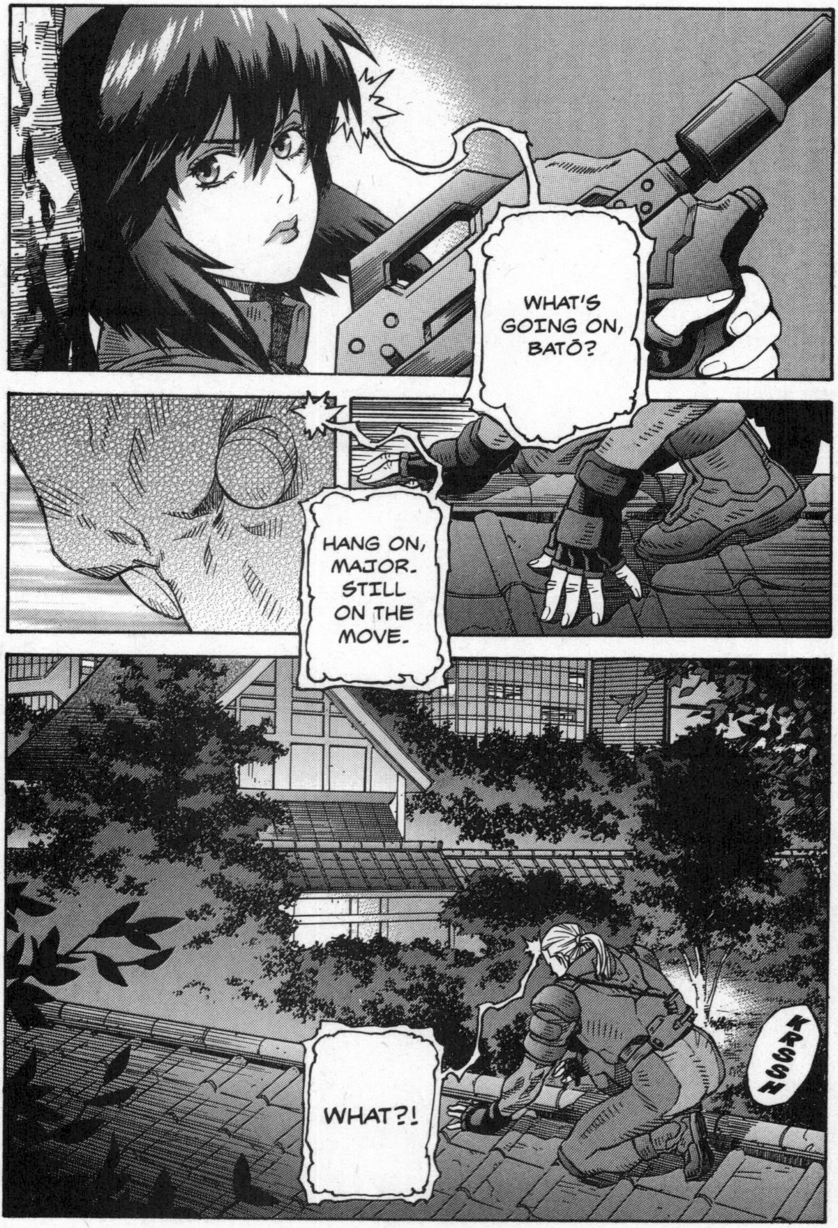
WHAT'S GOING ON, BATŌ?
HANG ON, MAJOR. STILL ON THE MOVE.
KRSSH
WHAT?!

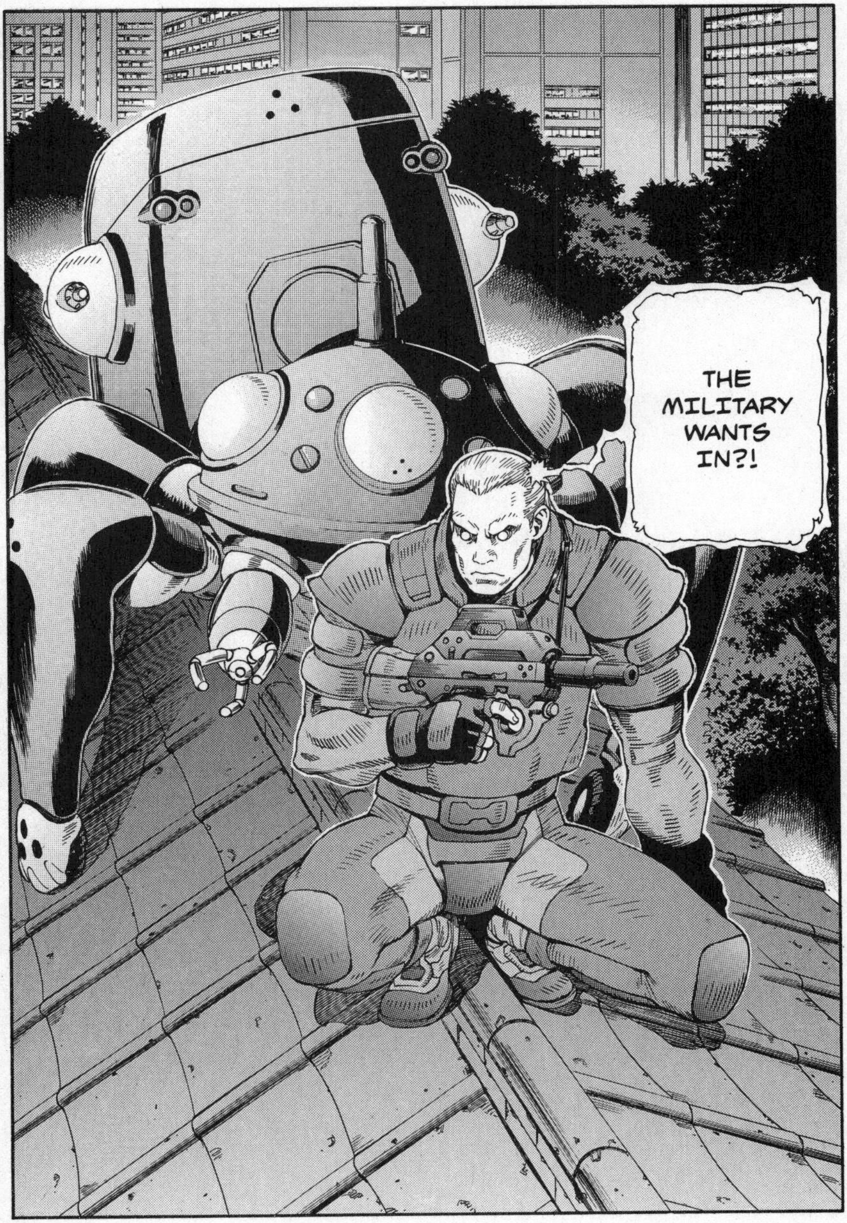
THE MILITARY WANTS IN?!

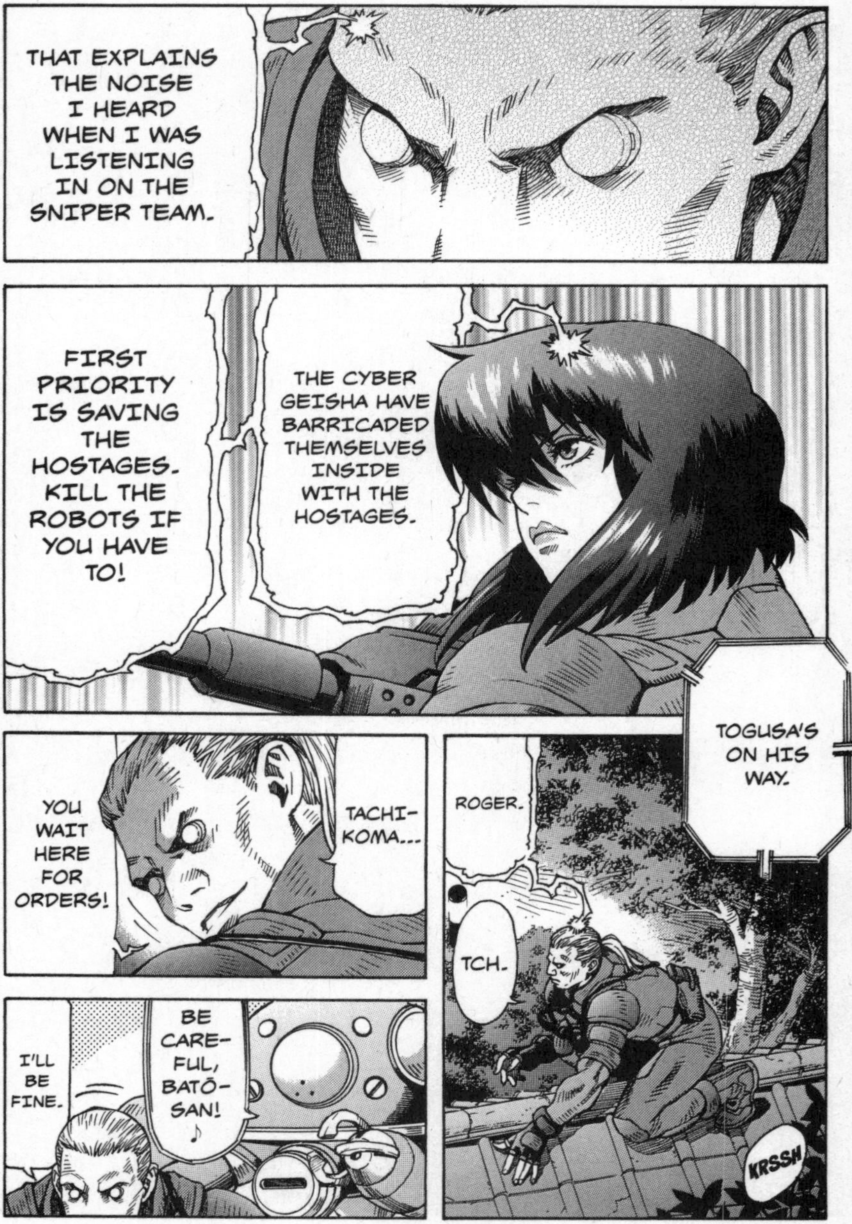
THAT EXPLAINS THE NOISE I HEARD WHEN I WAS LISTENING IN ON THE SNIPER TEAM.
THE CYBER GEISHA HAVE BARRICADED THEMSELVES INSIDE WITH THE HOSTAGES.
FIRST PRIORITY IS SAVING THE HOSTAGES. KILL THE ROBOTS IF YOU HAVE TO!
TOGUSA'S ON HIS WAY.
ROGER.
TCH.
KRSSH
TACHI-KOMA...
YOU WAIT HERE FOR ORDERS!
BE CARE-FUL, BATŌ-SAN! ♪
I'LL BE FINE.

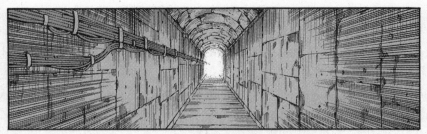

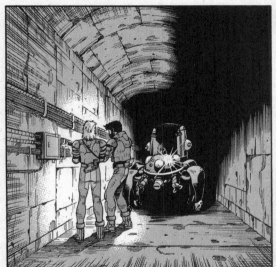

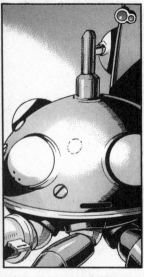

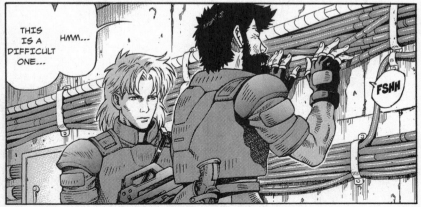

THIS IS A DIFFICULT ONE...

HMM...

FSHH

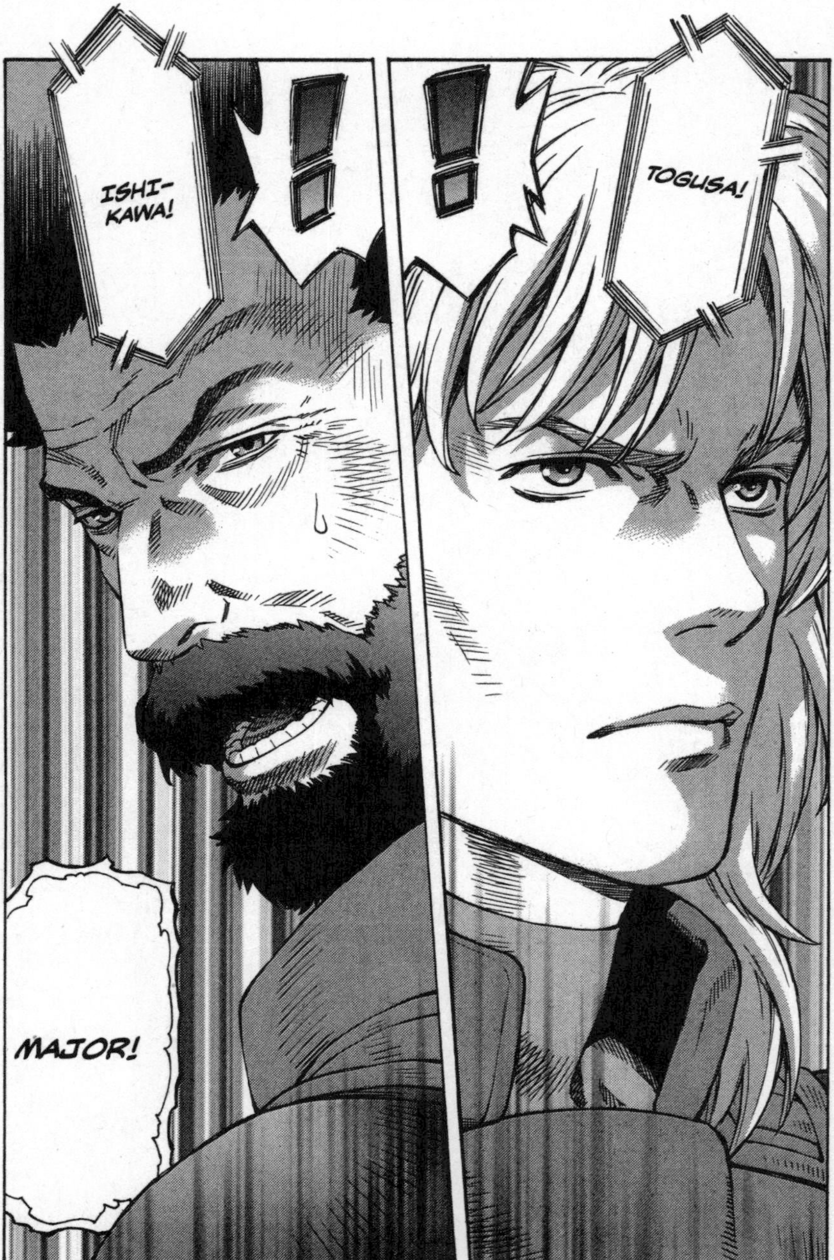
TOGUSA!
ISHI-
KAWA!
MAJOR!

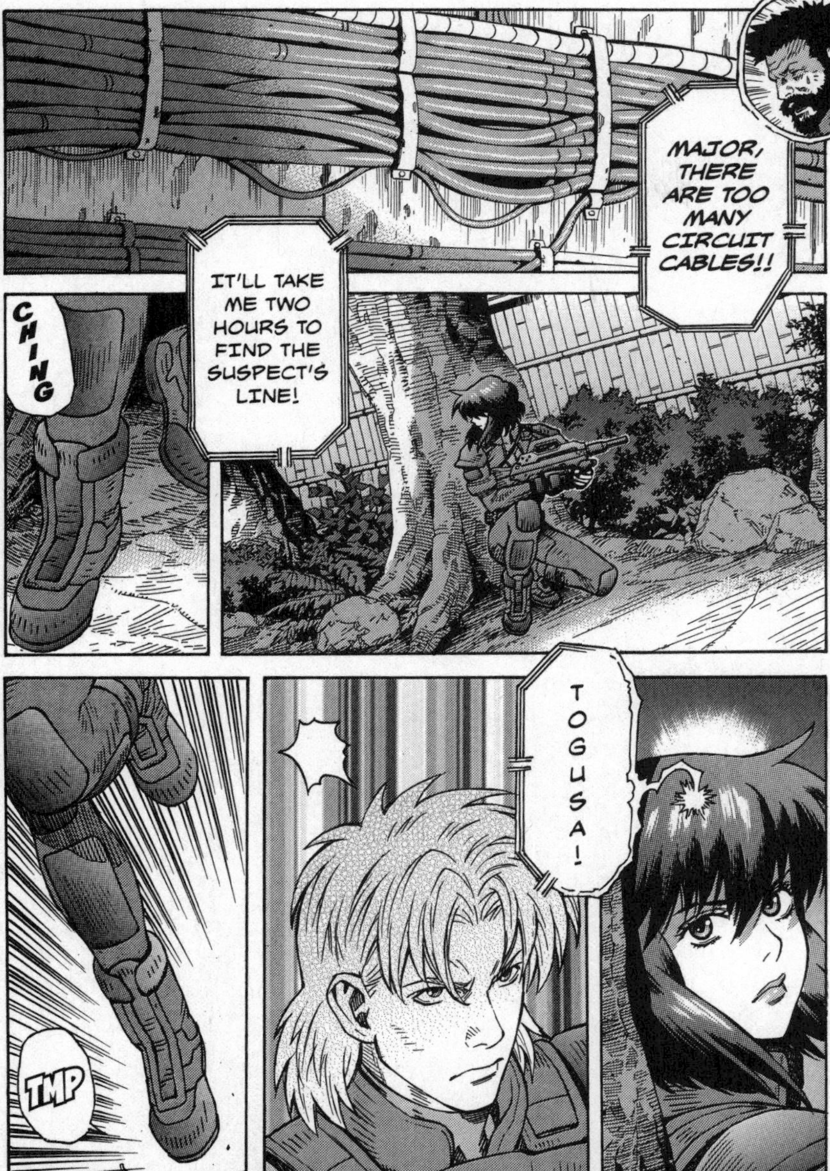
MAJOR, THERE ARE TOO MANY CIRCUIT CABLES!!
IT'LL TAKE ME TWO HOURS TO FIND THE SUSPECT'S LINE!
CHING
TOGUSA!
TMP

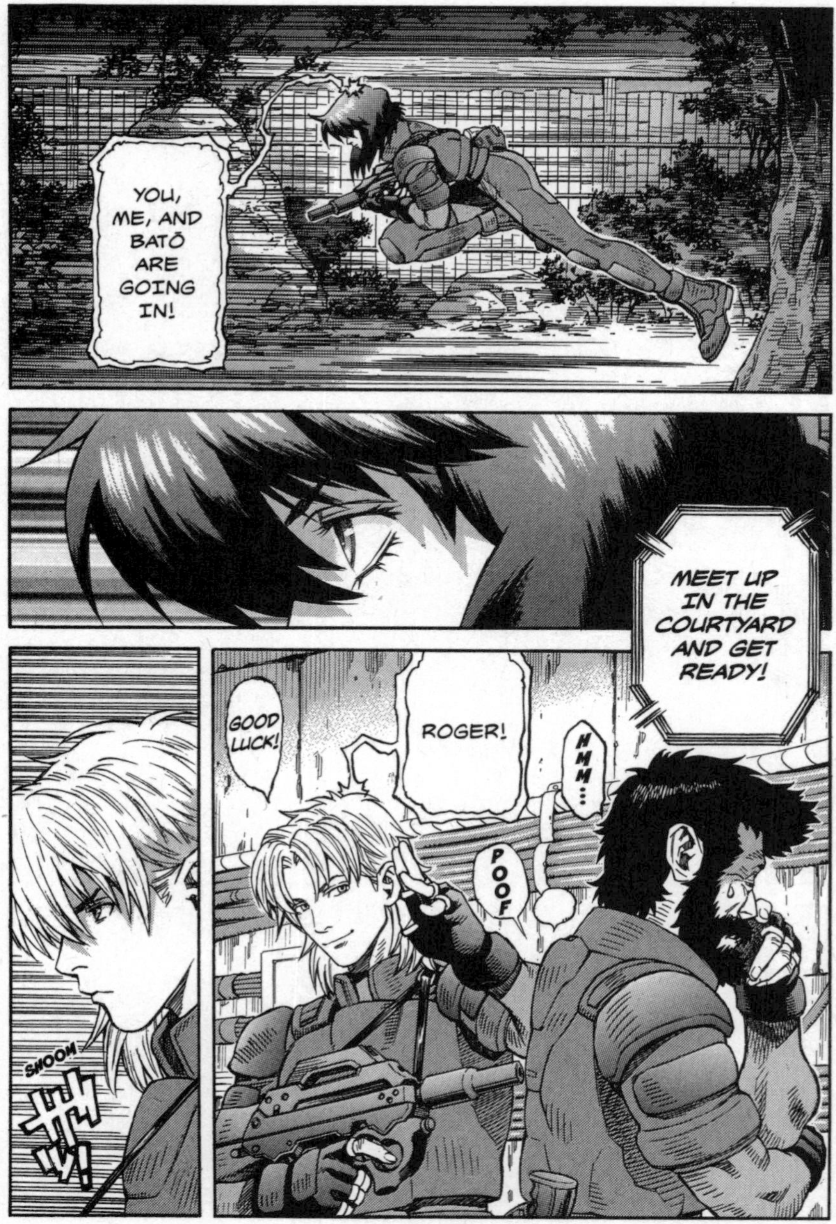
YOU, ME, AND BATŌ ARE GOING IN!
MEET UP IN THE COURTYARD AND GET READY!
HMM...
ROGER!
GOOD LUCK!
POOF
SHOOM

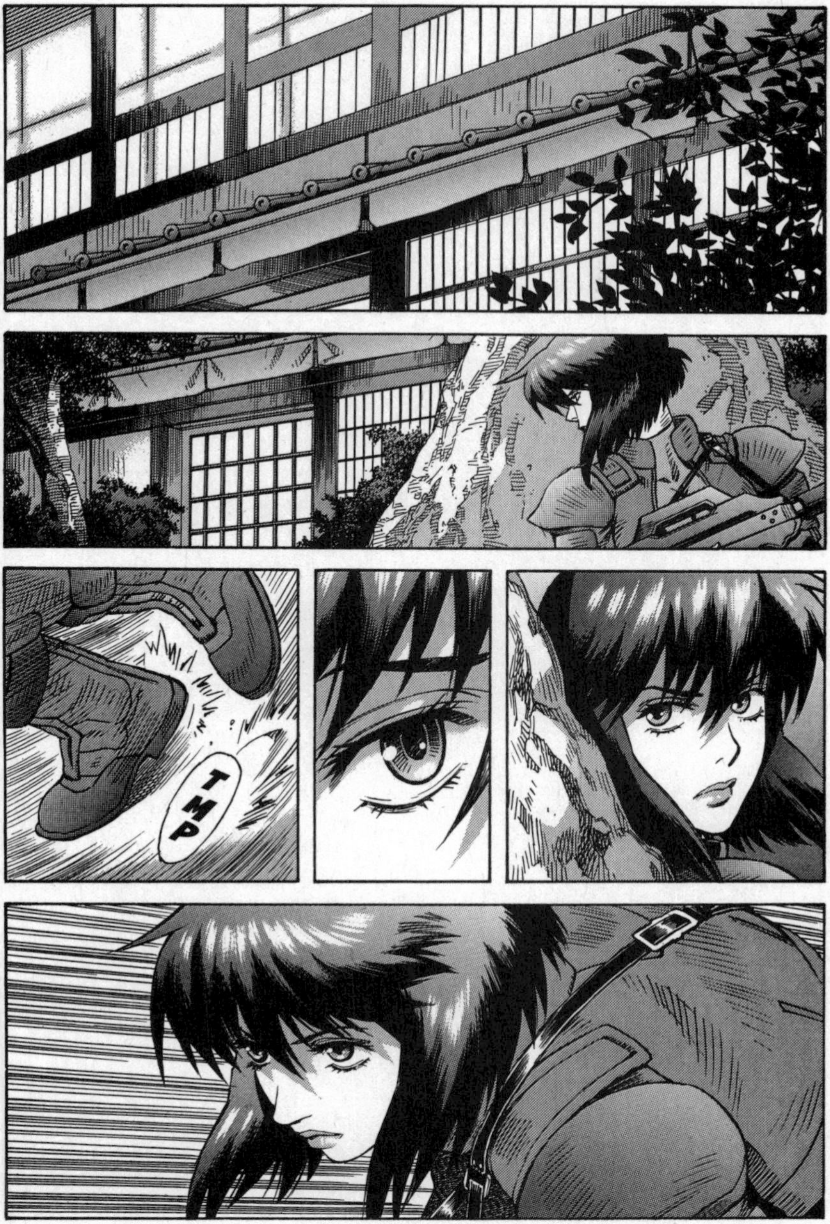
TMP

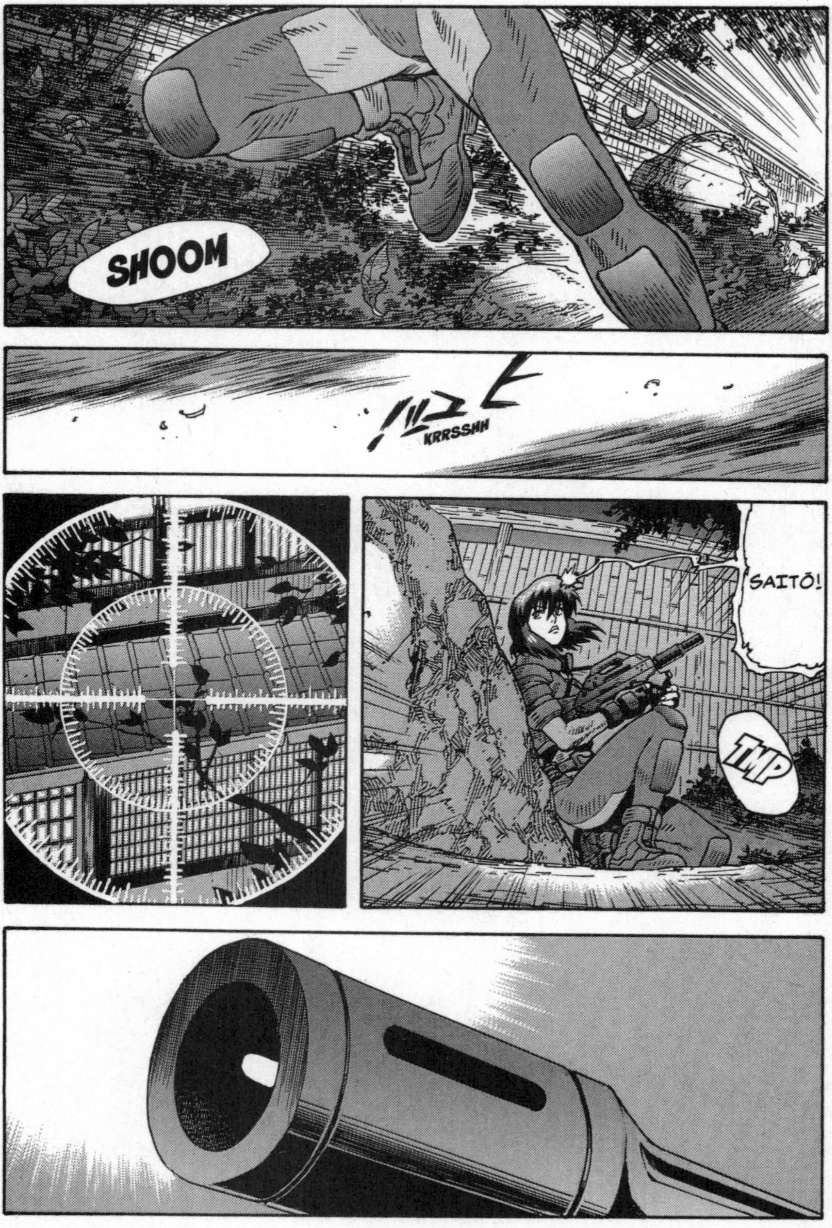
SHOOM
KRRSSHH
SAITŌ!
TMP

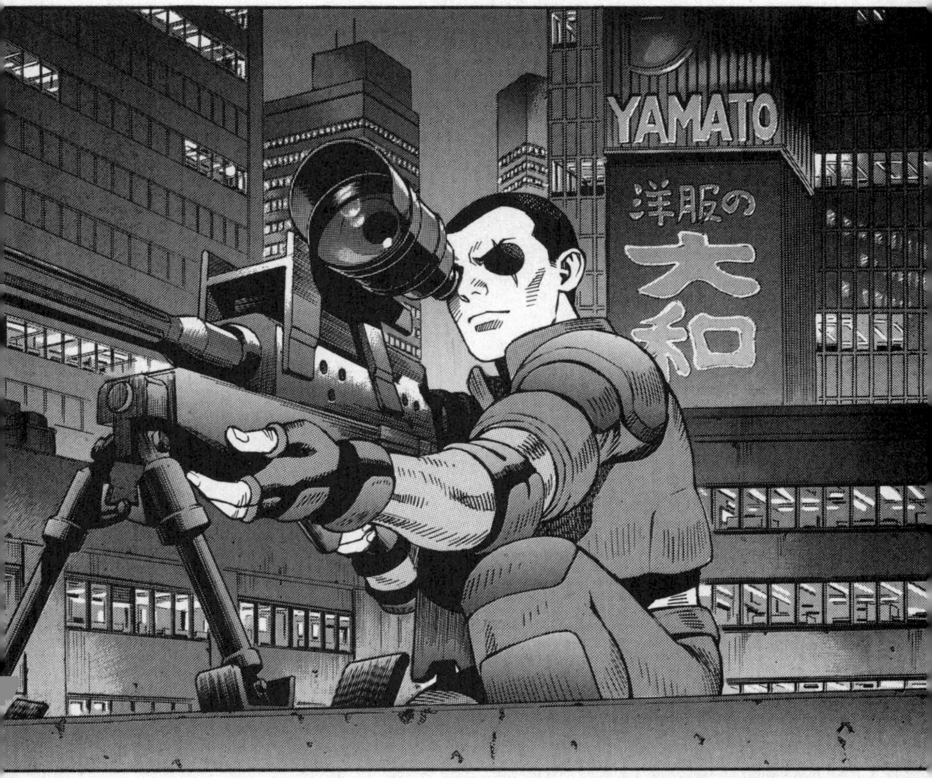
YAMATO
洋服の
大和

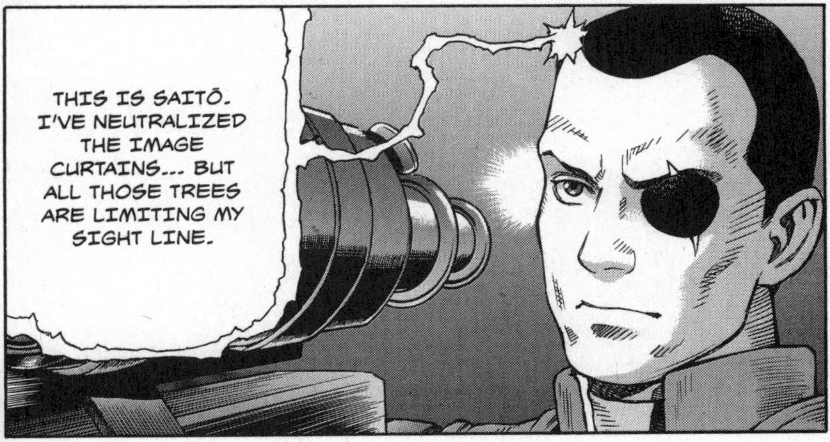
THIS IS SAITŌ. I'VE NEUTRALIZED THE IMAGE CURTAINS... BUT ALL THOSE TREES ARE LIMITING MY SIGHT LINE.

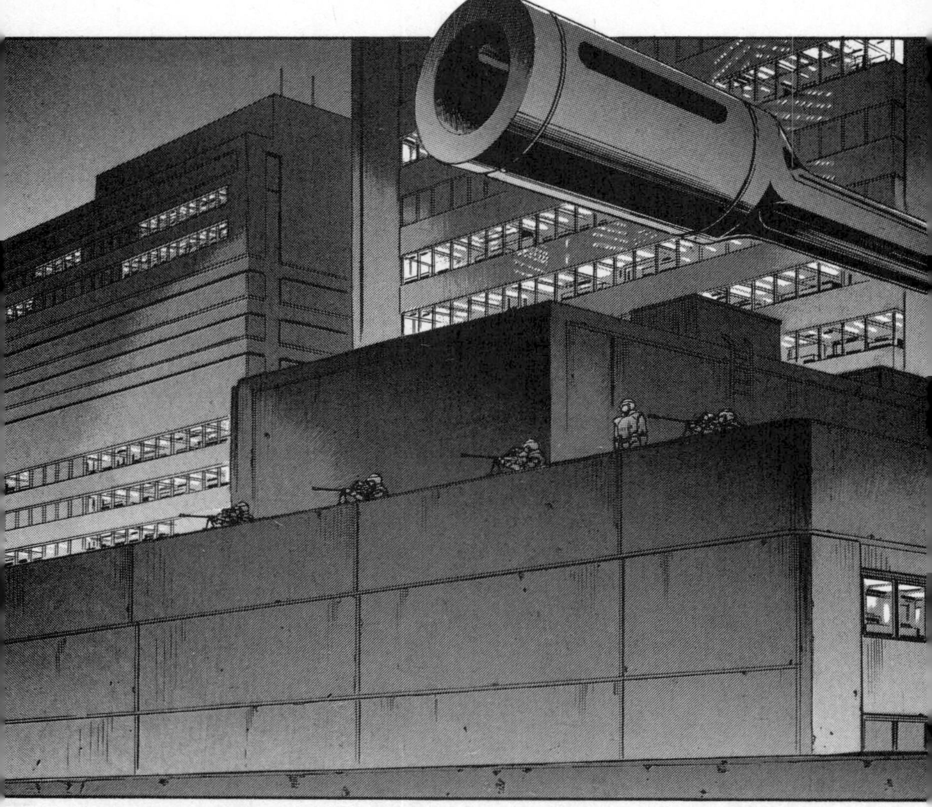

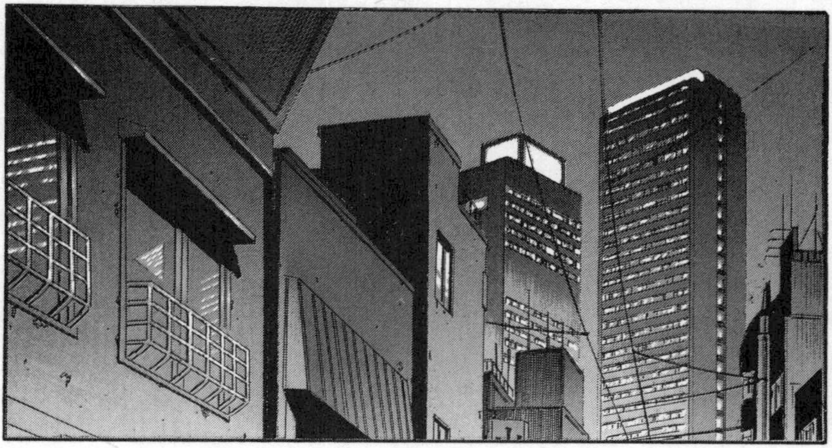

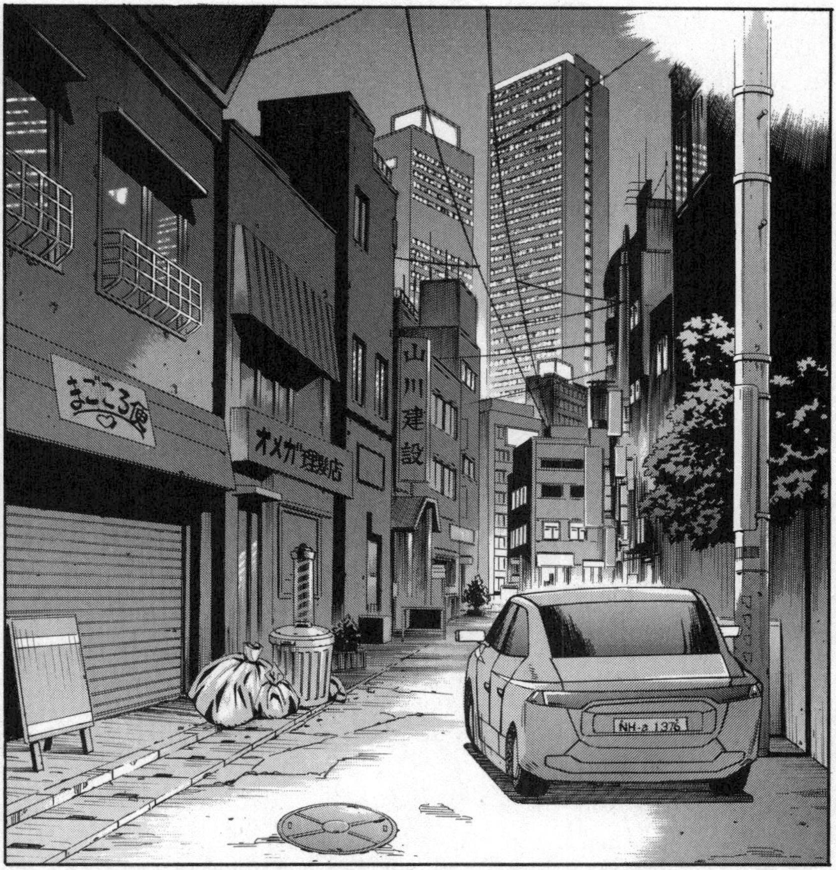
まごころ便
オメガ理髪店
山川建設
NH-a 1376

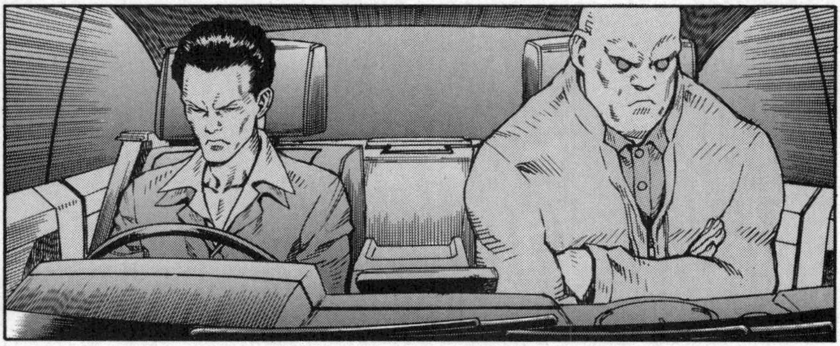

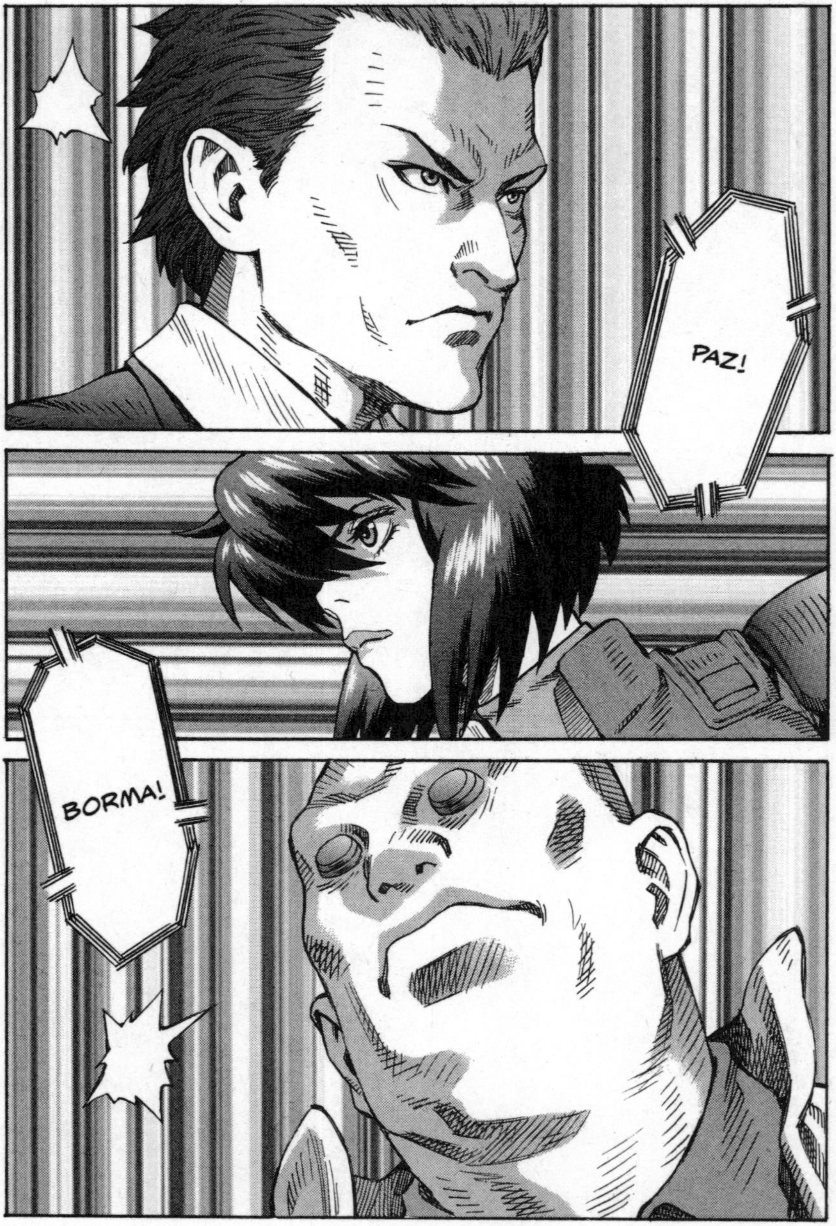
PAZ!
BORMA!

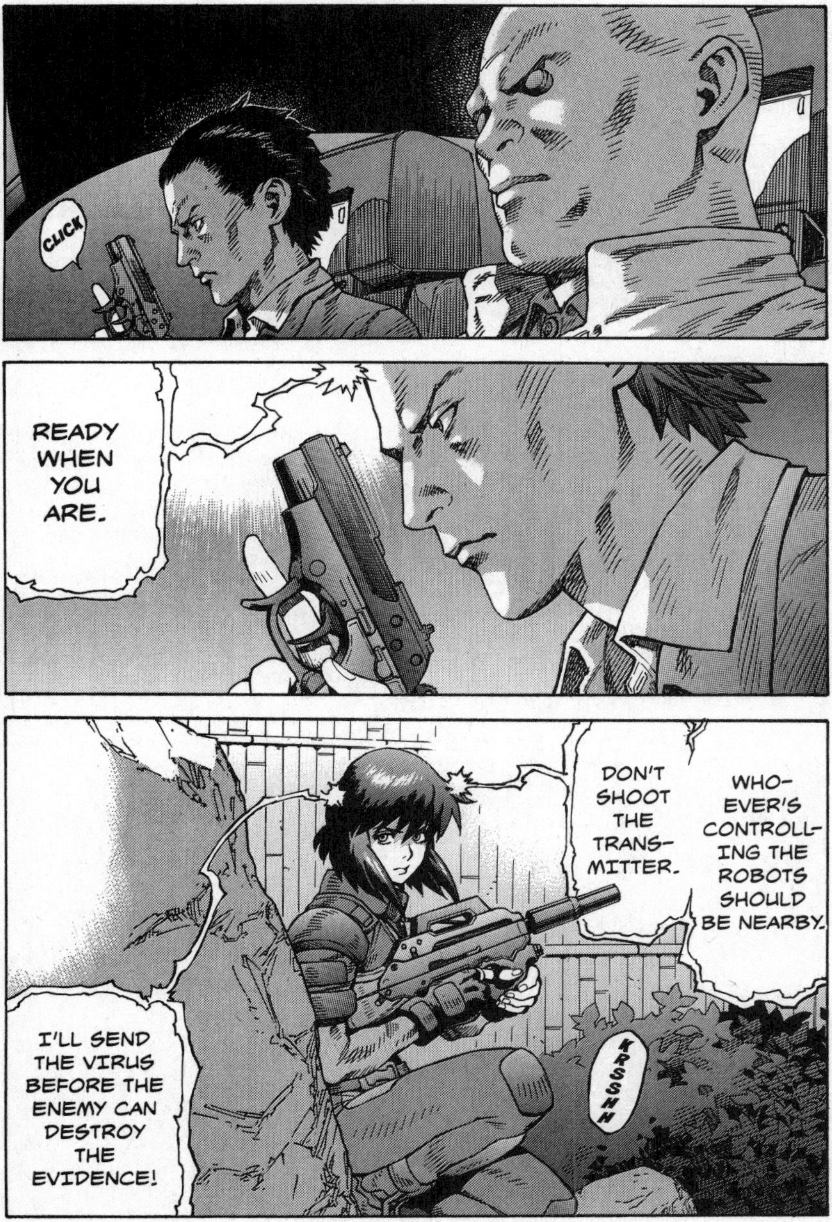

CLICK
READY WHEN YOU ARE.
WHO-EVER'S CONTROLL-ING THE ROBOTS SHOULD BE NEARBY.
DON'T SHOOT THE TRANS-MITTER.
KRSSHN
I'LL SEND THE VIRUS BEFORE THE ENEMY CAN DESTROY THE EVIDENCE!

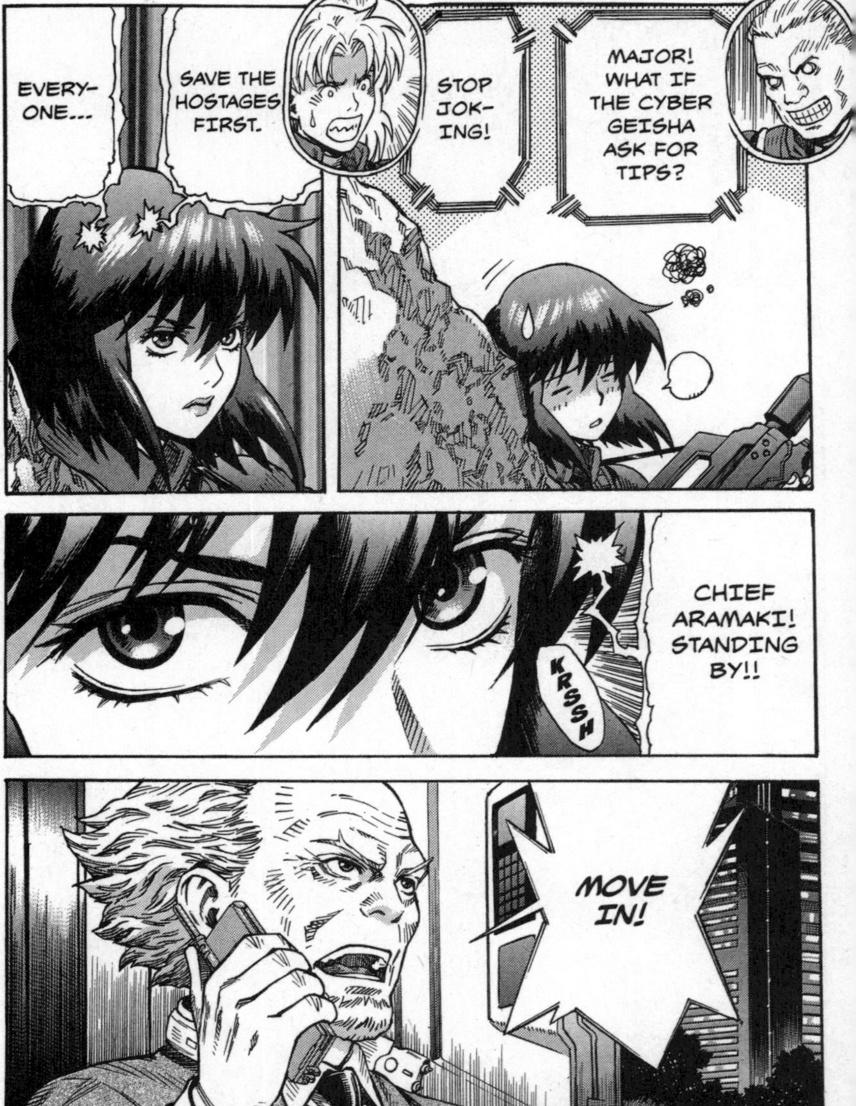
MAJOR! WHAT IF THE CYBER GEISHA ASK FOR TIPS?
STOP JOK-ING!
EVERY-ONE...
SAVE THE HOSTAGES FIRST.
CHIEF ARAMAKI! STANDING BY!!
KRSSH
MOVE IN!

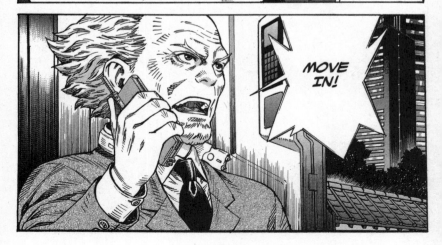

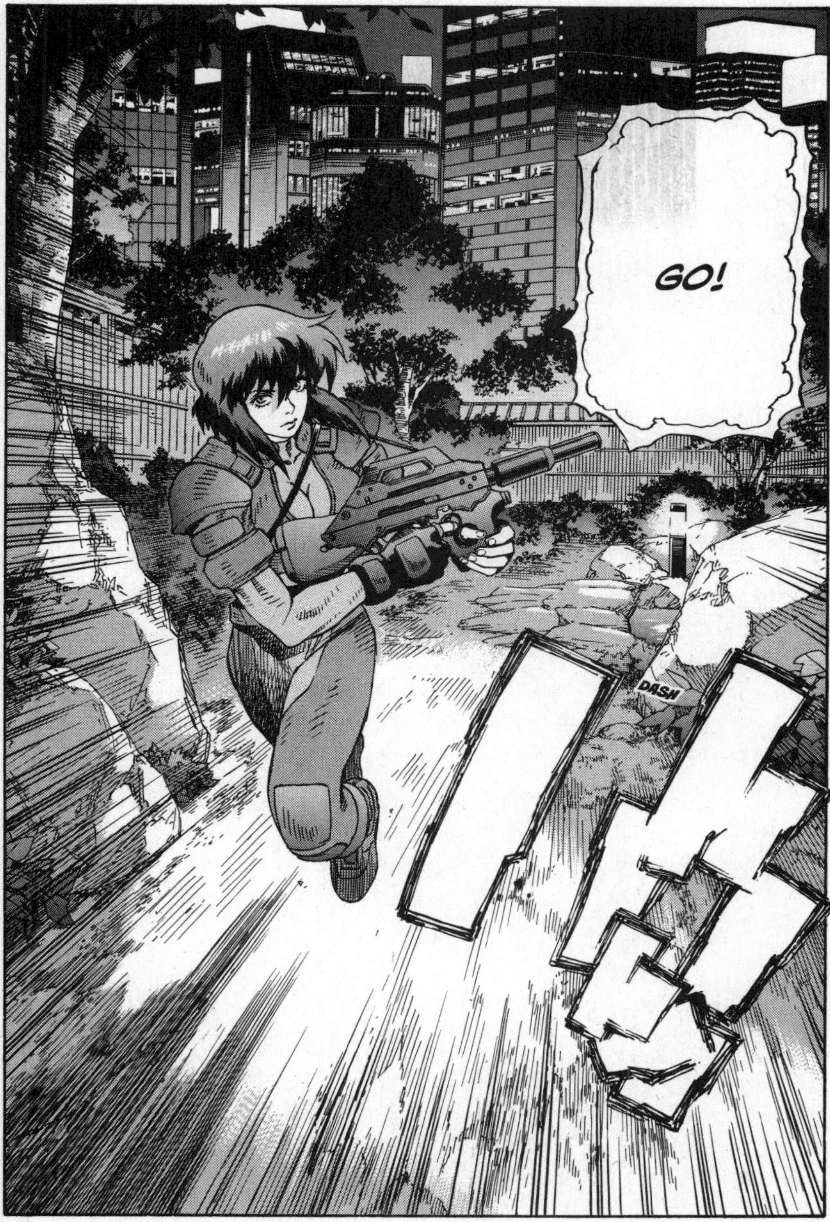
GO!
DASH

#002 / End

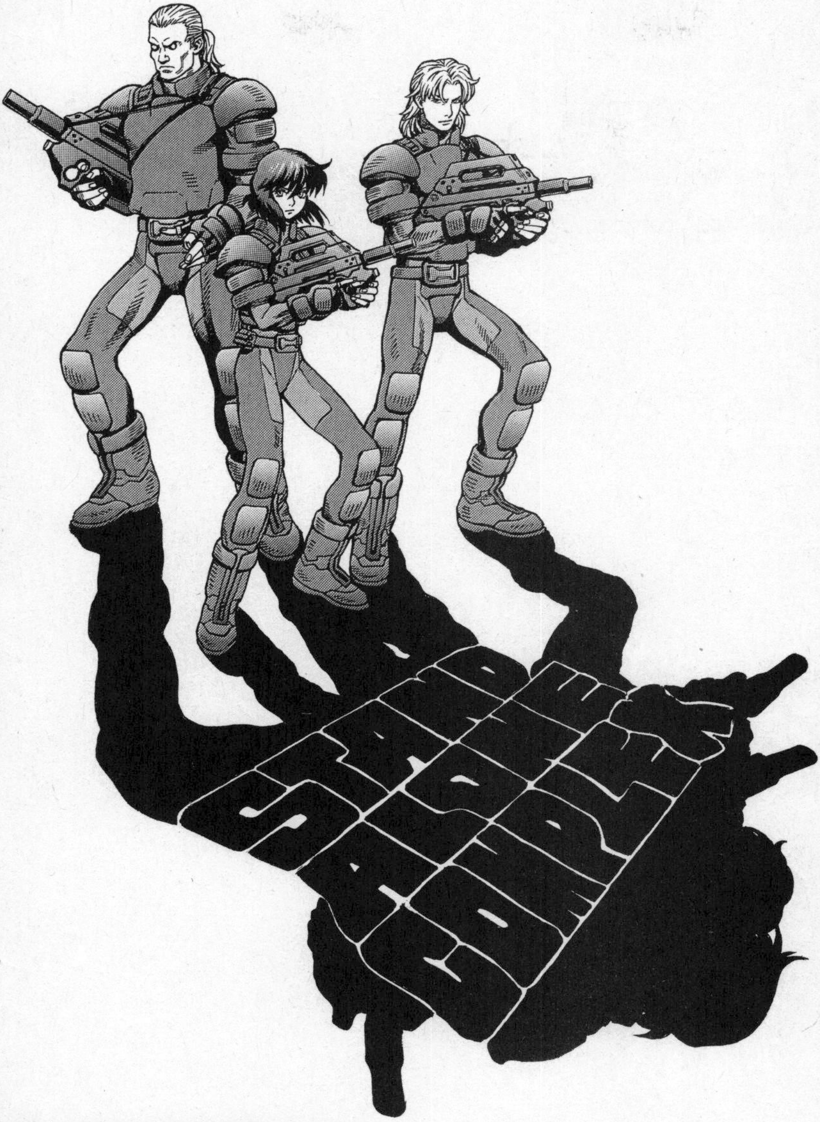
STAND
ALONE
COMPLEX

#003: Move In

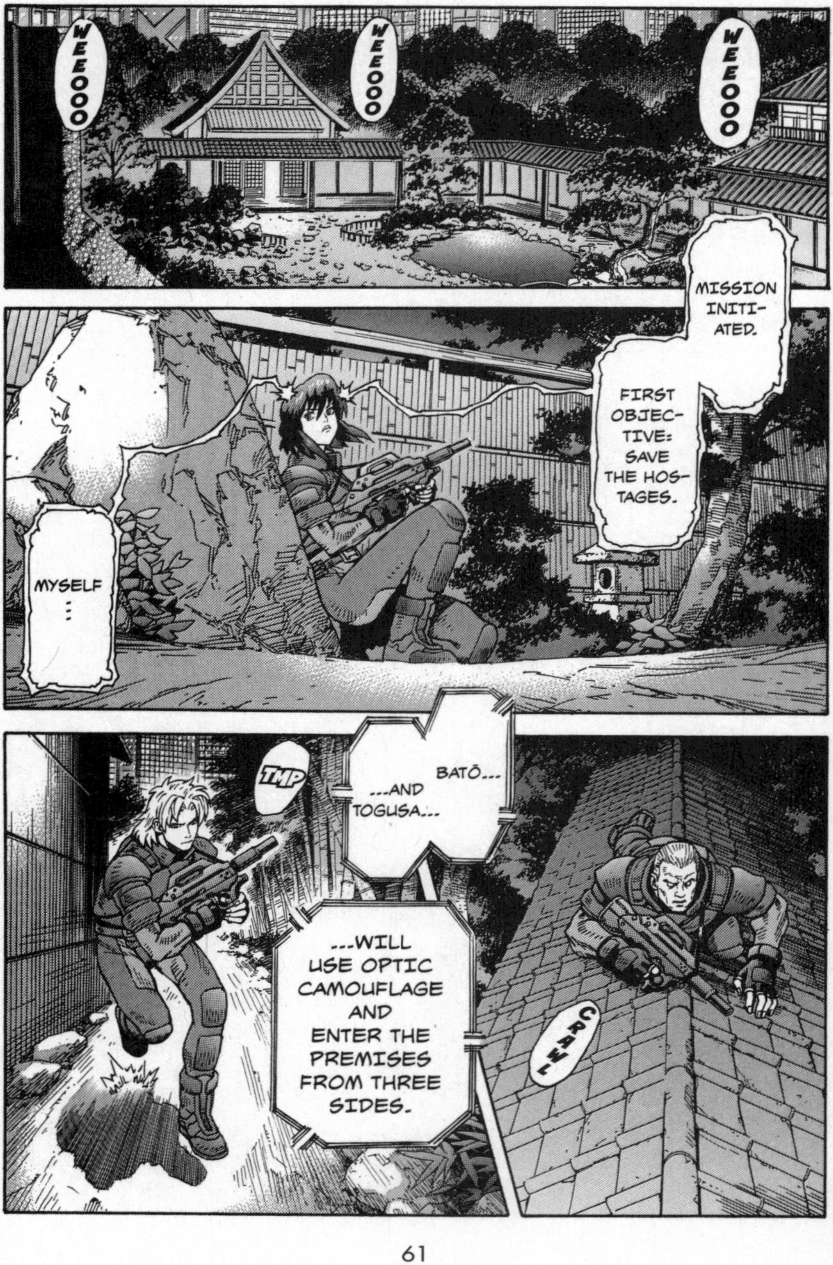
WEEOOO
WEEOOO
WEEOOO
MISSION INITI-ATED.
FIRST OBJEC-TIVE: SAVE THE HOS-TAGES.
MYSELF ...
BATŌ...
...AND TOGUSA...
...WILL USE OPTIC CAMOUFLAGE AND ENTER THE PREMISES FROM THREE SIDES.
CRAWL
TMP

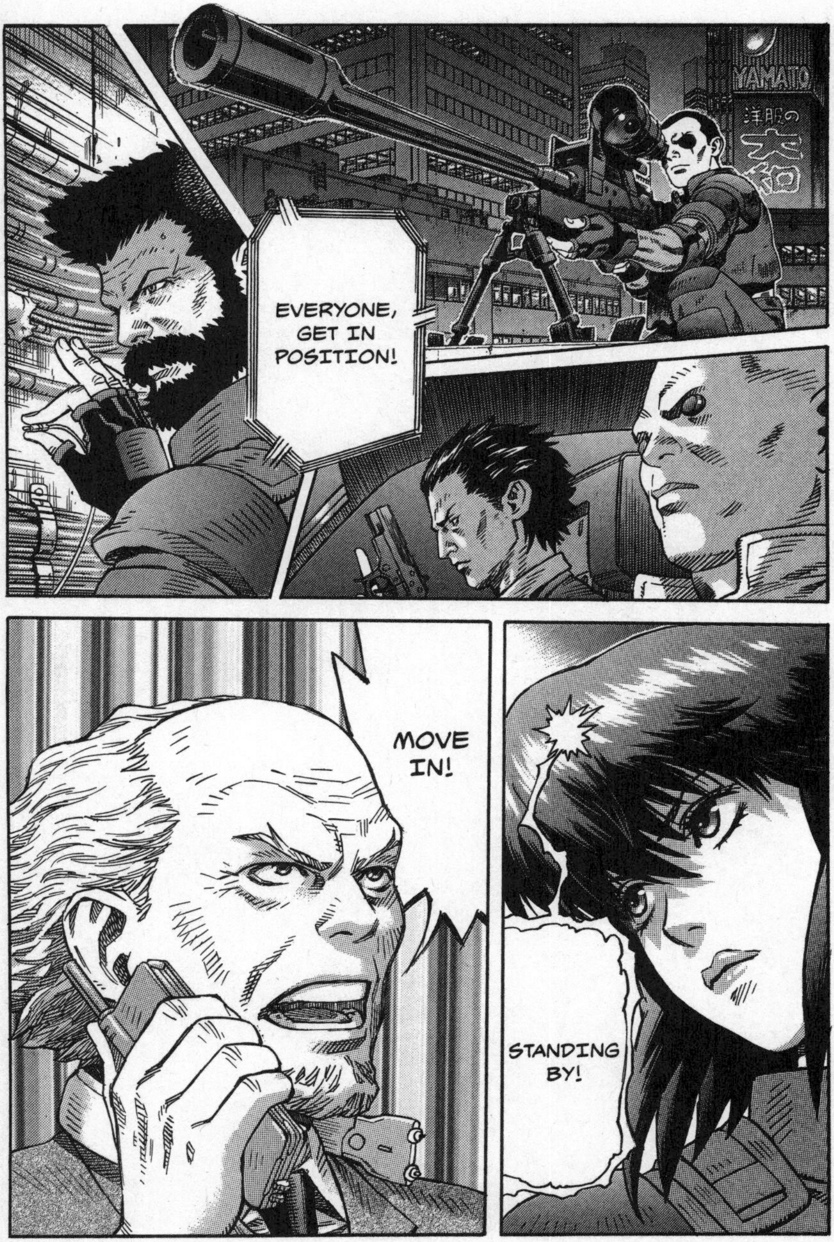
YAMATO
洋服の
EVERYONE, GET IN POSITION!
STANDING BY!
MOVE IN!

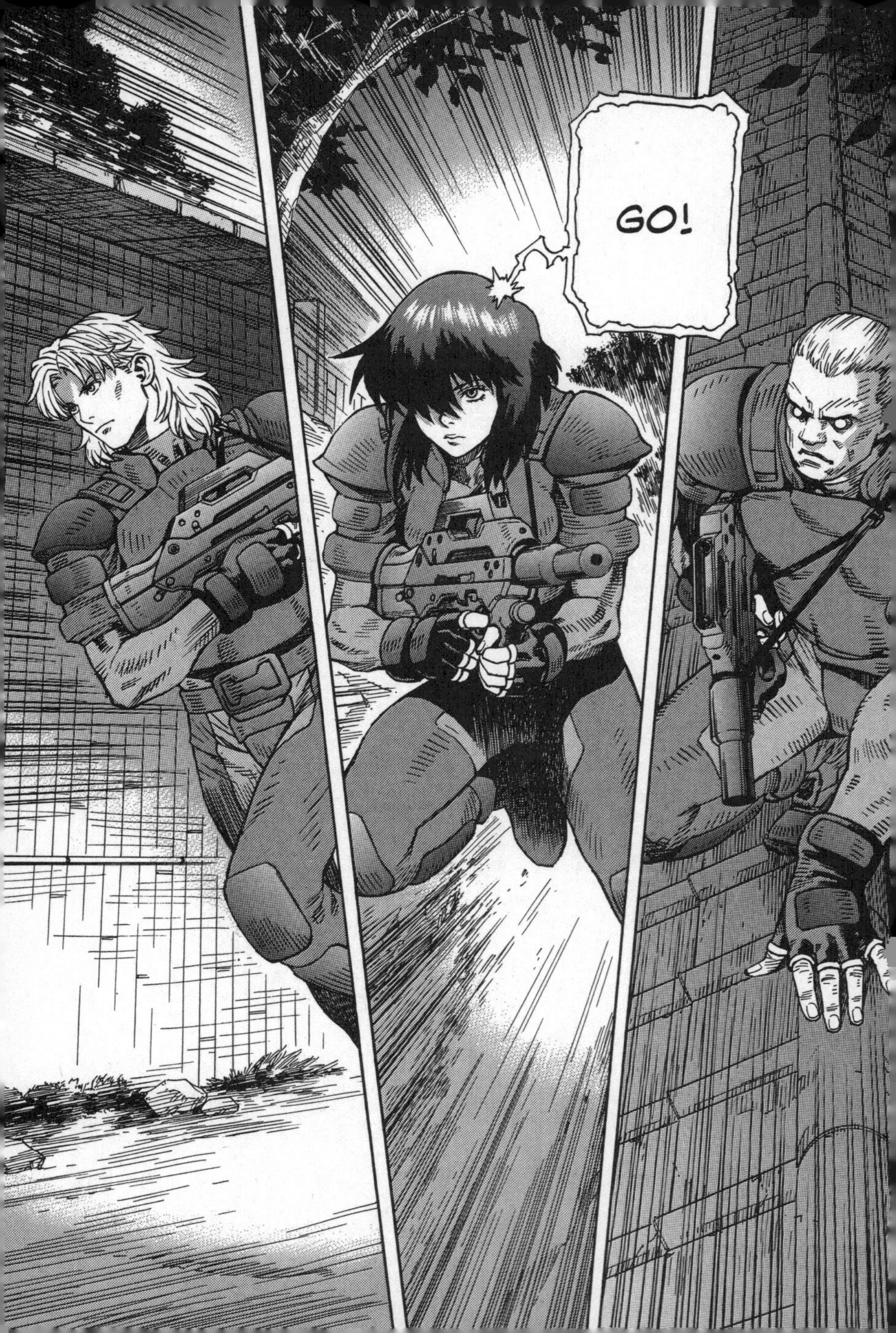
GO!

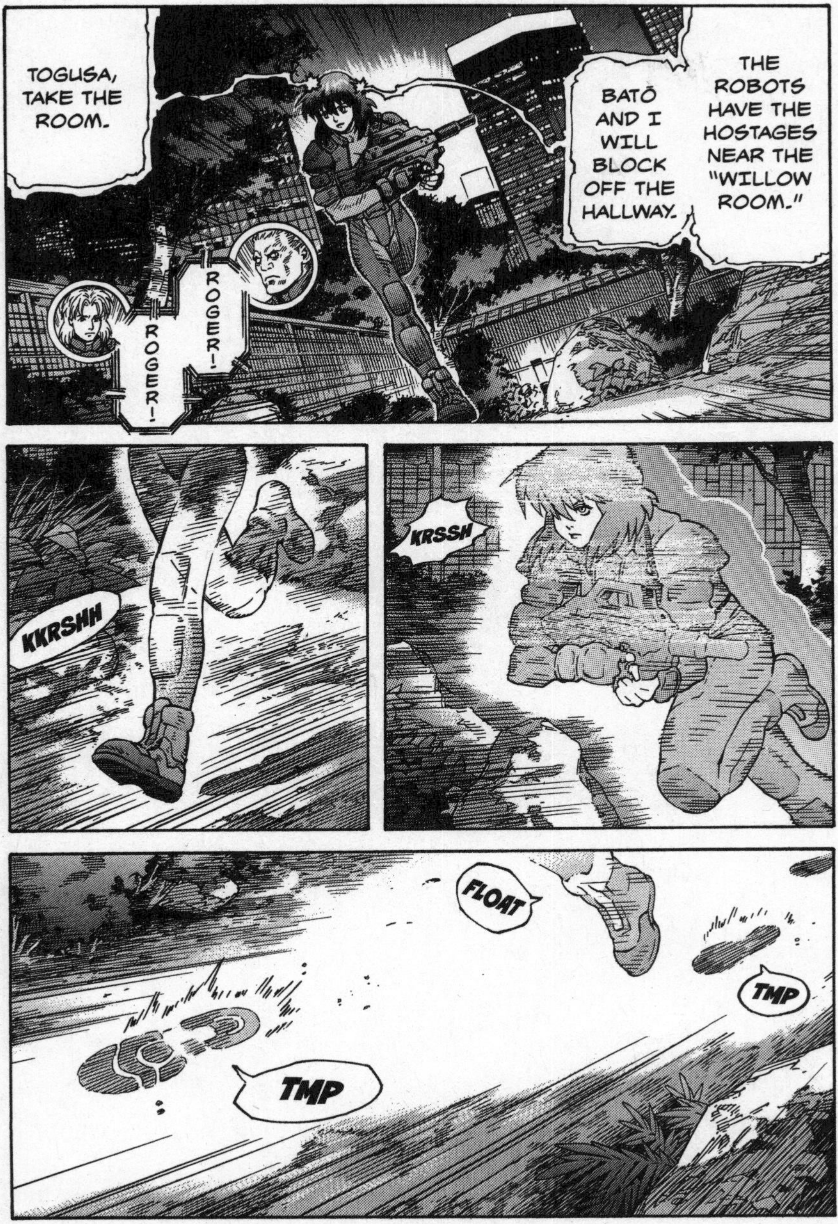
THE ROBOTS HAVE THE HOSTAGES NEAR THE "WILLOW ROOM."
BATŌ AND I WILL BLOCK OFF THE HALLWAY.
TOGUSA, TAKE THE ROOM.
ROGER!
ROGER!
KRSSH
KKRSHH
FLOAT
TMP
TMP

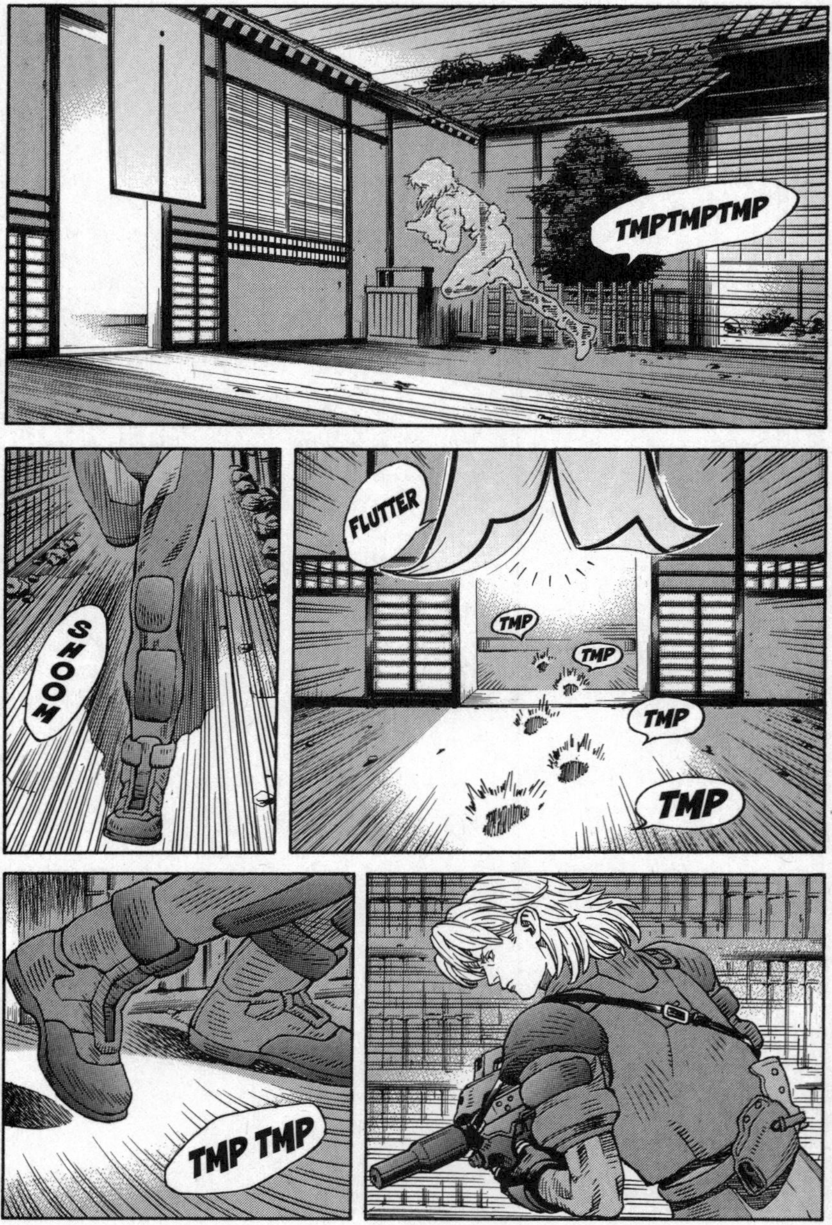
TMPTMPTMP
FLUTTER
TMP
TMP
TMP
TMP
SHOOM
TMP TMP

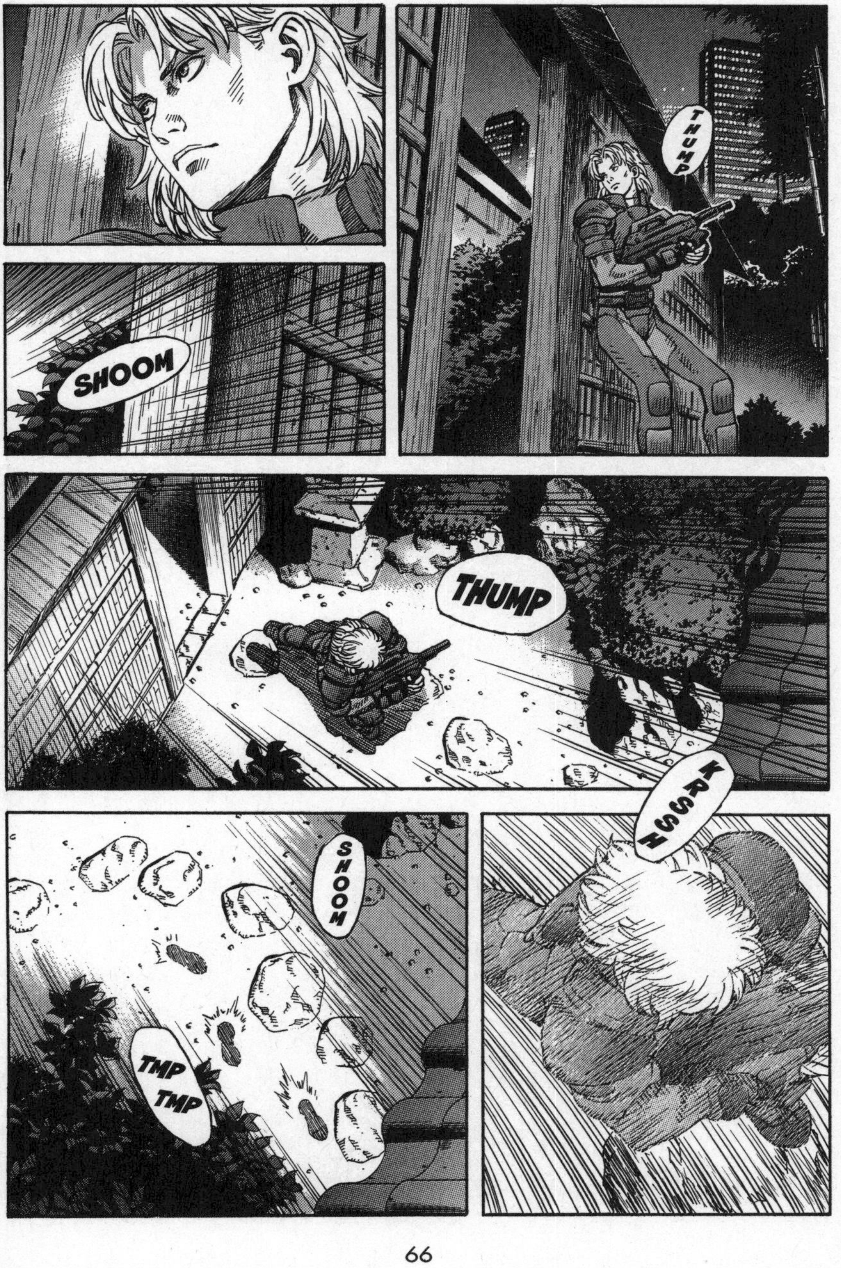
THUMP
SHOOM
THUMP
KRSSH
SHOOM
TMP TMP

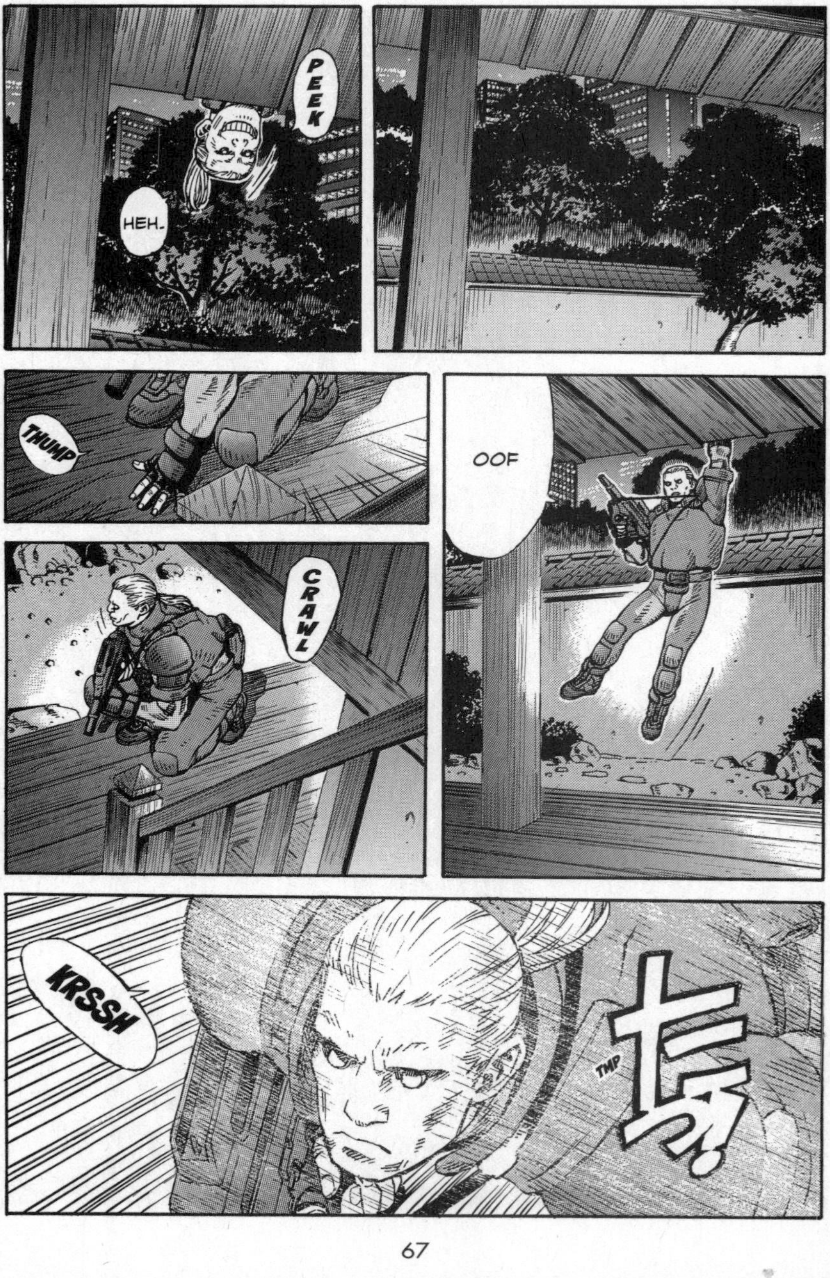
PEEK
HEH.
OOF
THUMP
CRAWL
TMP
KRSSH

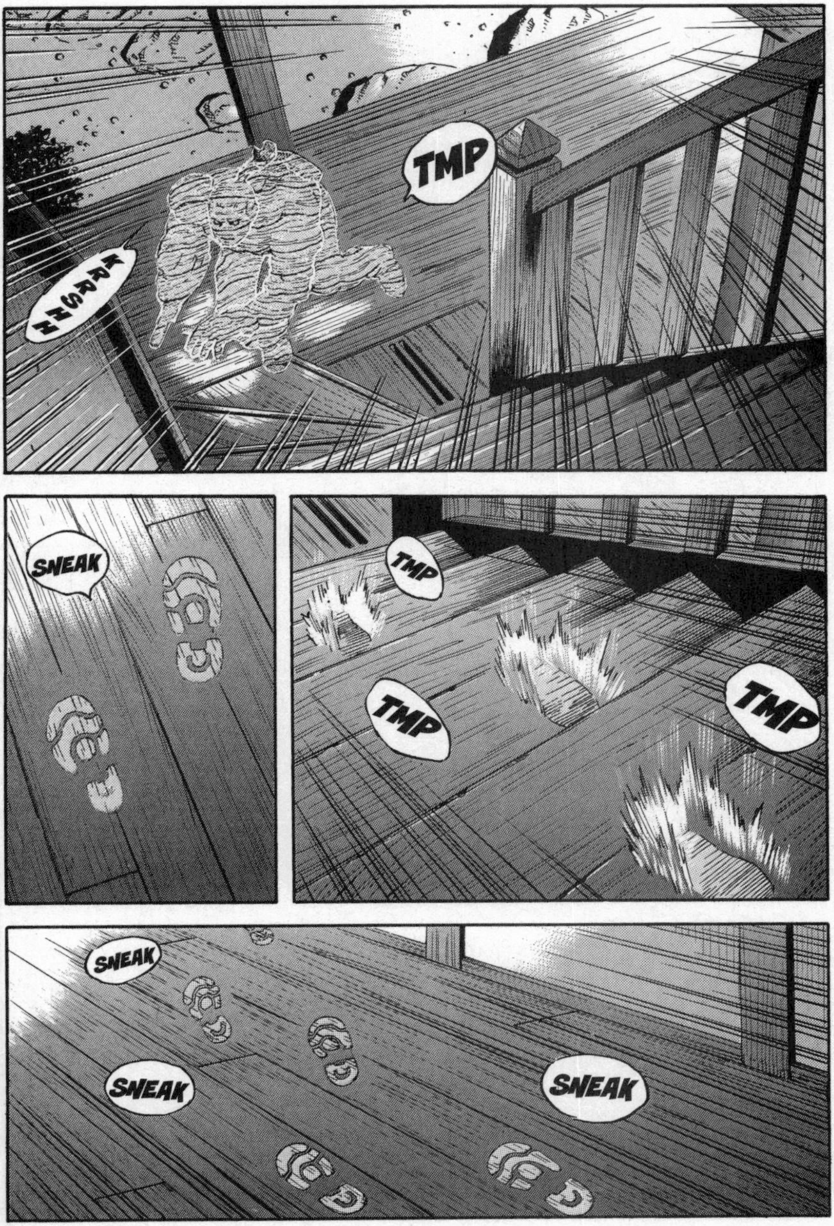
TMP
KRSH
TMP
TMP
TMP
SNEAK
SNEAK
SNEAK
SNEAK

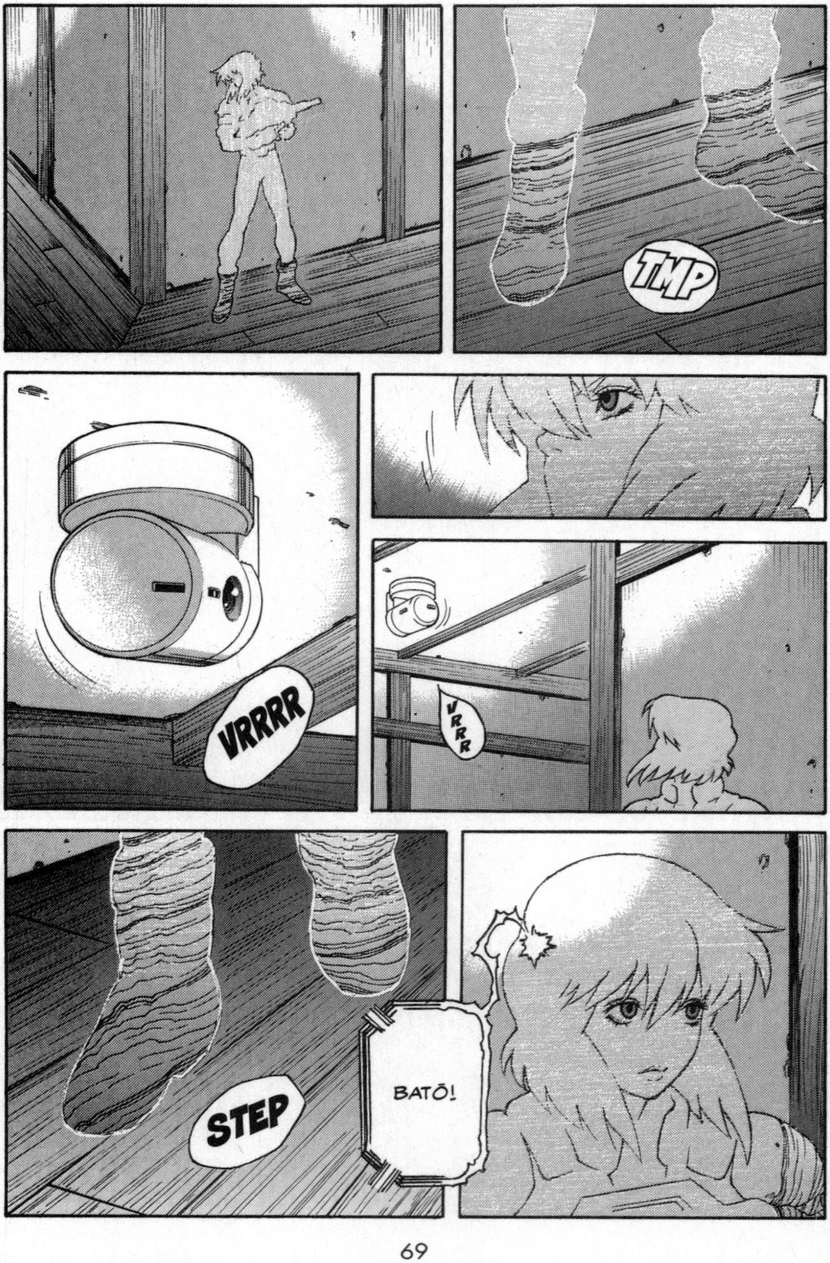
TMP
VRRR
VRRRR
BATŌ!
STEP

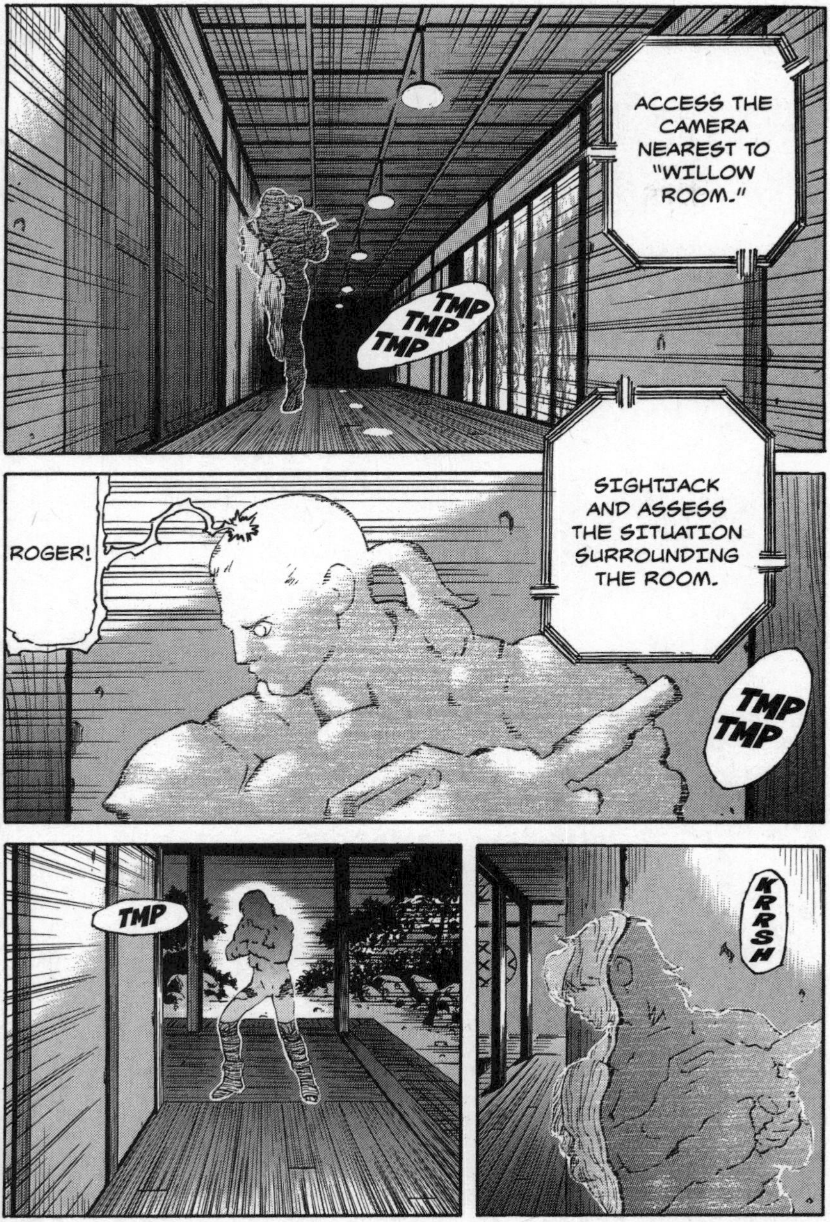

ACCESS THE CAMERA NEAREST TO "WILLOW ROOM."
TMP TMP TMP
SIGHTJACK AND ASSESS THE SITUATION SURROUNDING THE ROOM.
TMP TMP
ROGER!
KRRSH
TMP

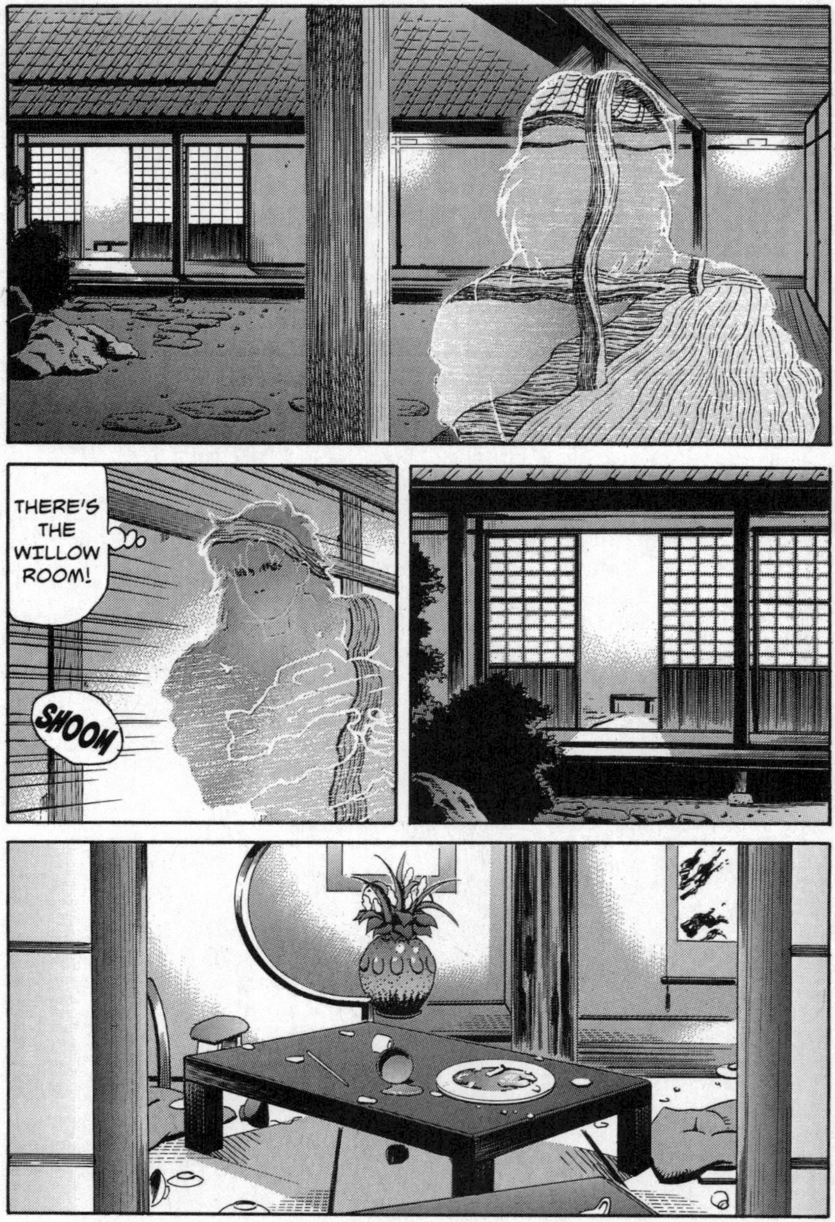
THERE'S THE WILLOW ROOM!
SHOOM

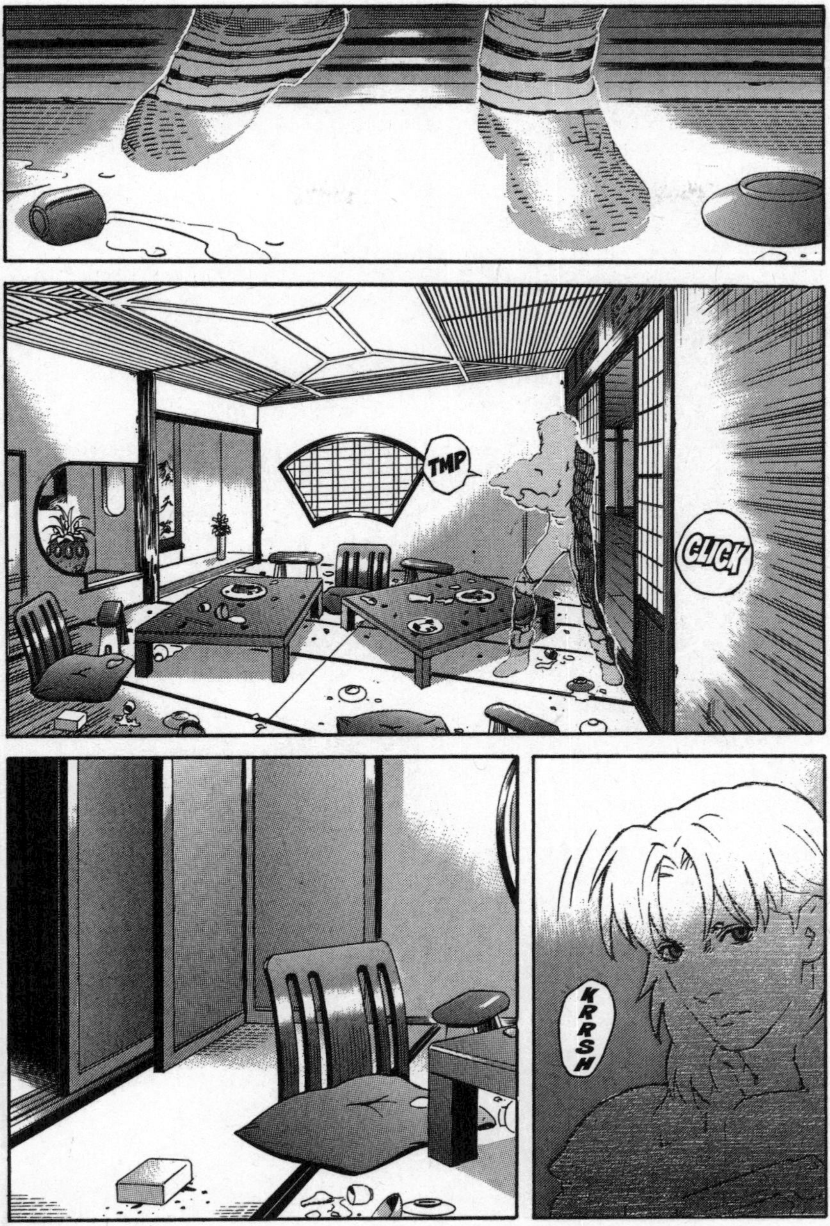
CLICK
TMP
KRRSH

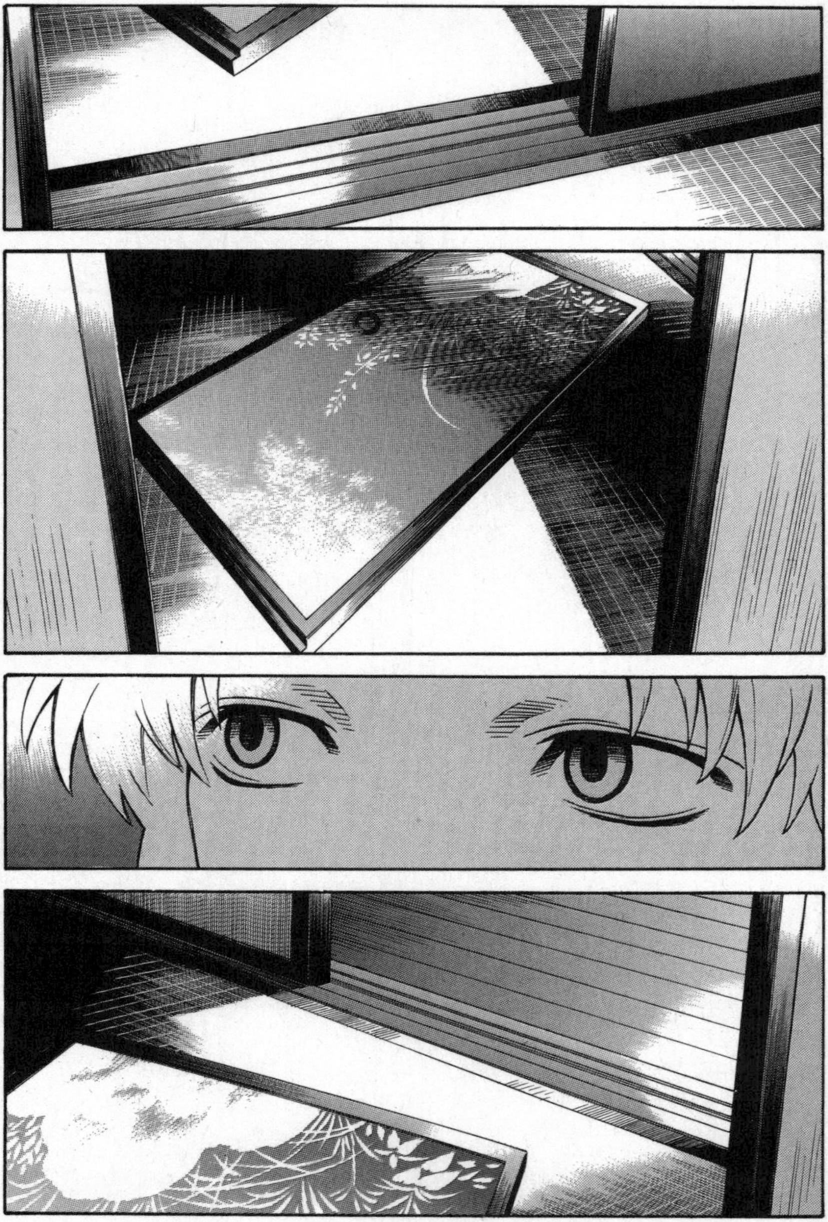

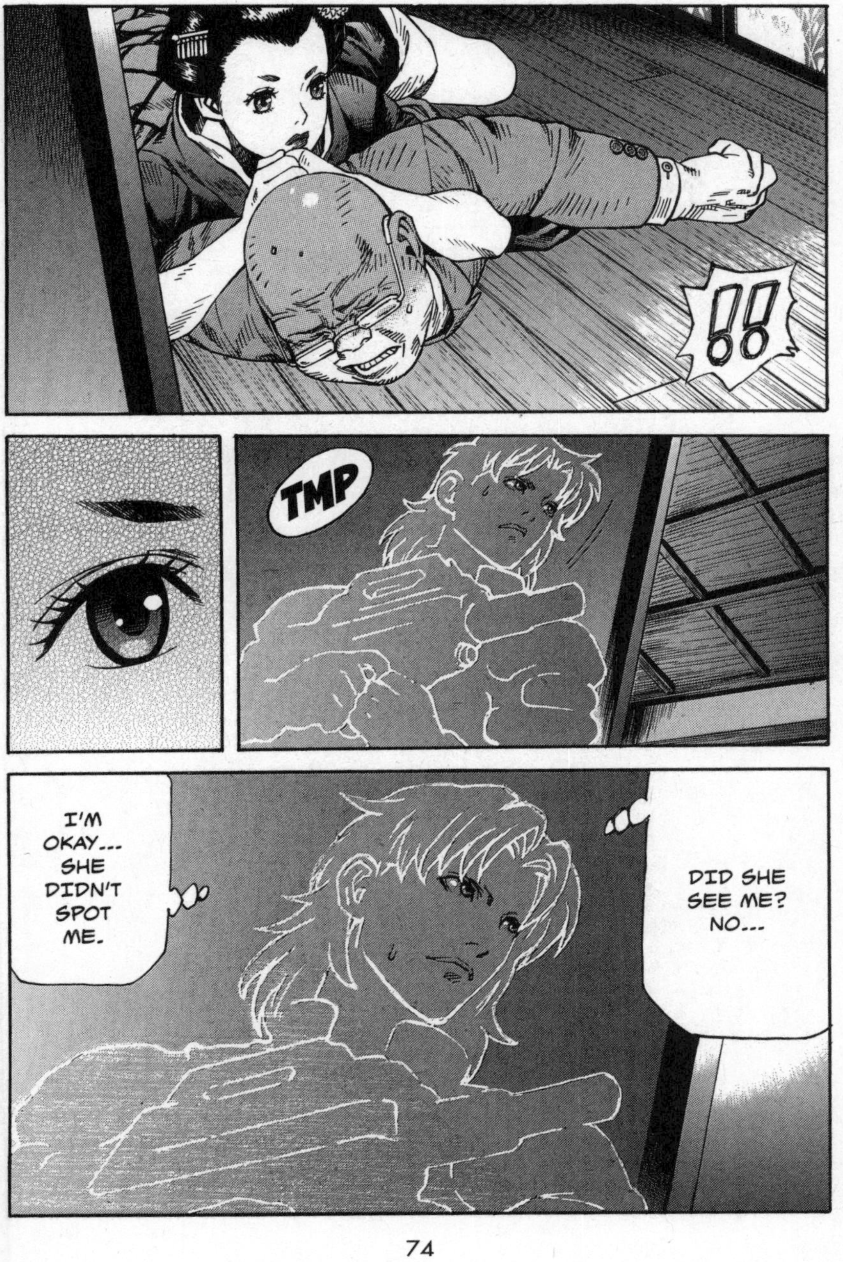
!!
TMP
DID SHE SEE ME? NO...
I'M OKAY... SHE DIDN'T SPOT ME.

KRRSH
CHHHN
BZZN
BZZN
BZZN
BZZN
BZZN
BZZN...

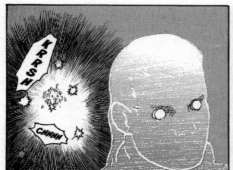

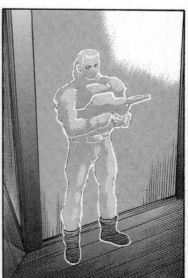

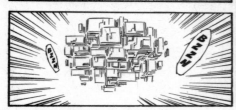

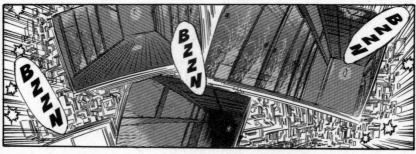

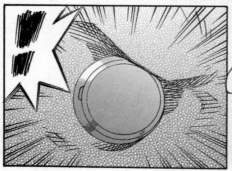

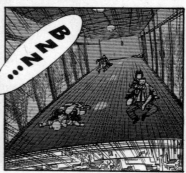

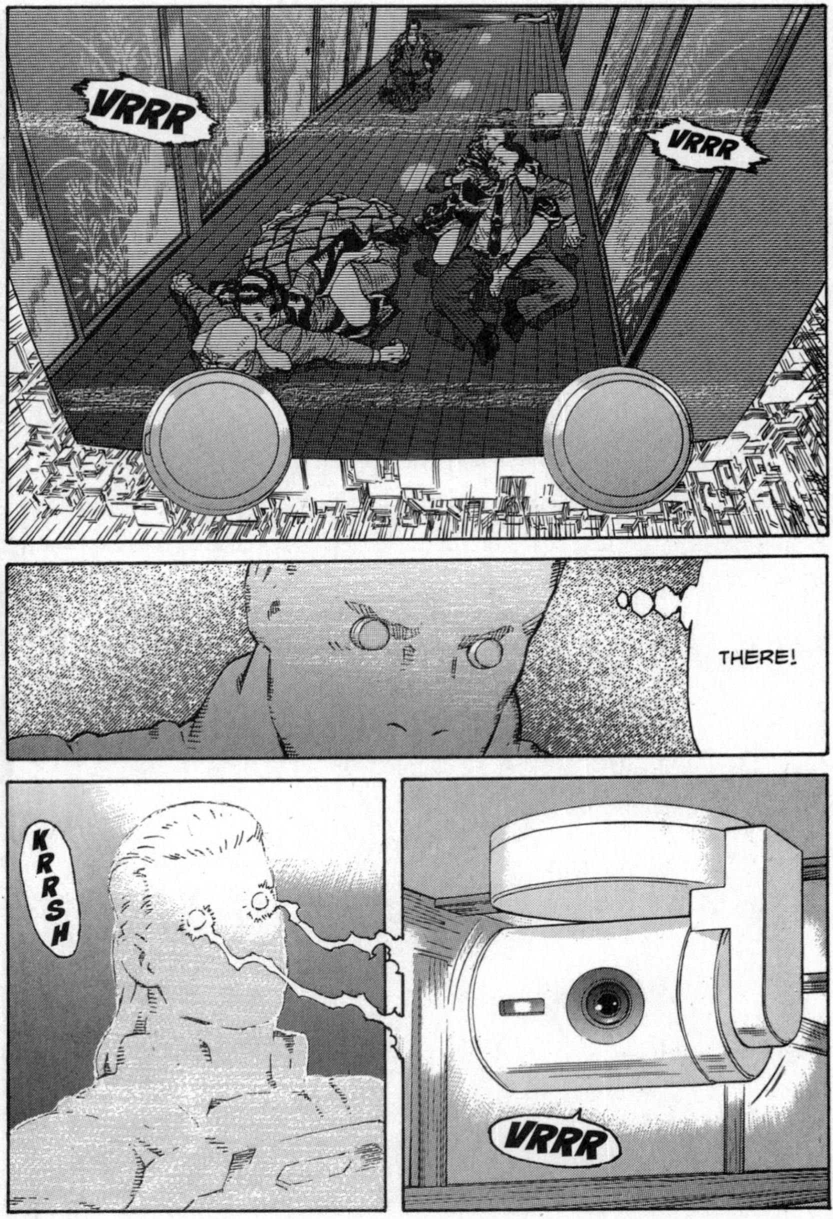
VRRR
VRRR
THERE!
VRRR
KRRSH

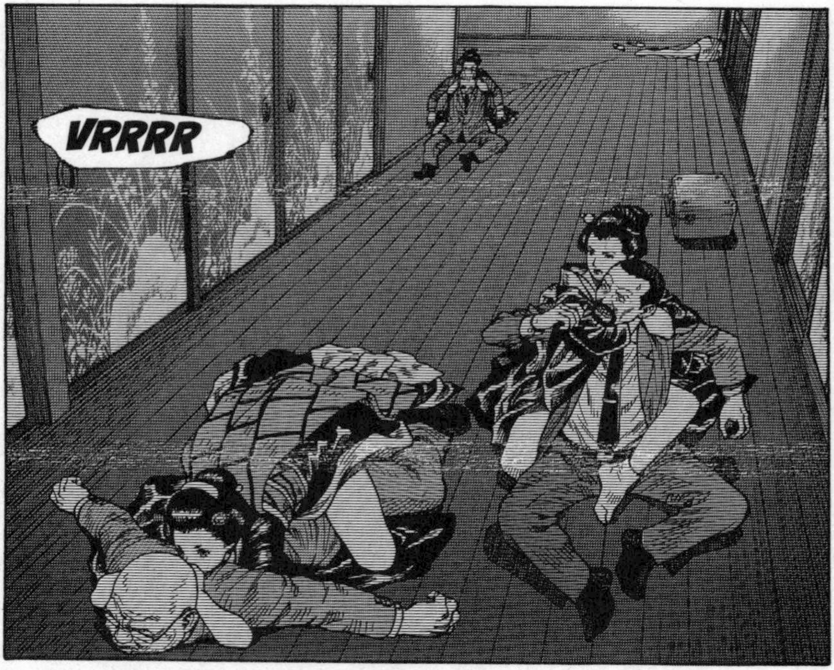
VRRRR
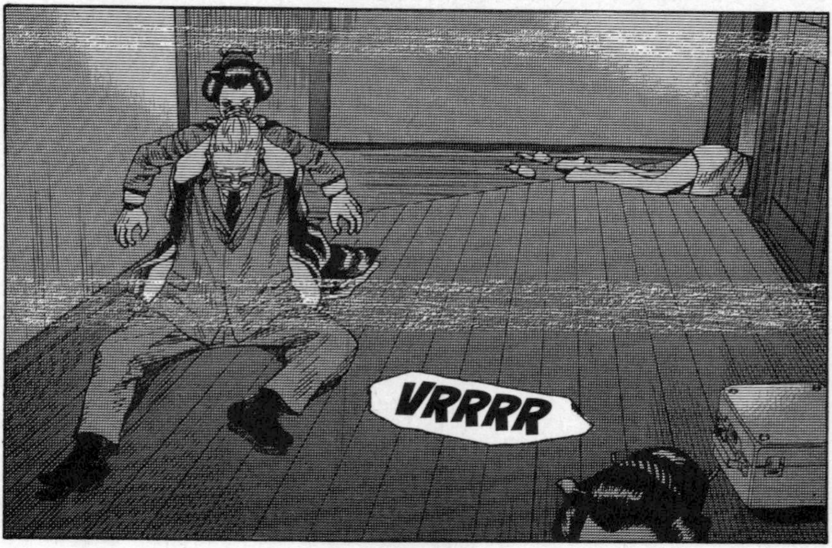
VRRRR

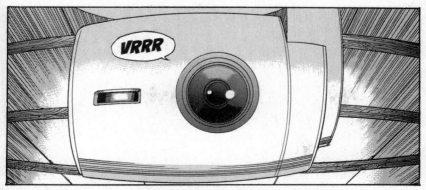

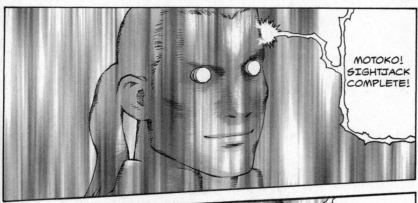

MOTOKO! SIGHTJACK COMPLETE!

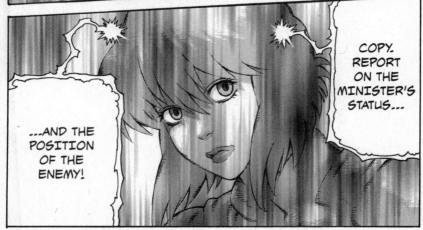

COPY. REPORT ON THE MINISTER'S STATUS...

...AND THE POSITION OF THE ENEMY!

#003 / End

#004: Launching Attack

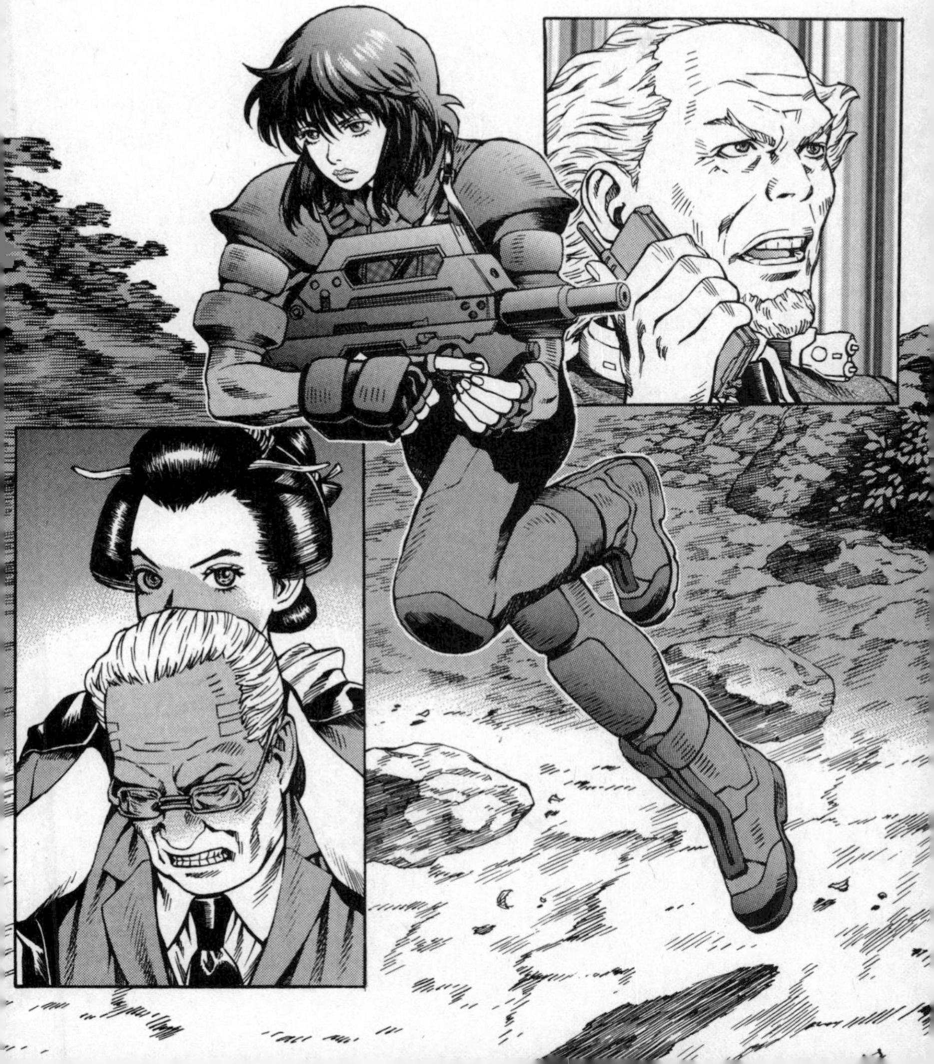

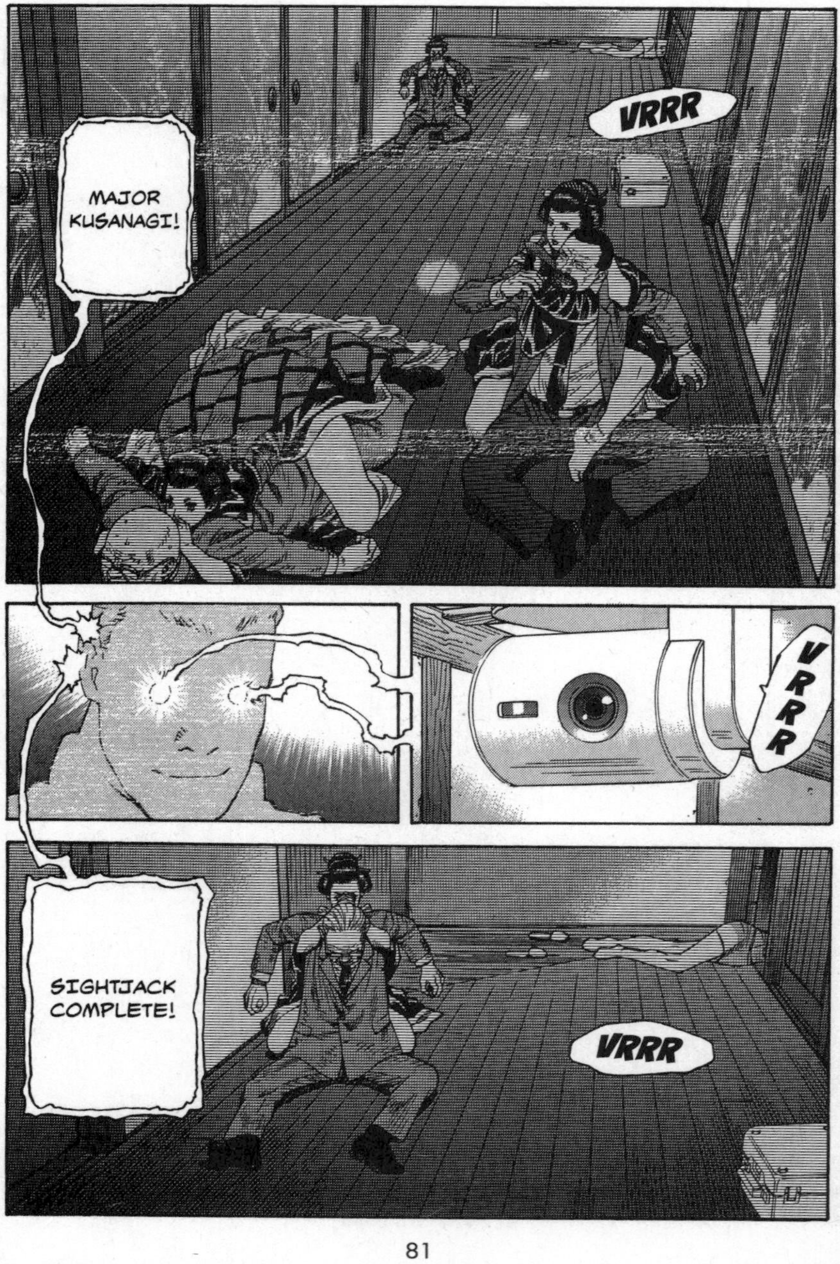
VRRR
MAJOR KUSANAGI!
VRRR
VRRR
SIGHTJACK COMPLETE!

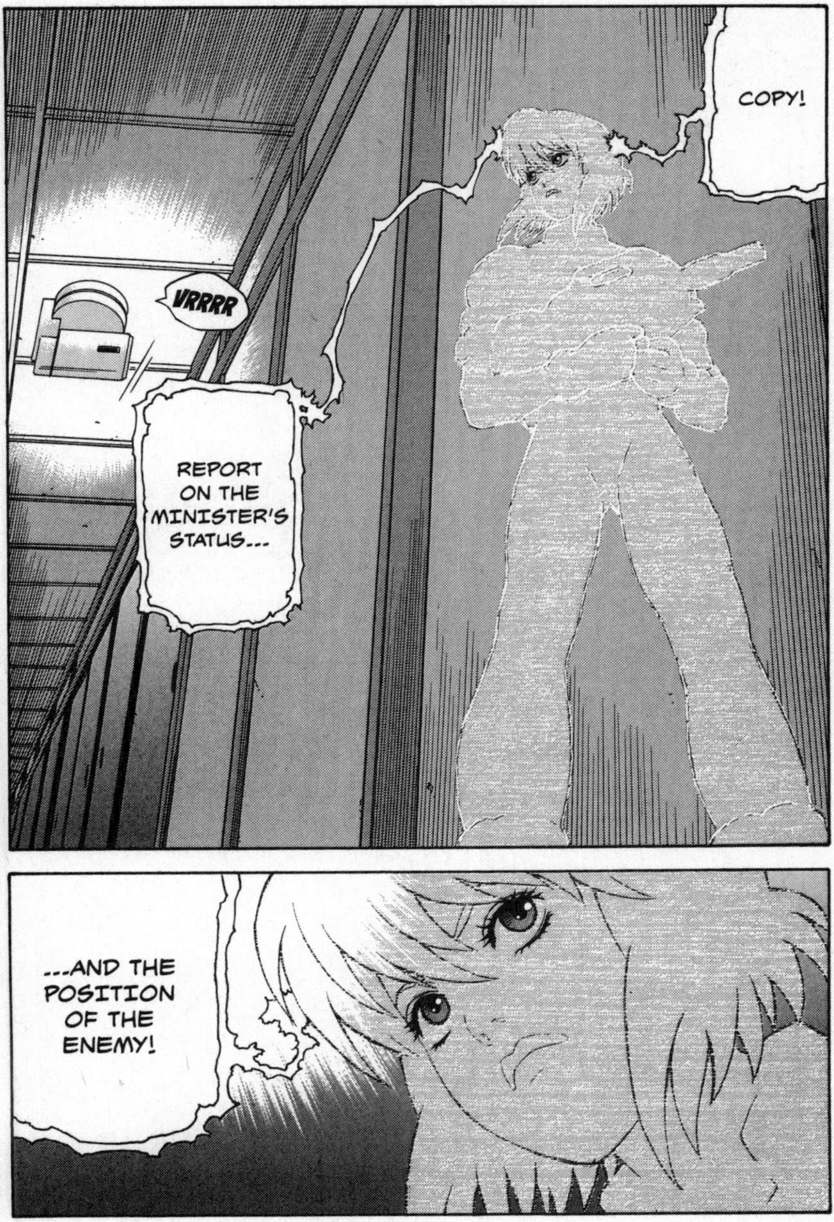
COPY!
VRRRR
REPORT ON THE MINISTER'S STATUS...
...AND THE POSITION OF THE ENEMY!

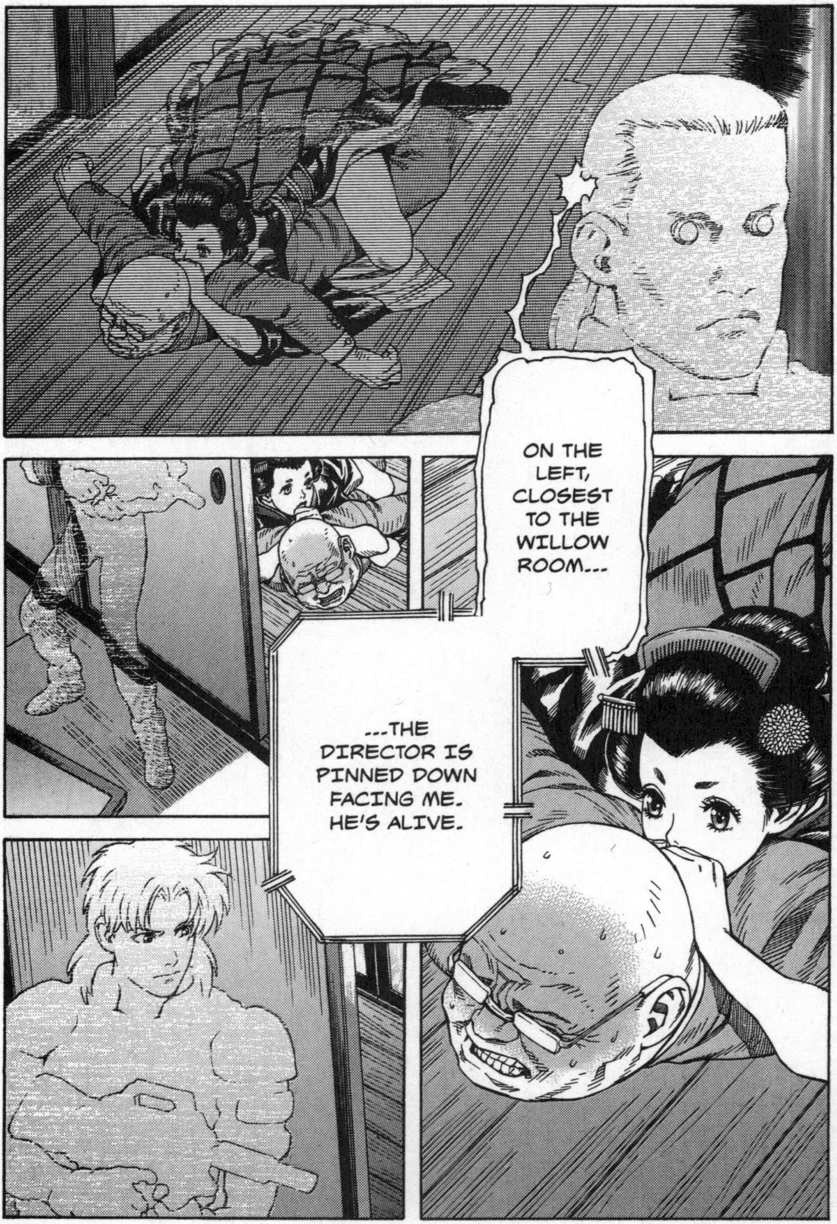
ON THE LEFT, CLOSEST TO THE WILLOW ROOM...
...THE DIRECTOR IS PINNED DOWN FACING ME. HE'S ALIVE.

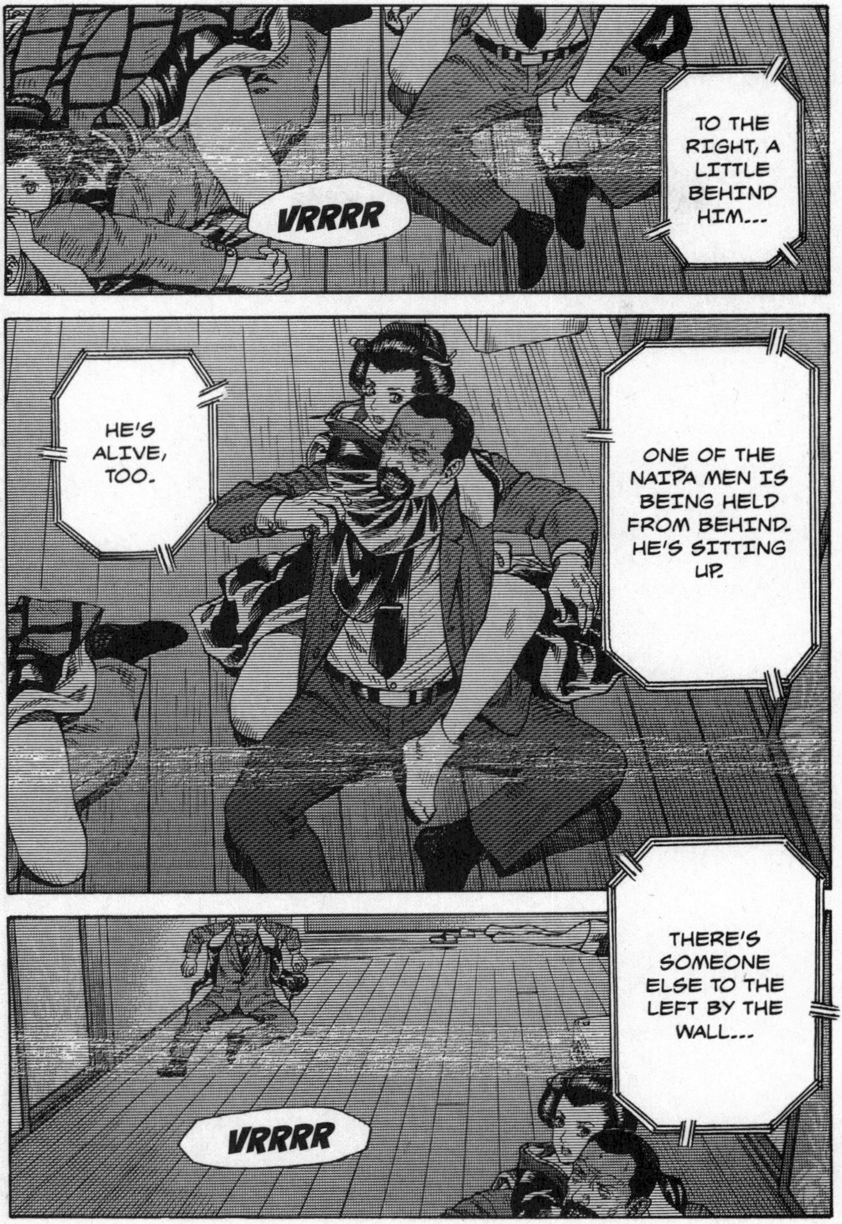
TO THE RIGHT, A LITTLE BEHIND HIM...
VRRRR
ONE OF THE NAIPA MEN IS BEING HELD FROM BEHIND. HE'S SITTING UP.
HE'S ALIVE, TOO.
THERE'S SOMEONE ELSE TO THE LEFT BY THE WALL...
VRRRR

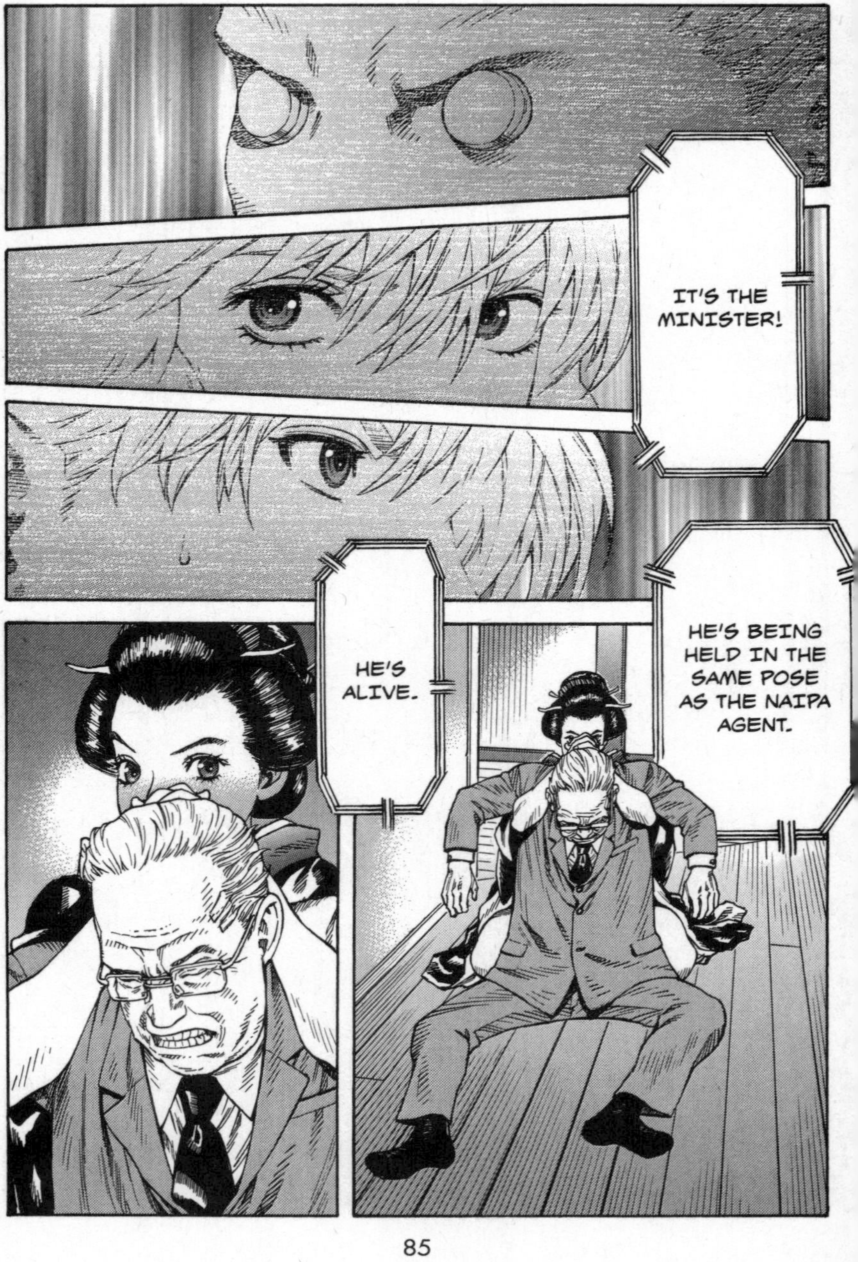
IT'S THE MINISTER!
HE'S BEING HELD IN THE SAME POSE AS THE NAIPA AGENT.
HE'S ALIVE.

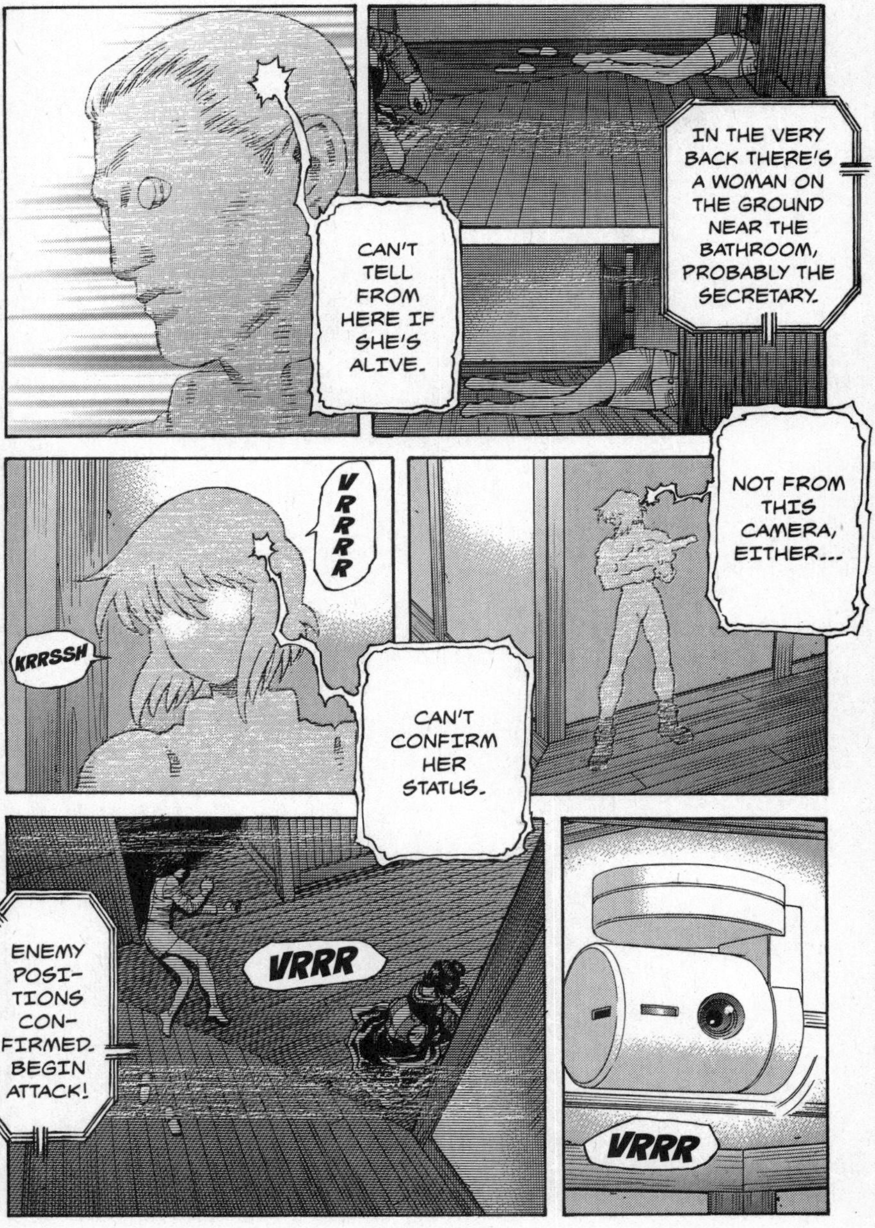
IN THE VERY BACK THERE'S A WOMAN ON THE GROUND NEAR THE BATHROOM, PROBABLY THE SECRETARY.
CAN'T TELL FROM HERE IF SHE'S ALIVE.
NOT FROM THIS CAMERA, EITHER...
VRRRR
KRRSSH
CAN'T CONFIRM HER STATUS.
VRRR
VRRR
ENEMY POSITIONS CONFIRMED. BEGIN ATTACK!

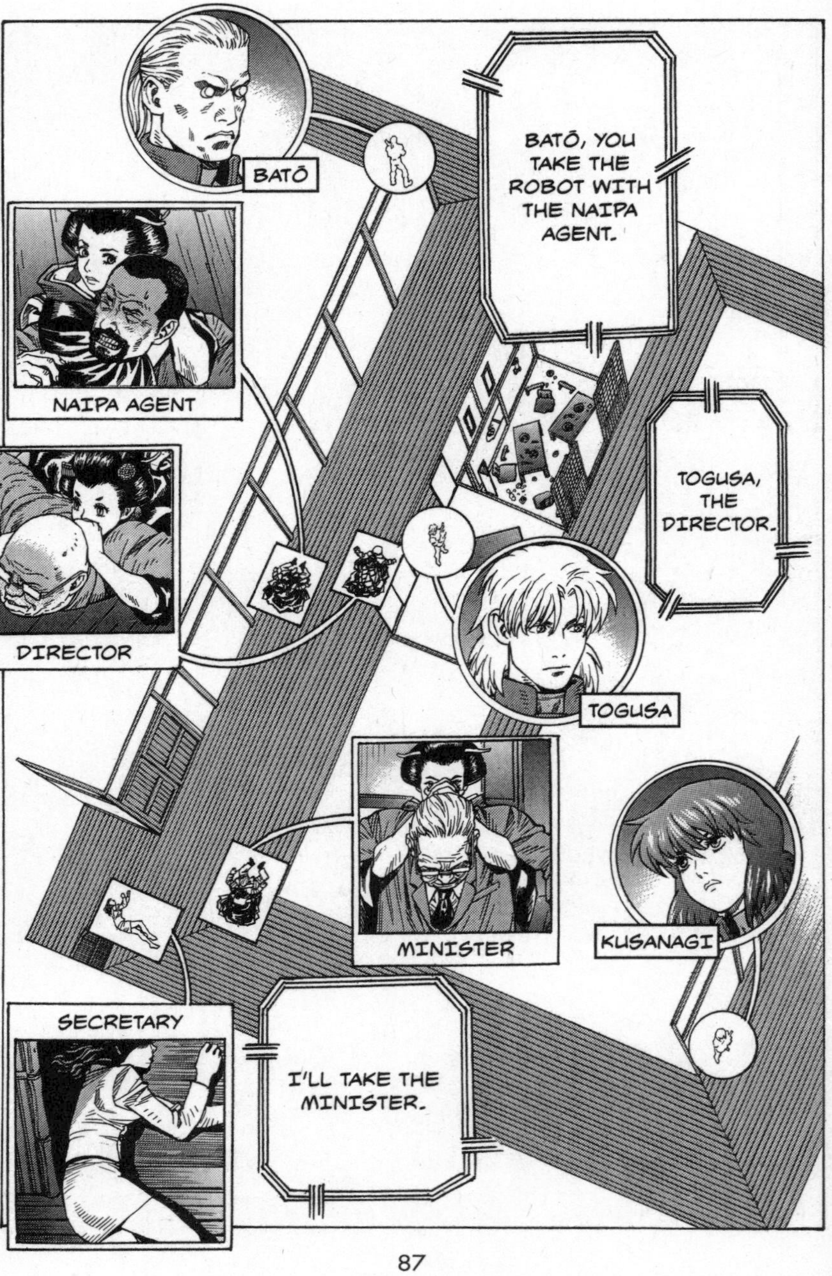
BATŌ, YOU TAKE THE ROBOT WITH THE NAIPA AGENT.
BATŌ
NAIPA AGENT
TOGUSA, THE DIRECTOR.
TOGUSA
DIRECTOR
KUSANAGI
MINISTER
I'LL TAKE THE MINISTER.
SECRETARY

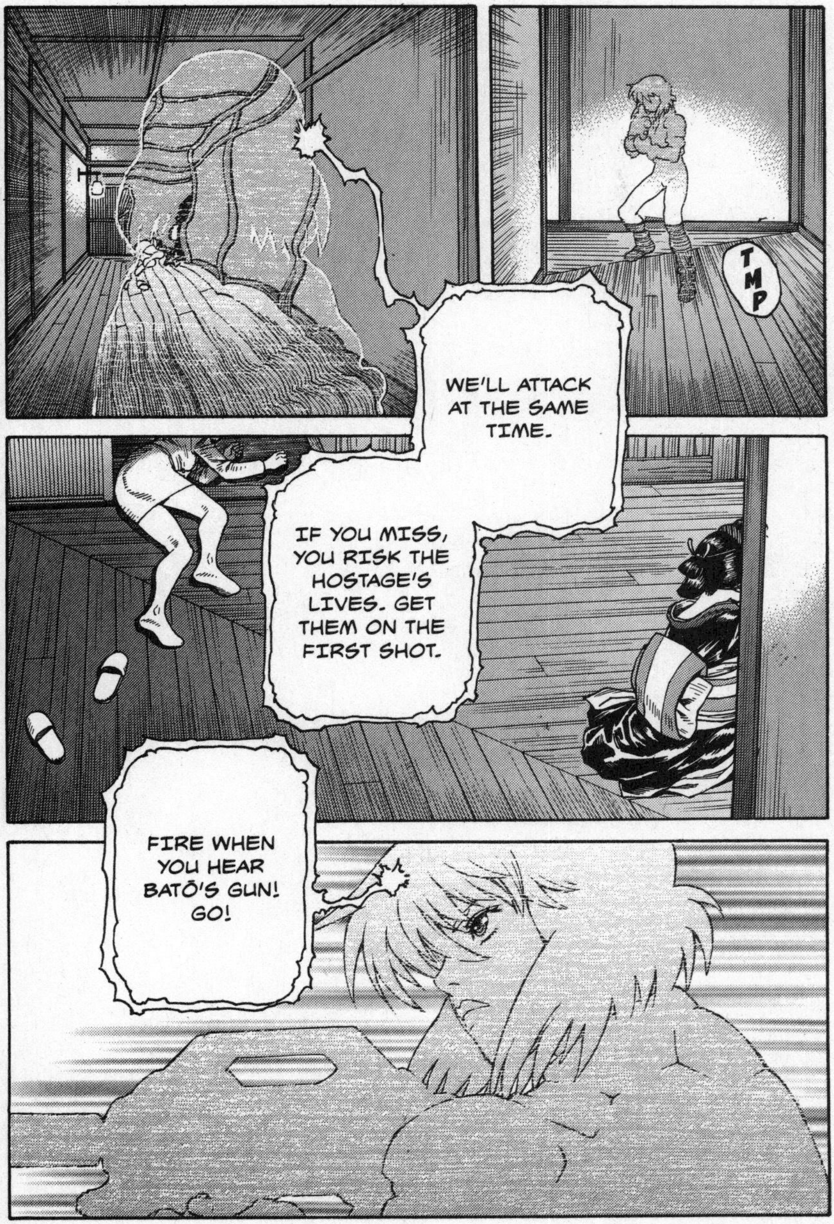
TMP
WE'LL ATTACK AT THE SAME TIME.
IF YOU MISS, YOU RISK THE HOSTAGE'S LIVES. GET THEM ON THE FIRST SHOT.
FIRE WHEN YOU HEAR BATŌ'S GUN! GO!

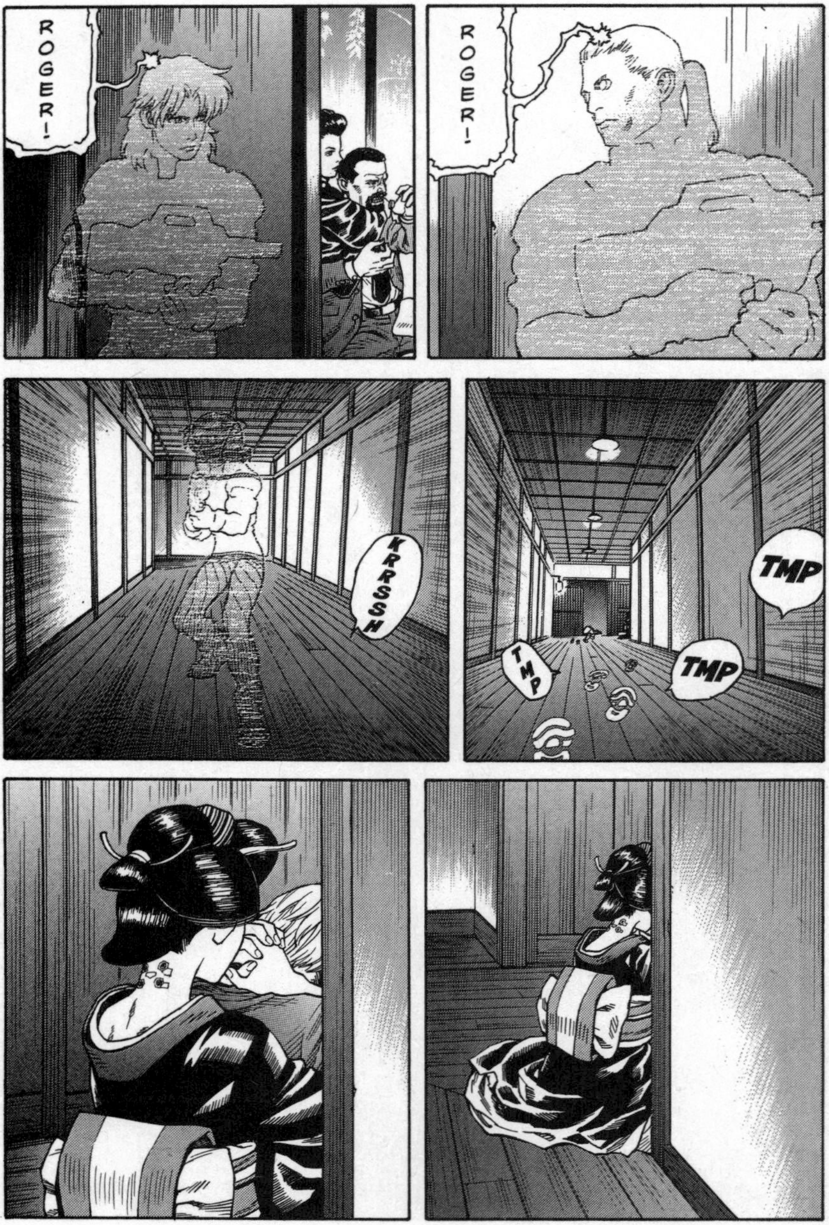
ROGER!
ROGER!
TMP
TMP
TMP
KRRSSH

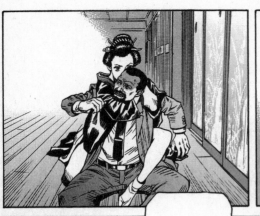

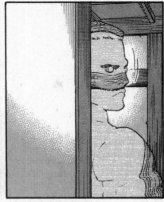

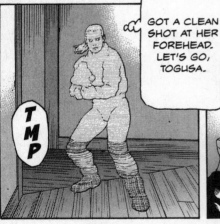

GOT A CLEAN SHOT AT HER FOREHEAD. LET'S GO, TOGUSA.

TMP

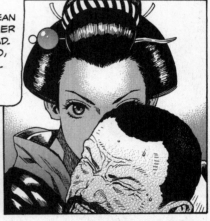

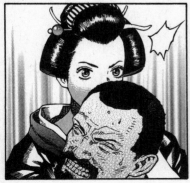

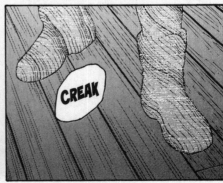

CREAK

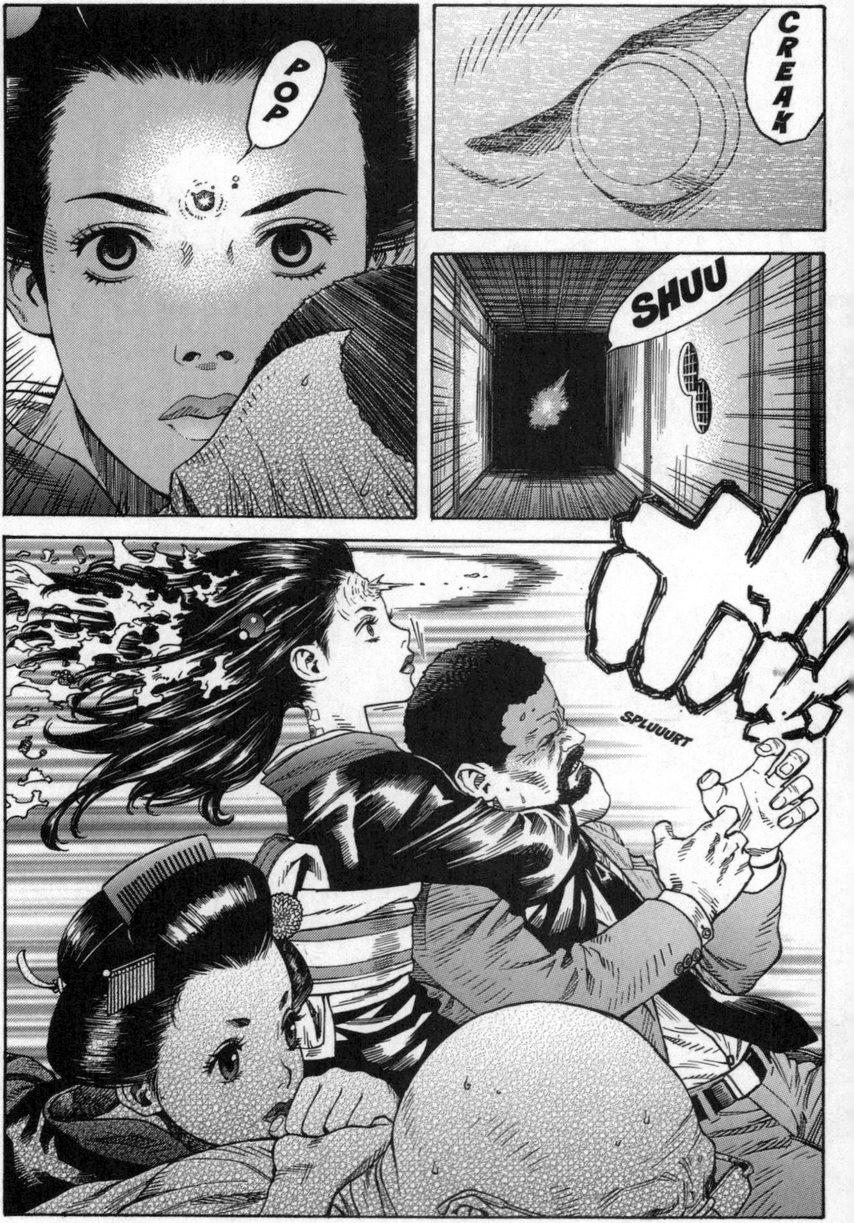
CREAK
SHUU
POP
SPLUUURT

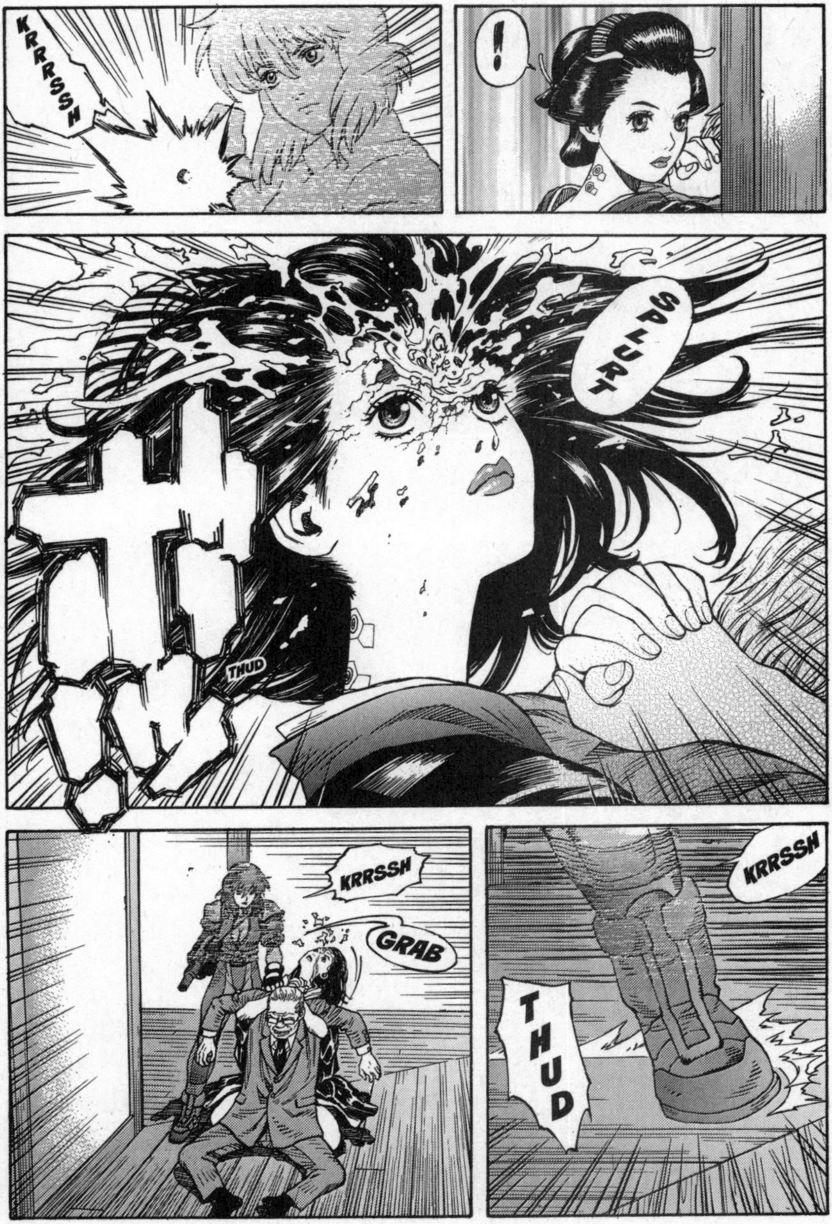
!
KRRRSSH
SPLURT
THUD
KRRSSH
THUD
KRRSSH
GRAB

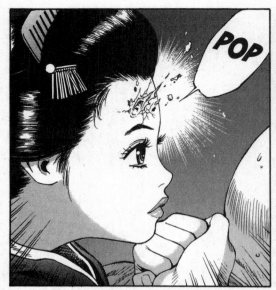

CHIKA CHIKA
POP
!
DAMN IT...
TOGUSA! YOU DIDN'T KILL HER!
TMP
SHE'LL GET AWAY!
THUMP

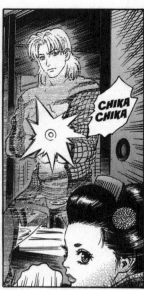

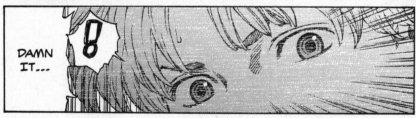

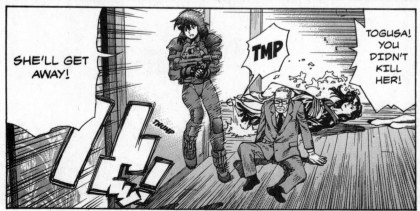

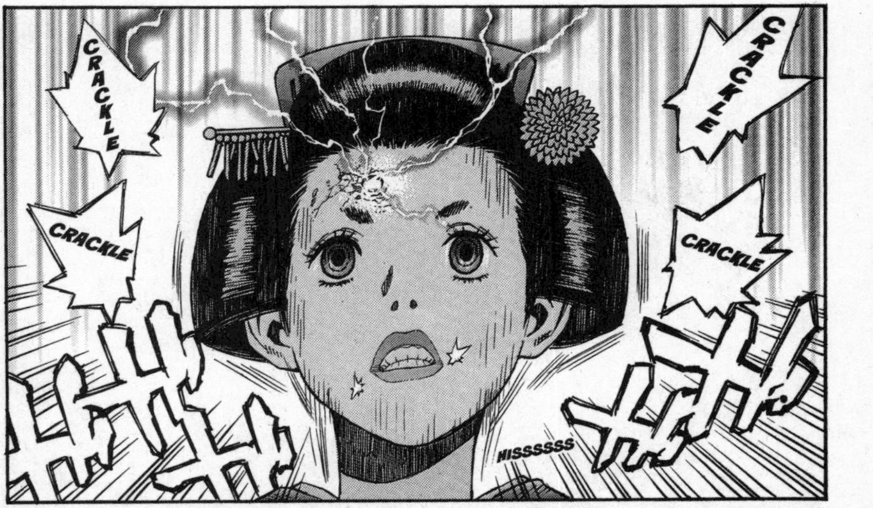
CRACKLE
CRACKLE
CRACKLE
CRACKLE
HISSSSSS

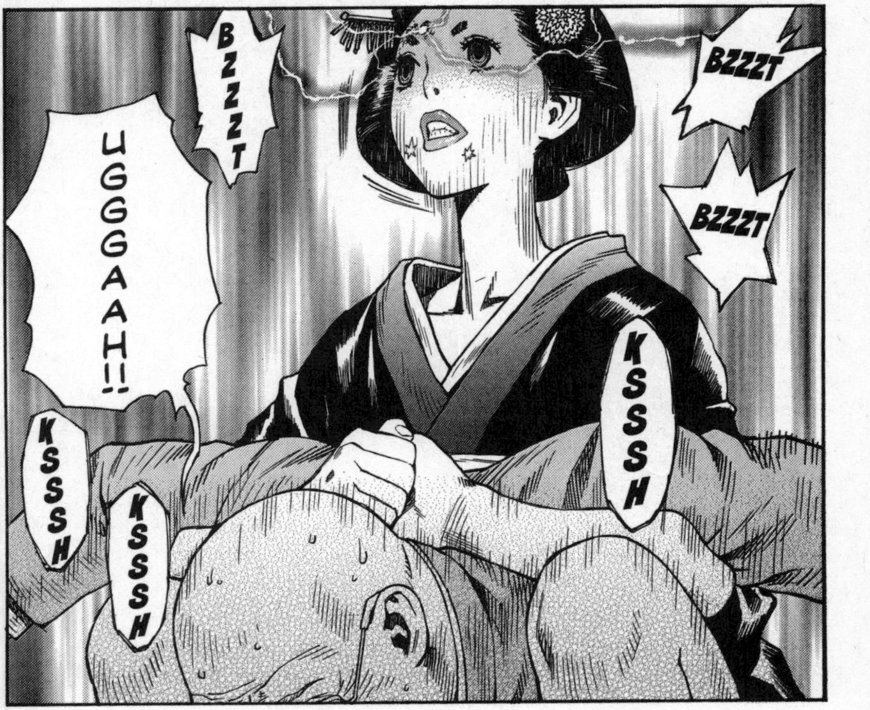
BZZZT
BZZZT
BZZZT
UGGGAAH!!
KSSSH
KSSSH
KSSSH

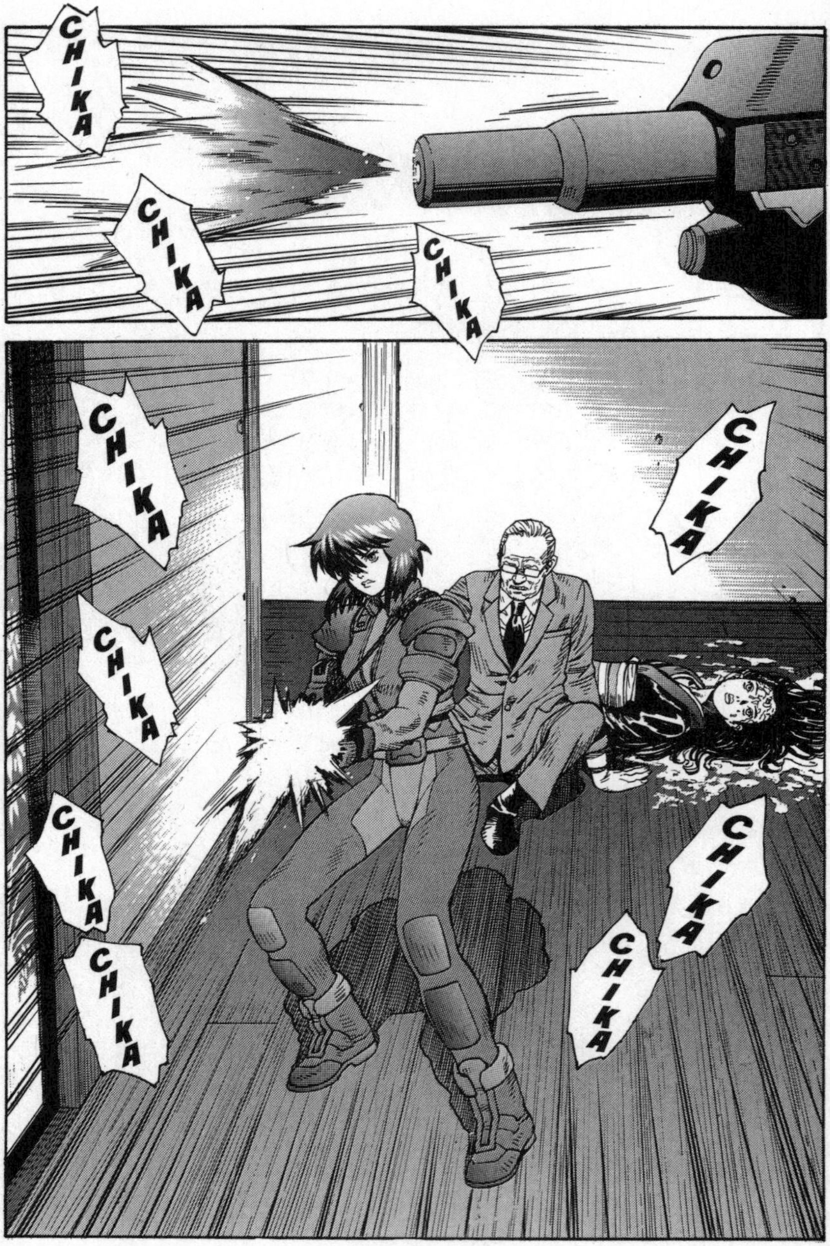
CHIKA
CHIKA
CHIKA
CHIKA
CHIKA
CHIKA
CHIKA
CHIKA
CHIKA
CHIKA

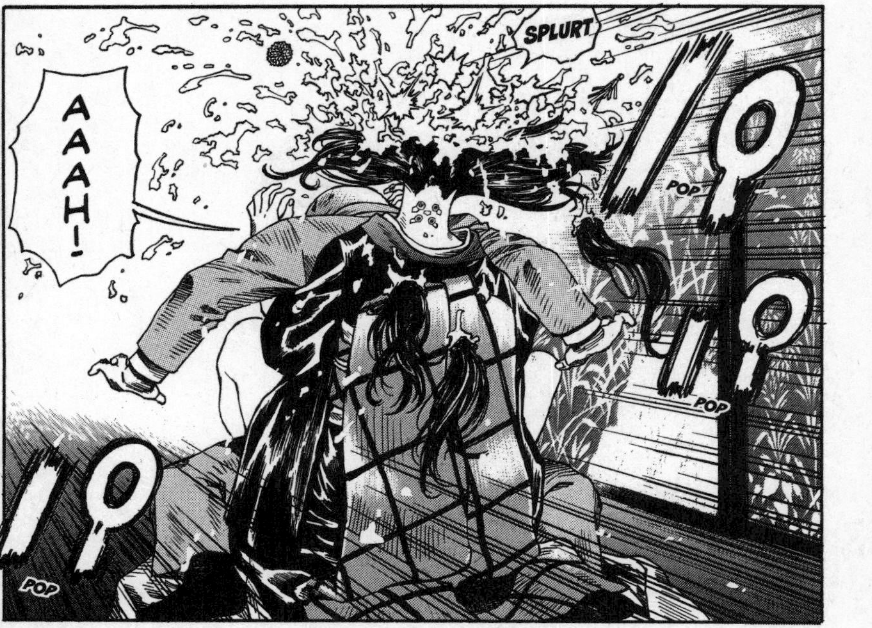
POP
POP
SPLURT
AAAH!
POP
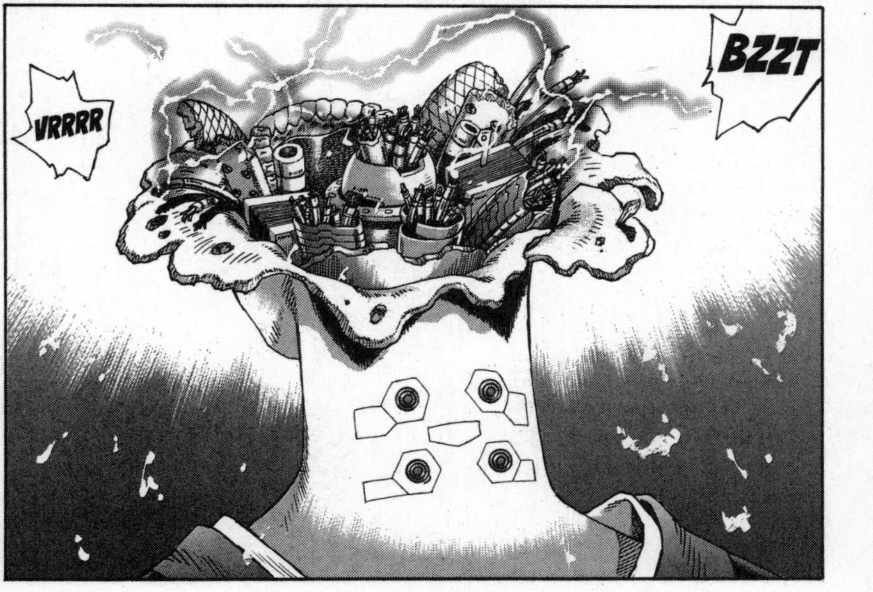
BZZT
VRRRR

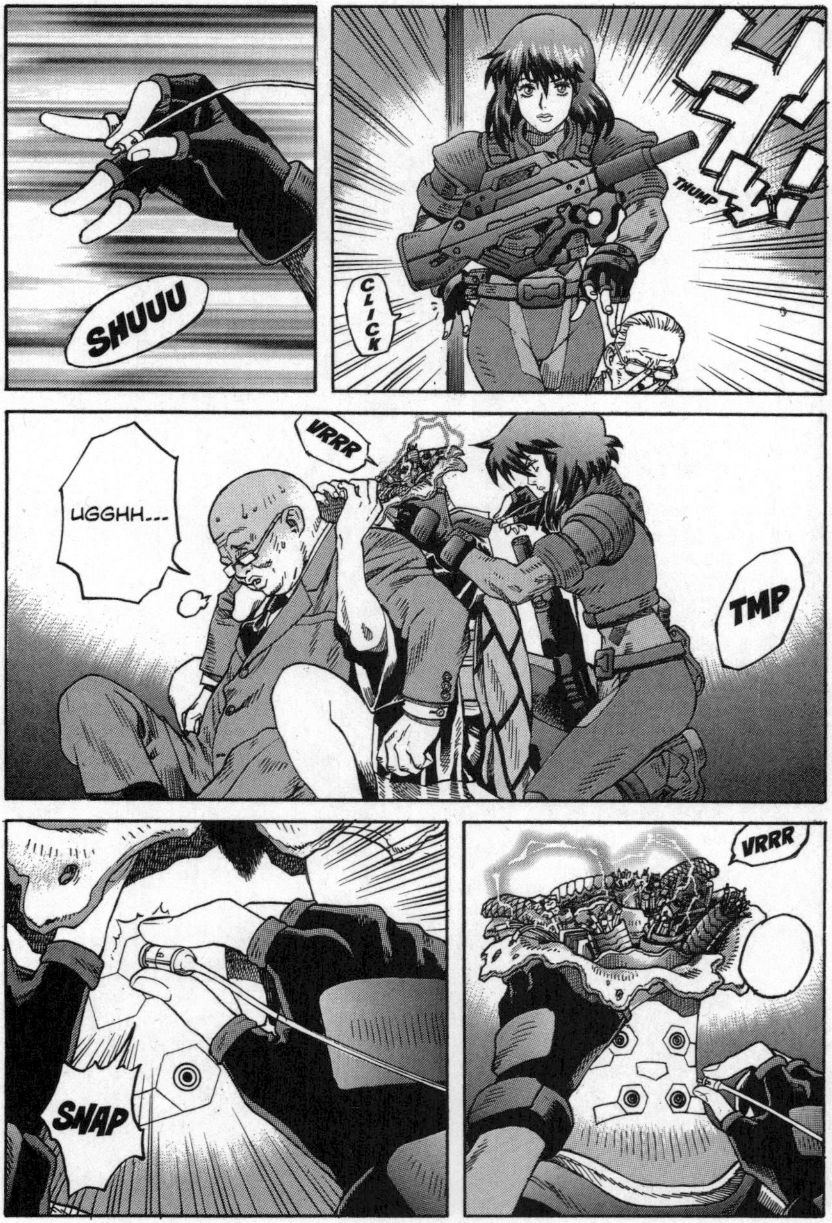
THUMP
CLICK
SHUUU
VRRR
UGGHH...
TMP
VRRR
SNAP

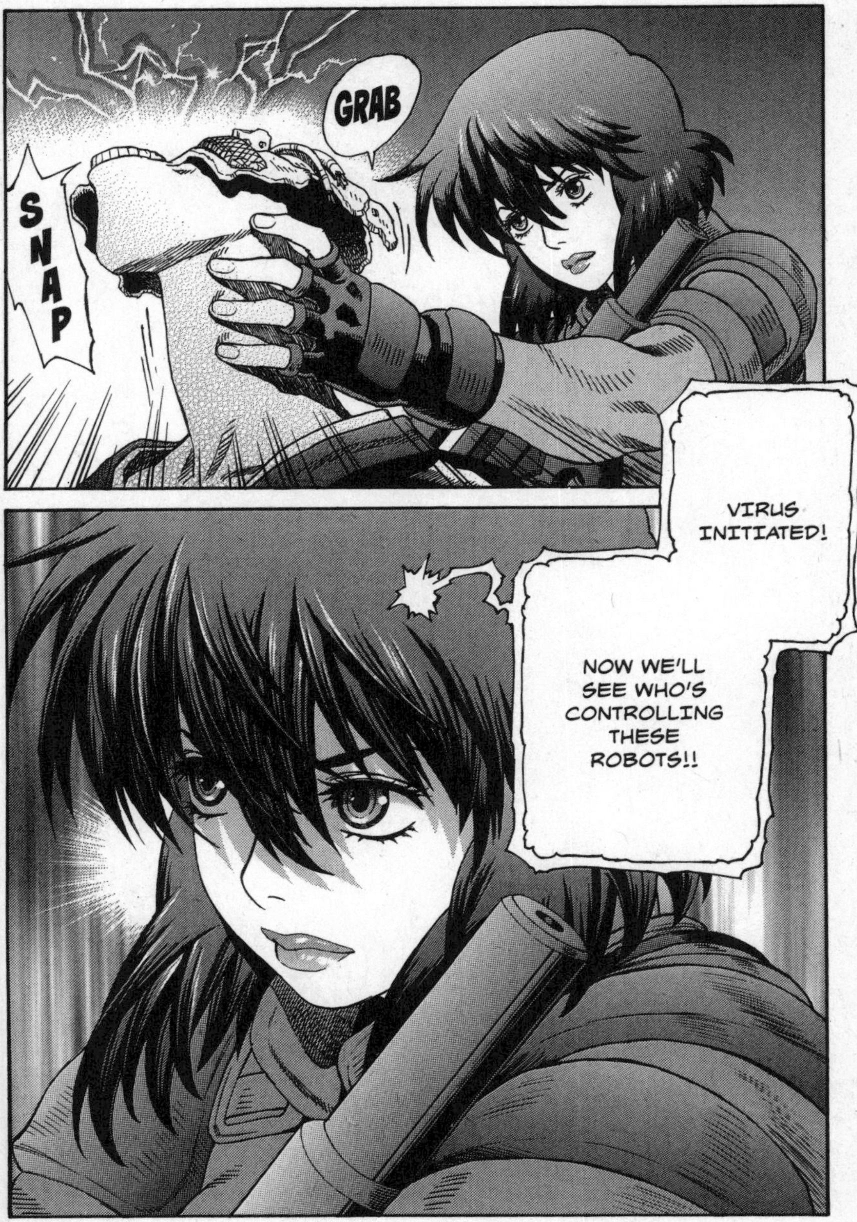
GRAB
SNAP
VIRUS INITIATED!
NOW WE'LL SEE WHO'S CONTROLLING THESE ROBOTS!!

#004 / End

#005: Search Initiated

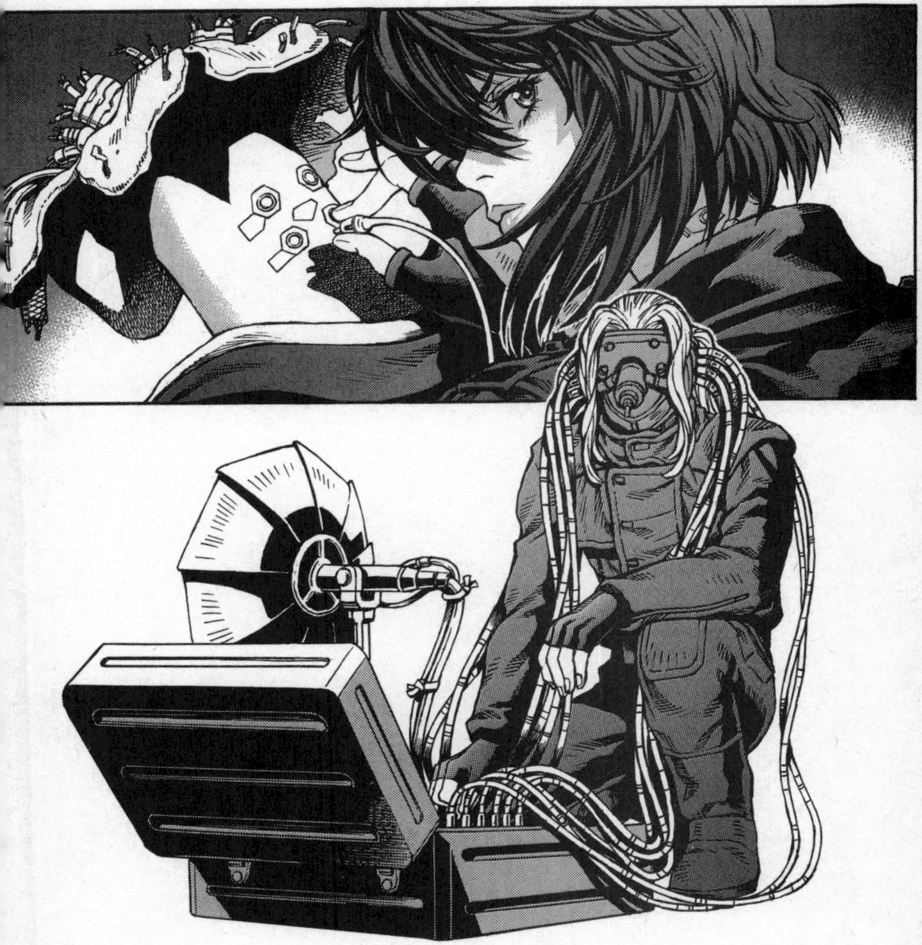

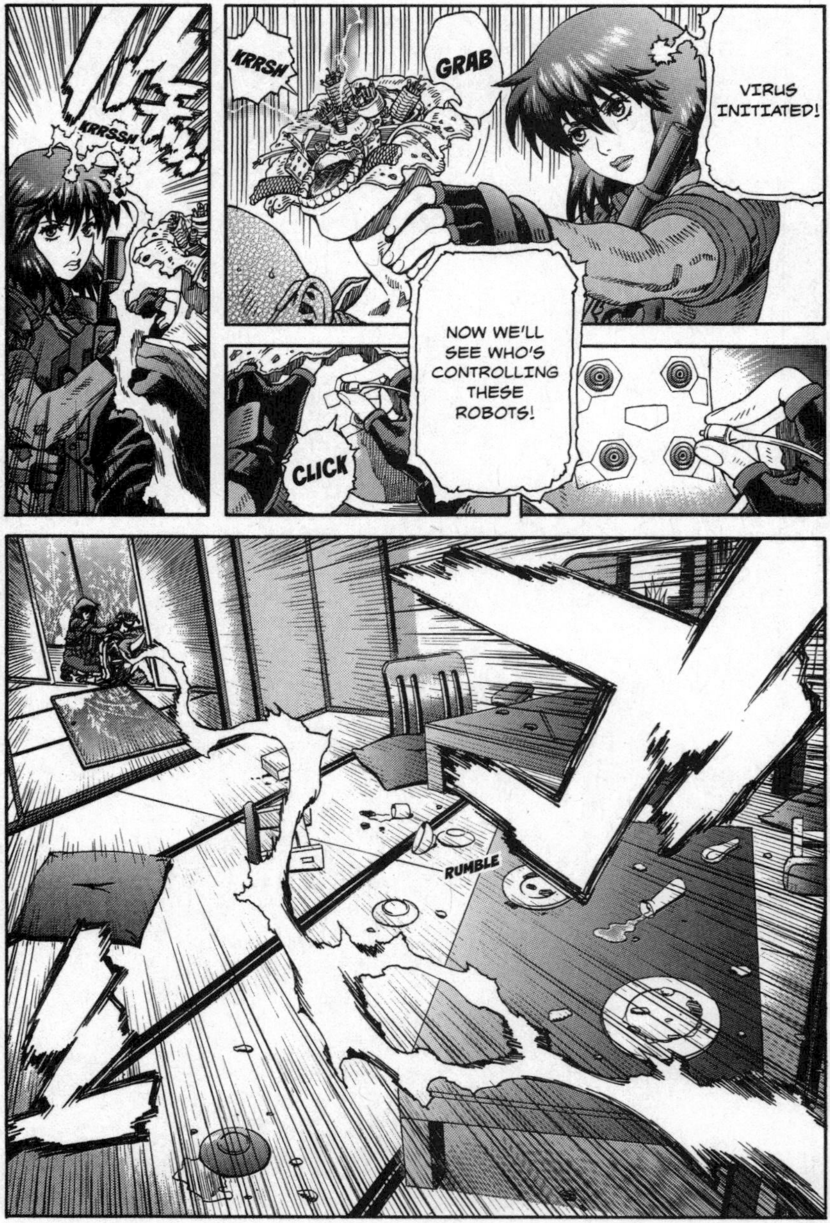
VIRUS INITIATED!
GRAB
KRRSH
NOW WE'LL SEE WHO'S CONTROLLING THESE ROBOTS!
CLICK
KRRSSH
RUMBLE

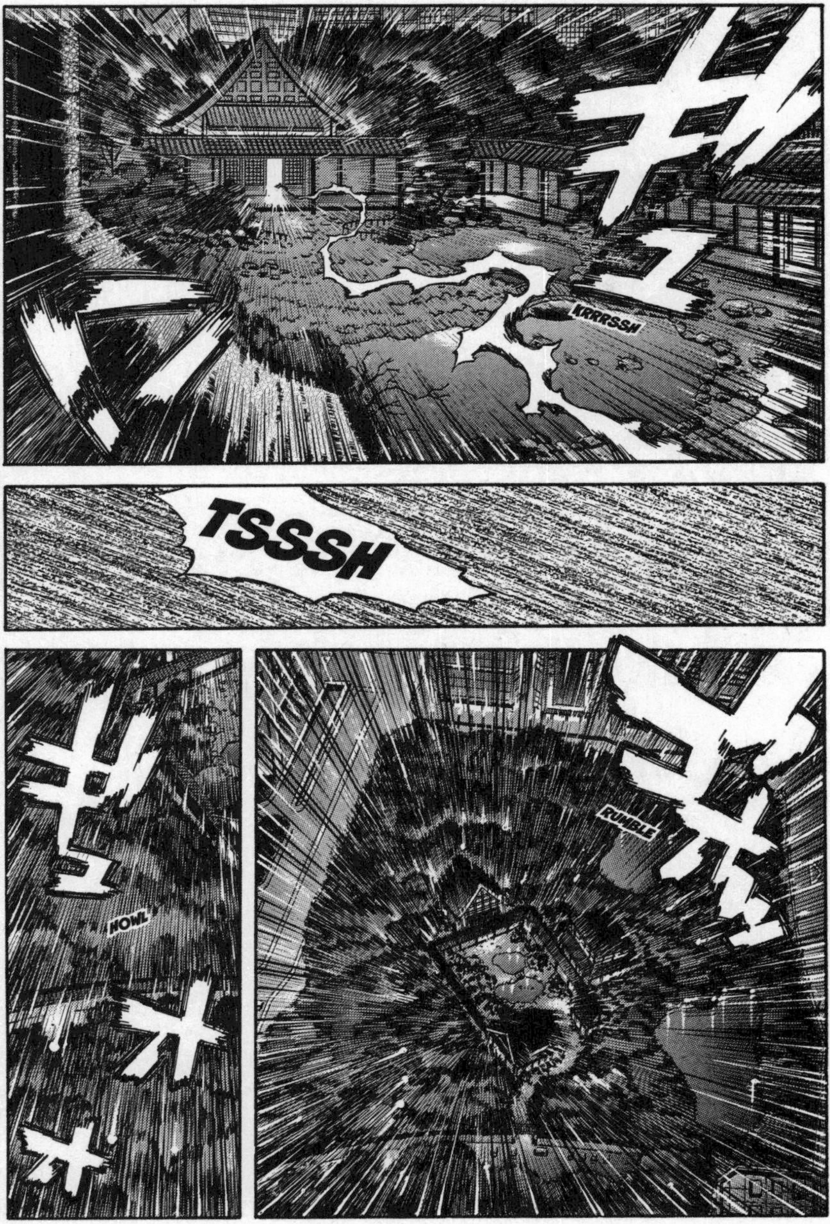
KRRRSSH
TSSSH
RUMBLE
HOWL

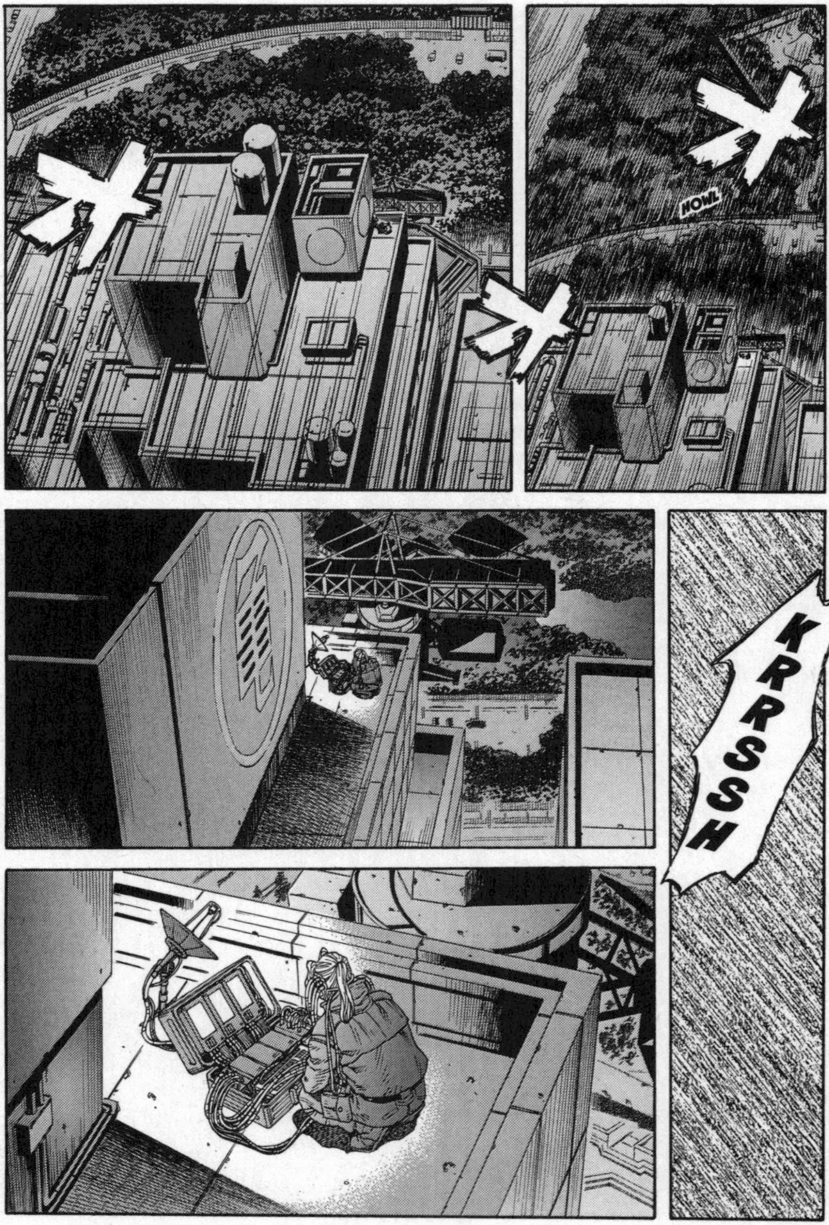
HOWL
KRRSSH

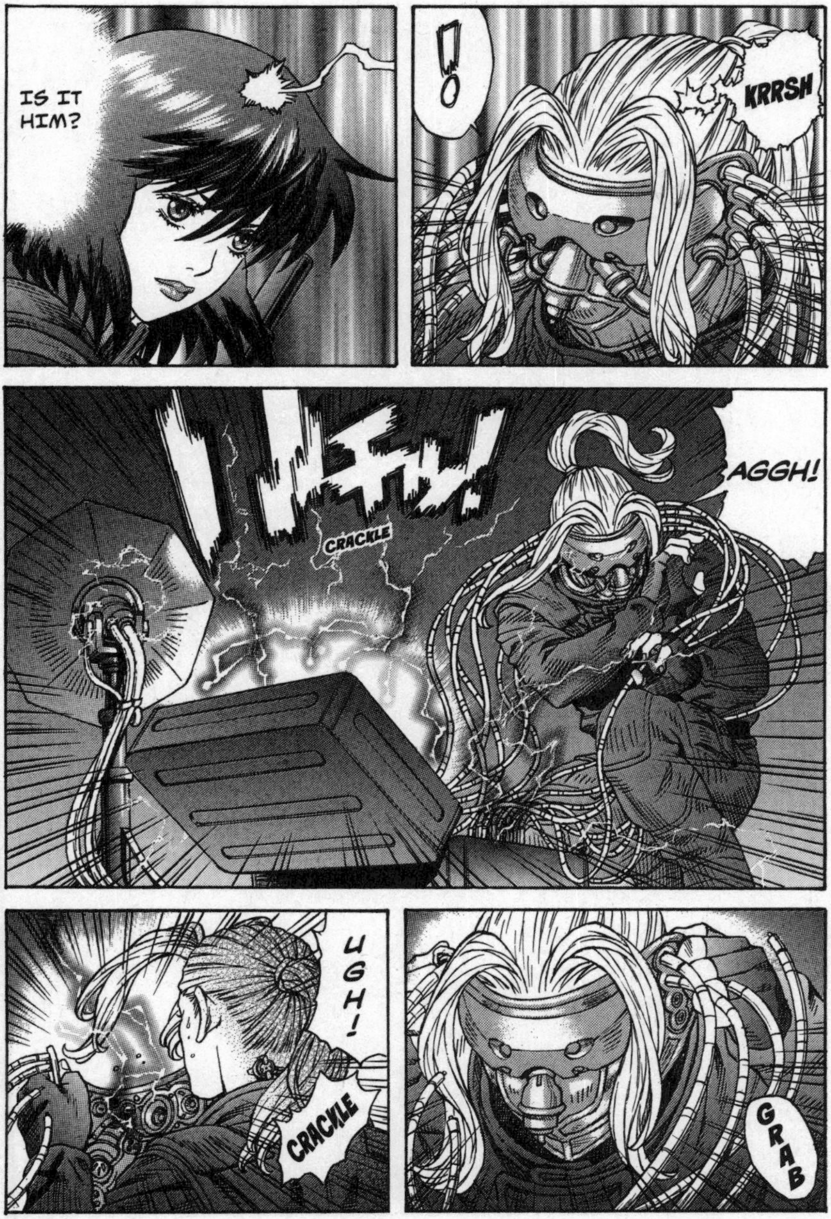
!?
KRRSH
IS IT HIM?
AGGH!
CRACKLE
GRAB
UGH!
CRACKLE

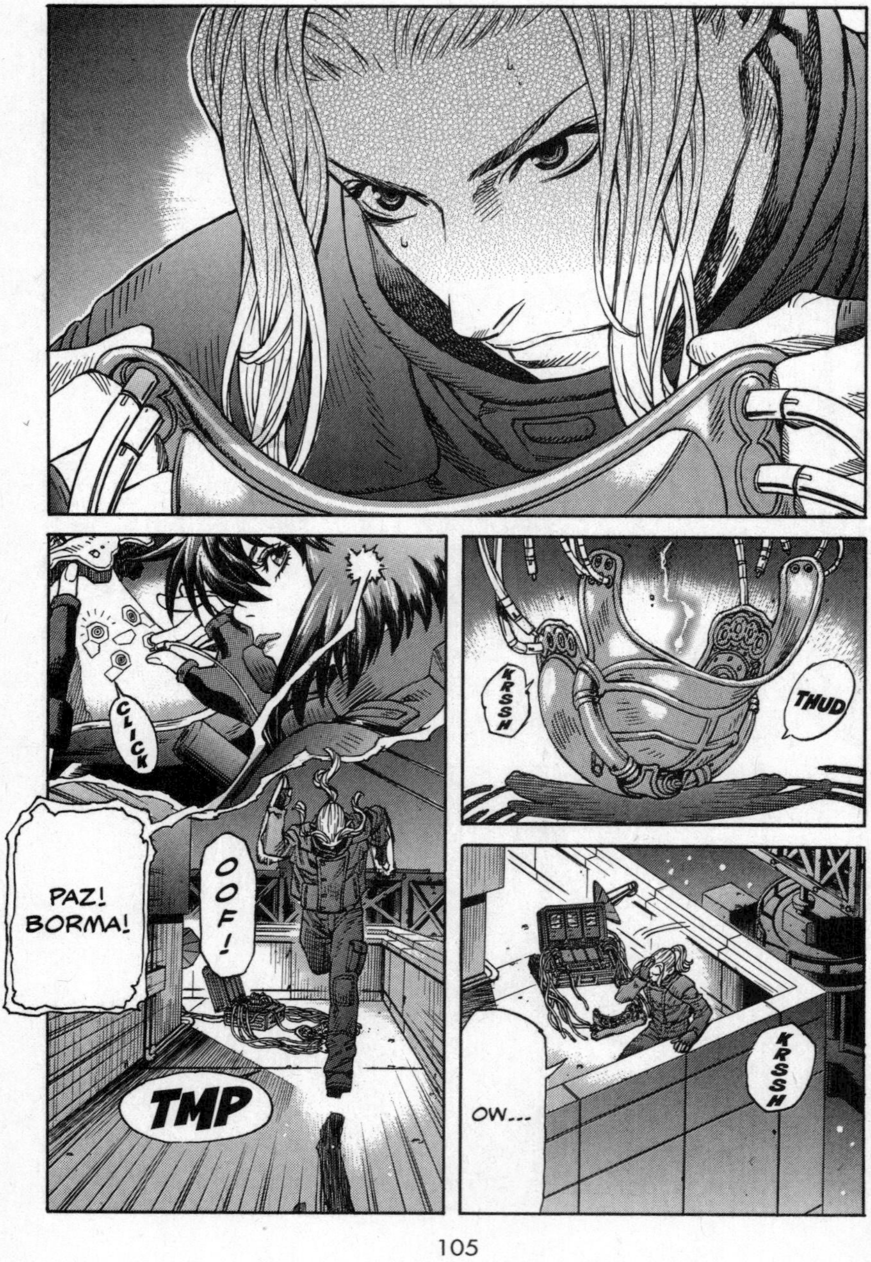
THUD
KRSSH
KRSSH
OW...
CLICK
OOF!
PAZ! BORMA!
TMP

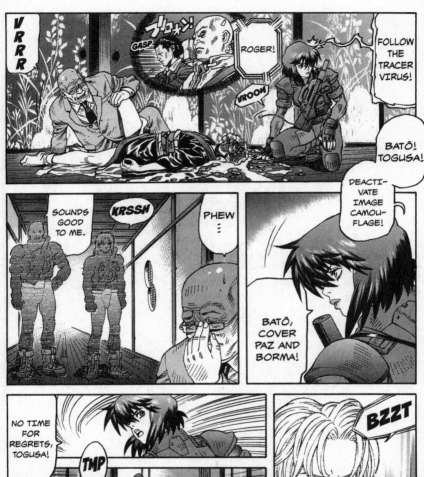

FOLLOW THE TRACER VIRUS!
BATŌ! TOGUSA!
ROGER!
VROOM
GASP
VRRR
DEACTIVATE IMAGE CAMOUFLAGE!
BATŌ, COVER PAZ AND BORMA!
PHEW ...
KRSSH
SOUNDS GOOD TO ME.
BZZT
MAJOR, I MISSED ...
NO TIME FOR REGRETS, TOGUSA!
TMP

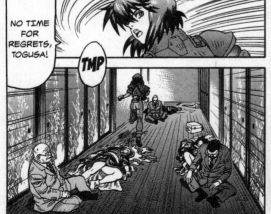

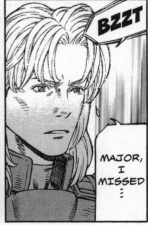

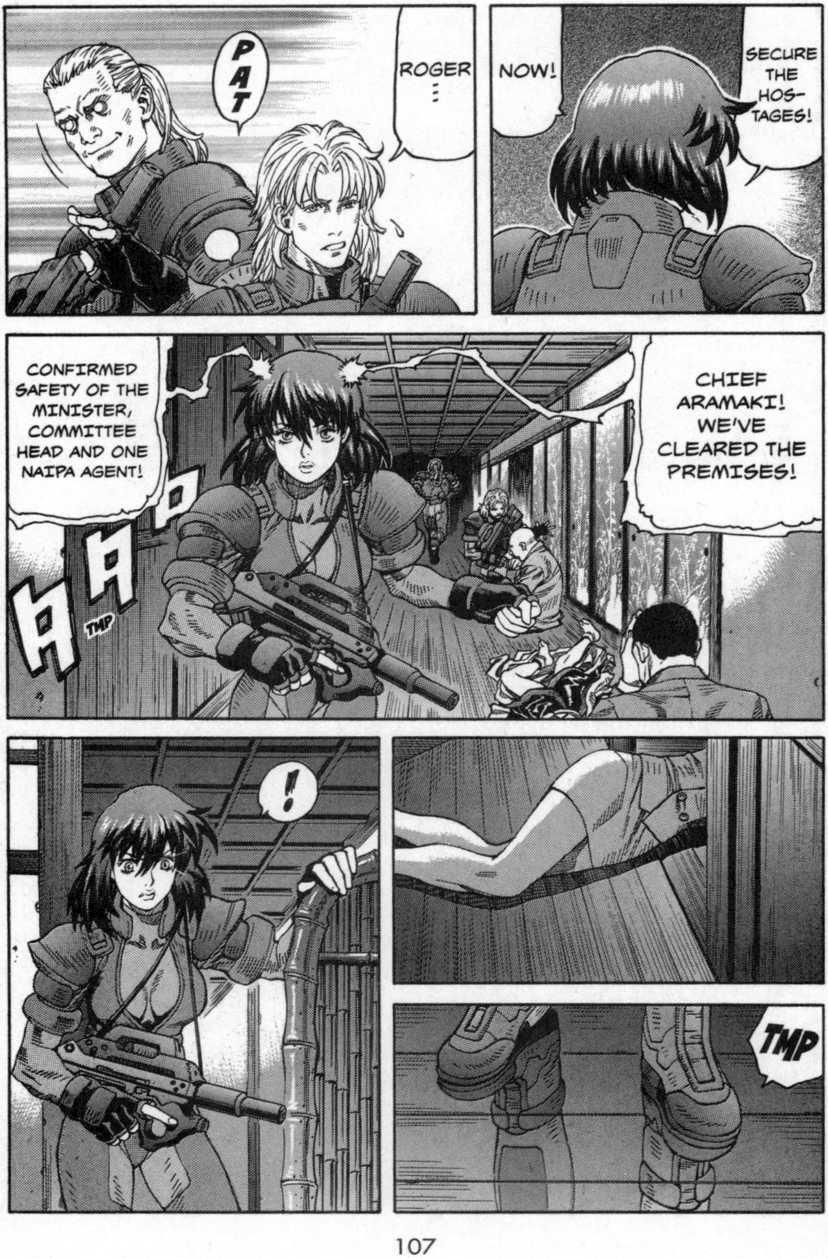
SECURE THE HOS- TAGES!
NOW!
ROGER ...
PAT
CHIEF ARAMAKI! WE'VE CLEARED THE PREMISES!
CONFIRMED SAFETY OF THE MINISTER, COMMITTEE HEAD AND ONE NAIPA AGENT!
TMP
TMP
!

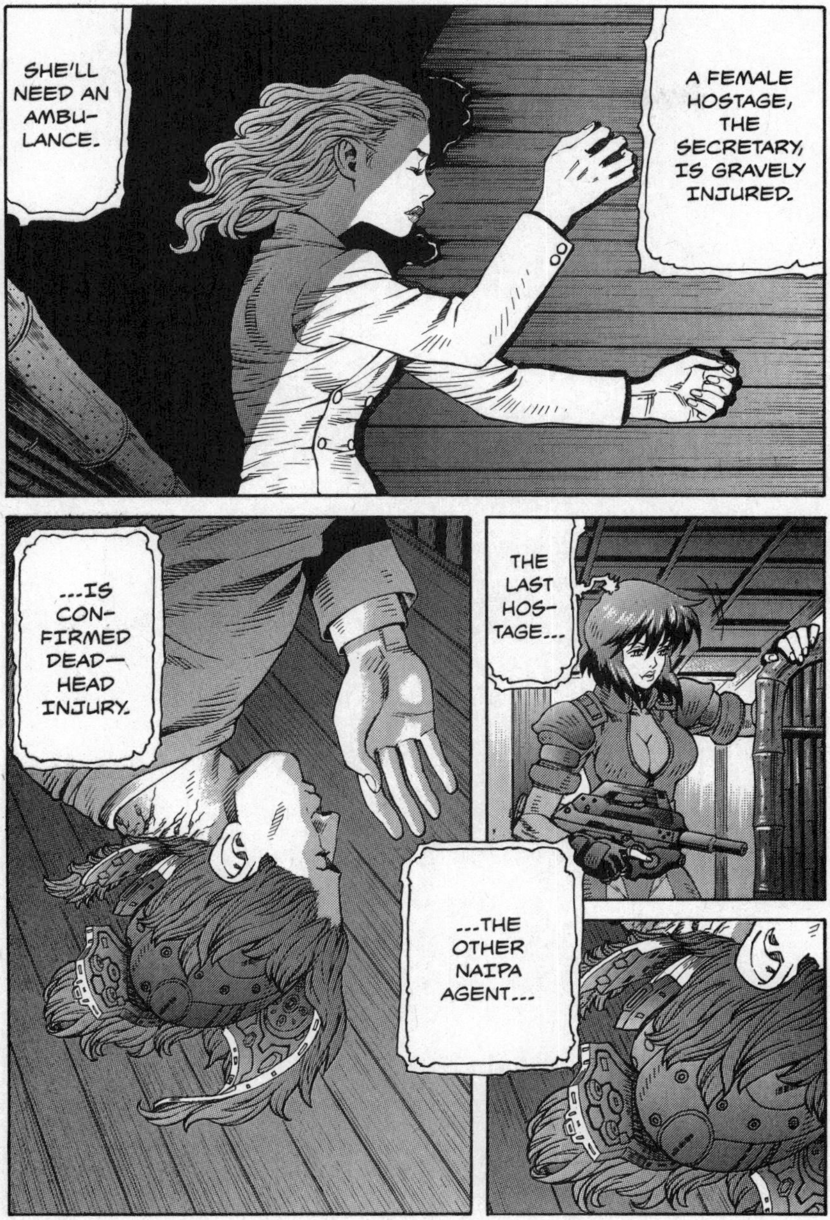
A FEMALE HOSTAGE, THE SECRETARY, IS GRAVELY INJURED.
SHE'LL NEED AN AMBU-LANCE.
THE LAST HOS-TAGE...
...THE OTHER NAIPA AGENT...
...IS CON-FIRMED DEAD—HEAD INJURY.

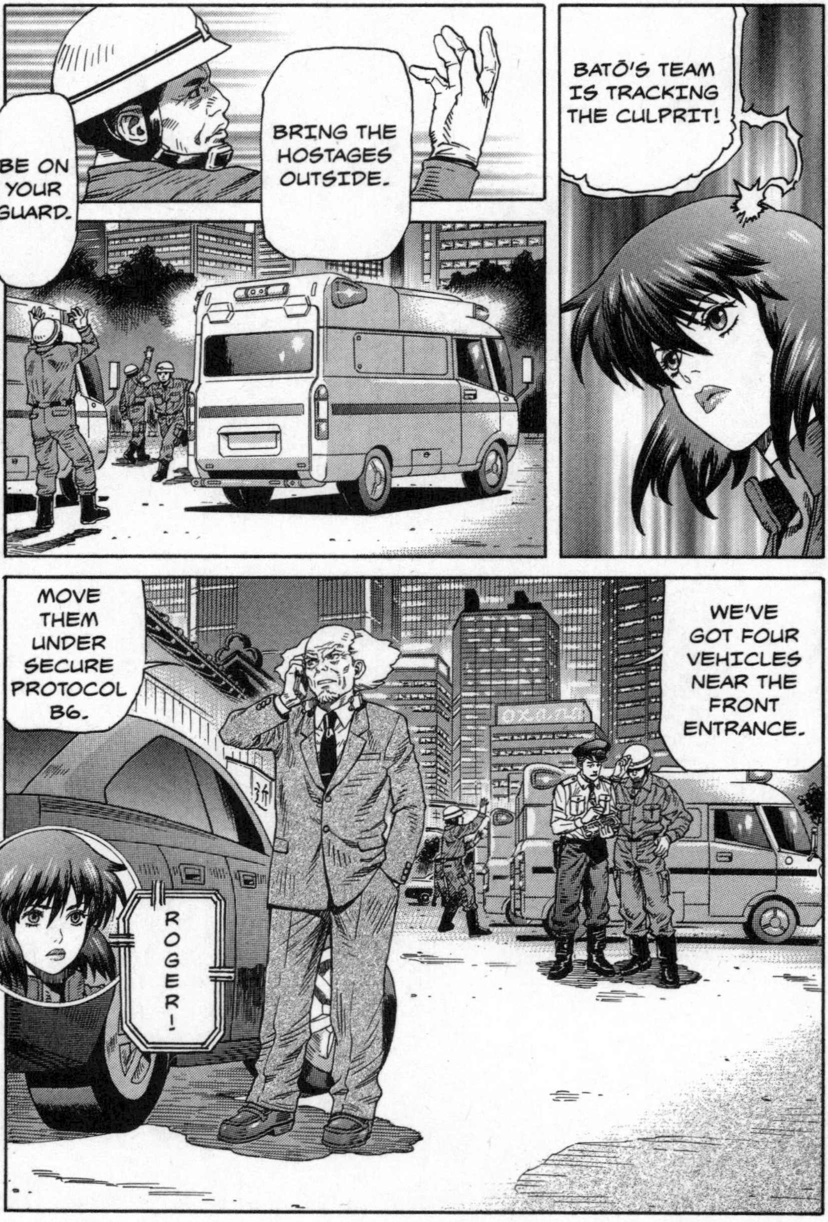
BATŌ'S TEAM IS TRACKING THE CULPRIT!
BRING THE HOSTAGES OUTSIDE.
BE ON YOUR GUARD.
WE'VE GOT FOUR VEHICLES NEAR THE FRONT ENTRANCE.
MOVE THEM UNDER SECURE PROTOCOL B6.
ROGER!

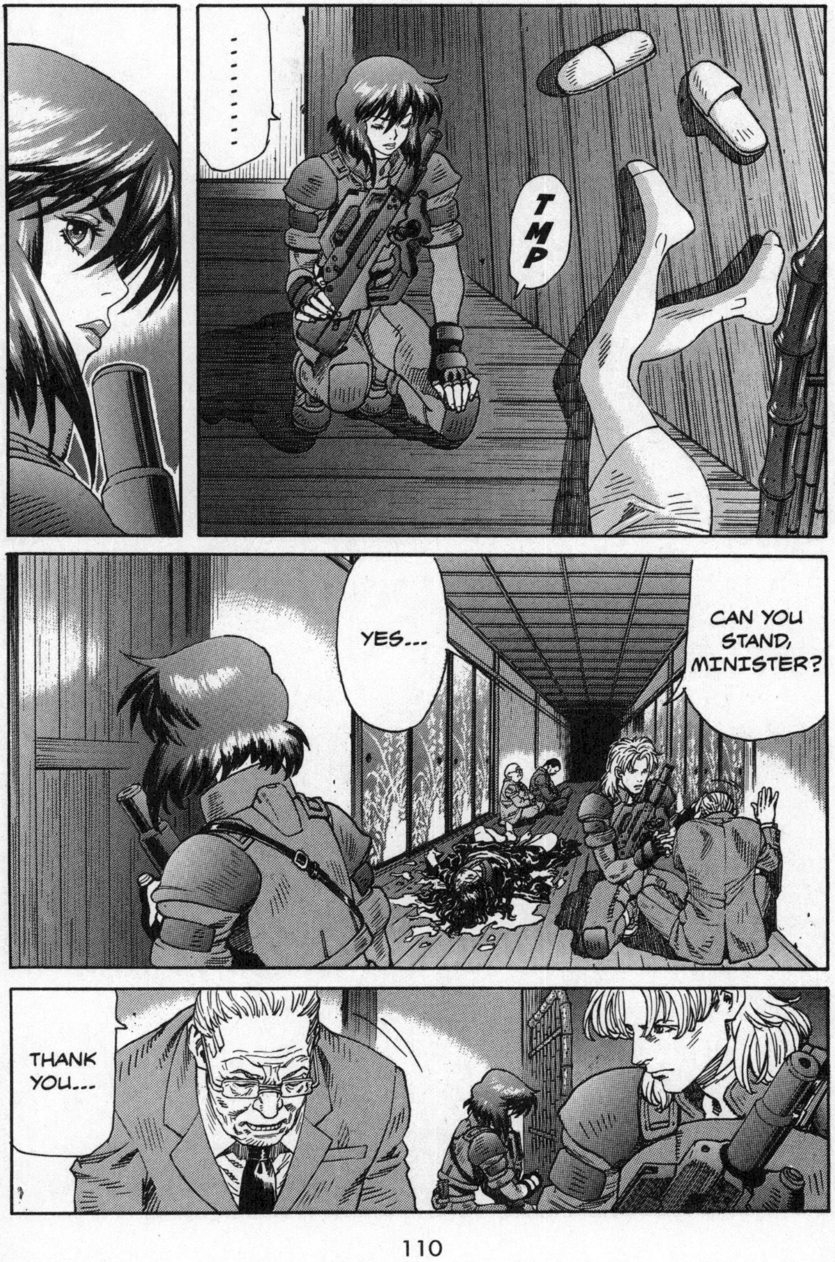
TMP
......
CAN YOU STAND, MINISTER?
YES...
THANK YOU...

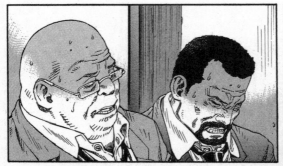

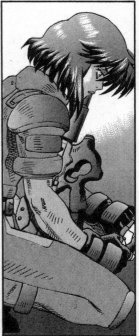

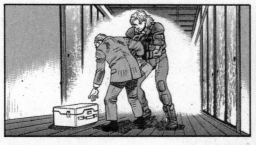

WAIT A
MINUTE,
PLEASE.

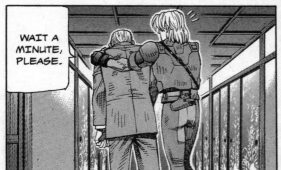

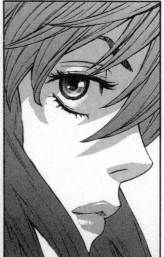

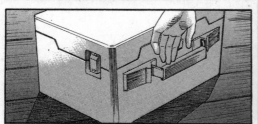

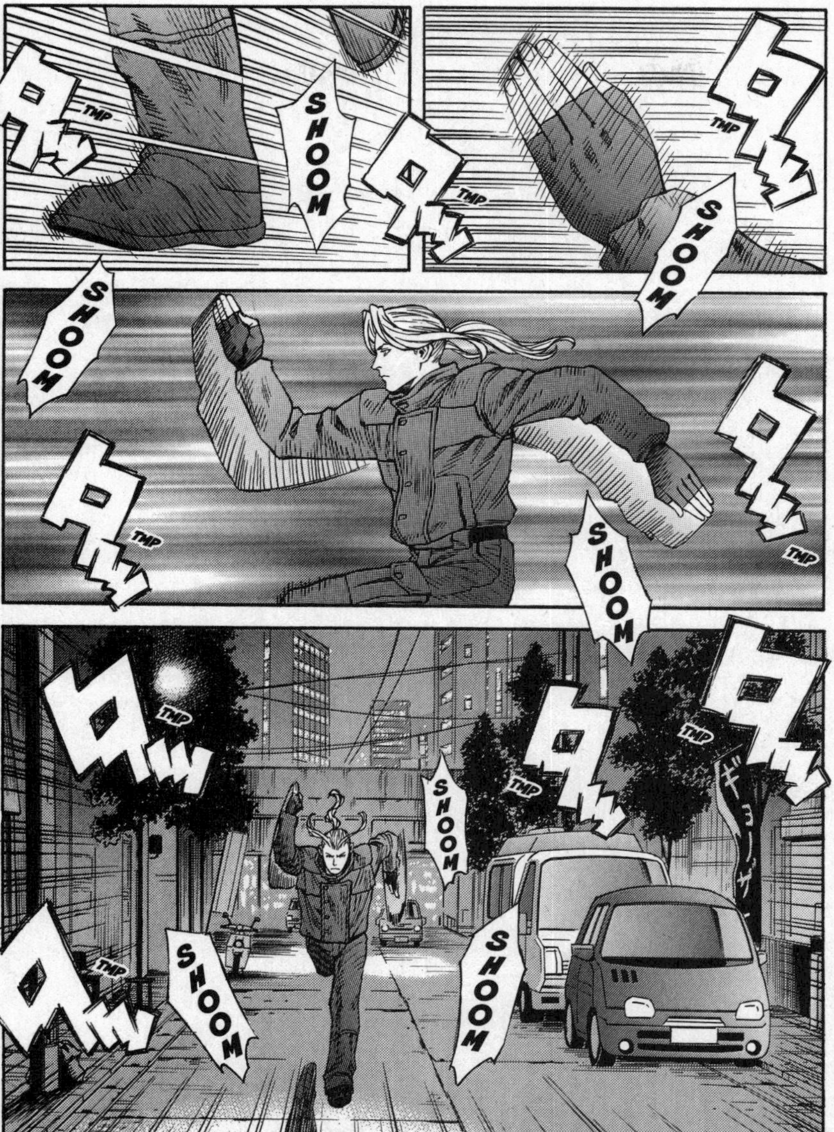

ダッ
TMP
SHOOM
ダッ
TMP
SHOOM
ダッ
TMP
SHOOM
ダッ
TMP
SHOOM
ダッ
TMP
SHOOM
ダッ
TMP
SHOOM
ダッ
TMP
SHOOM
ダッ
TMP
SHOOM
ダッ
TMP
SHOOM

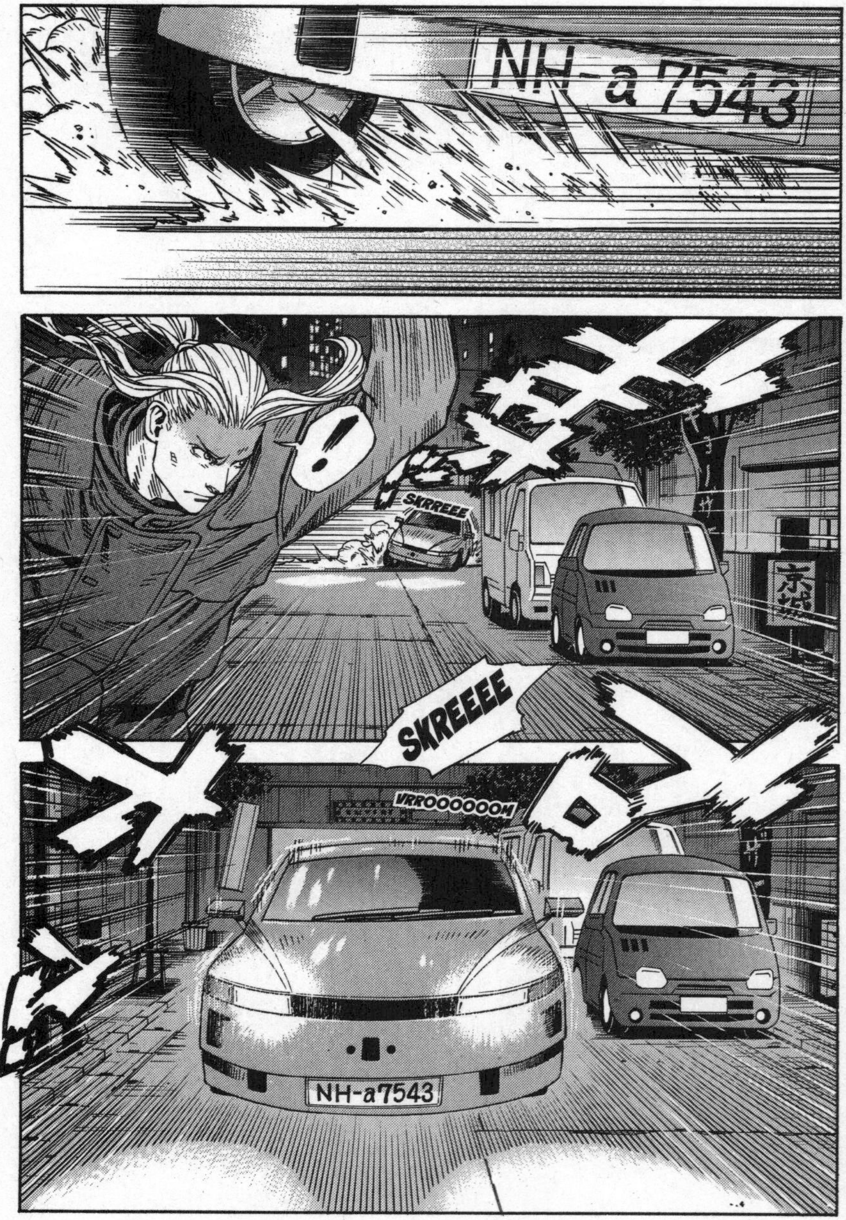
NH-a 7543
!
SKRREEE
SKREEEE
VRROOOOOOOM
NH-a7543

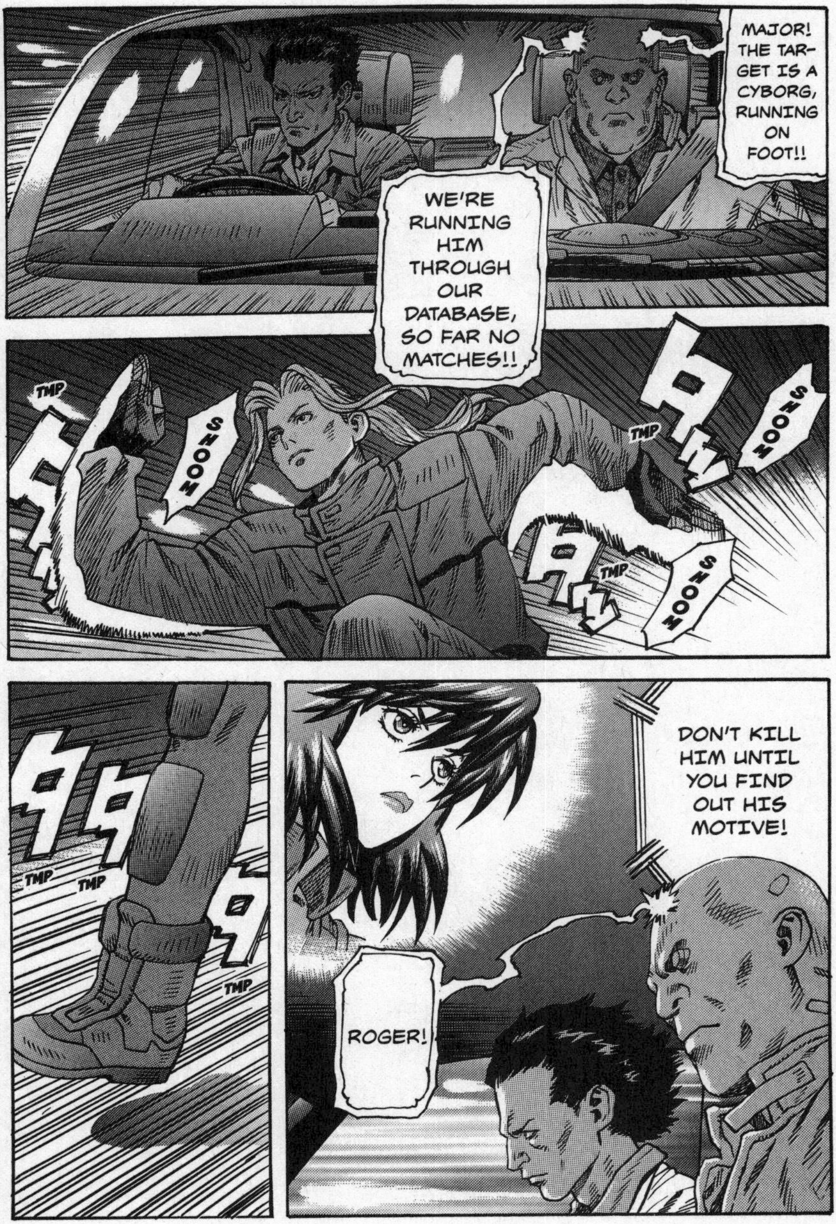
MAJOR! THE TAR-GET IS A CYBORG, RUNNING ON FOOT!!
WE'RE RUNNING HIM THROUGH OUR DATABASE, SO FAR NO MATCHES!!
SHOOM
TMP
SHOOM
TMP
SHOOM
TMP
DON'T KILL HIM UNTIL YOU FIND OUT HIS MOTIVE!
ROGER!
TMP
TMP
TMP

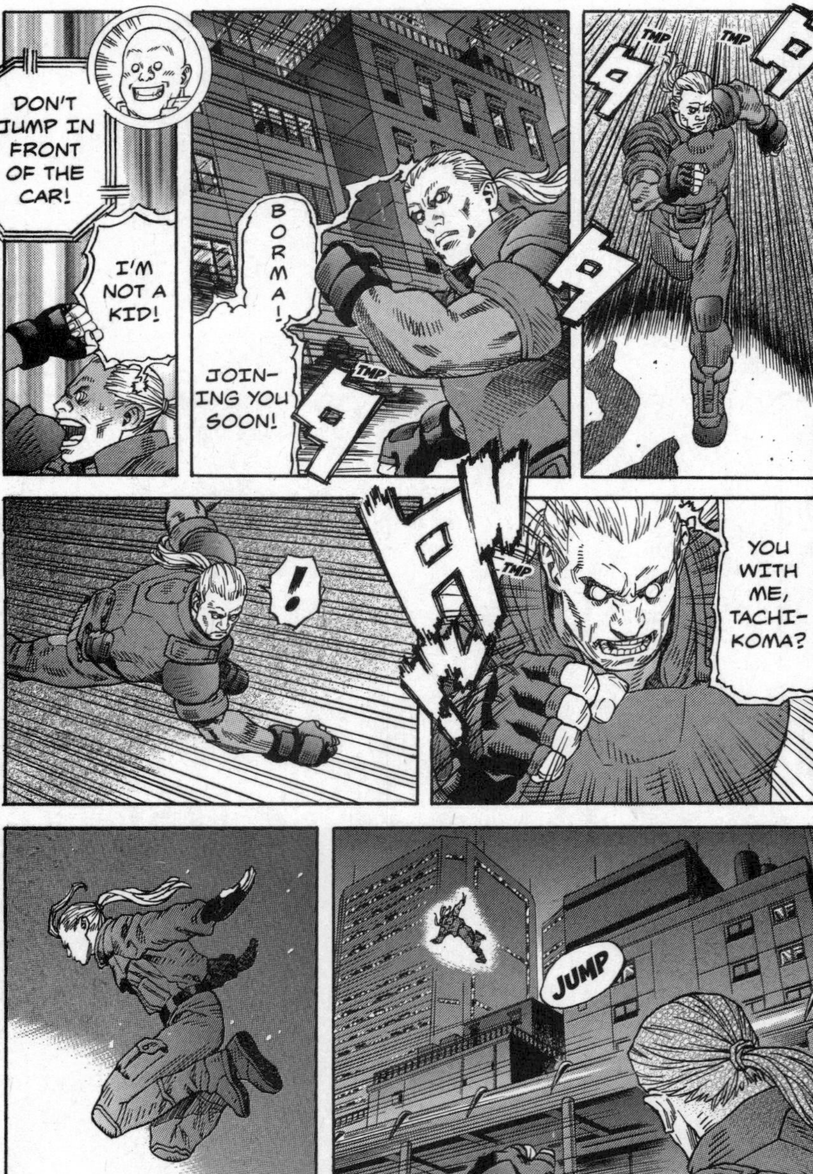

TMP
TMP
BORMA!
JOINING YOU SOON!
TMP
DON'T JUMP IN FRONT OF THE CAR!
I'M NOT A KID!
TMP
YOU WITH ME, TACHIKOMA?
!
JUMP

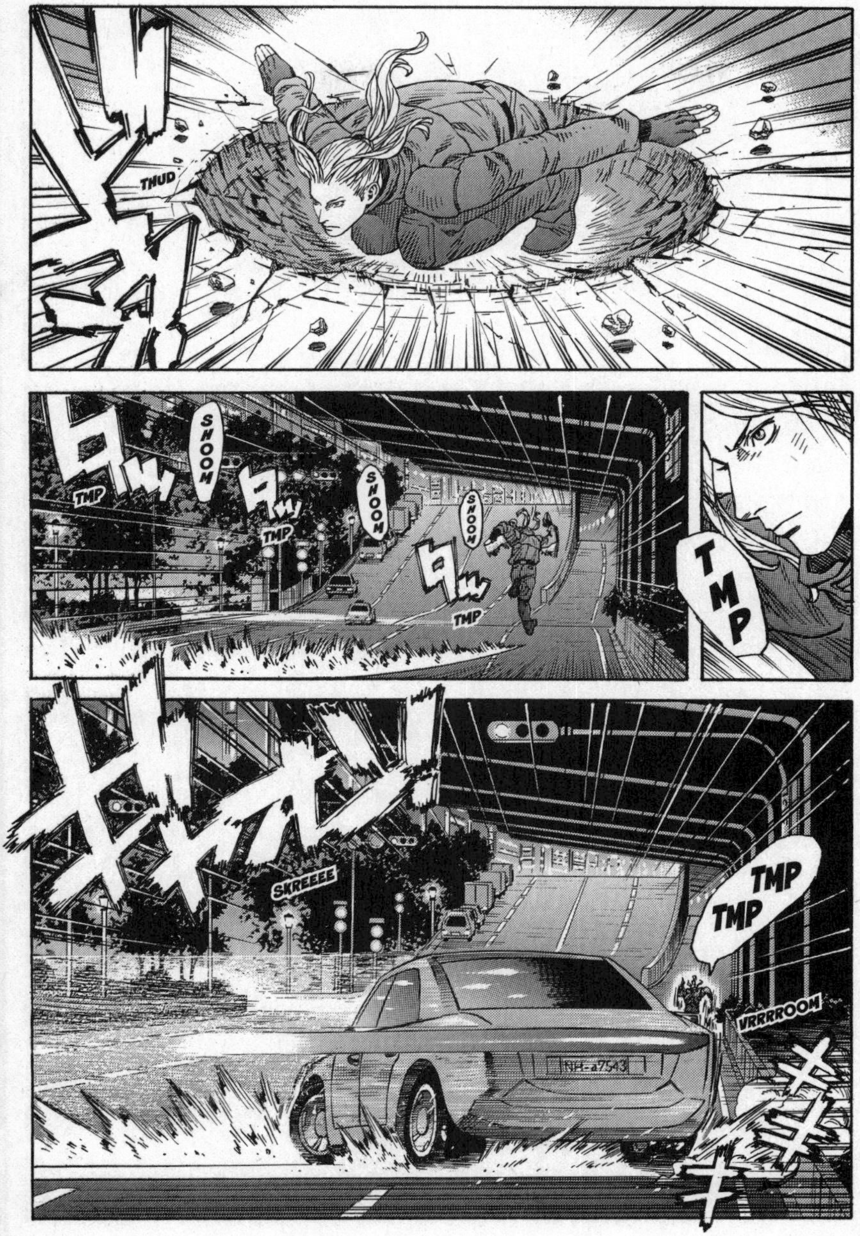
THUD
TMP
SHOOM
TMP
SHOOM
TMP
SHOOM
TMP
TMP
TMP
VRRRROOM
SKREEEE
NH-a7543

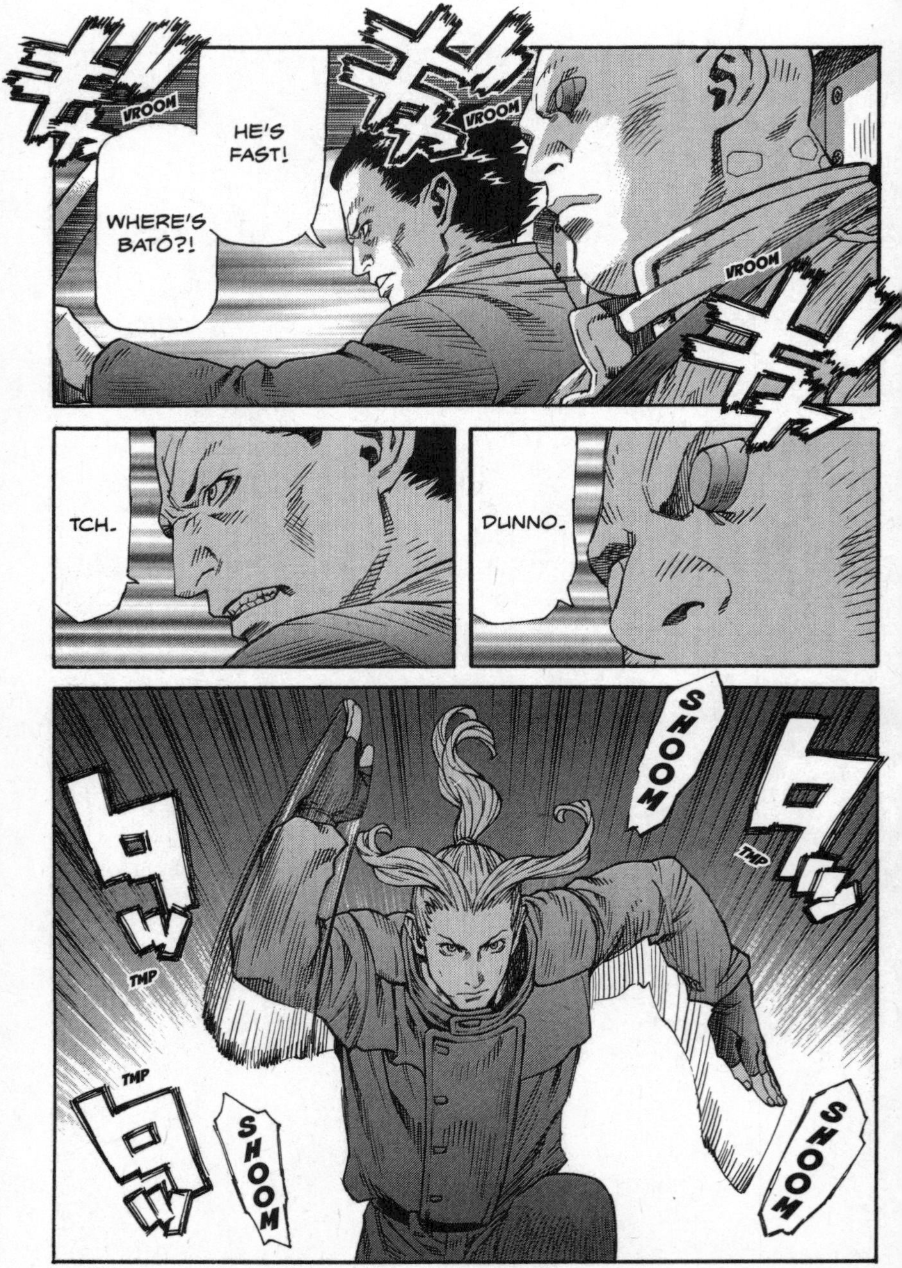
VROOM
VROOM
HE'S FAST!
VROOM
WHERE'S BATŌ?!
DUNNO.
TCH.
SHOOM
TMP
SHOOM
TMP
TMP
SHOOM

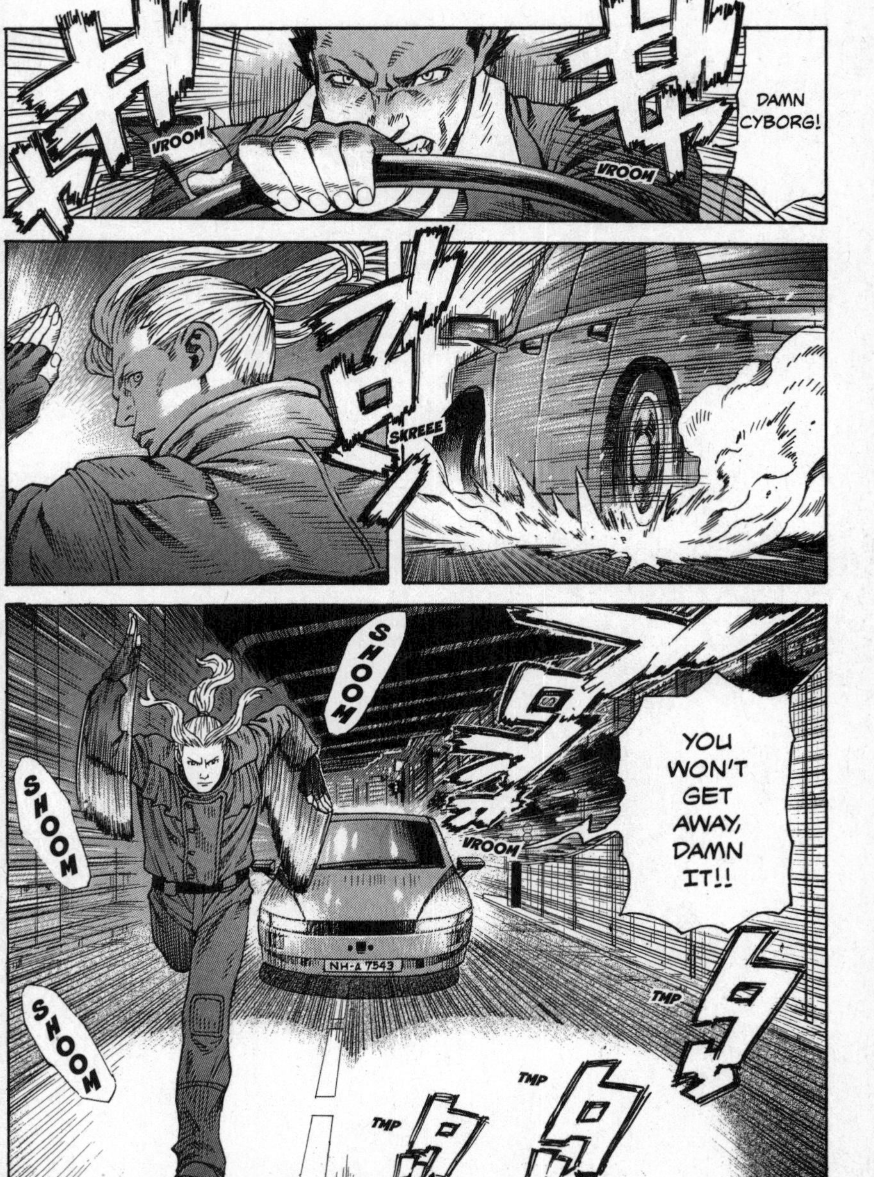
DAMN CYBORG!
VROOM
VROOM
SKREEE
YOU WON'T GET AWAY, DAMN IT!!
SHOOM
VROOM
TMP
TMP
TMP
SHOOM
SHOOM

#005 / End

#006: Loose Cannon

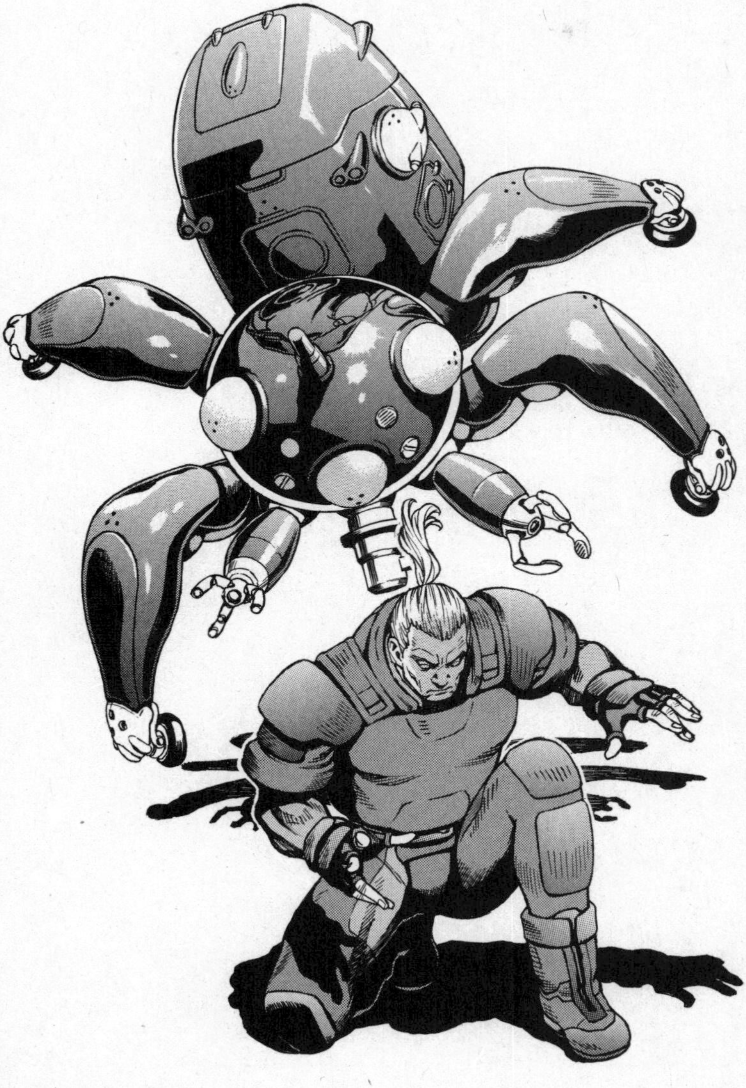

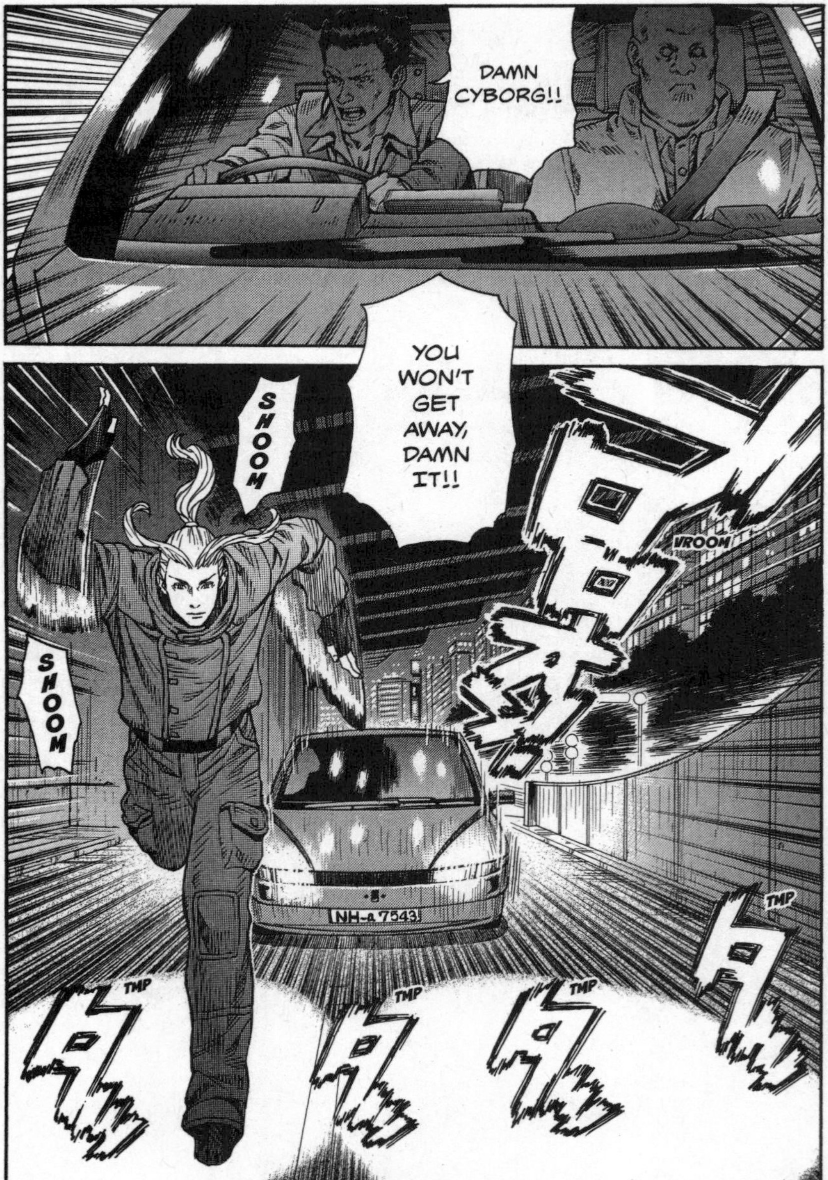
DAMN CYBORG!!
YOU WON'T GET AWAY, DAMN IT!!
VROOM
SHOOM
SHOOM
NH-a 7543
TMP
TMP
TMP
TMP

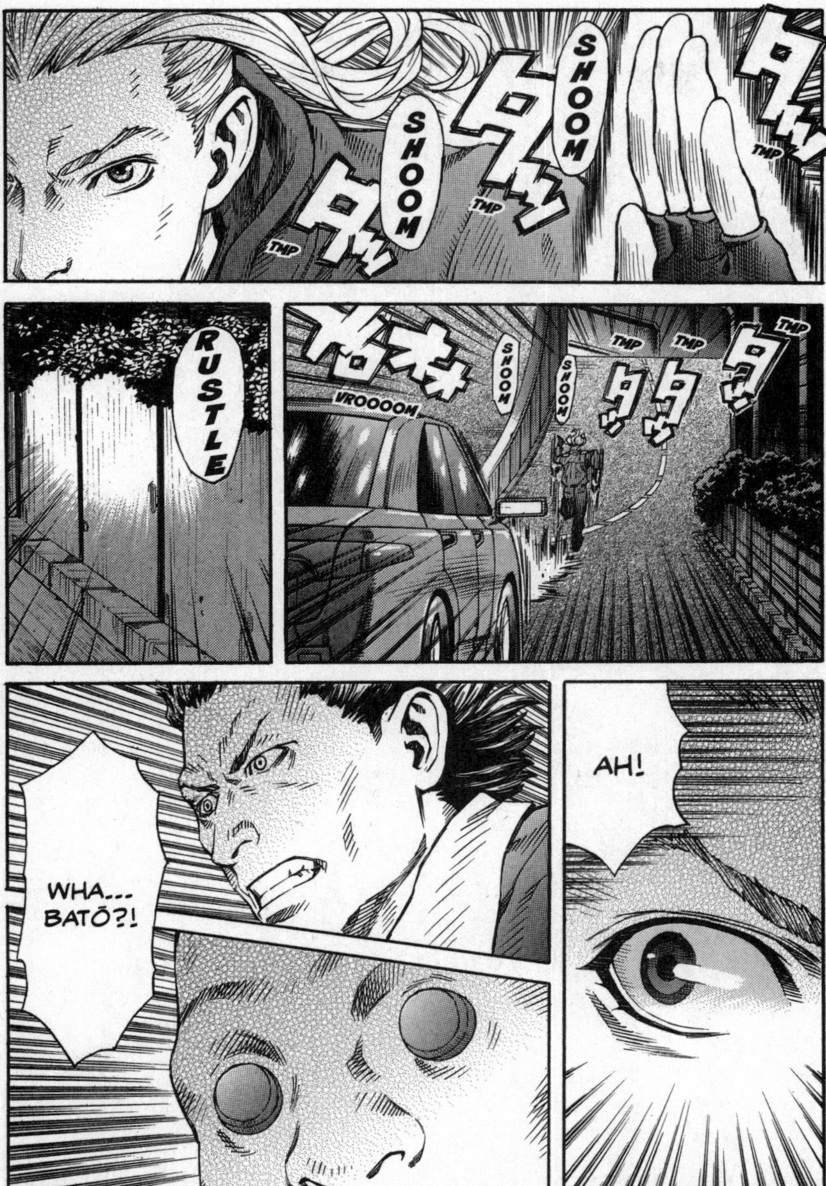
TMP
SHOOM
TMP
SHOOM
TMP
TMP
TMP
TMP
SHOOM
SHOOM
VROOOOM
RUSTLE
AH!
WHA...
BATŌ?!

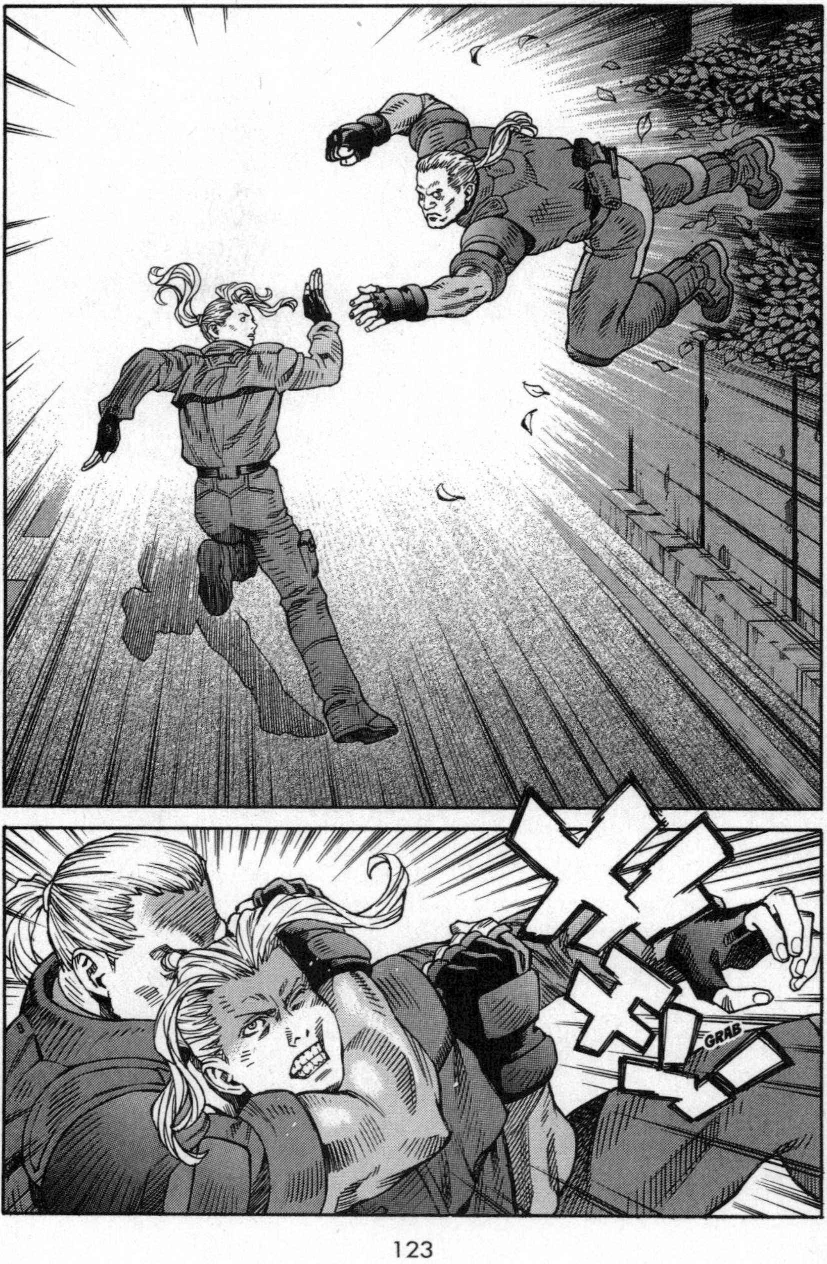
GRAB

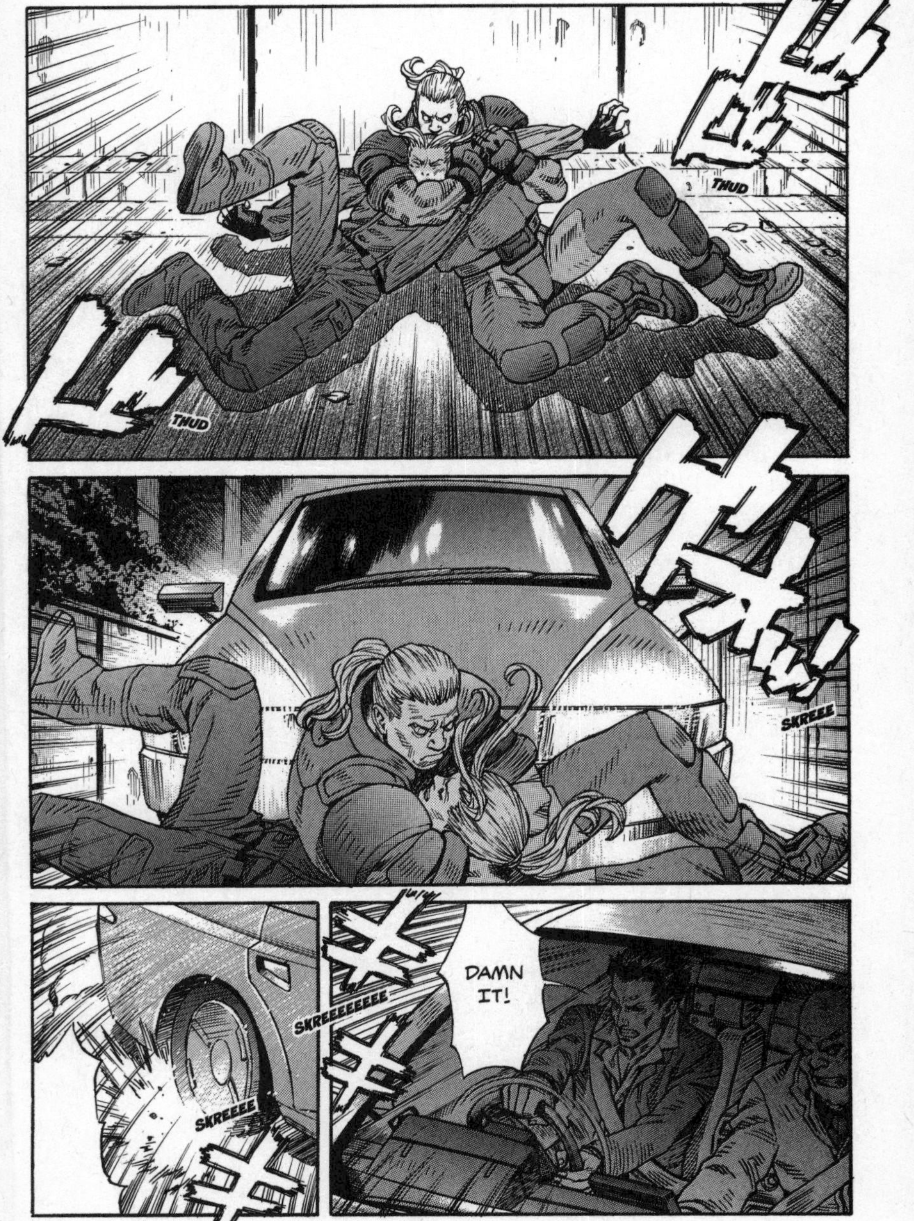
THUD
THUD
SKREEE
DAMN IT!
SKREEEEEEEEE
SKREEEE

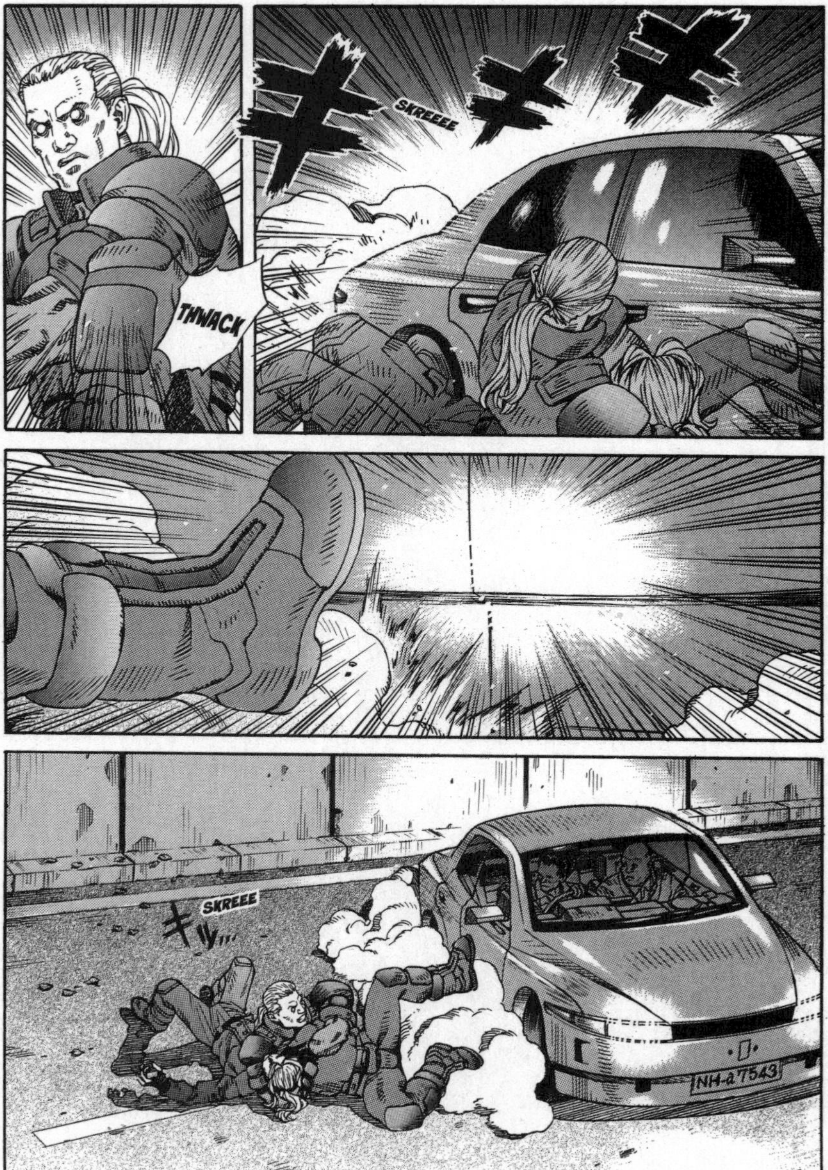
SKREEEE
THWACK
SKREEE
NH-a 7543

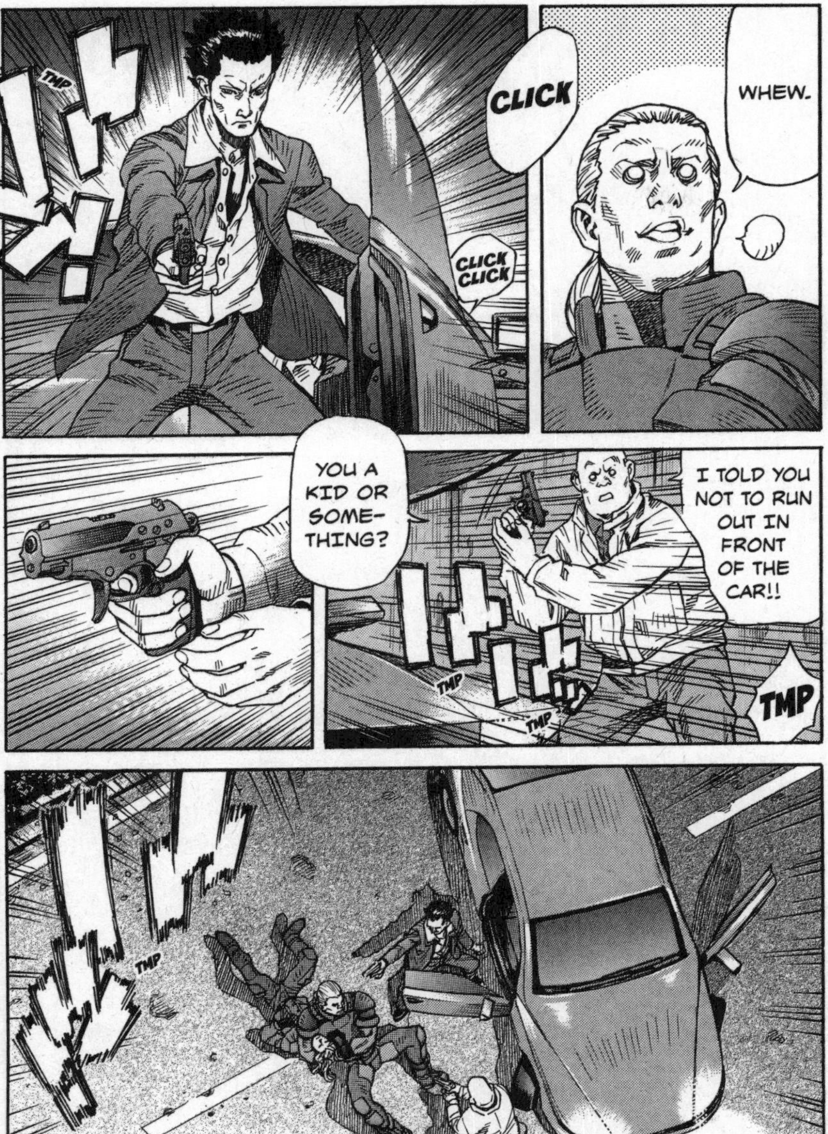
WHEW.
CLICK
TMP
CLICK CLICK
I TOLD YOU NOT TO RUN OUT IN FRONT OF THE CAR!!
YOU A KID OR SOME-THING?
TMP
TMP
TMP
TMP

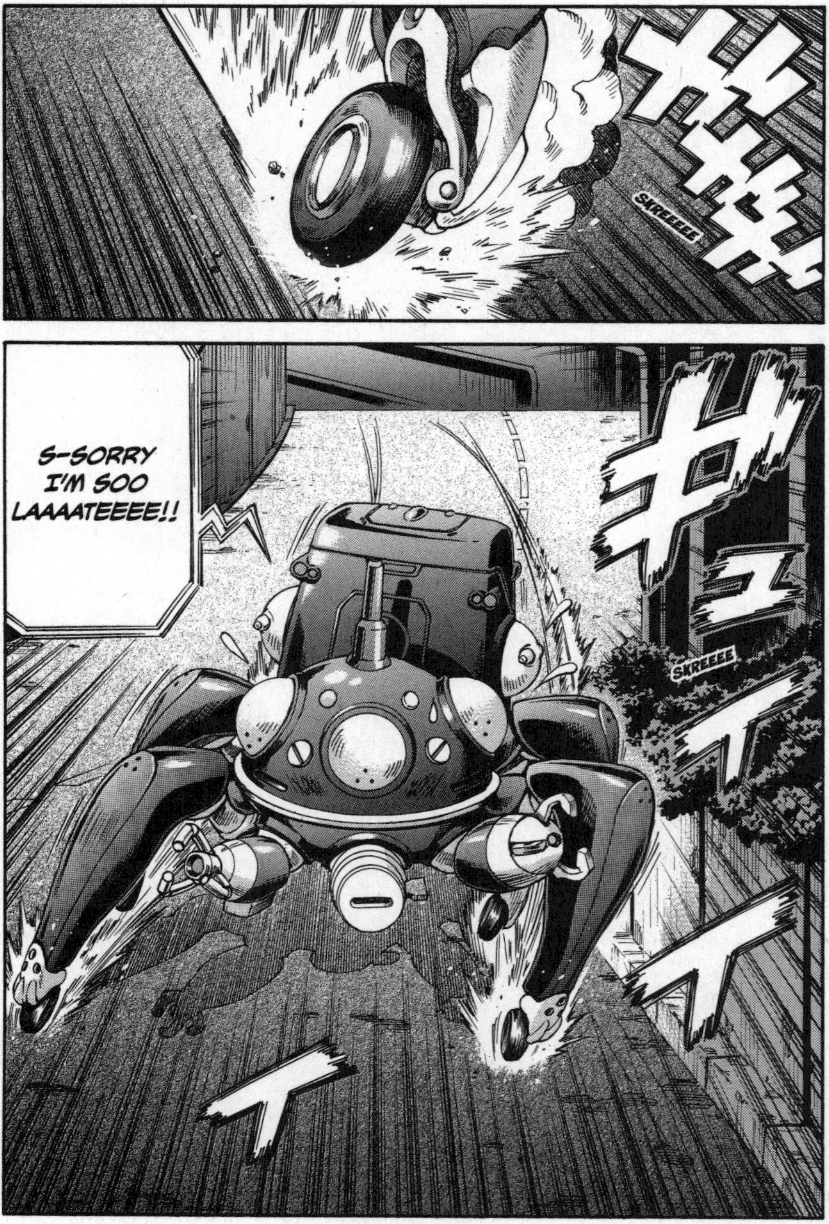
SKREEEEE
SKREEEE
S-SORRY
I'M SOO
LAAAATEEEE!!

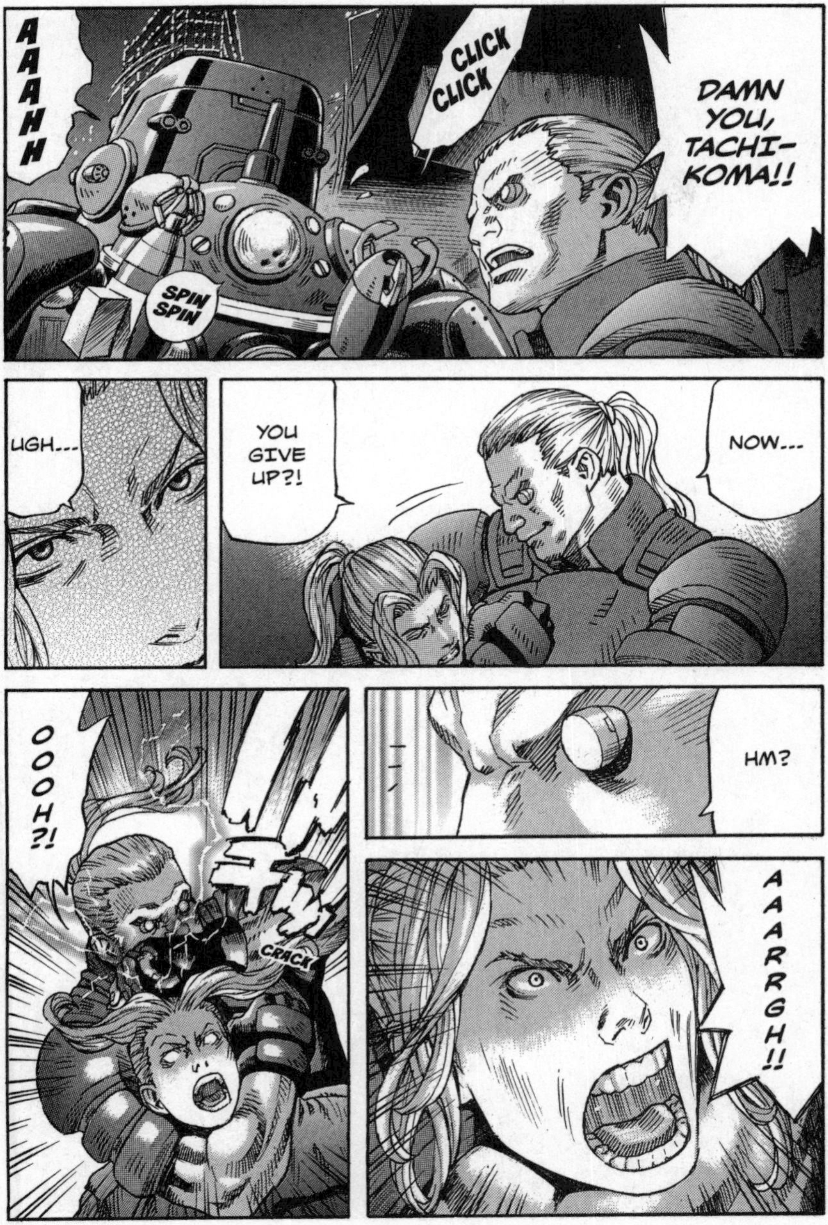
DAMN YOU, TACHI-KOMA!!
CLICK CLICK
AAAAHH
SPIN SPIN
NOW...
YOU GIVE UP?!
UGH...
HM?
AAAARRGH!!
OOOOH?!
CRACK

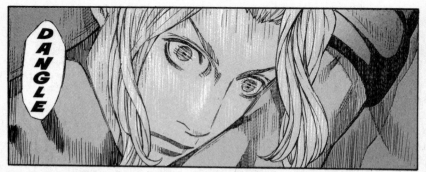

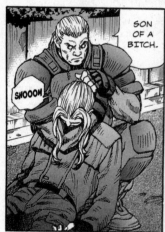

SON OF A BITCH.

SHOOOM

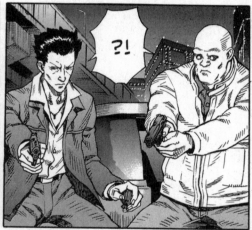

?!

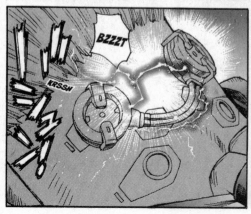

BZZZT

KRSSH

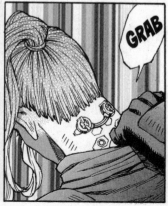

GRAB

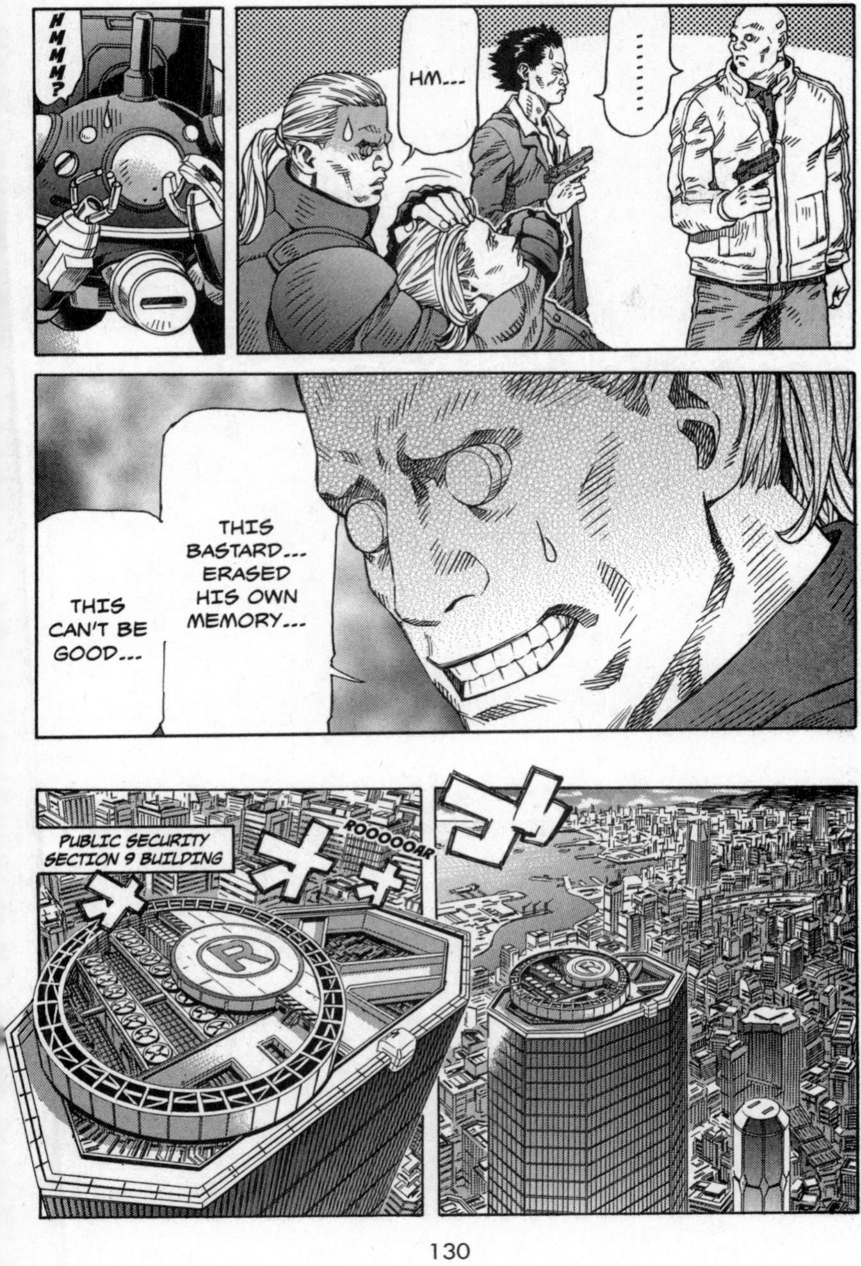
......
HM...
HMMM?
THIS BASTARD... ERASED HIS OWN MEMORY...
THIS CAN'T BE GOOD...
ROOOOOAR
PUBLIC SECURITY SECTION 9 BUILDING

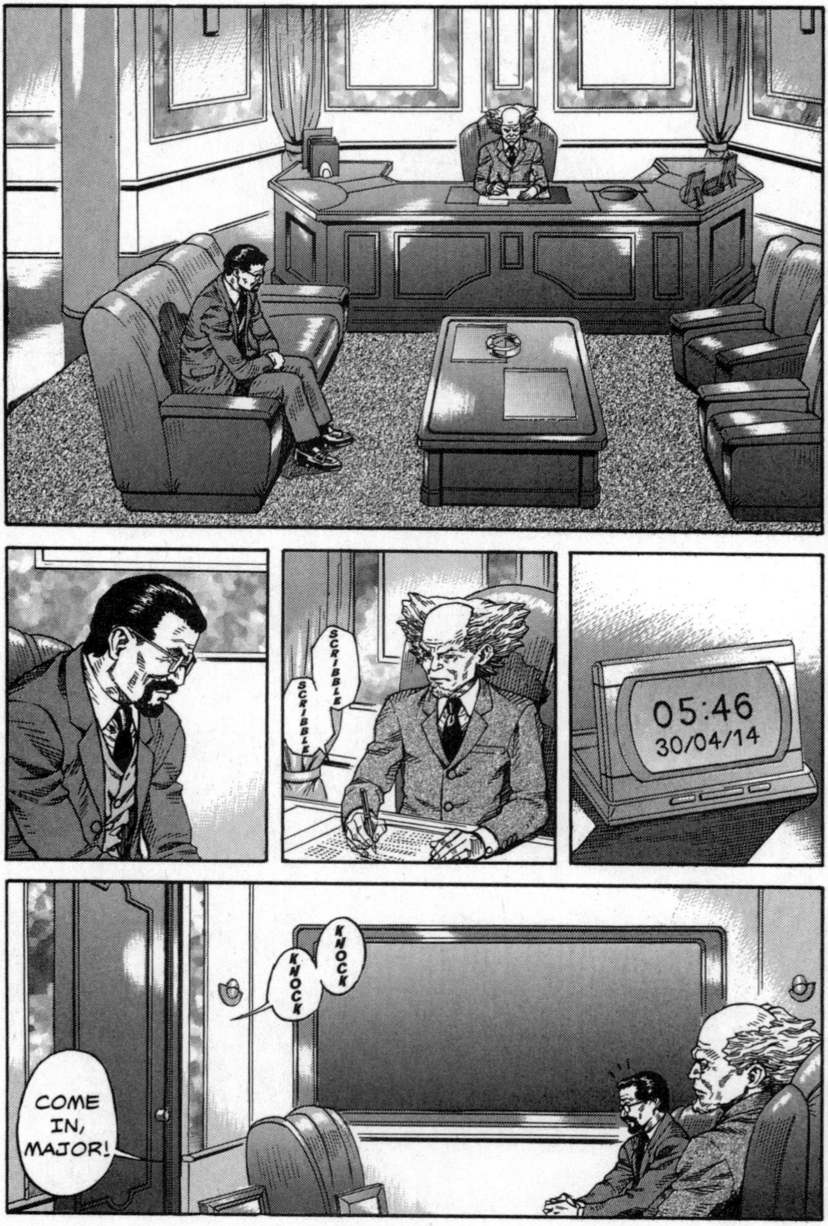
05:46
30/04/14
SCRIBBLE
SCRIBBLE
KNOCK
KNOCK
COME IN, MAJOR!

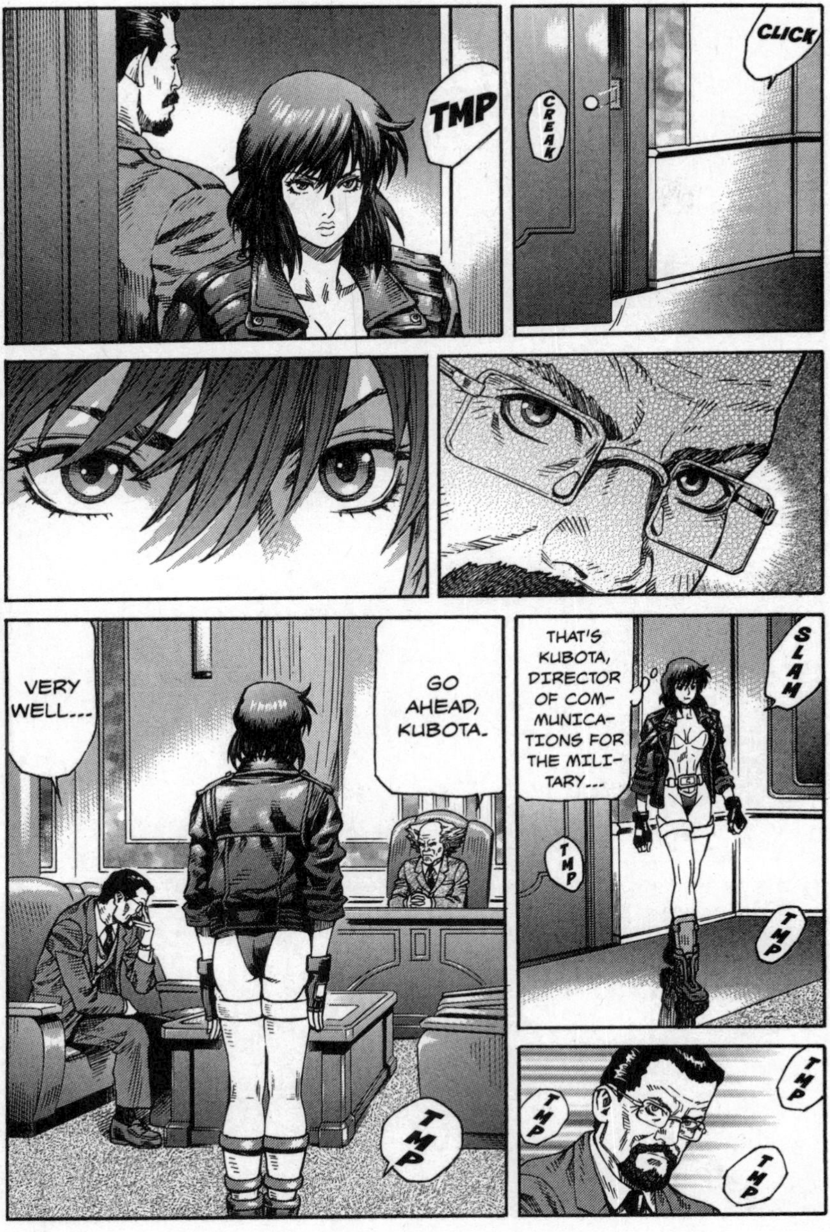
CLICK
CREAK
TMP
SLAM
THAT'S KUBOTA, DIRECTOR OF COMMUNICATIONS FOR THE MILITARY...
TMP
TMP
TMP
TMP
TMP
GO AHEAD, KUBOTA.
VERY WELL...
TMP

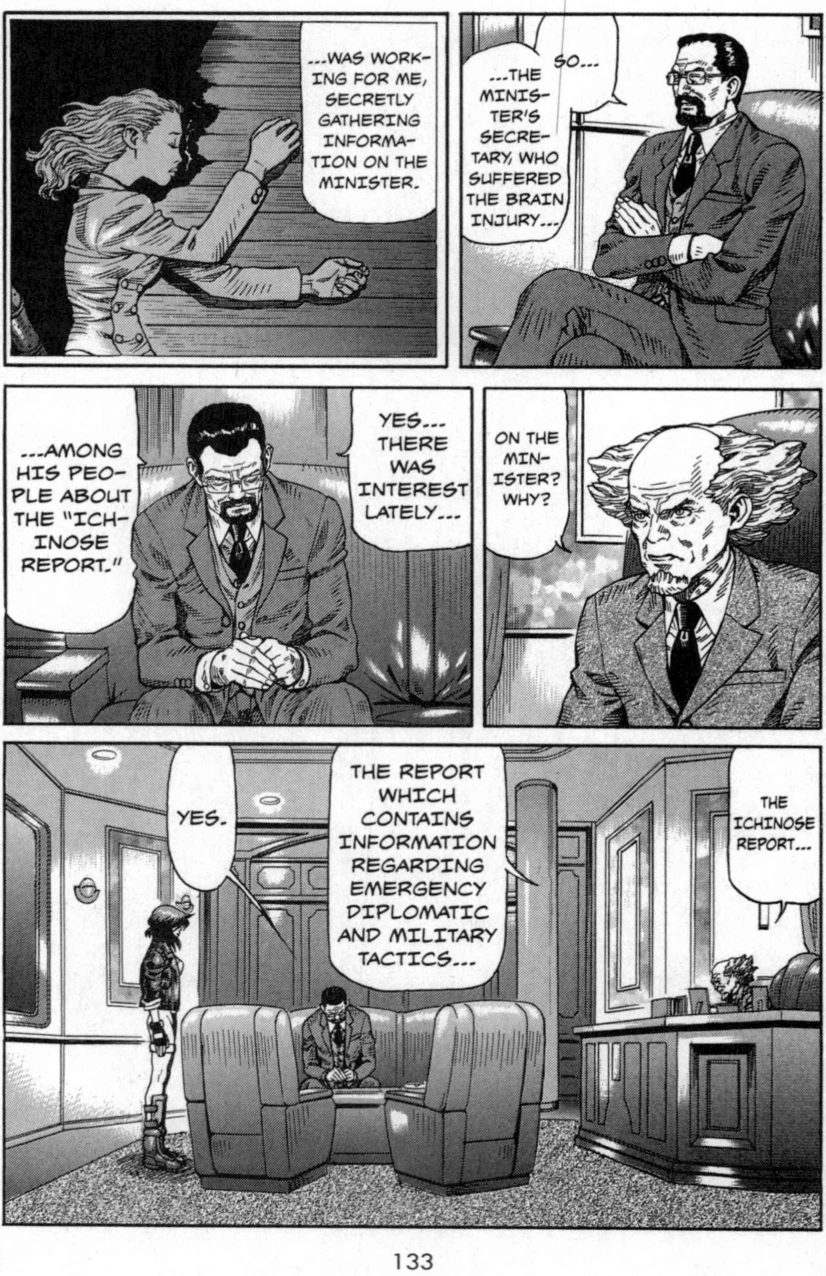
SO...
...THE MINISTER'S SECRETARY, WHO SUFFERED THE BRAIN INJURY...
...WAS WORKING FOR ME, SECRETLY GATHERING INFORMATION ON THE MINISTER.
ON THE MINISTER? WHY?
YES... THERE WAS INTEREST LATELY...
...AMONG HIS PEOPLE ABOUT THE "ICHINOSE REPORT."
THE ICHINOSE REPORT...
THE REPORT WHICH CONTAINS INFORMATION REGARDING EMERGENCY DIPLOMATIC AND MILITARY TACTICS...
YES.

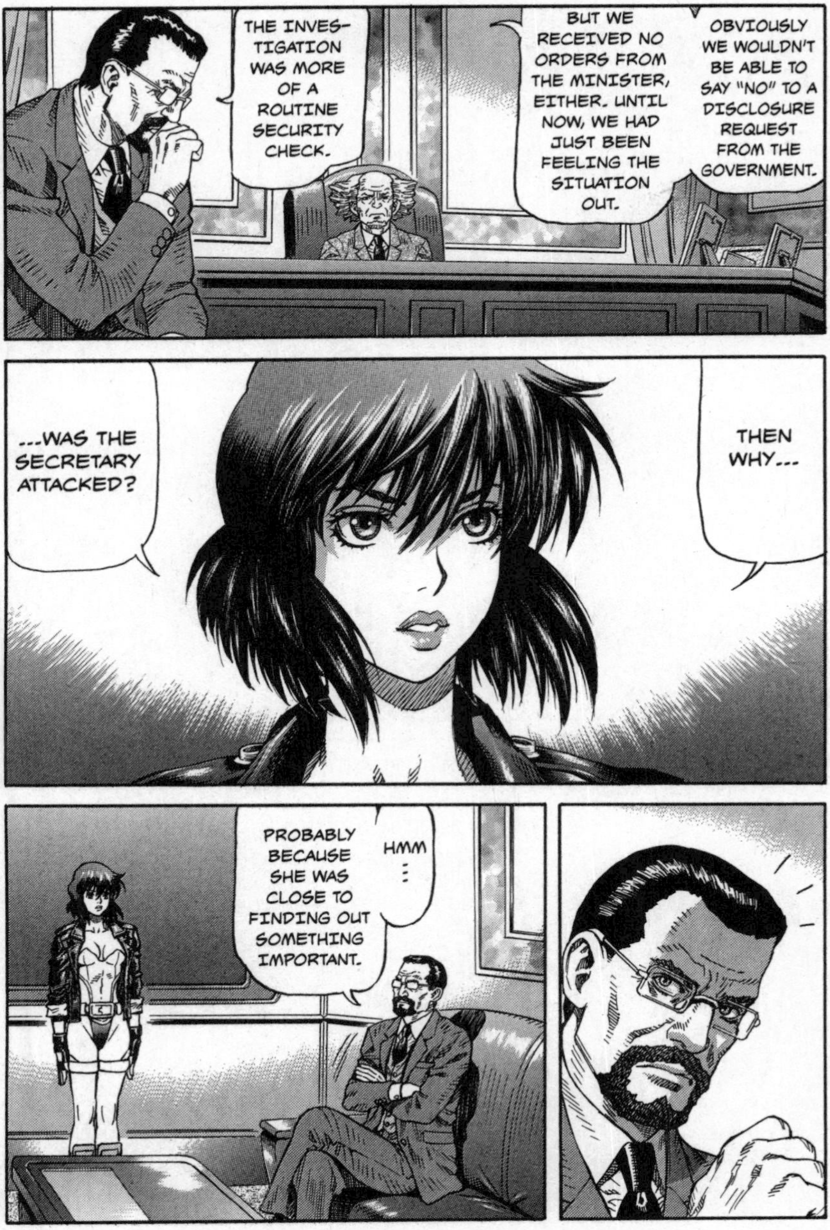
OBVIOUSLY WE WOULDN'T BE ABLE TO SAY "NO" TO A DISCLOSURE REQUEST FROM THE GOVERNMENT.
BUT WE RECEIVED NO ORDERS FROM THE MINISTER, EITHER. UNTIL NOW, WE HAD JUST BEEN FEELING THE SITUATION OUT.
THE INVES-TIGATION WAS MORE OF A ROUTINE SECURITY CHECK.
THEN WHY...
...WAS THE SECRETARY ATTACKED?
HMM...
PROBABLY BECAUSE SHE WAS CLOSE TO FINDING OUT SOMETHING IMPORTANT.

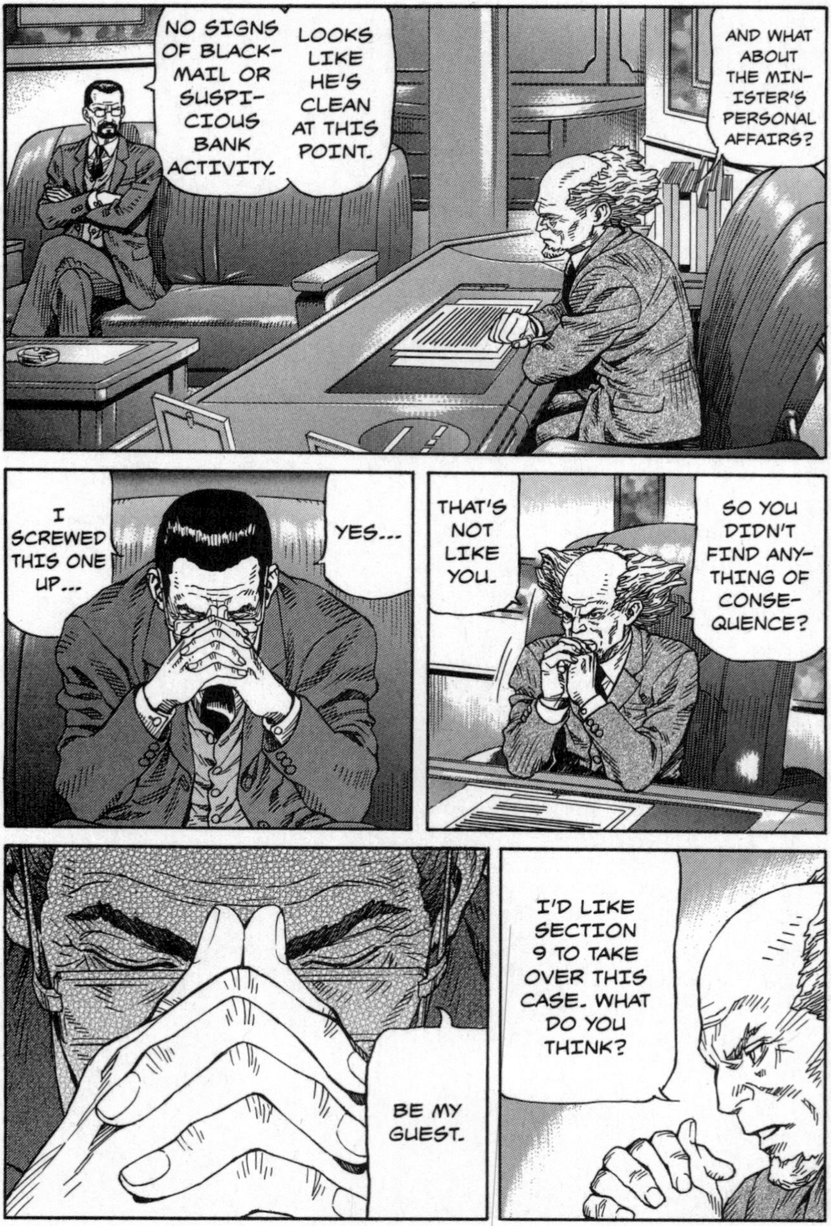
AND WHAT ABOUT THE MIN-ISTER'S PERSONAL AFFAIRS?
LOOKS LIKE HE'S CLEAN AT THIS POINT.
NO SIGNS OF BLACK-MAIL OR SUSPI-CIOUS BANK ACTIVITY.
SO YOU DIDN'T FIND ANY-THING OF CONSE-QUENCE?
THAT'S NOT LIKE YOU.
YES...
I SCREWED THIS ONE UP...
I'D LIKE SECTION 9 TO TAKE OVER THIS CASE. WHAT DO YOU THINK?
BE MY GUEST.

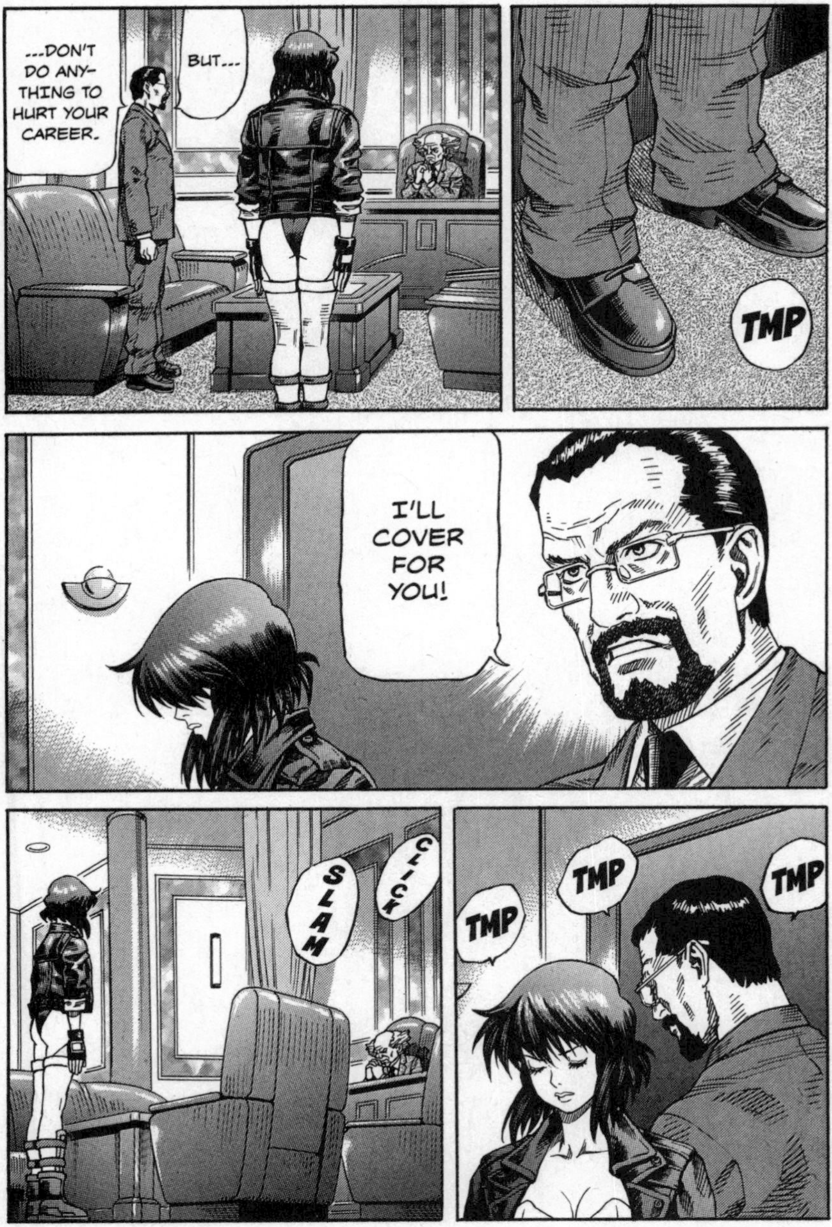
TMP
BUT...
...DON'T DO ANYTHING TO HURT YOUR CAREER.
I'LL COVER FOR YOU!
TMP
TMP
TMP
CLICK
SLAM

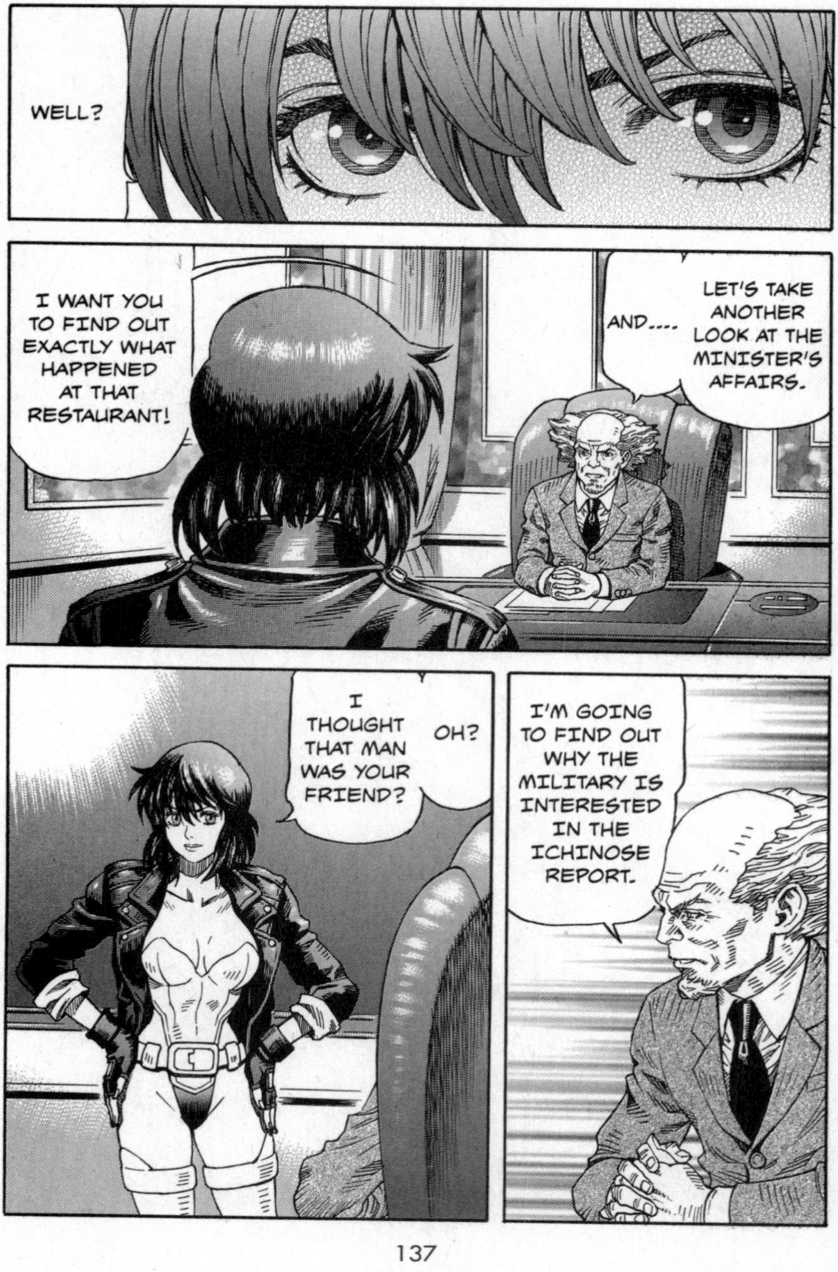
WELL?
AND.... LET'S TAKE ANOTHER LOOK AT THE MINISTER'S AFFAIRS.
I WANT YOU TO FIND OUT EXACTLY WHAT HAPPENED AT THAT RESTAURANT!
I'M GOING TO FIND OUT WHY THE MILITARY IS INTERESTED IN THE ICHINOSE REPORT.
OH?
I THOUGHT THAT MAN WAS YOUR FRIEND?

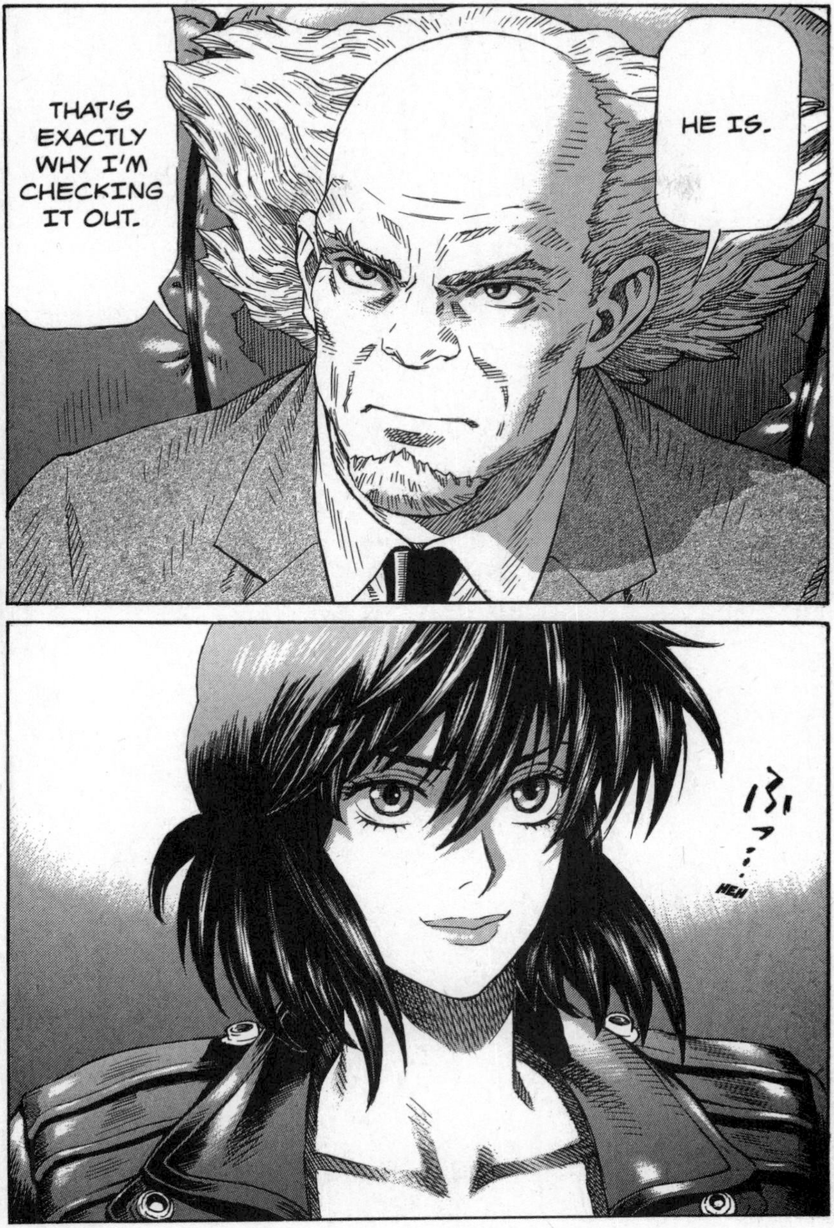
HE IS.
THAT'S EXACTLY WHY I'M CHECKING IT OUT.
HEH

#006 / End

#007: Searching for Evidence

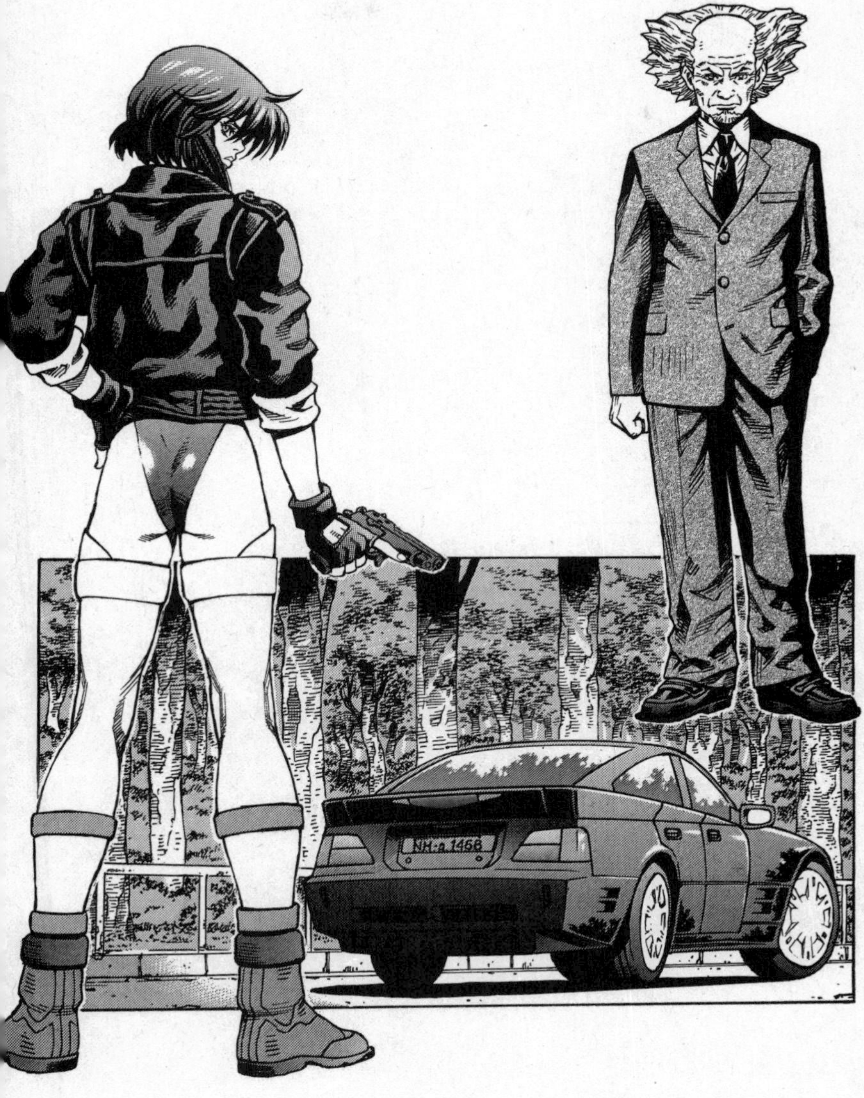

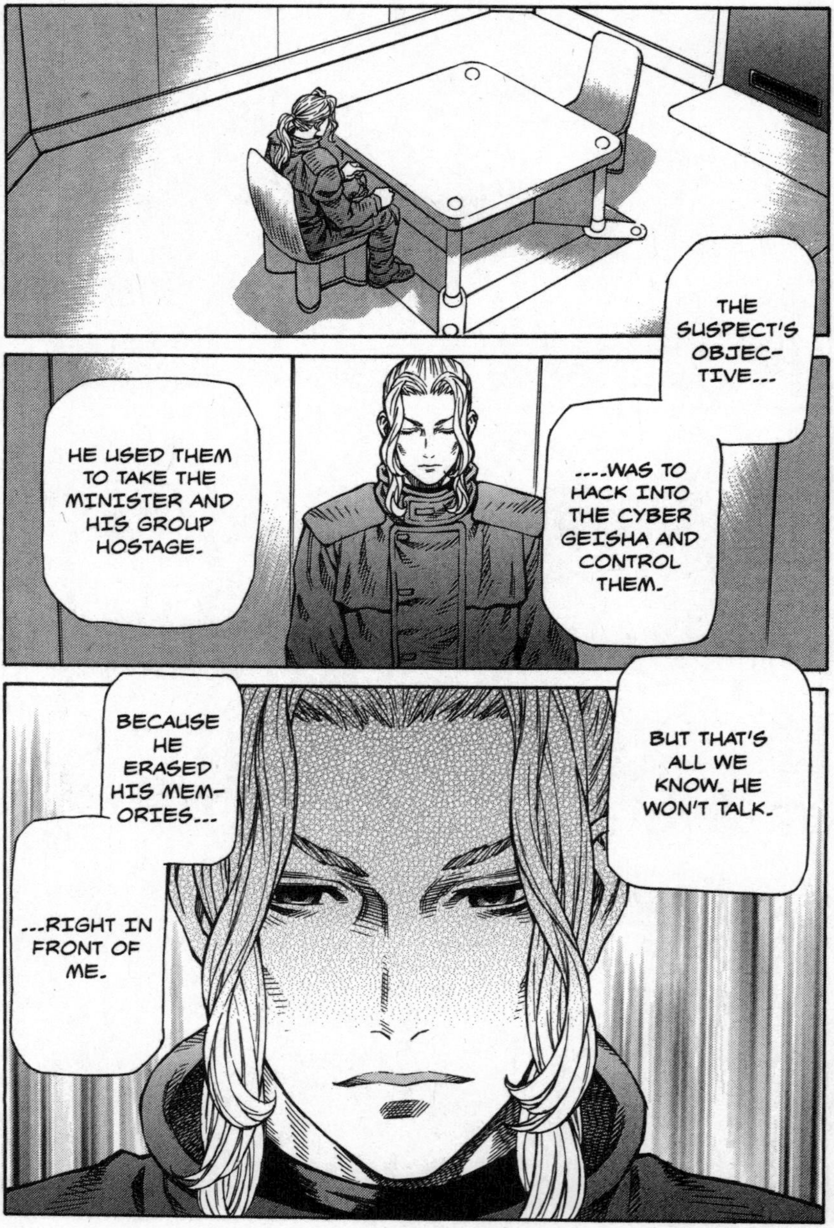
THE SUSPECT'S OBJECTIVE...
....WAS TO HACK INTO THE CYBER GEISHA AND CONTROL THEM.
HE USED THEM TO TAKE THE MINISTER AND HIS GROUP HOSTAGE.
BUT THAT'S ALL WE KNOW. HE WON'T TALK.
BECAUSE HE ERASED HIS MEMORIES...
...RIGHT IN FRONT OF ME.

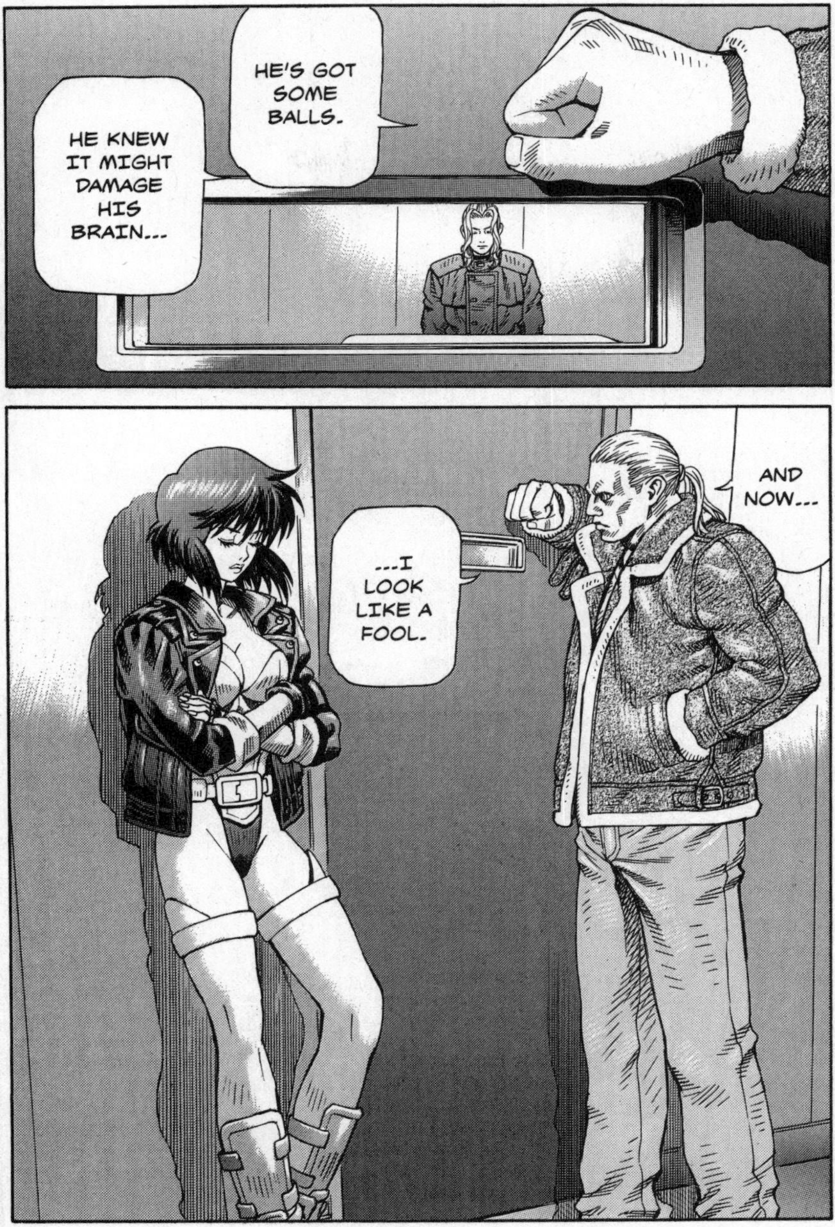
HE'S GOT SOME BALLS.
HE KNEW IT MIGHT DAMAGE HIS BRAIN...
AND NOW...
...I LOOK LIKE A FOOL.

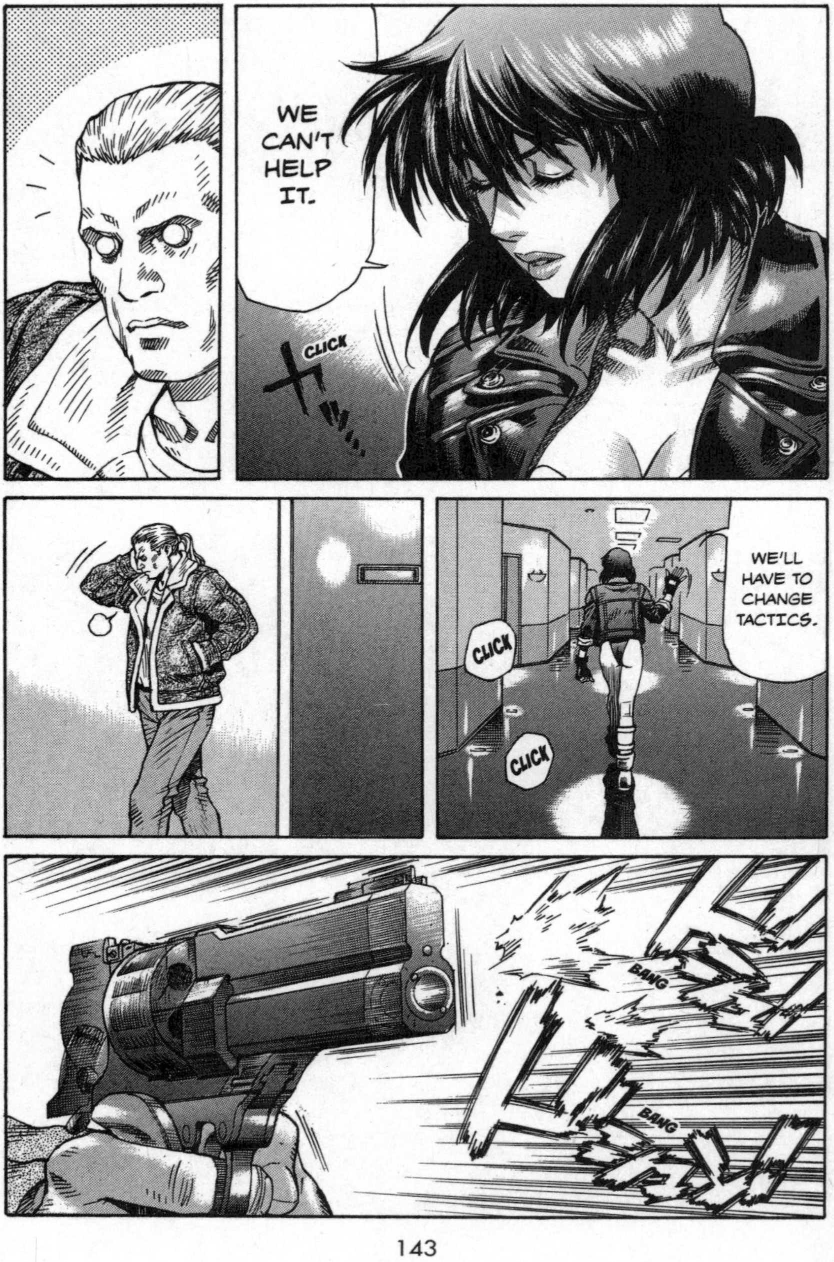
WE CAN'T HELP IT.
CLICK
WE'LL HAVE TO CHANGE TACTICS.
CLICK
CLICK
BANG
BANG

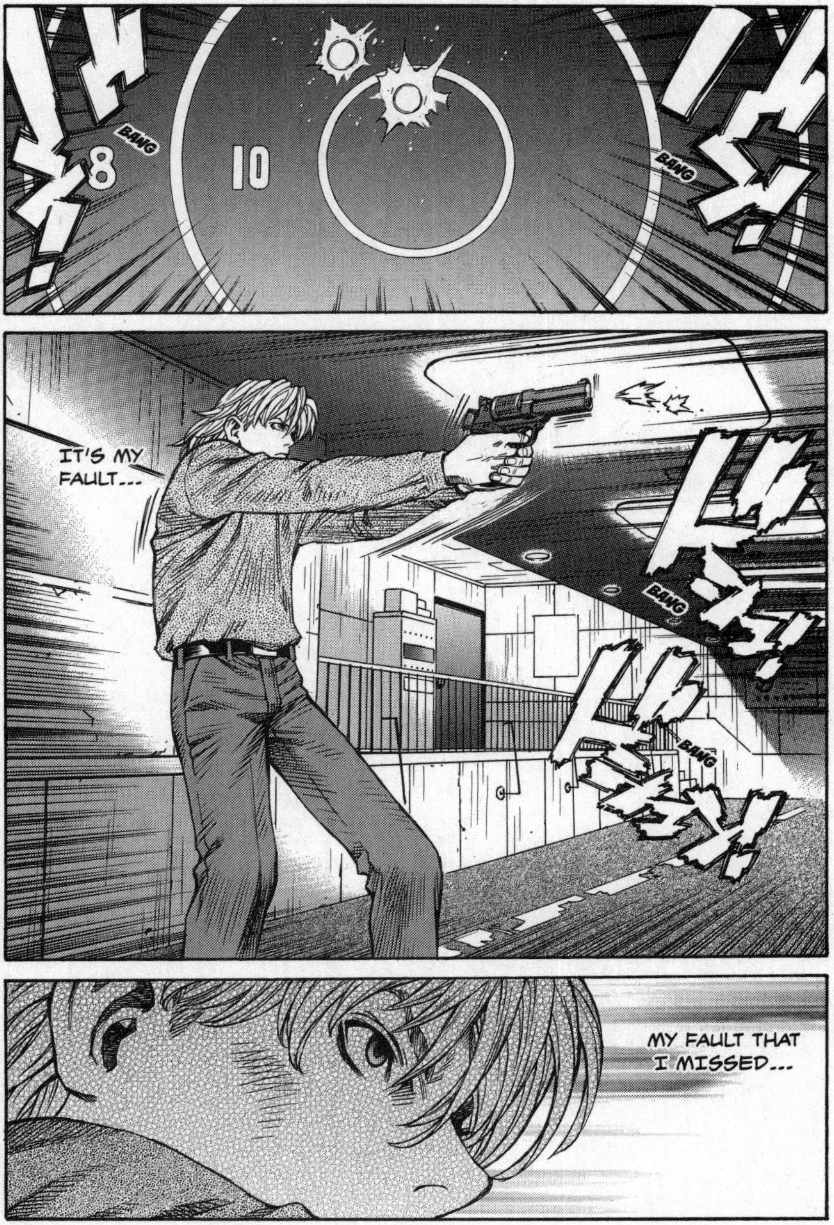
BANG
10
8
BANG
BANG
BANG
IT'S MY FAULT...
MY FAULT THAT I MISSED...

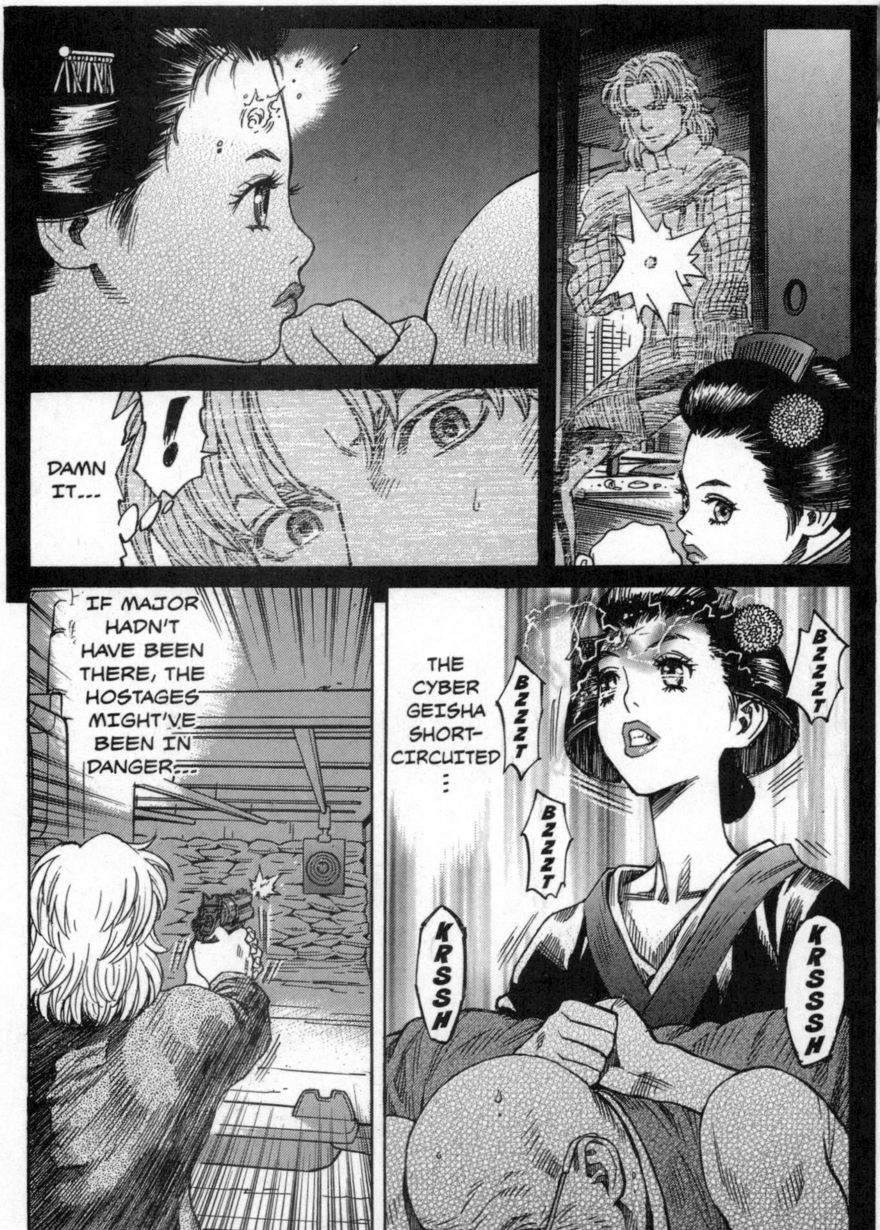
!
DAMN IT...
BZZZT
BZZZT
THE CYBER GEISHA SHORT-CIRCUITED ...
BZZZT
KRSSSH
KRSSH
IF MAJOR HADN'T HAVE BEEN THERE, THE HOSTAGES MIGHT'VE BEEN IN DANGER...

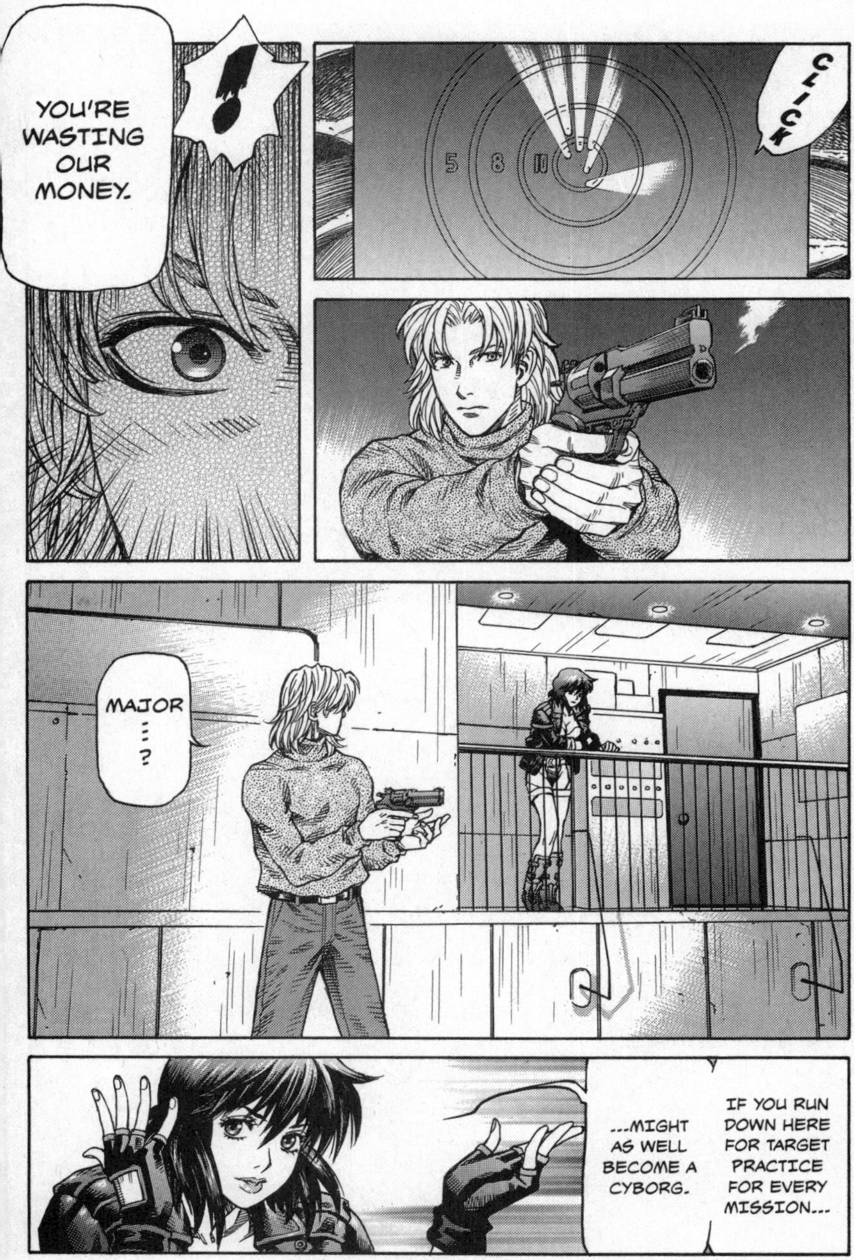
CLICK
!
YOU'RE WASTING OUR MONEY.
MAJOR ...?
IF YOU RUN DOWN HERE FOR TARGET PRACTICE FOR EVERY MISSION...
...MIGHT AS WELL BECOME A CYBORG.

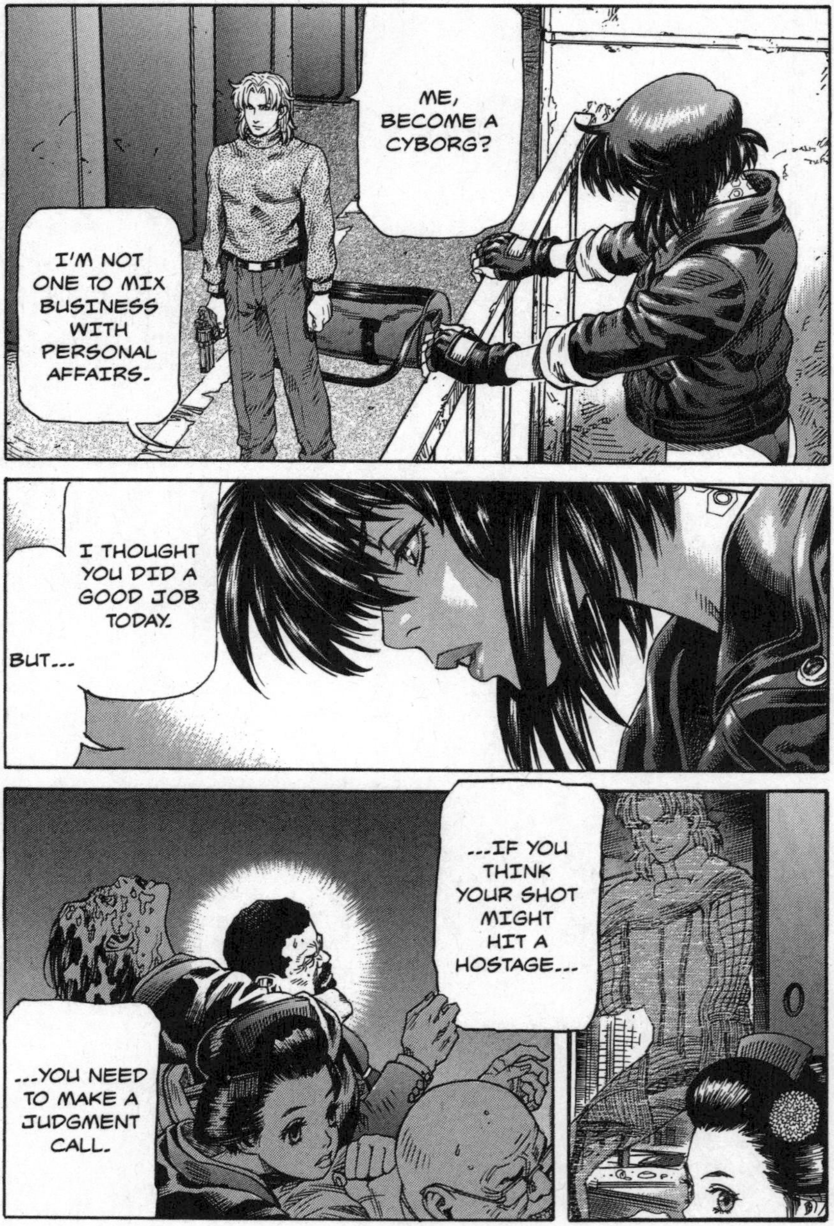
ME, BECOME A CYBORG?
I'M NOT ONE TO MIX BUSINESS WITH PERSONAL AFFAIRS.
I THOUGHT YOU DID A GOOD JOB TODAY.
BUT...
...IF YOU THINK YOUR SHOT MIGHT HIT A HOSTAGE...
...YOU NEED TO MAKE A JUDGMENT CALL.

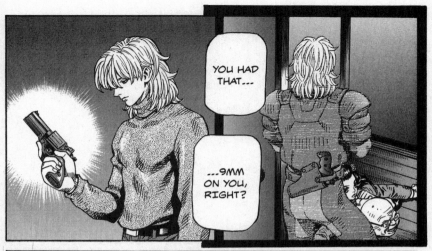

YOU HAD THAT...
...9MM ON YOU, RIGHT?
REALLY...
WHY DO YOU THINK WE HIRED YOU FROM THE POLICE HEADQUARTERS?
STOP MOPING AROUND DOWN HERE...

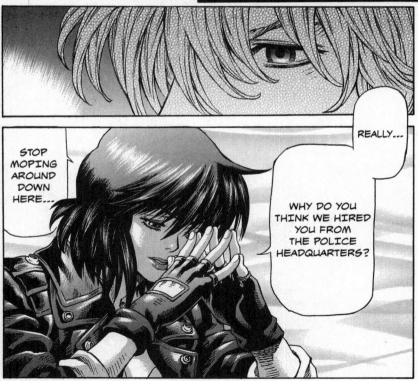

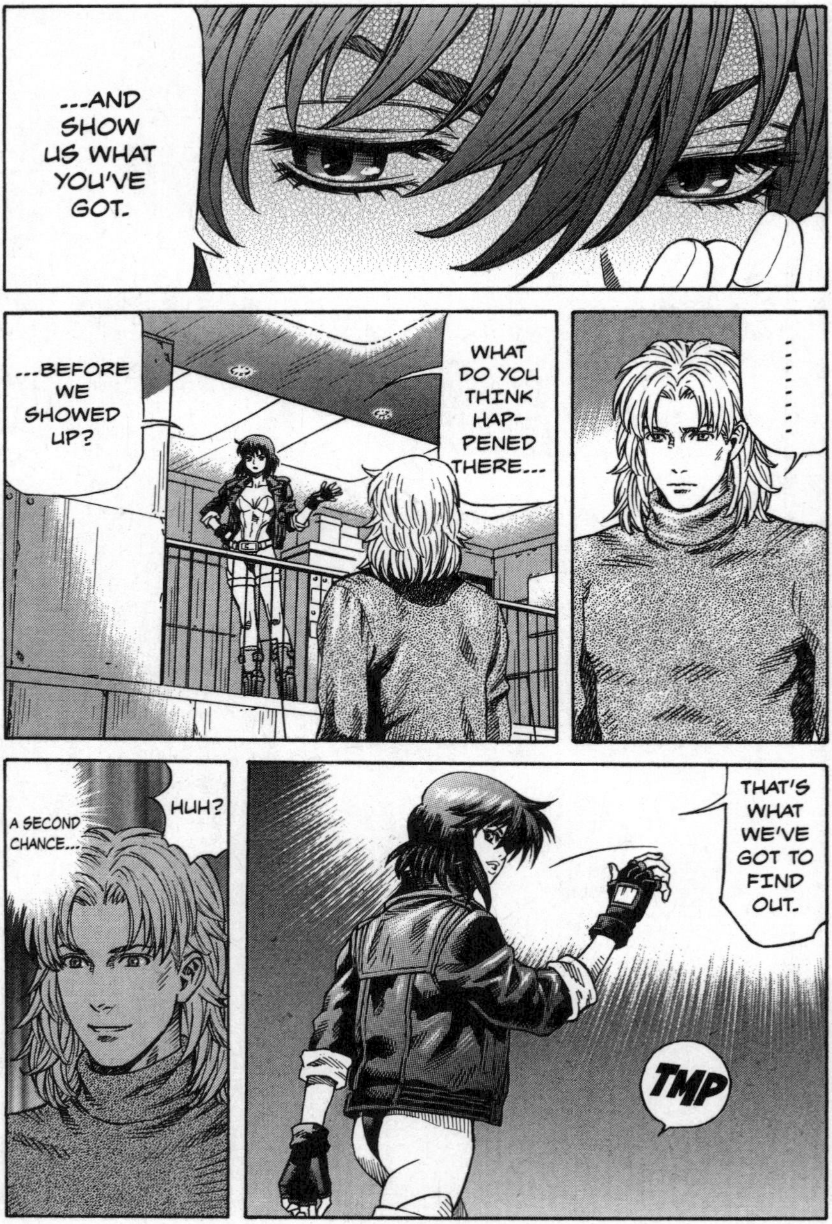
...AND SHOW US WHAT YOU'VE GOT.
....
WHAT DO YOU THINK HAPPENED THERE...
...BEFORE WE SHOWED UP?
THAT'S WHAT WE'VE GOT TO FIND OUT.
TMP
HUH?
A SECOND CHANCE...

SLAM
CLICK
TMP
TMP
TMP

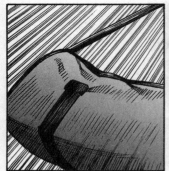

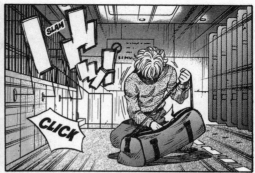

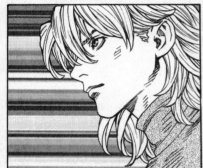

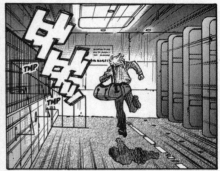

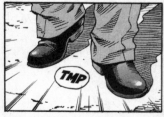

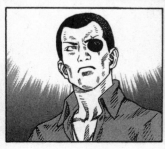

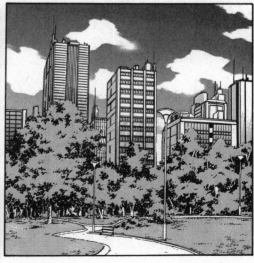

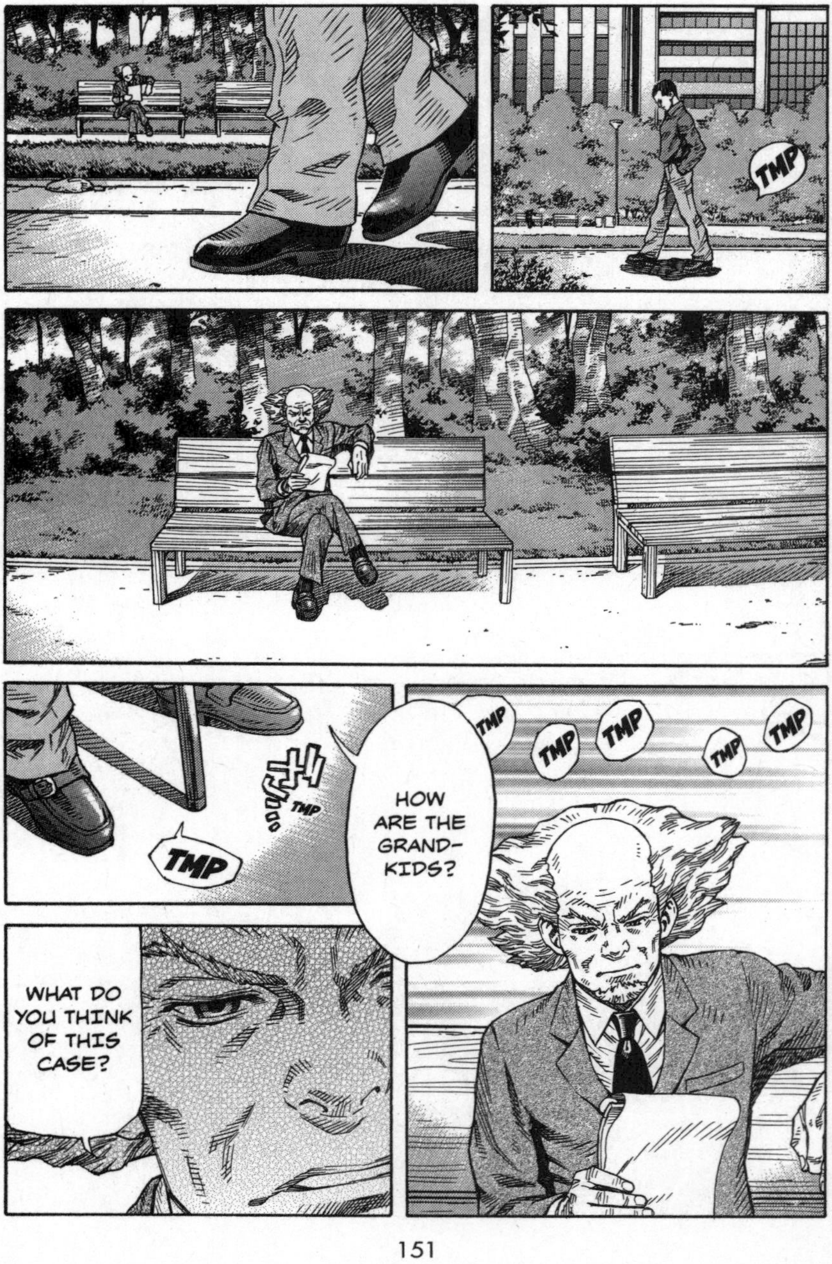
TMP
TMP
TMP
TMP
TMP
TMP
HOW ARE THE GRAND-KIDS?
TMP
TMP
WHAT DO YOU THINK OF THIS CASE?

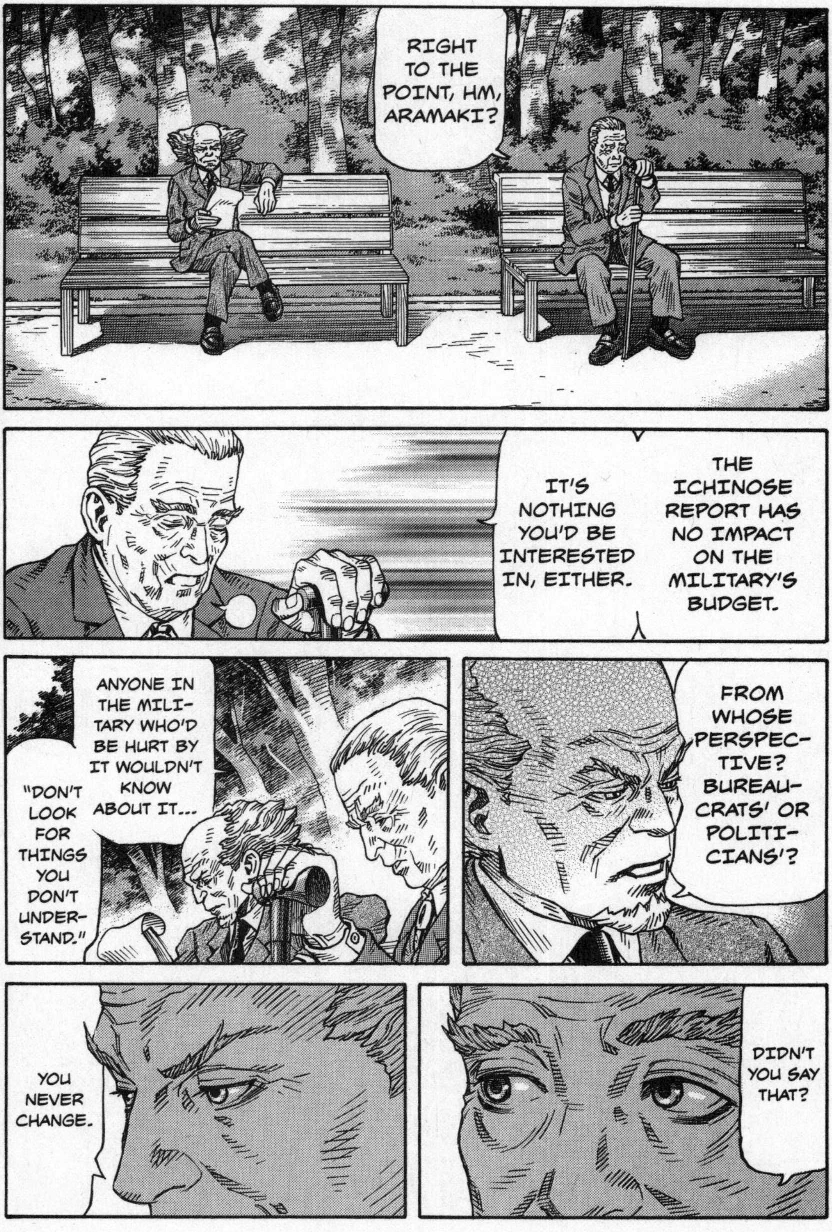
RIGHT TO THE POINT, HM, ARAMAKI?
THE ICHINOSE REPORT HAS NO IMPACT ON THE MILITARY'S BUDGET.
IT'S NOTHING YOU'D BE INTERESTED IN, EITHER.
FROM WHOSE PERSPECTIVE? BUREAUCRATS' OR POLITICIANS'?
ANYONE IN THE MILITARY WHO'D BE HURT BY IT WOULDN'T KNOW ABOUT IT...
"DON'T LOOK FOR THINGS YOU DON'T UNDERSTAND."
DIDN'T YOU SAY THAT?
YOU NEVER CHANGE.

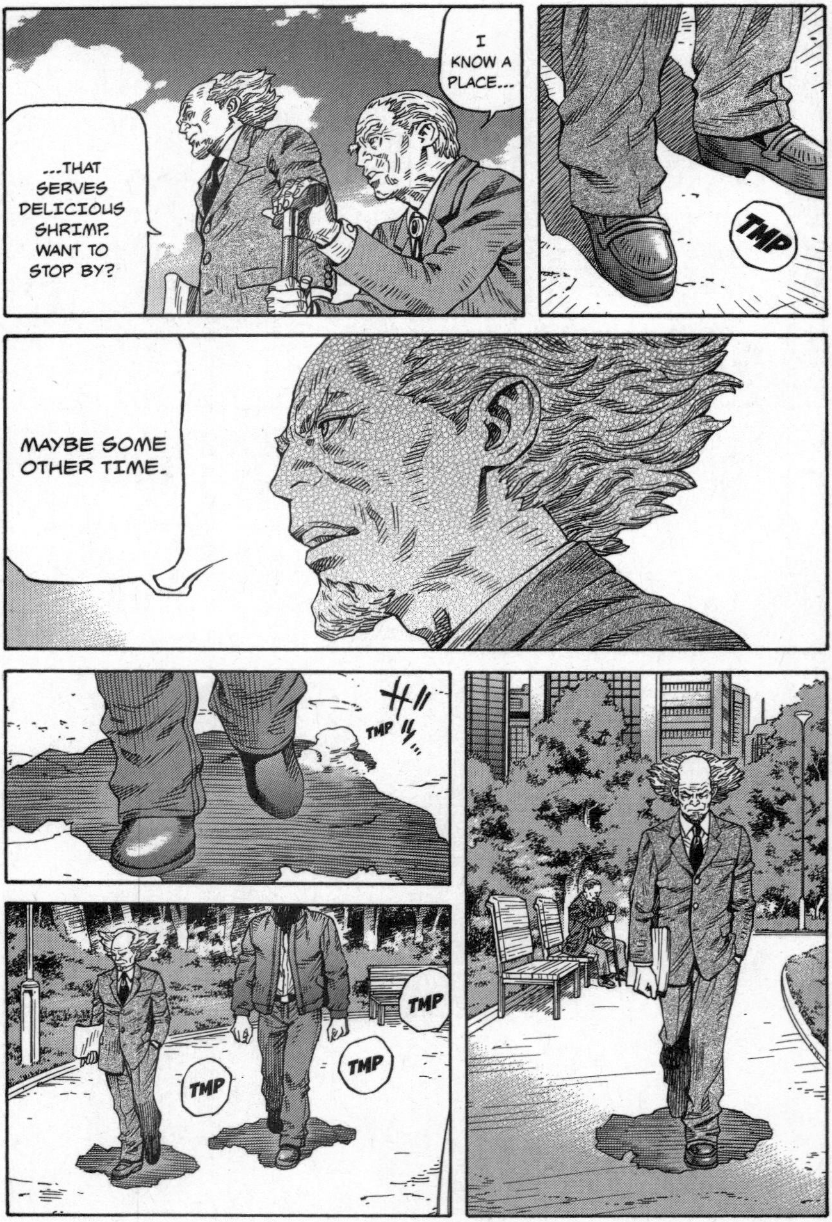
TMP
I KNOW A PLACE...
...THAT SERVES DELICIOUS SHRIMP. WANT TO STOP BY?
MAYBE SOME OTHER TIME.
TMP
TMP
TMP
TMP

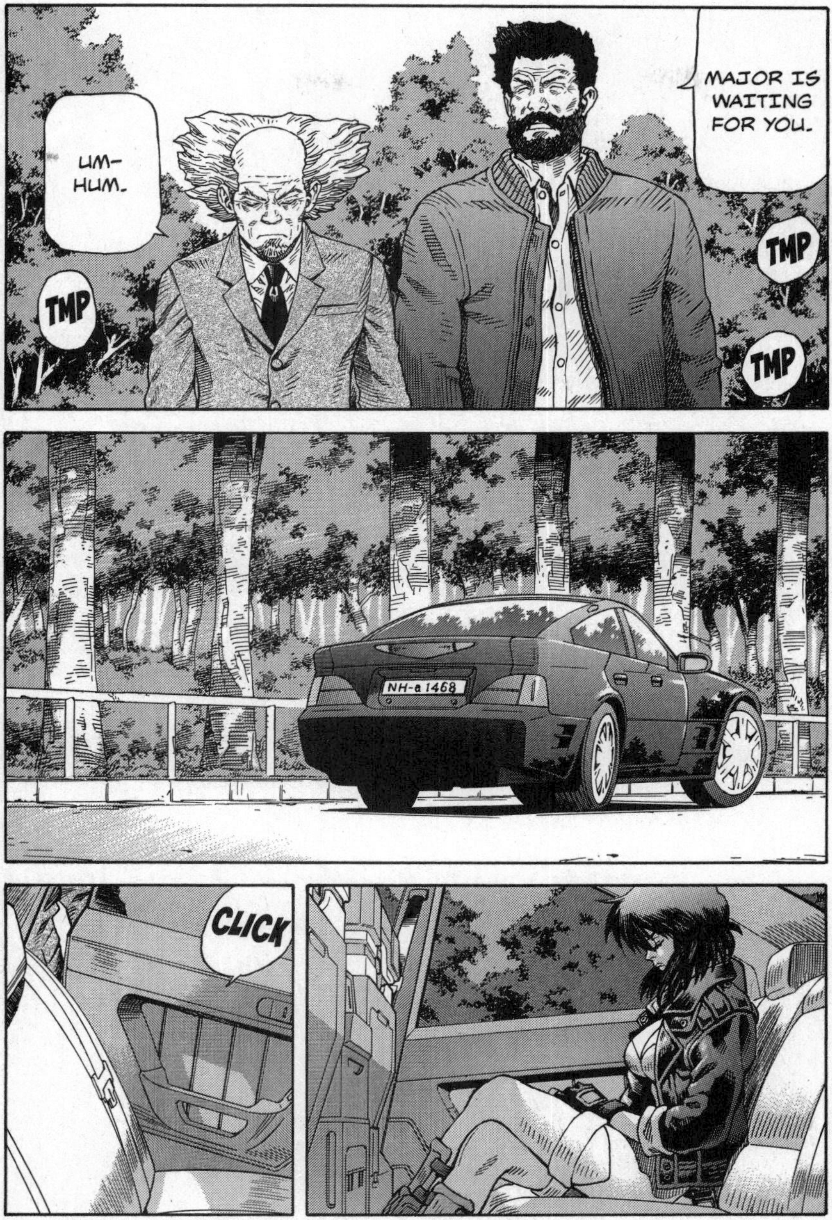
MAJOR IS WAITING FOR YOU.
TMP
TMP
UM-HUM.
TMP
NH-a 1468
CLICK

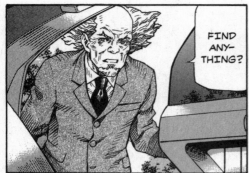

FIND ANY- THING?

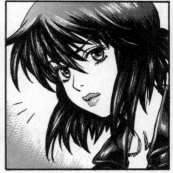

VIDEO OF THE WILLOW ROOM IM- MEDIATELY FOLLOWING. PLUS...

SHOOM

...SOMETHING DISTURBING FROM THE SURVEILLANCE CAMERAS.

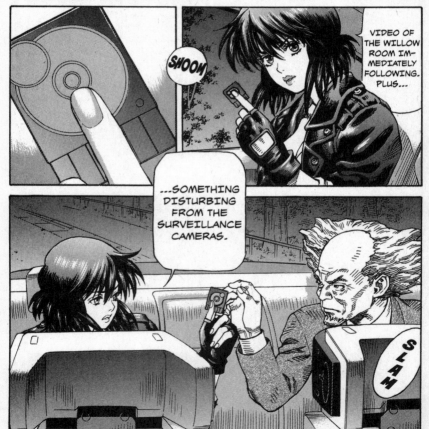

S L A M

155

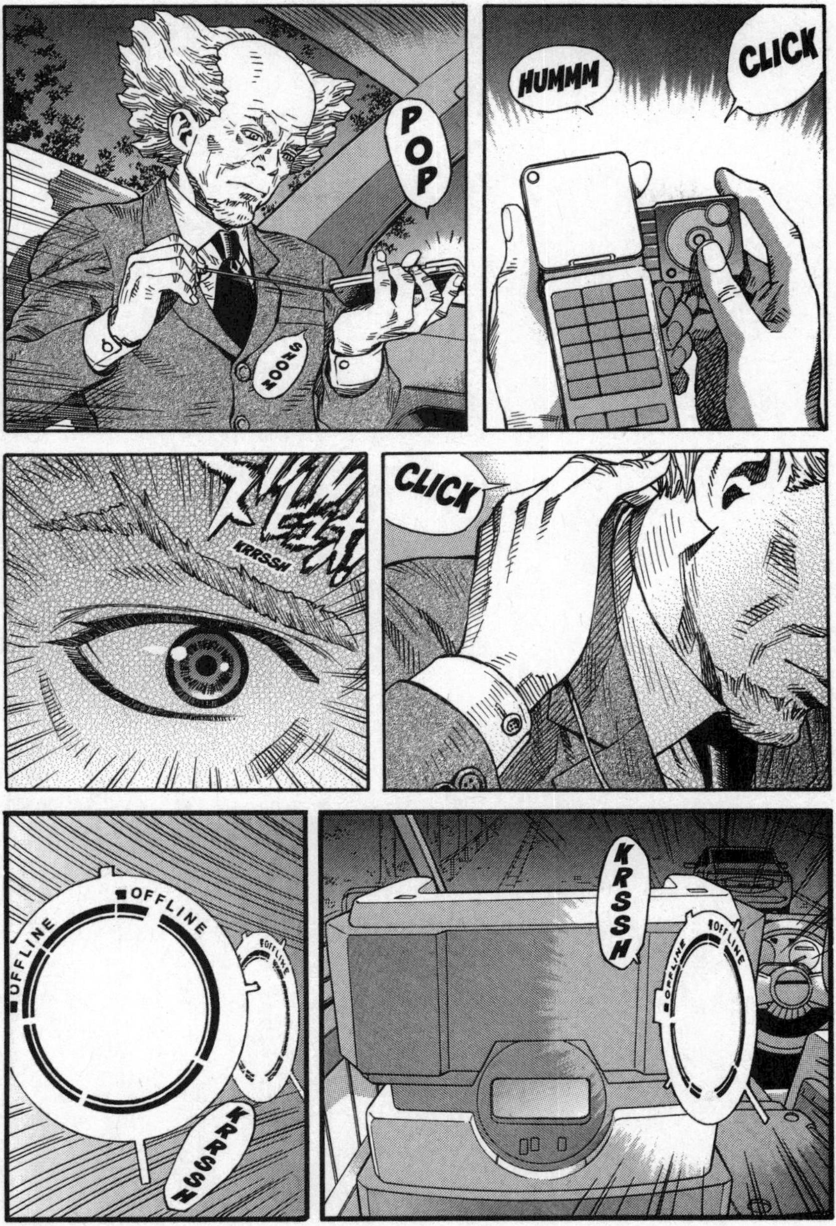
HUMMM
CLICK
POP
SNOOK
CLICK
KRRSSH
KRSSH
OFFLINE
OFFLINE
OFFLINE
OFFLINE
OFFLINE
KRRSSH

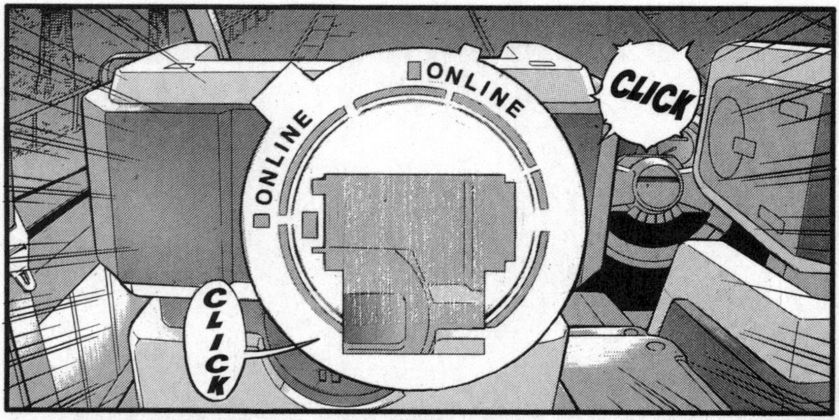
CLICK
ONLINE
ONLINE
CLICK

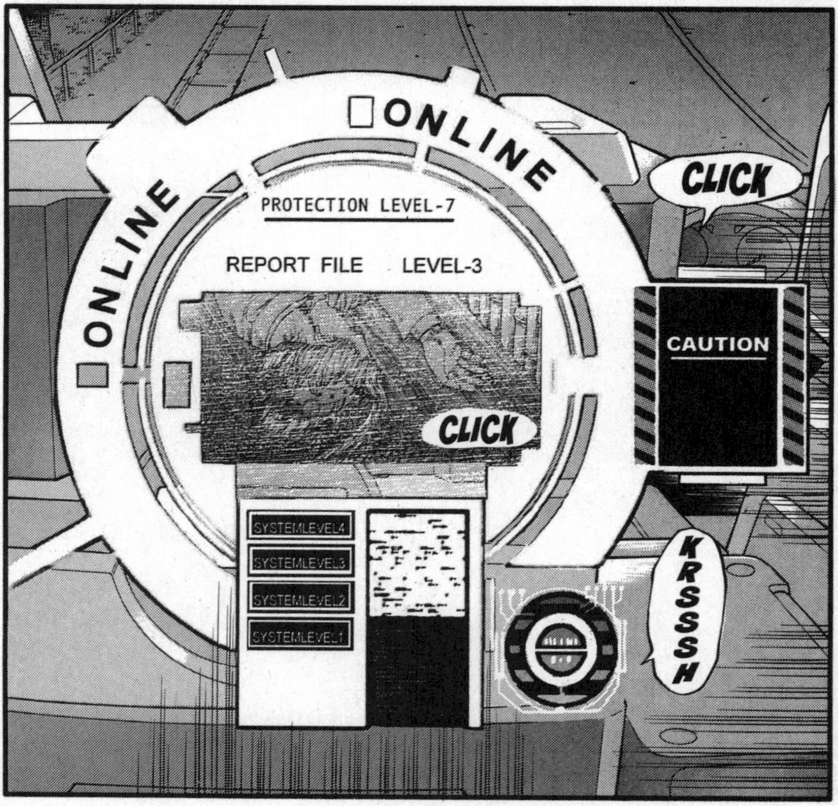
CLICK
ONLINE
ONLINE
PROTECTION LEVEL-7
REPORT FILE LEVEL-3
CAUTION
CLICK
KRSSSH
SYSTEMLEVEL4
SYSTEMLEVEL3
SYSTEMLEVEL2
SYSTEMLEVEL1

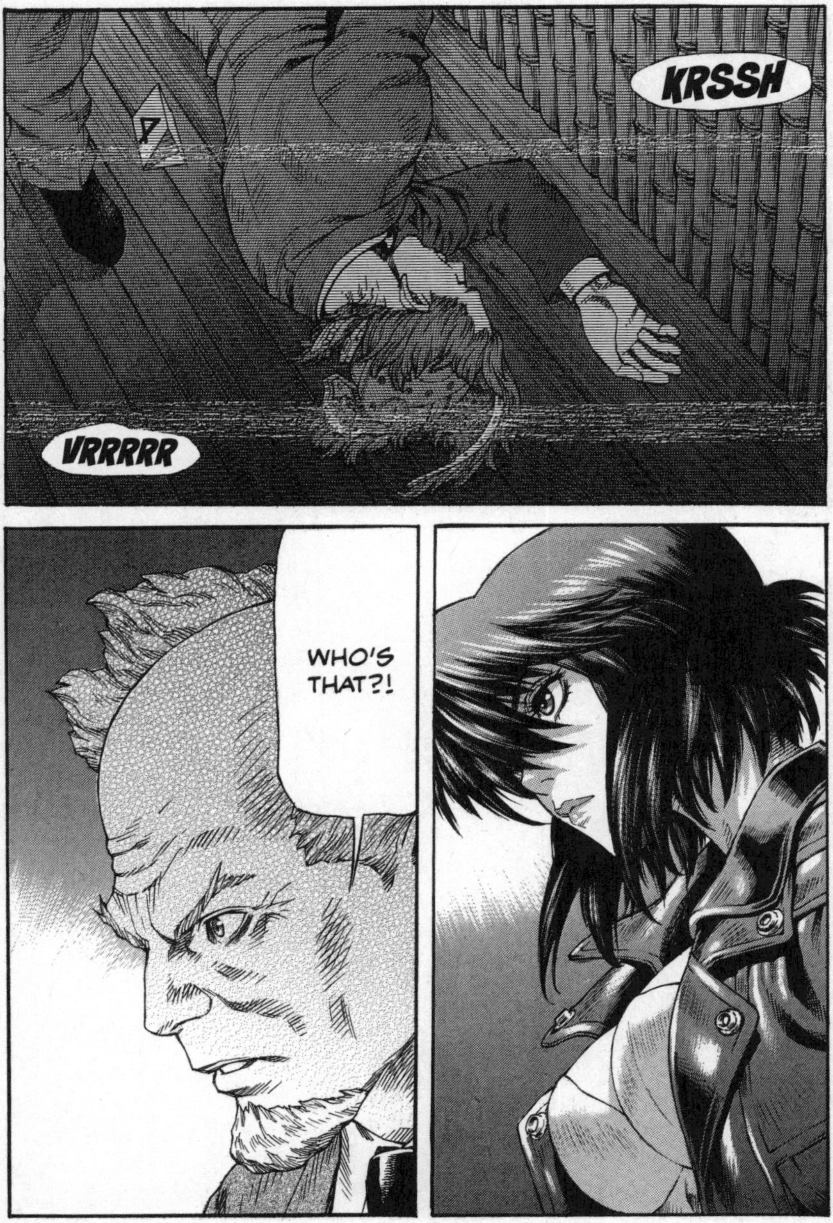
KRSSH
VRRRRR
WHO'S THAT?!

#007 / End

#008: Blind Spot

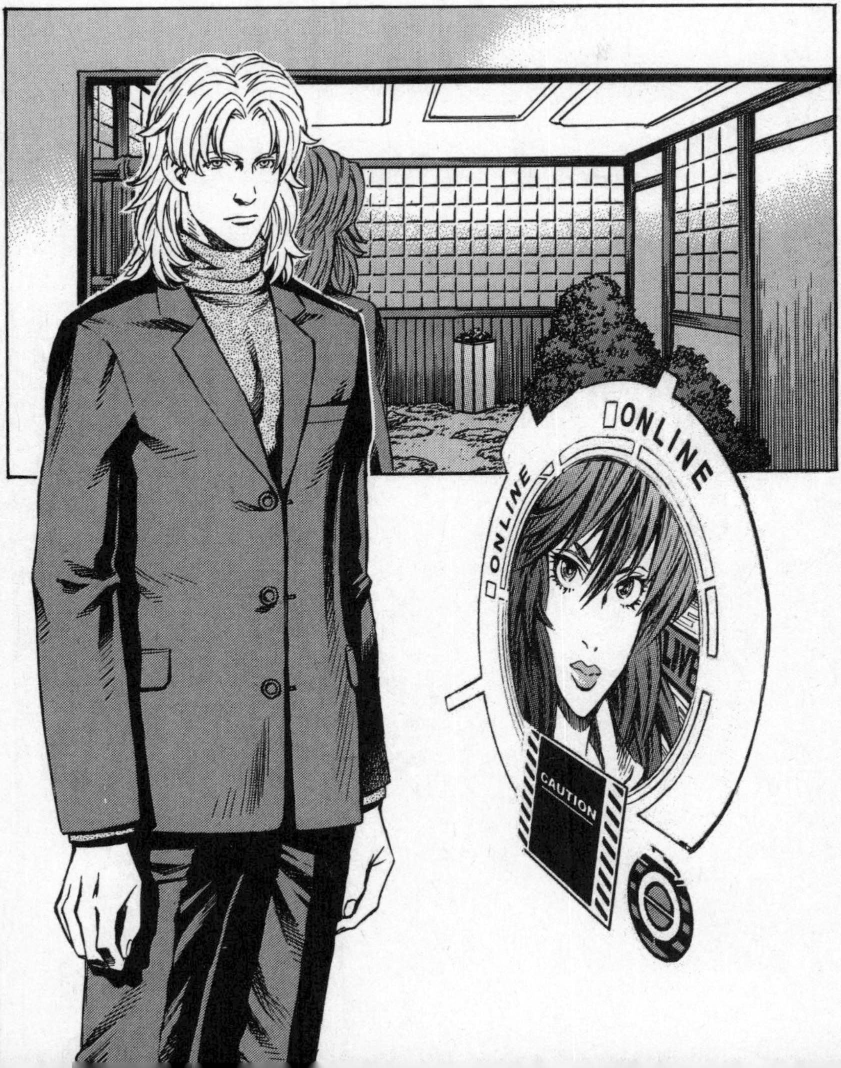
ONLINE
ONLINE
CAUTION

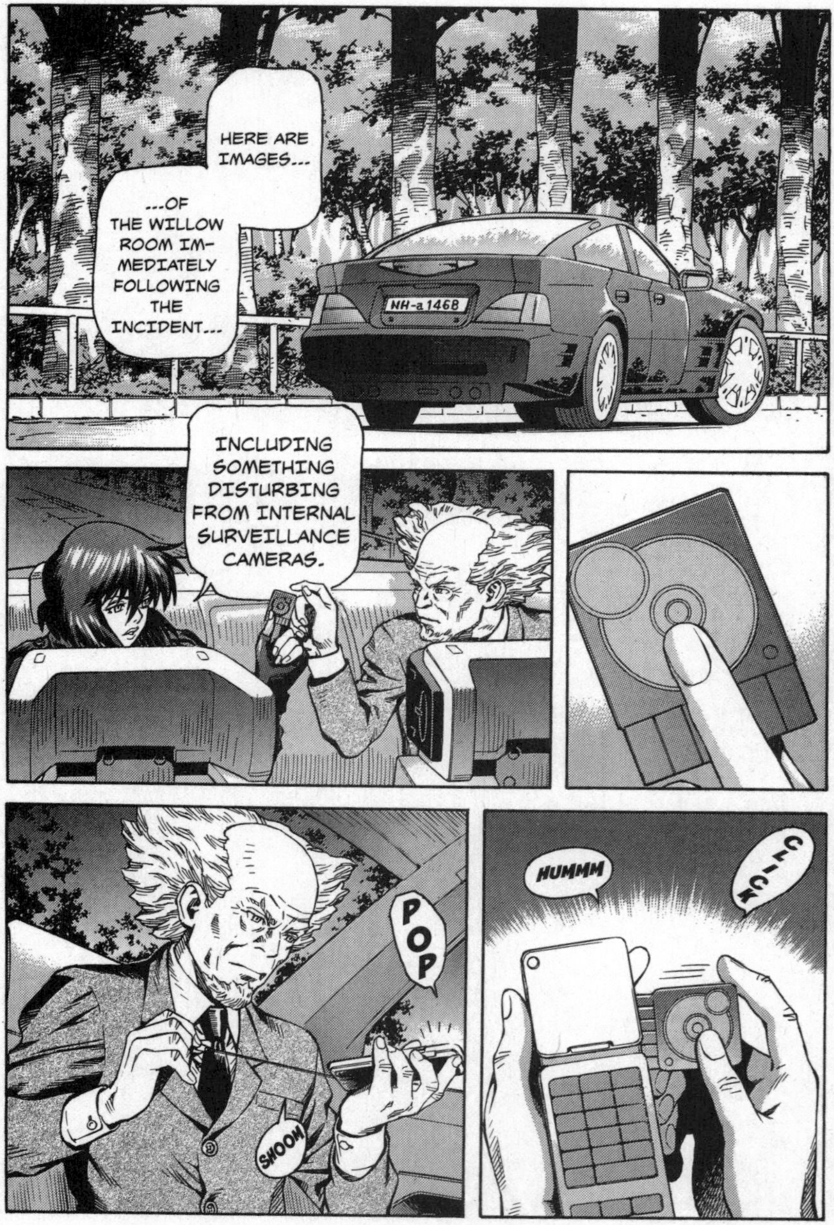
HERE ARE IMAGES...
...OF THE WILLOW ROOM IM-MEDIATELY FOLLOWING THE INCIDENT...
NH-a 1468
INCLUDING SOMETHING DISTURBING FROM INTERNAL SURVEILLANCE CAMERAS.
CLICK
HUMMM
POP
SHOOM

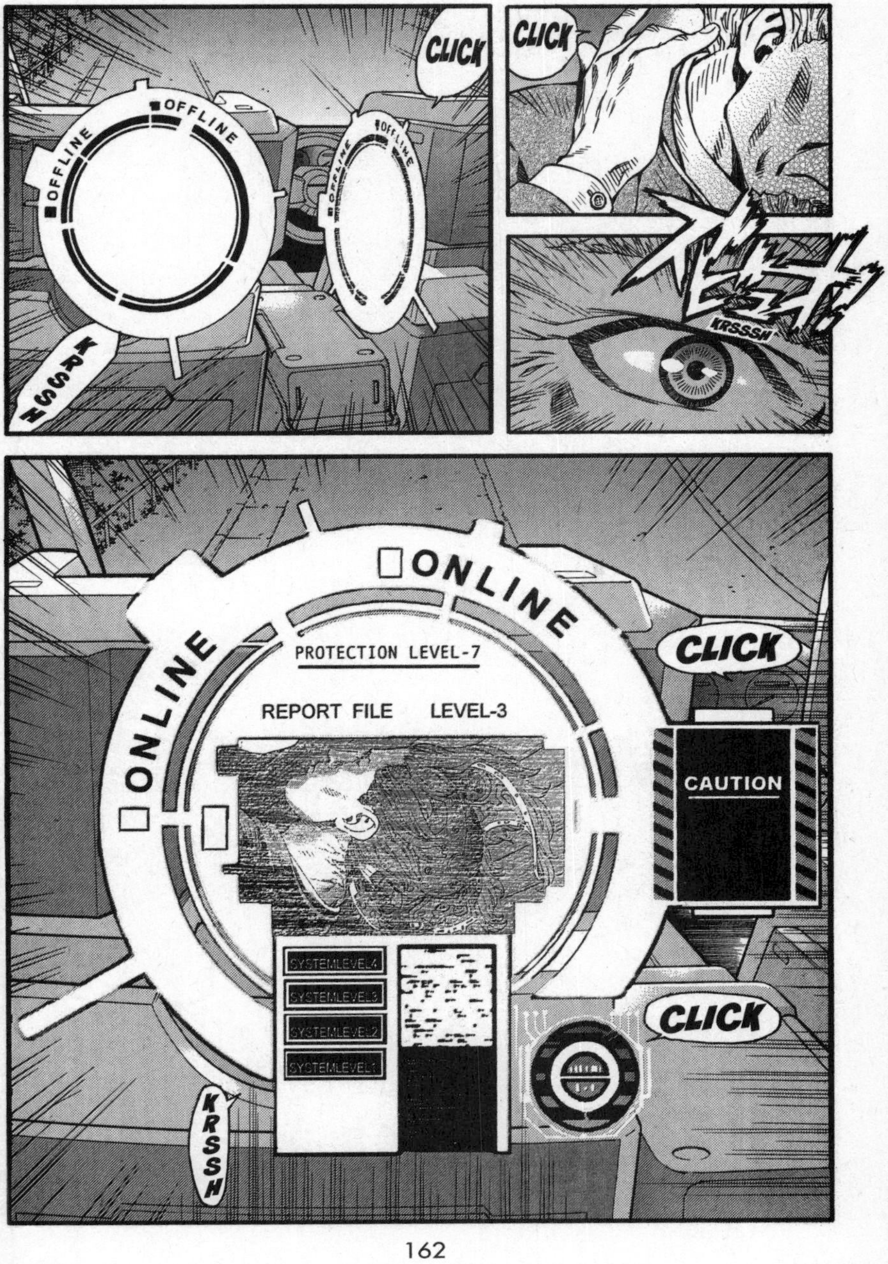
CLICK
KRSSSH
CLICK
OFFLINE
OFFLINE
OFFLINE
OFFLINE
KRSSH
CLICK
ONLINE
ONLINE
PROTECTION LEVEL-7
REPORT FILE LEVEL-3
CAUTION
CLICK
SYSTEMLEVEL4
SYSTEMLEVEL3
SYSTEMLEVEL2
SYSTEMLEVEL1
KRSSH

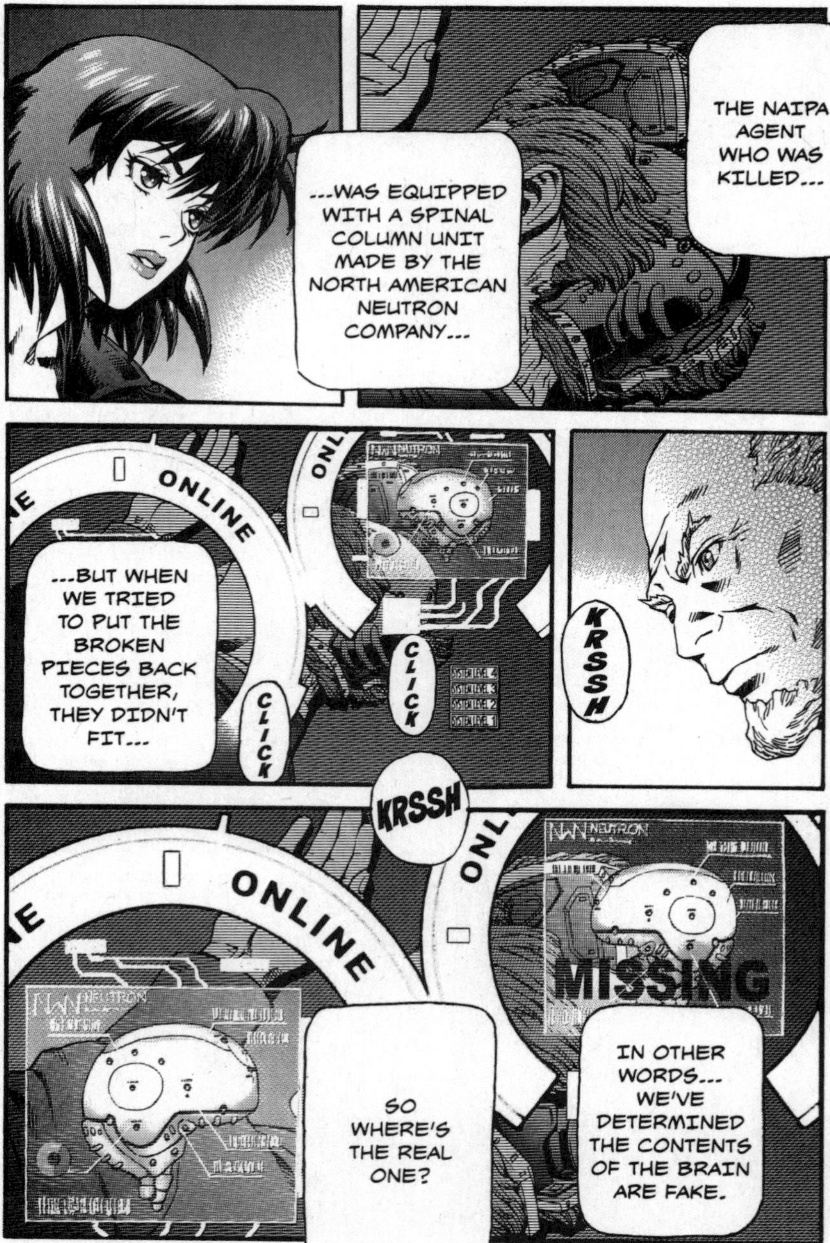
THE NAIPA AGENT WHO WAS KILLED...
...WAS EQUIPPED WITH A SPINAL COLUMN UNIT MADE BY THE NORTH AMERICAN NEUTRON COMPANY...
KRSSH
ONLINE
NEUTRON
CLICK
SYSTEM LEVEL 4
SYSTEM LEVEL 3
SYSTEM LEVEL 2
SYSTEM LEVEL 1
CLICK
...BUT WHEN WE TRIED TO PUT THE BROKEN PIECES BACK TOGETHER, THEY DIDN'T FIT...
KRSSH
ONLINE
NEUTRON
MISSING
IN OTHER WORDS... WE'VE DETERMINED THE CONTENTS OF THE BRAIN ARE FAKE.
NEUTRON
SO WHERE'S THE REAL ONE?

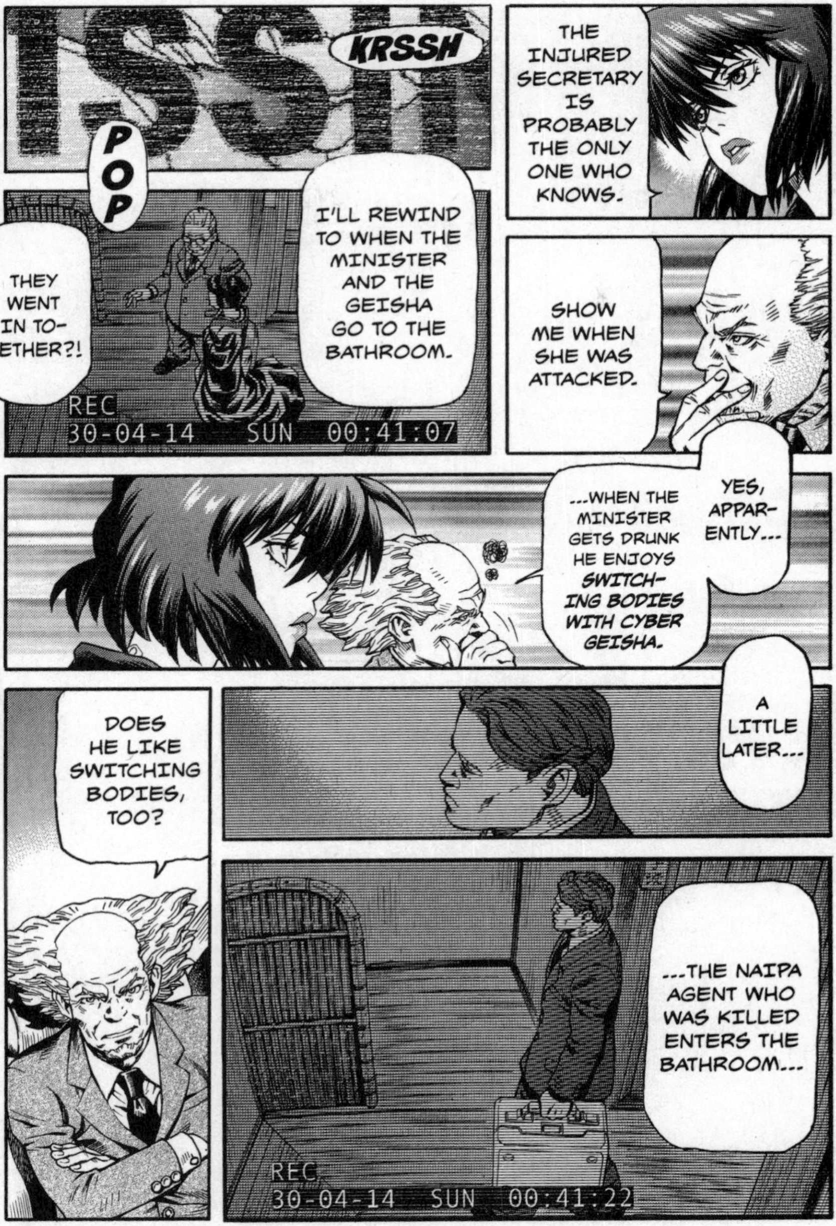
THE INJURED SECRETARY IS PROBABLY THE ONLY ONE WHO KNOWS.
KRSSH
POP
SHOW ME WHEN SHE WAS ATTACKED.
I'LL REWIND TO WHEN THE MINISTER AND THE GEISHA GO TO THE BATHROOM.
THEY WENT IN TO-GETHER?!
REC
30-04-14 SUN 00:41:07
YES, APPAR-ENTLY...
...WHEN THE MINISTER GETS DRUNK HE ENJOYS SWITCH-ING BODIES WITH CYBER GEISHA.
A LITTLE LATER...
...THE NAIPA AGENT WHO WAS KILLED ENTERS THE BATHROOM...
REC
30-04-14 SUN 00:41:22
DOES HE LIKE SWITCHING BODIES, TOO?

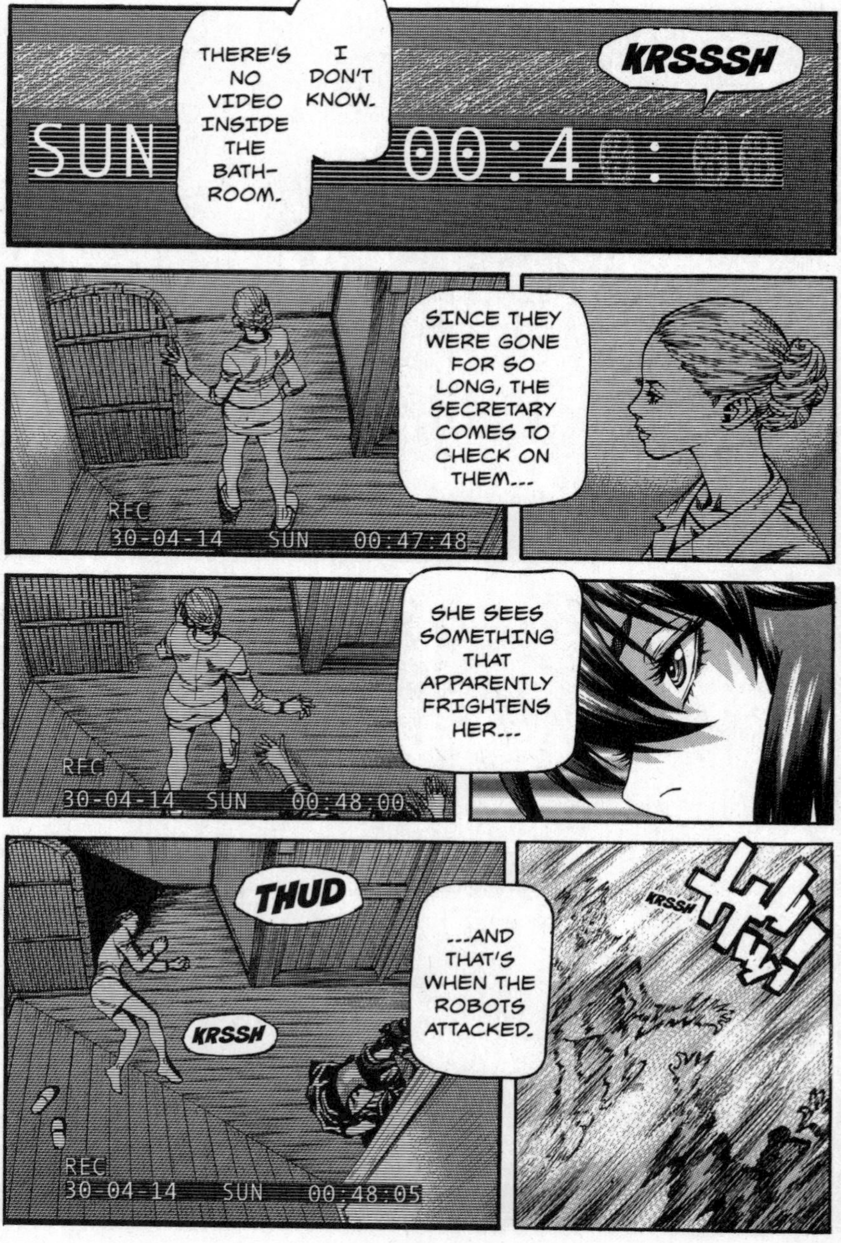
KRSSSH
SUN 00:4
I DON'T KNOW.
THERE'S NO VIDEO INSIDE THE BATH-ROOM.
SINCE THEY WERE GONE FOR SO LONG, THE SECRETARY COMES TO CHECK ON THEM...
REC
30-04-14 SUN 00:47:48
SHE SEES SOMETHING THAT APPARENTLY FRIGHTENS HER...
REC
30-04-14 SUN 00:48:00
KRSSH
...AND THAT'S WHEN THE ROBOTS ATTACKED.
THUD
KRSSH
REC
30-04-14 SUN 00:48:05

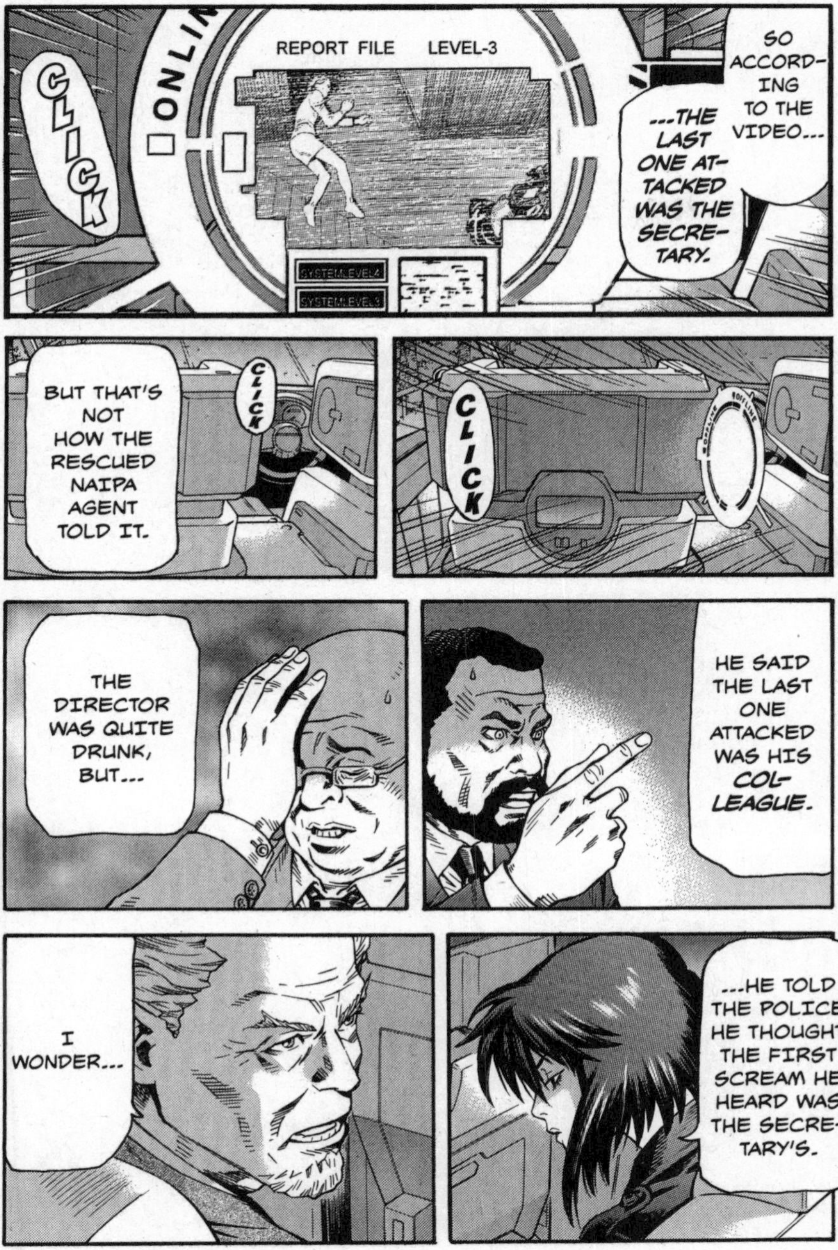
SO ACCORDING TO THE VIDEO...
...THE LAST ONE ATTACKED WAS THE SECRETARY.
REPORT FILE LEVEL-3
ONLIN
SYSTEM LEVEL4
SYSTEM LEVEL3
CLICK
CLICK
CLICK
BUT THAT'S NOT HOW THE RESCUED NAIPA AGENT TOLD IT.
HE SAID THE LAST ONE ATTACKED WAS HIS COLLEAGUE.
THE DIRECTOR WAS QUITE DRUNK, BUT...
...HE TOLD THE POLICE HE THOUGHT THE FIRST SCREAM HE HEARD WAS THE SECRETARY'S.
I WONDER...

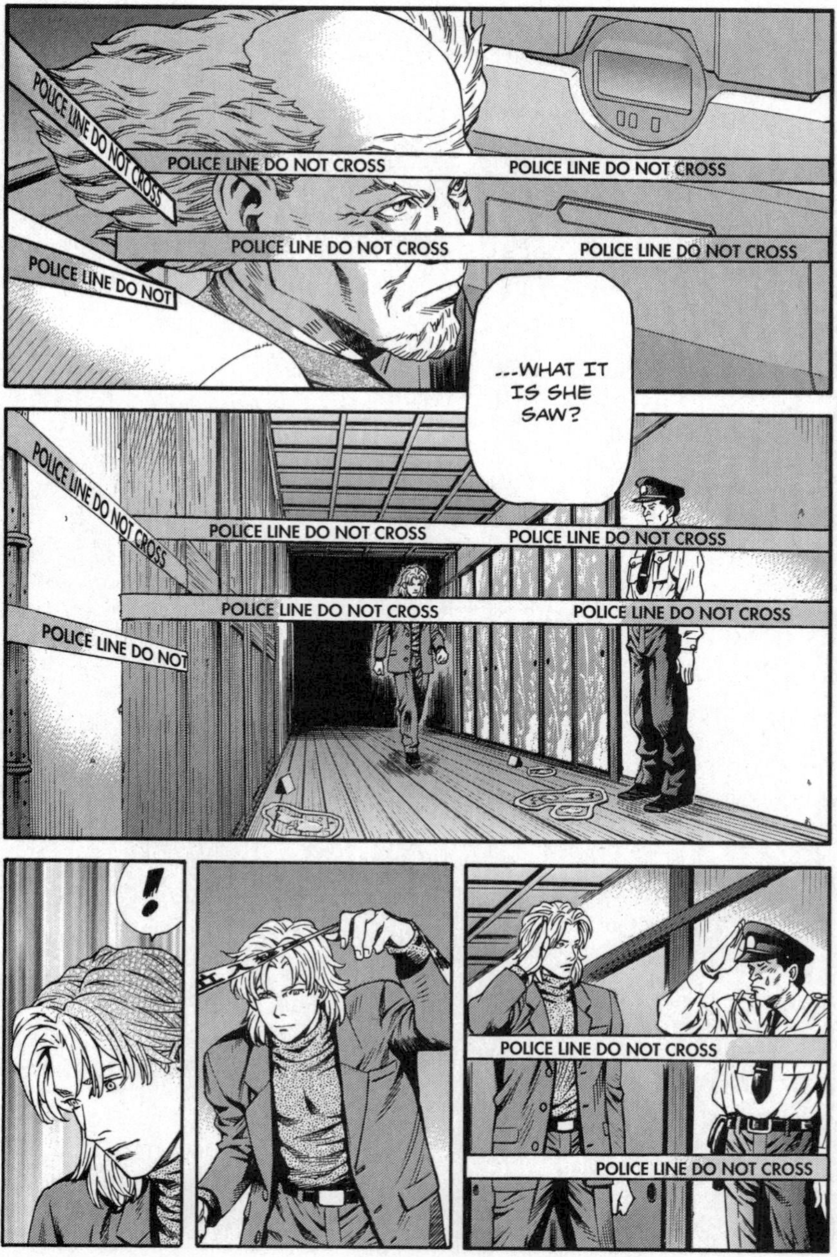

POLICE LINE DO NOT CROSS
POLICE LINE DO NOT CROSS
POLICE LINE DO NOT CROSS
POLICE LINE DO NOT CROSS
POLICE LINE DO NOT CROSS
POLICE LINE DO NOT
---WHAT IT IS SHE SAW?
POLICE LINE DO NOT CROSS
POLICE LINE DO NOT CROSS
POLICE LINE DO NOT CROSS
POLICE LINE DO NOT CROSS
POLICE LINE DO NOT CROSS
POLICE LINE DO NOT
POLICE LINE DO NOT CROSS
POLICE LINE DO NOT CROSS
!

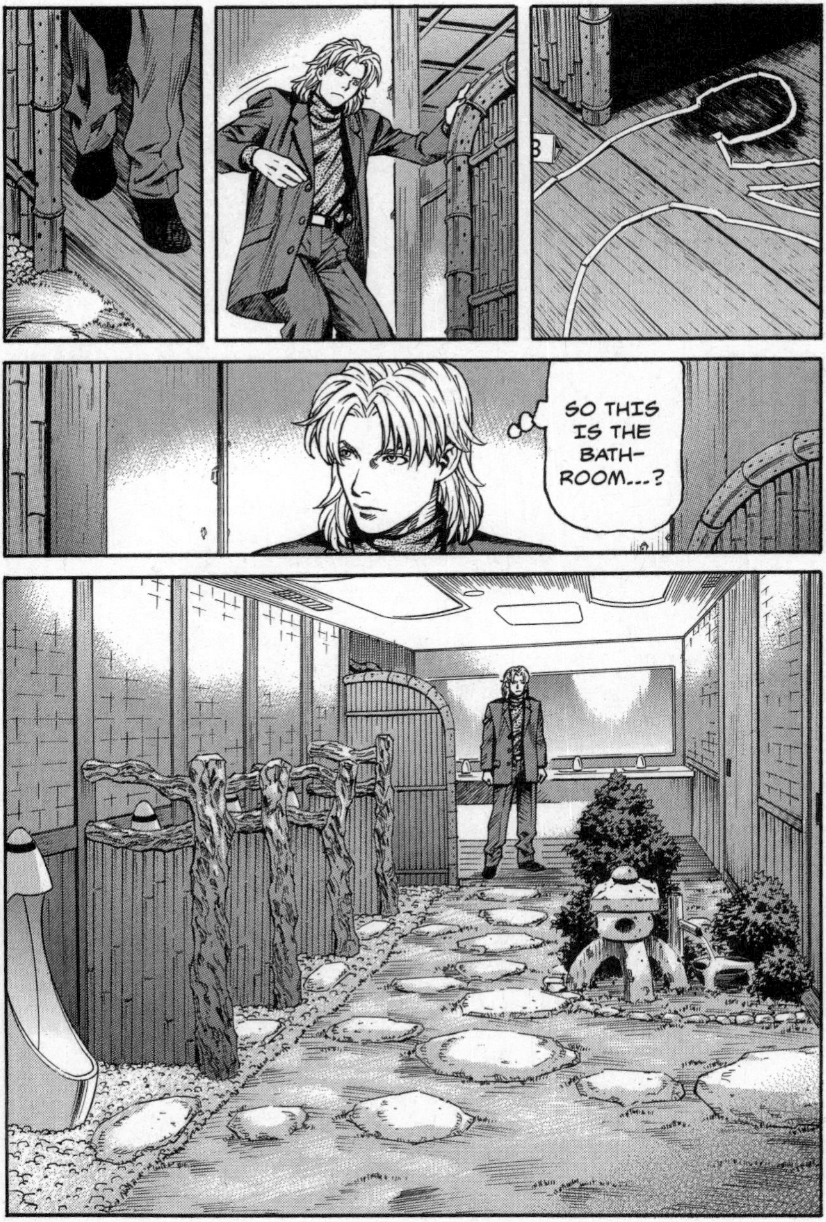
SO THIS IS THE BATH-ROOM...?

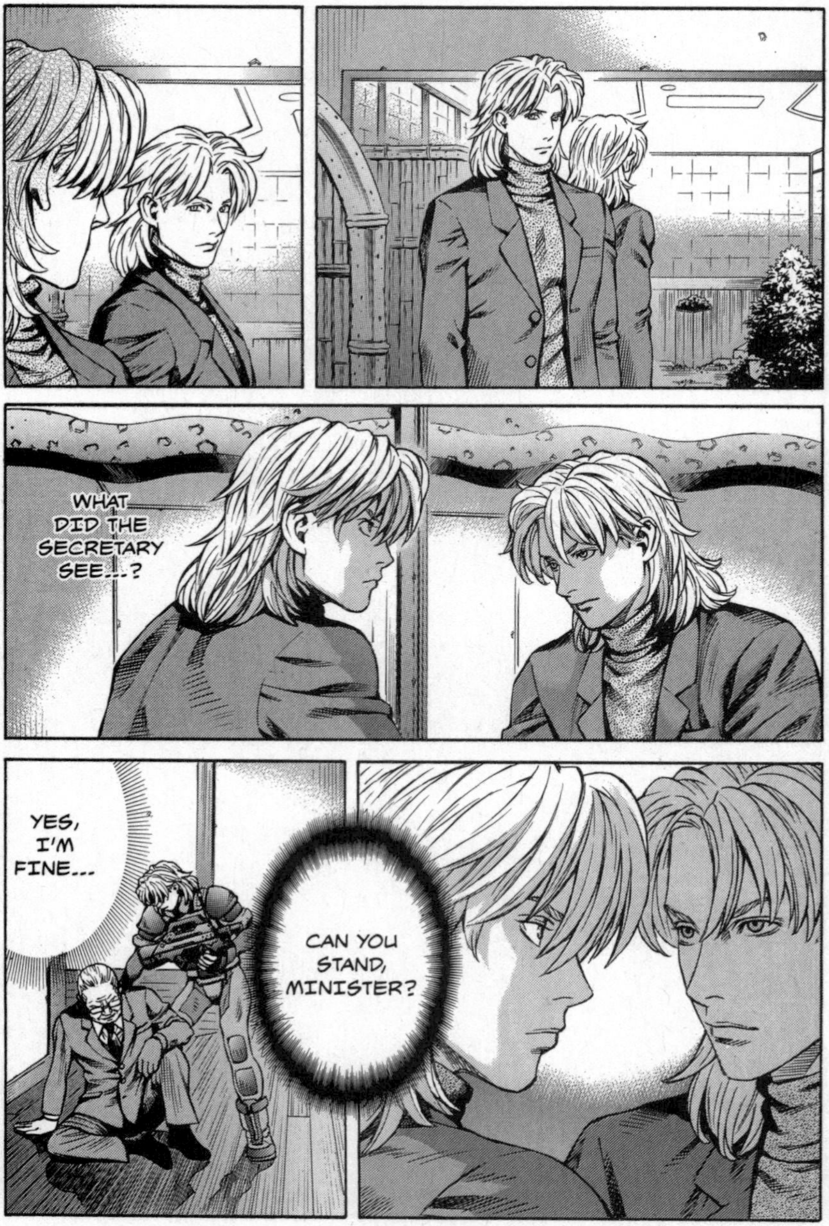
WHAT DID THE SECRETARY SEE...?
CAN YOU STAND, MINISTER?
YES, I'M FINE...

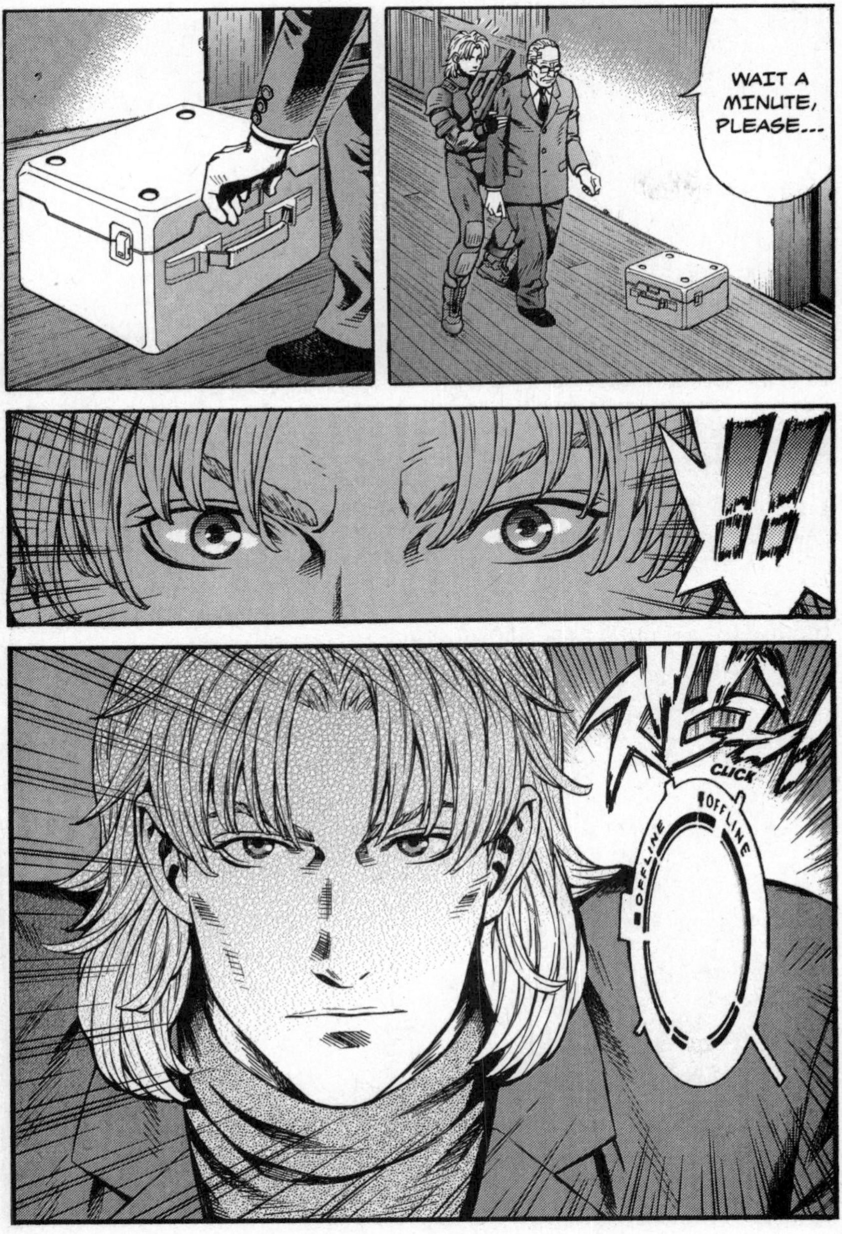
WAIT A MINUTE, PLEASE...
!!
CLICK
OFFLINE
OFFLINE

ONLINE
ONLINE
ONLINE
PROTECTION LEVEL-7
REPORT FILE LEVEL-3
CLICK
KRSSH
VRRR
REC
30-04-14 SUN 00:41:23
VRRRR
REC
30-04-14 SUN 00:41:
TMP
41:22
VRRRR
Zoomer
MATERIAL
BEEP
TARGE
REC
30-04-14 SUN 00:41:22

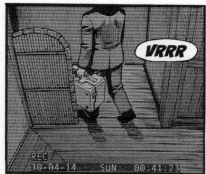

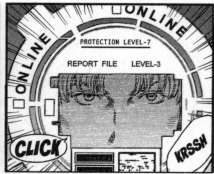

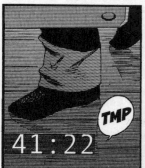

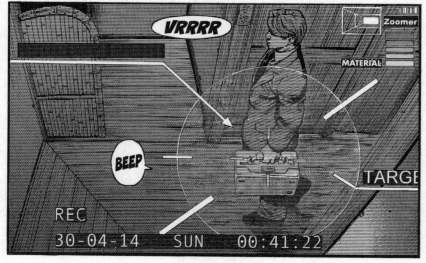

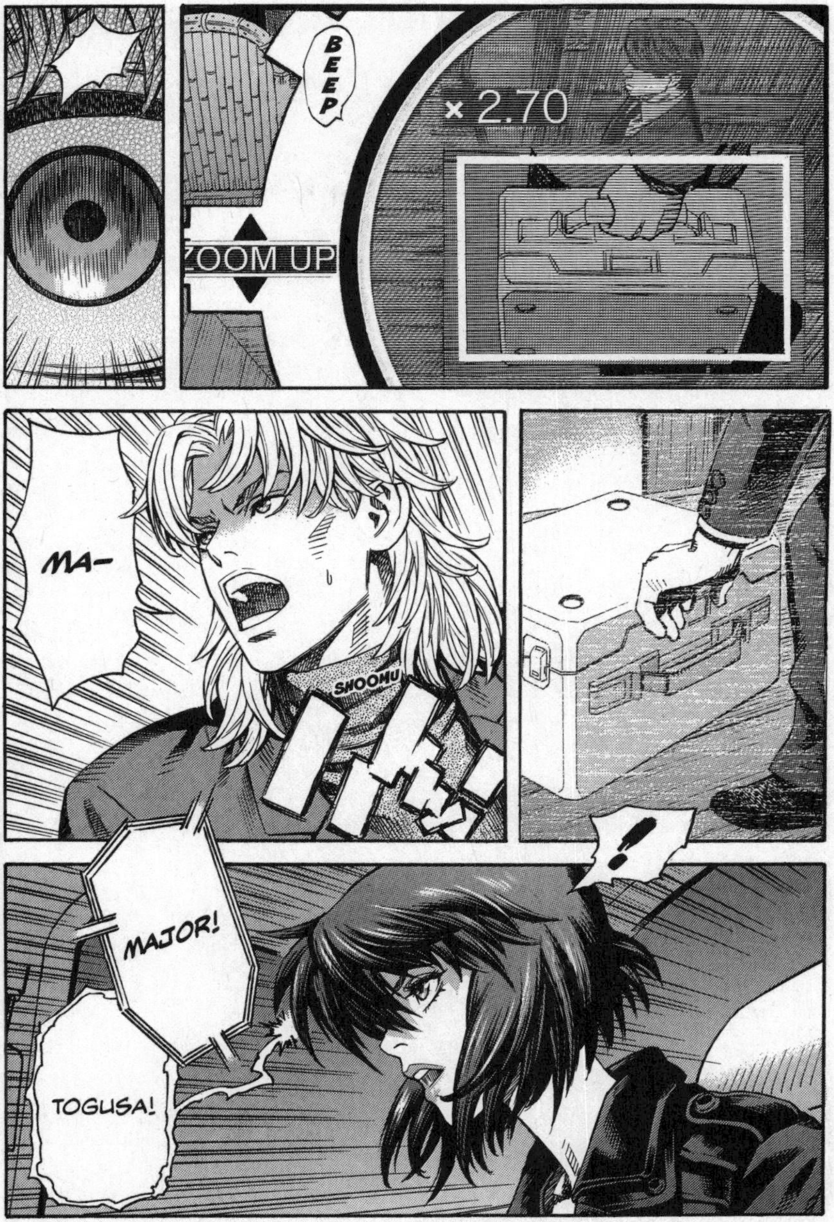
BEEP
× 2.70
ZOOM UP
MA-
SHOOMU
!
MAJOR!
TOGUSA!

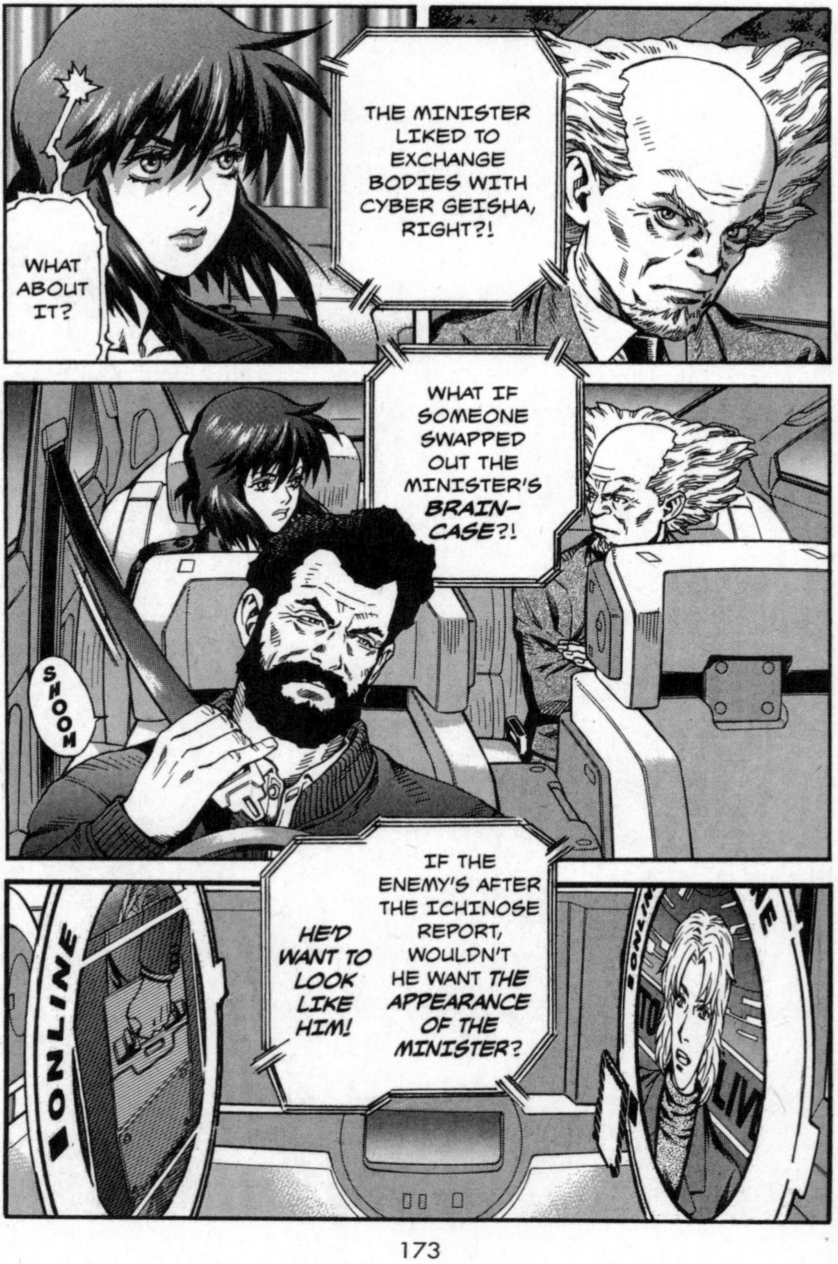
THE MINISTER LIKED TO EXCHANGE BODIES WITH CYBER GEISHA, RIGHT?!
WHAT ABOUT IT?
WHAT IF SOMEONE SWAPPED OUT THE MINISTER'S *BRAIN-CASE*?!
SHOOM
IF THE ENEMY'S AFTER THE ICHINOSE REPORT, WOULDN'T HE WANT *THE APPEARANCE OF THE MINISTER*?
HE'D WANT TO LOOK LIKE HIM!
ONLINE

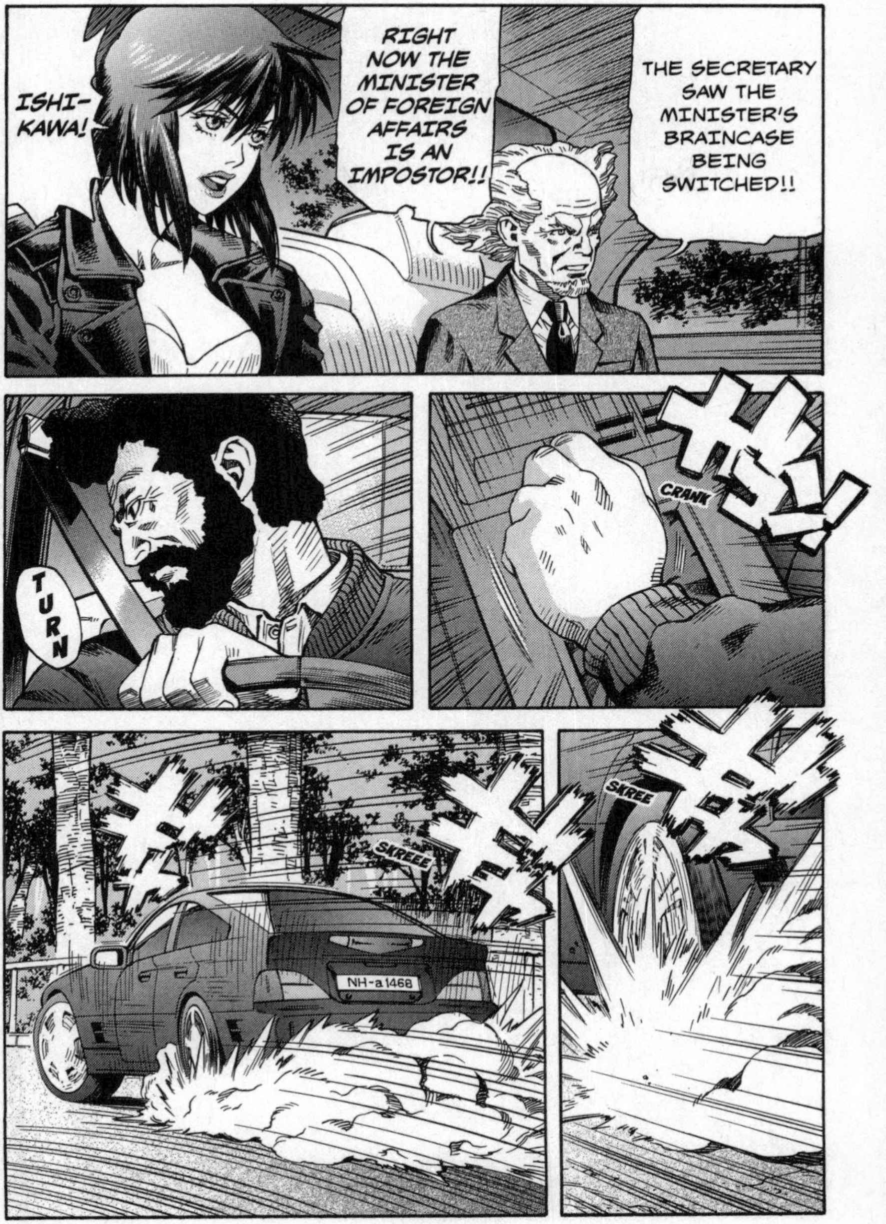
THE SECRETARY SAW THE MINISTER'S BRAINCASE BEING SWITCHED!!
RIGHT NOW THE MINISTER OF FOREIGN AFFAIRS IS AN IMPOSTOR!!
ISHI-KAWA!
CRANK
TURN
SKREE
SKREEE
NH-a 1468

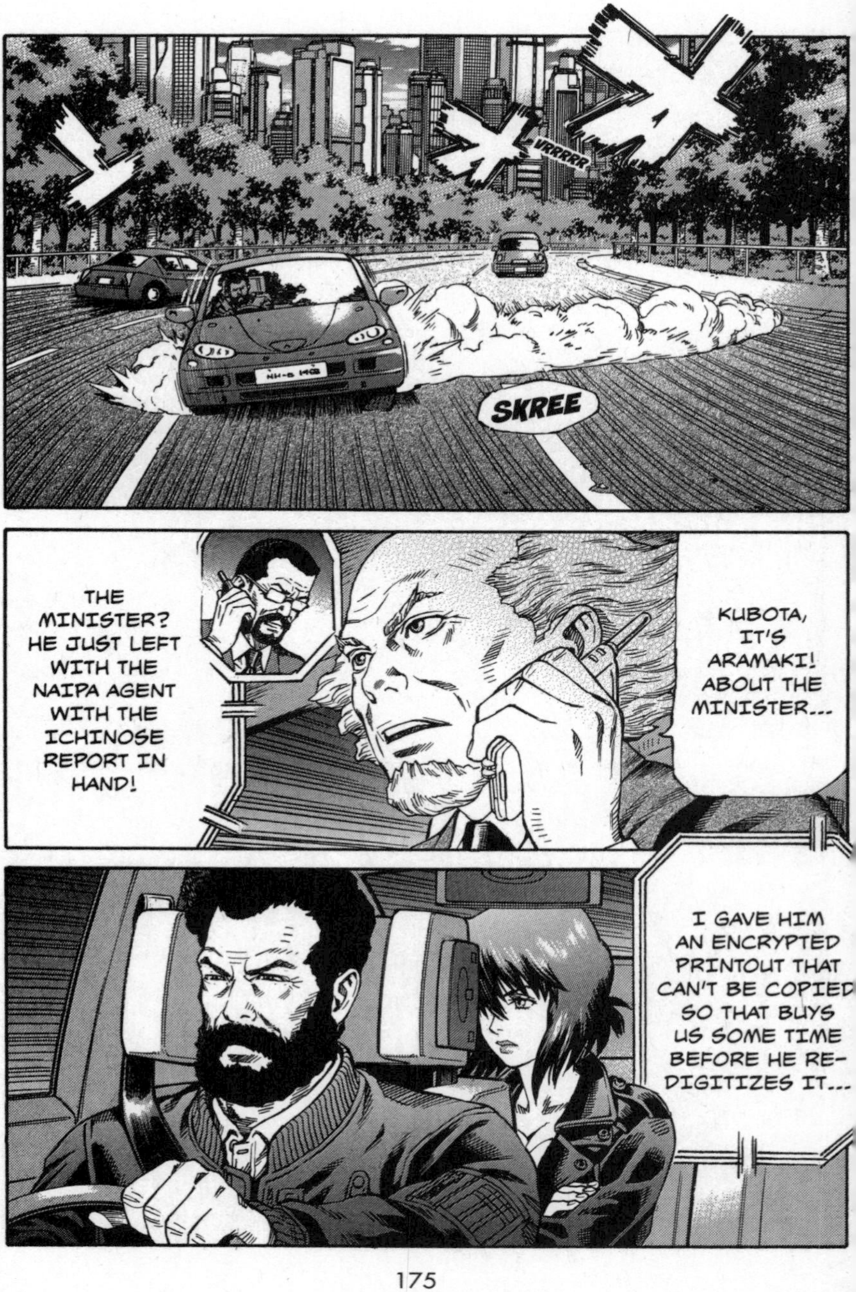
VRRRRR
SKREE
KUBOTA, IT'S ARAMAKI! ABOUT THE MINISTER...
THE MINISTER? HE JUST LEFT WITH THE NAIPA AGENT WITH THE ICHINOSE REPORT IN HAND!
I GAVE HIM AN ENCRYPTED PRINTOUT THAT CAN'T BE COPIED SO THAT BUYS US SOME TIME BEFORE HE RE-DIGITIZES IT...

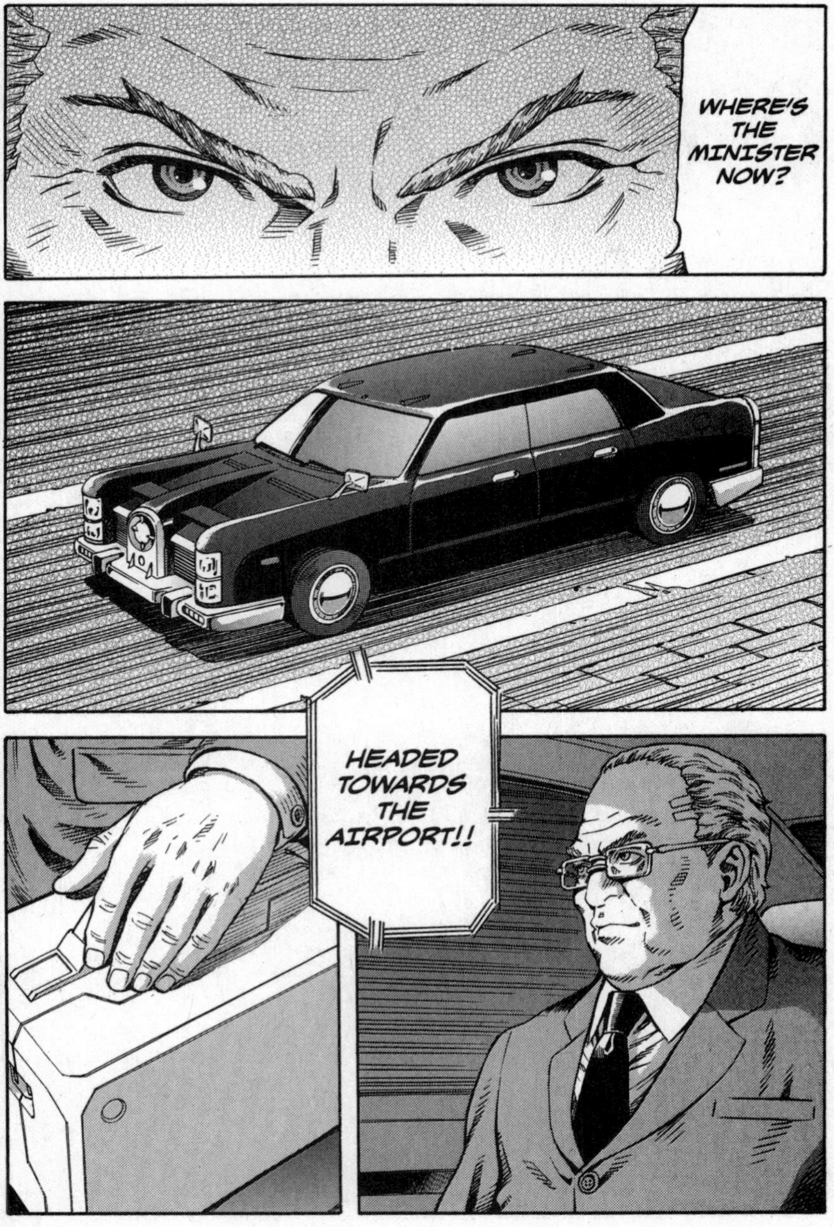
WHERE'S THE MINISTER NOW?
HEADED TOWARDS THE AIRPORT!!

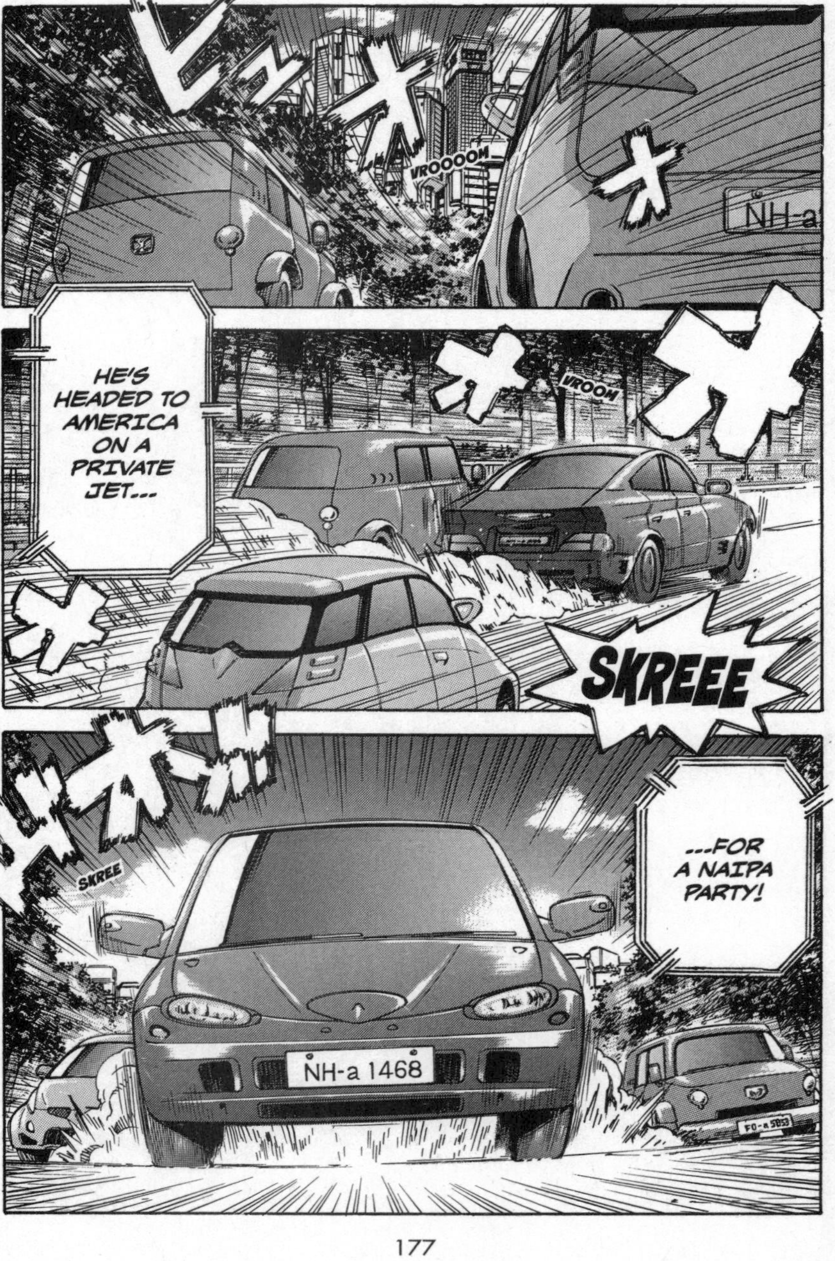
VROOOOM
VROOM
HE'S HEADED TO AMERICA ON A PRIVATE JET...
SKREEE
...FOR A NAIPA PARTY!
SKREE
NH-a 1468

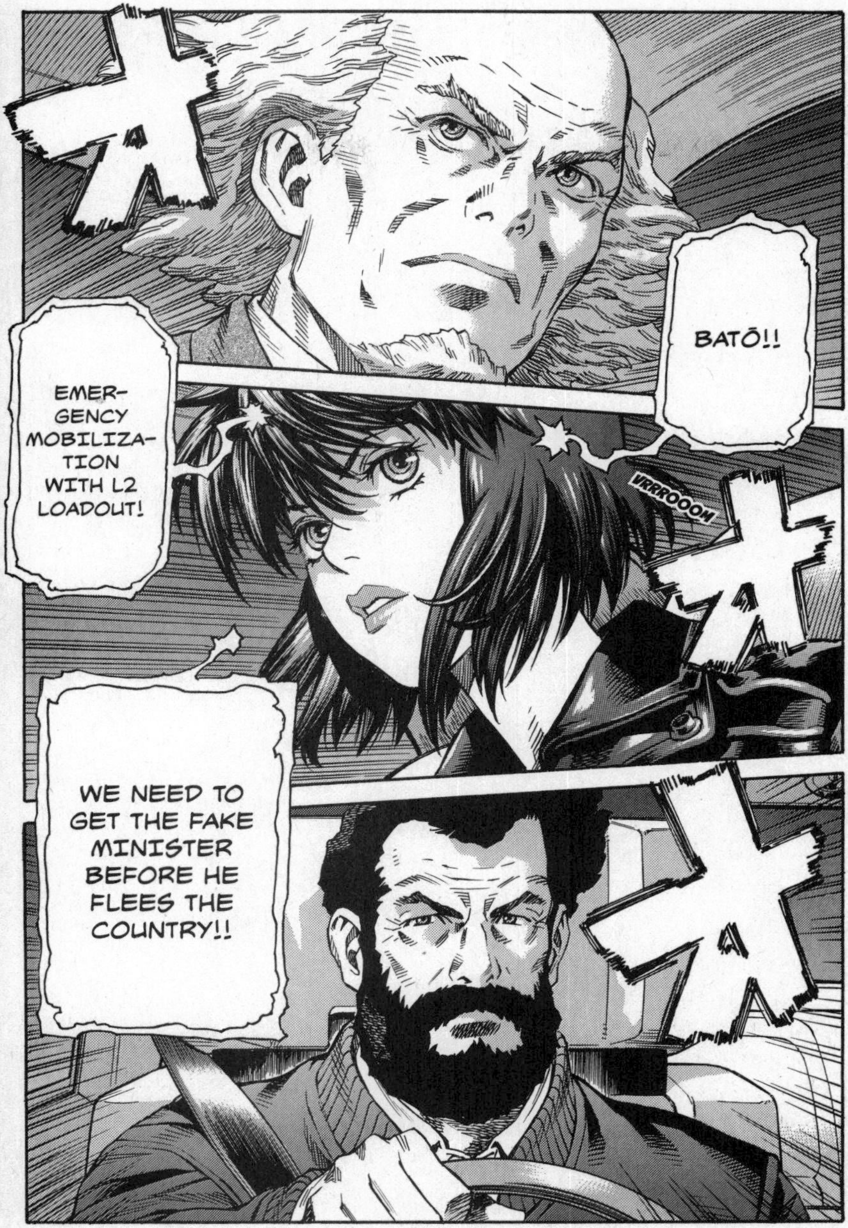
BATŌ!!
EMER-GENCY MOBILIZA-TION WITH L2 LOADOUT!
VRRROOOM
WE NEED TO GET THE FAKE MINISTER BEFORE HE FLEES THE COUNTRY!!

#008 / End

#009: Classified

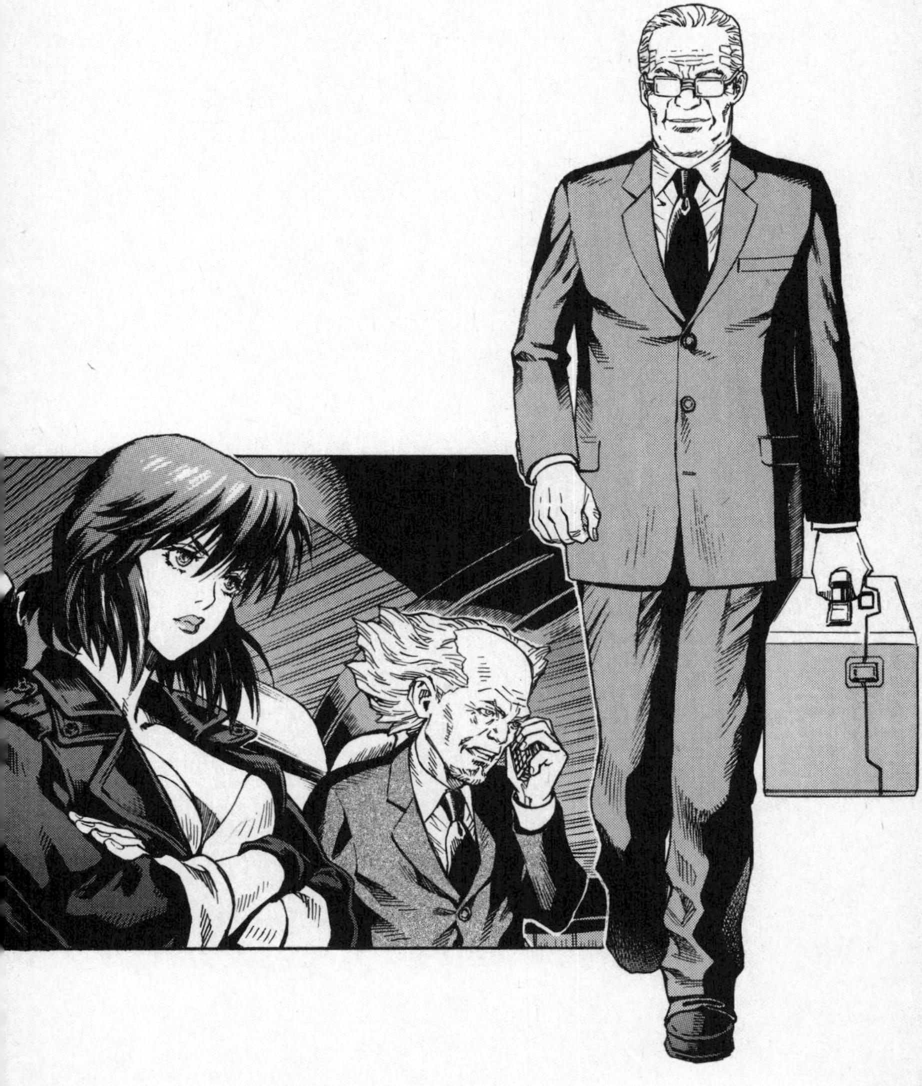

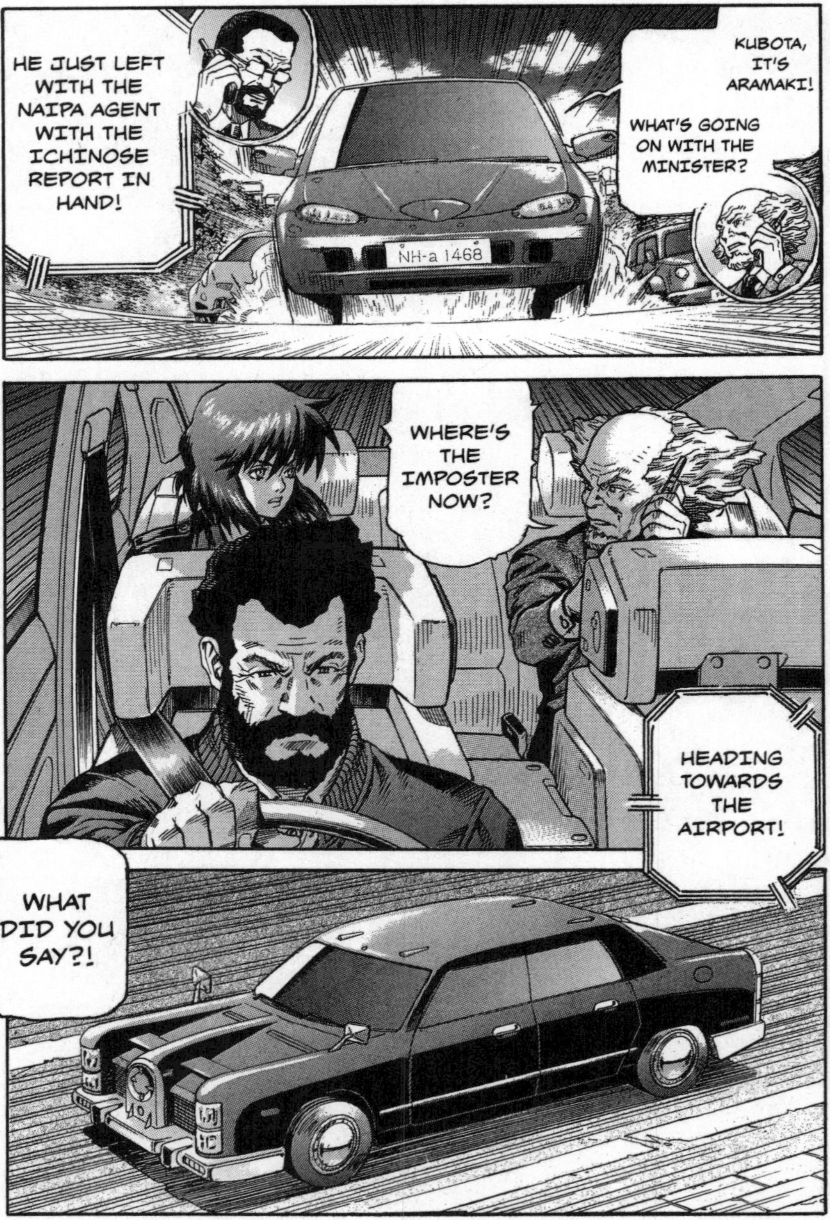
KUBOTA, IT'S ARAMAKI!
WHAT'S GOING ON WITH THE MINISTER?
HE JUST LEFT WITH THE NAIPA AGENT WITH THE ICHINOSE REPORT IN HAND!
NH-a 1468
WHERE'S THE IMPOSTER NOW?
HEADING TOWARDS THE AIRPORT!
WHAT DID YOU SAY?!

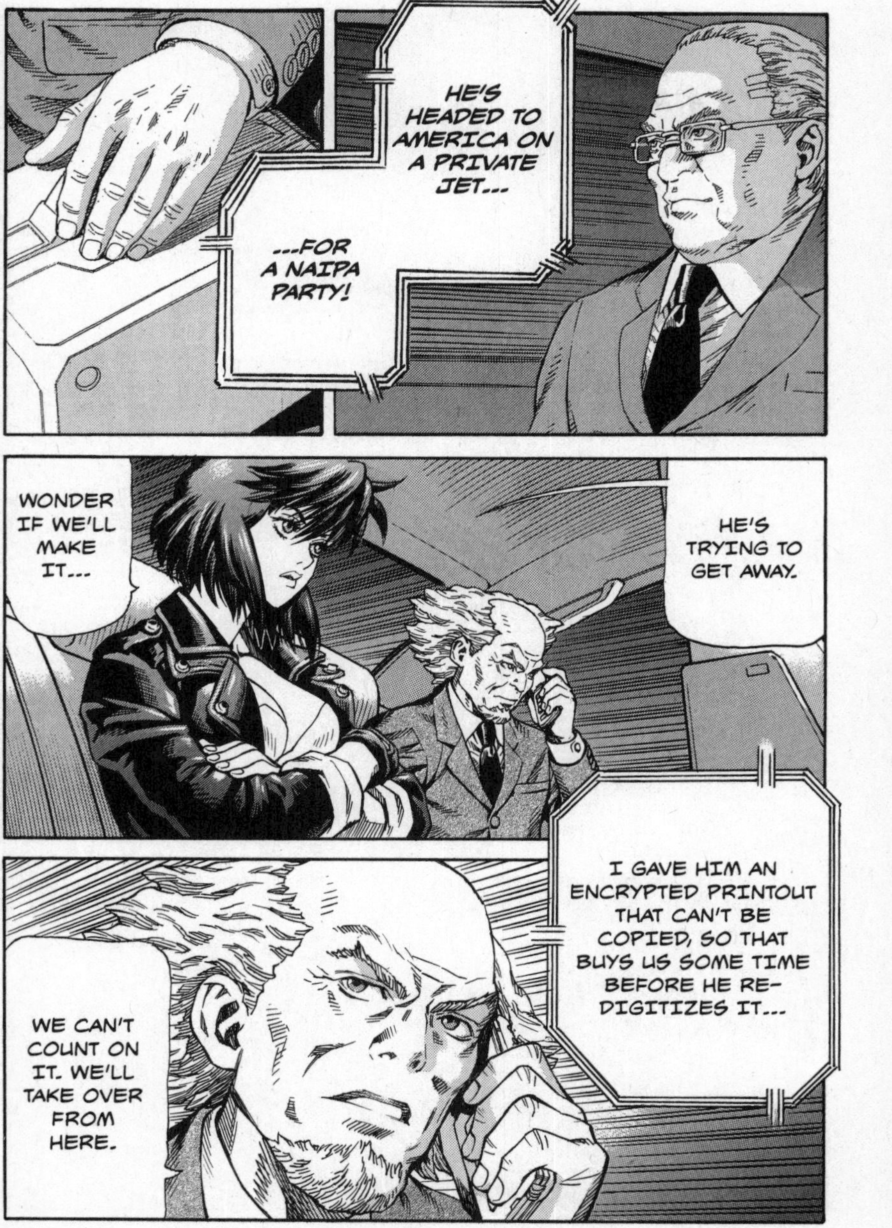

HE'S HEADED TO AMERICA ON A PRIVATE JET...
...FOR A NAIPA PARTY!
HE'S TRYING TO GET AWAY.
WONDER IF WE'LL MAKE IT...
I GAVE HIM AN ENCRYPTED PRINTOUT THAT CAN'T BE COPIED, SO THAT BUYS US SOME TIME BEFORE HE RE-DIGITIZES IT...
WE CAN'T COUNT ON IT. WE'LL TAKE OVER FROM HERE.

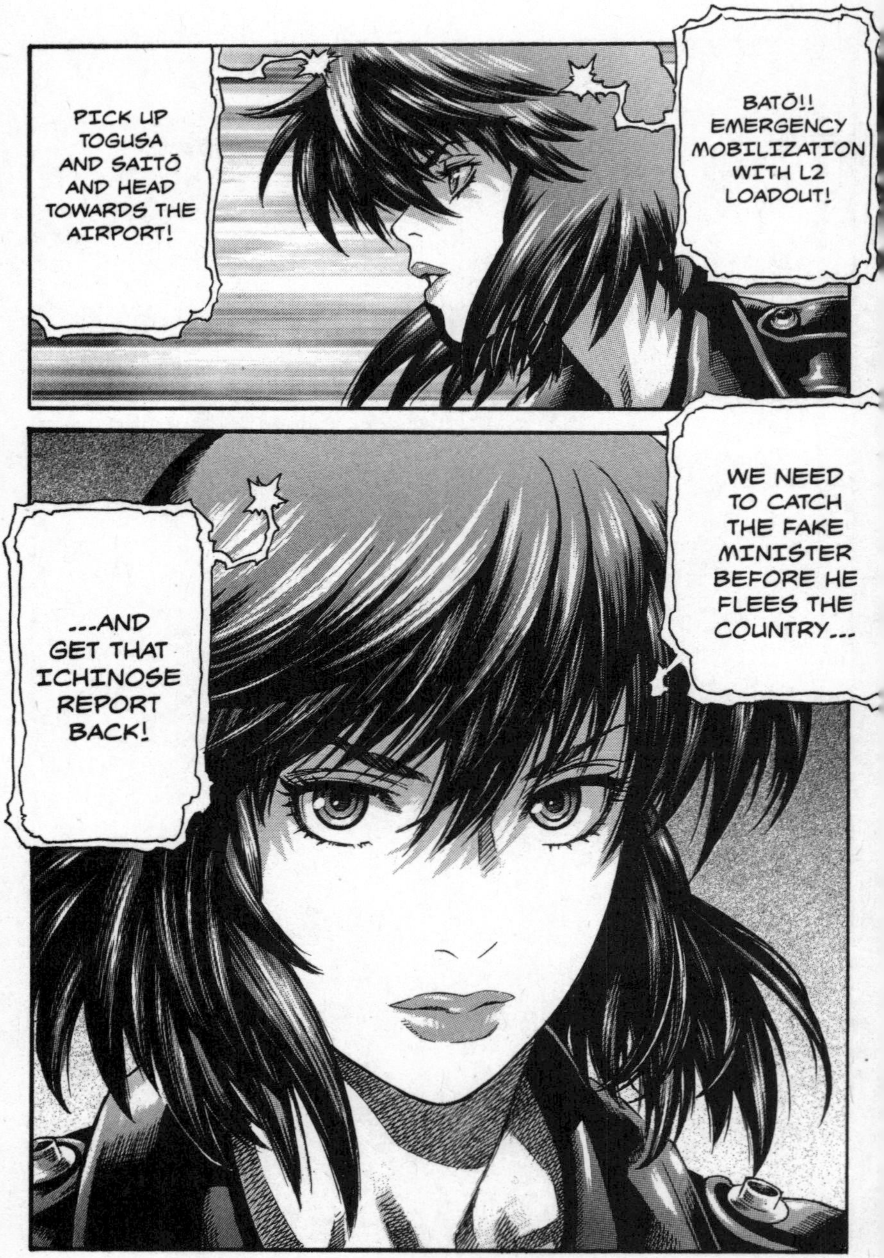
BATŌ!! EMERGENCY MOBILIZATION WITH L2 LOADOUT!
PICK UP TOGUSA AND SAITŌ AND HEAD TOWARDS THE AIRPORT!
WE NEED TO CATCH THE FAKE MINISTER BEFORE HE FLEES THE COUNTRY...
...AND GET THAT ICHINOSE REPORT BACK!

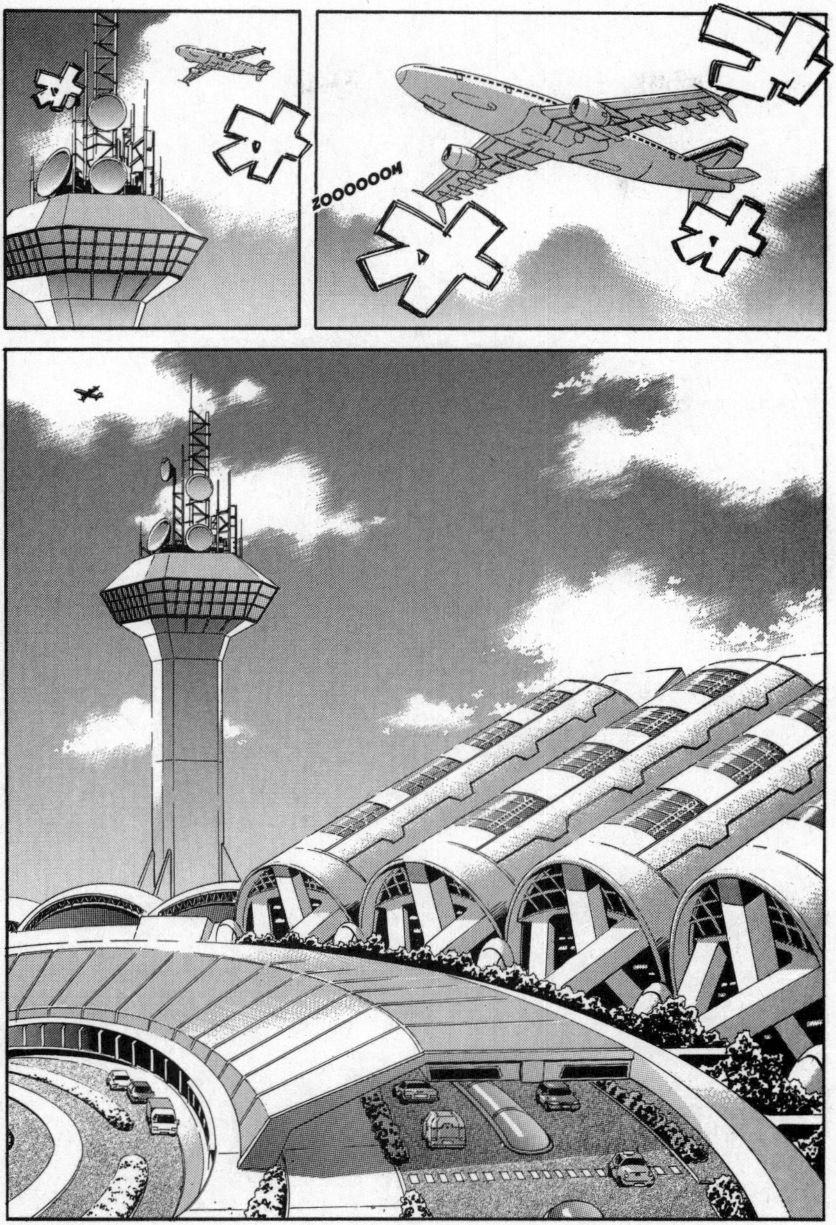
ZOOOOOOM

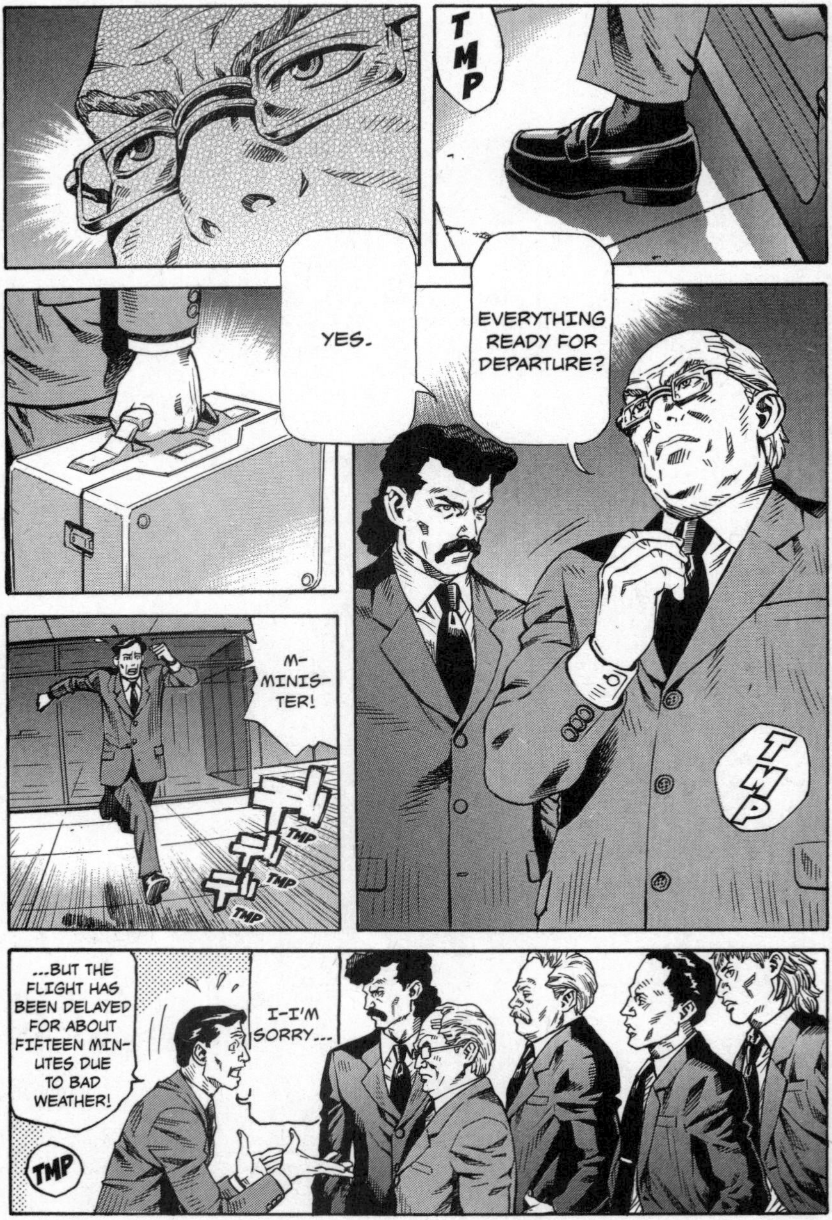
TMP
EVERYTHING READY FOR DEPARTURE?
YES.
TMP
M-MINISTER!
TMP
TMP
TMP
I-I'M SORRY...
...BUT THE FLIGHT HAS BEEN DELAYED FOR ABOUT FIFTEEN MINUTES DUE TO BAD WEATHER!
TMP

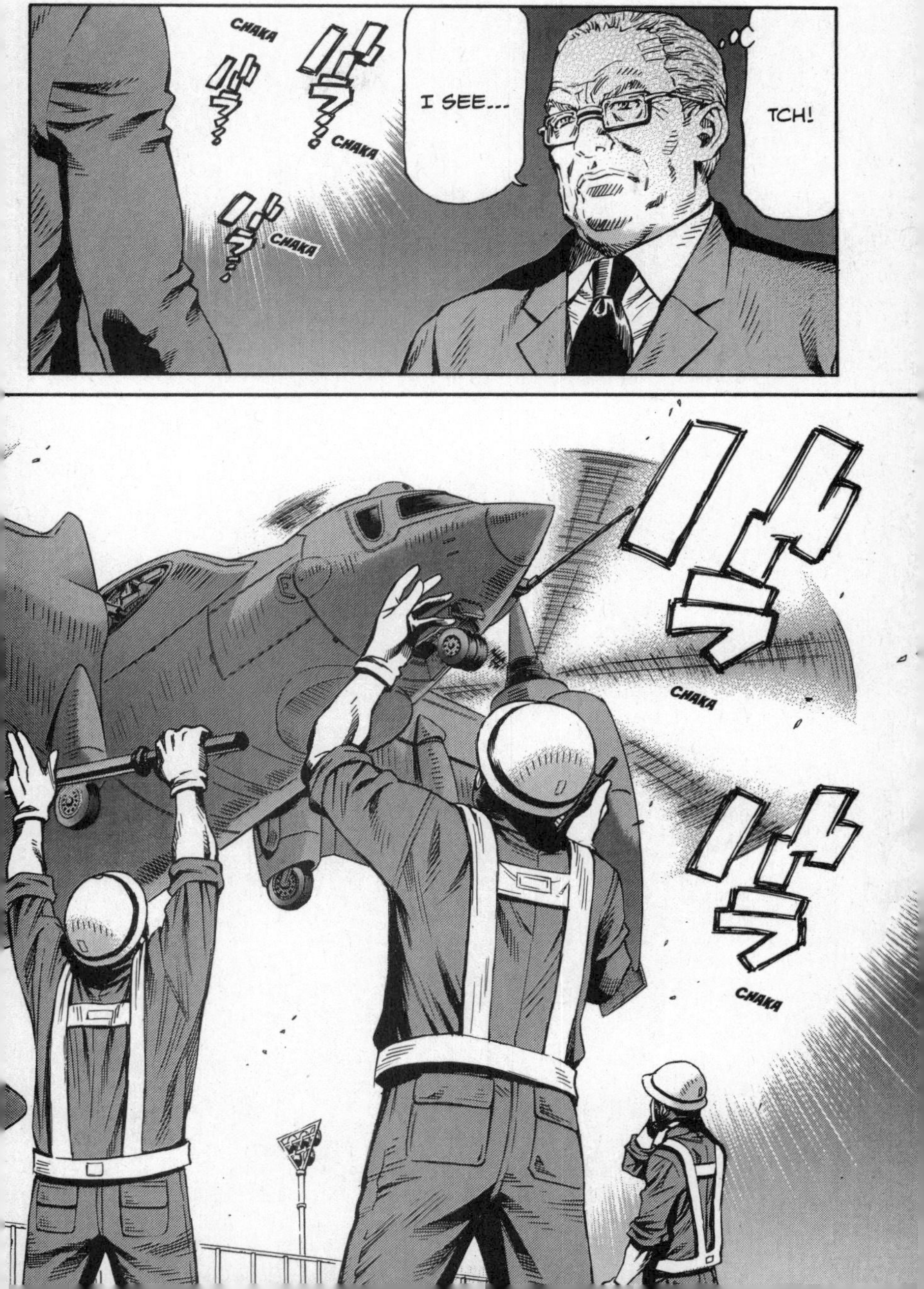
TCH!
I SEE...
CHAKA
CHAKA
CHAKA
CHAKA
CHAKA

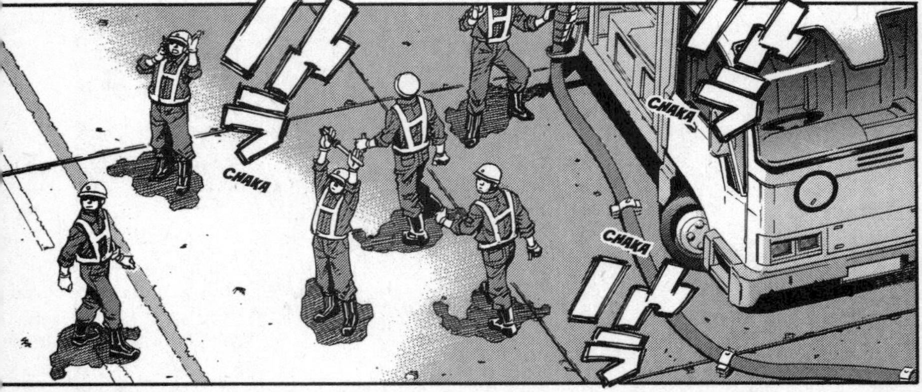
CHAKA
CHAKA
CHAKA
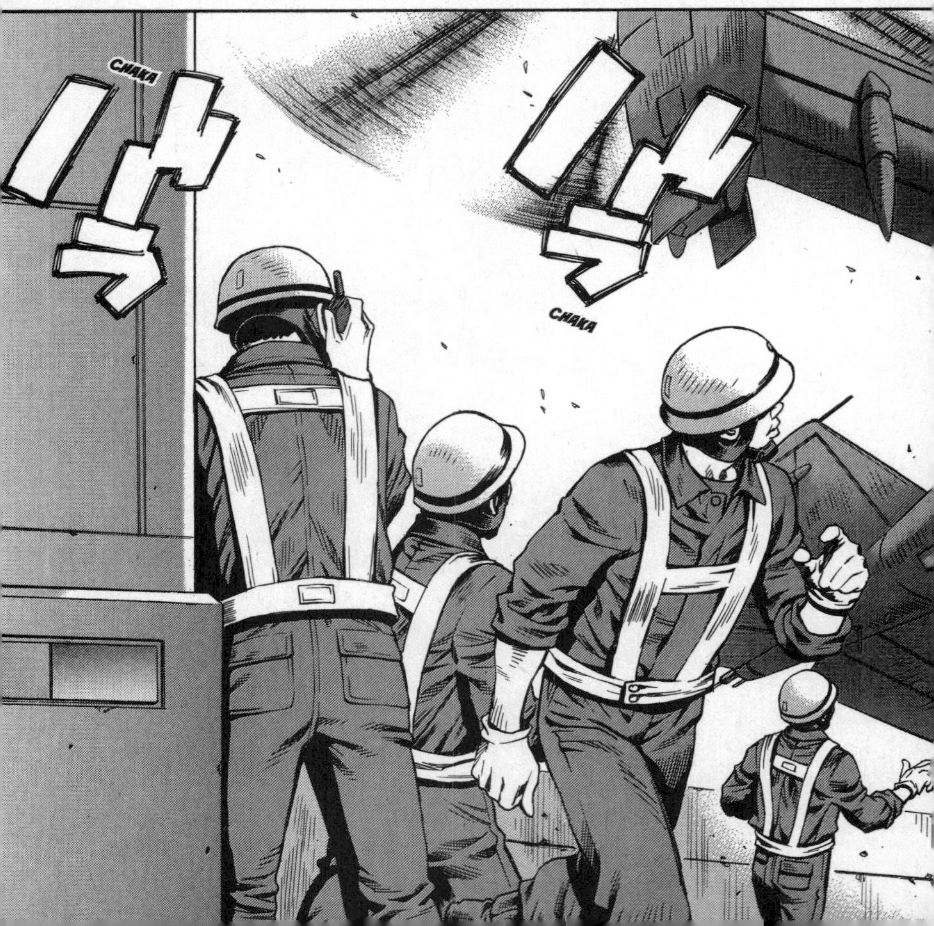
CHAKA
CHAKA

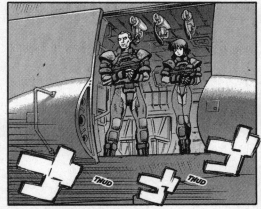
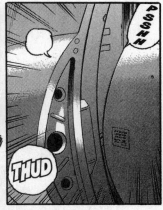

THUD

THUD

PSSHH

THUD

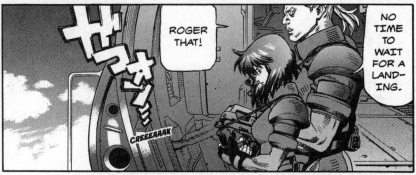

ROGER THAT!

NO TIME TO WAIT FOR A LANDING.

CREEEAAAK

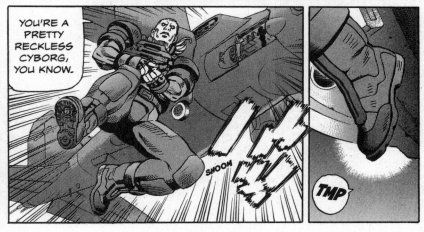

YOU'RE A PRETTY RECKLESS CYBORG, YOU KNOW.

SHOOM

TMP

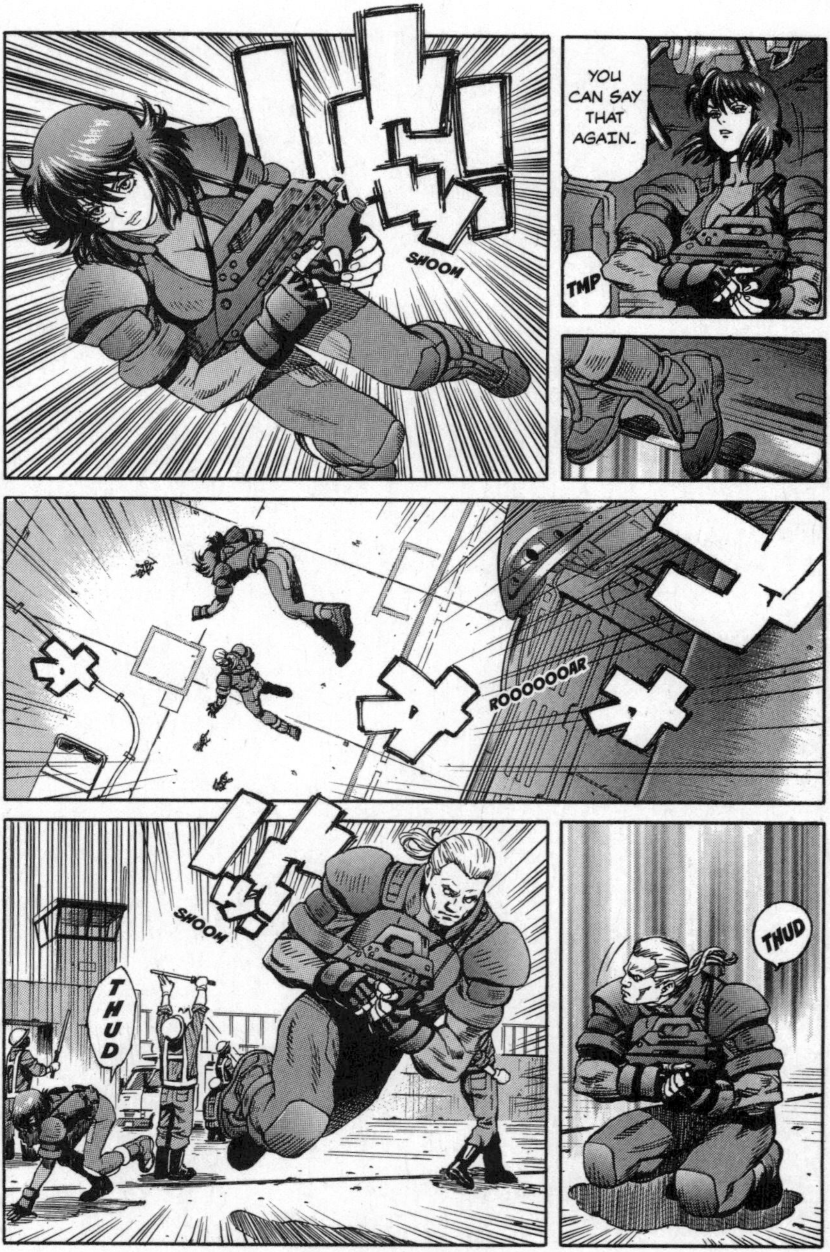
YOU CAN SAY THAT AGAIN.
TMP
SHOOM
ROOOOOOAR
THUD
SHOOM
THUD

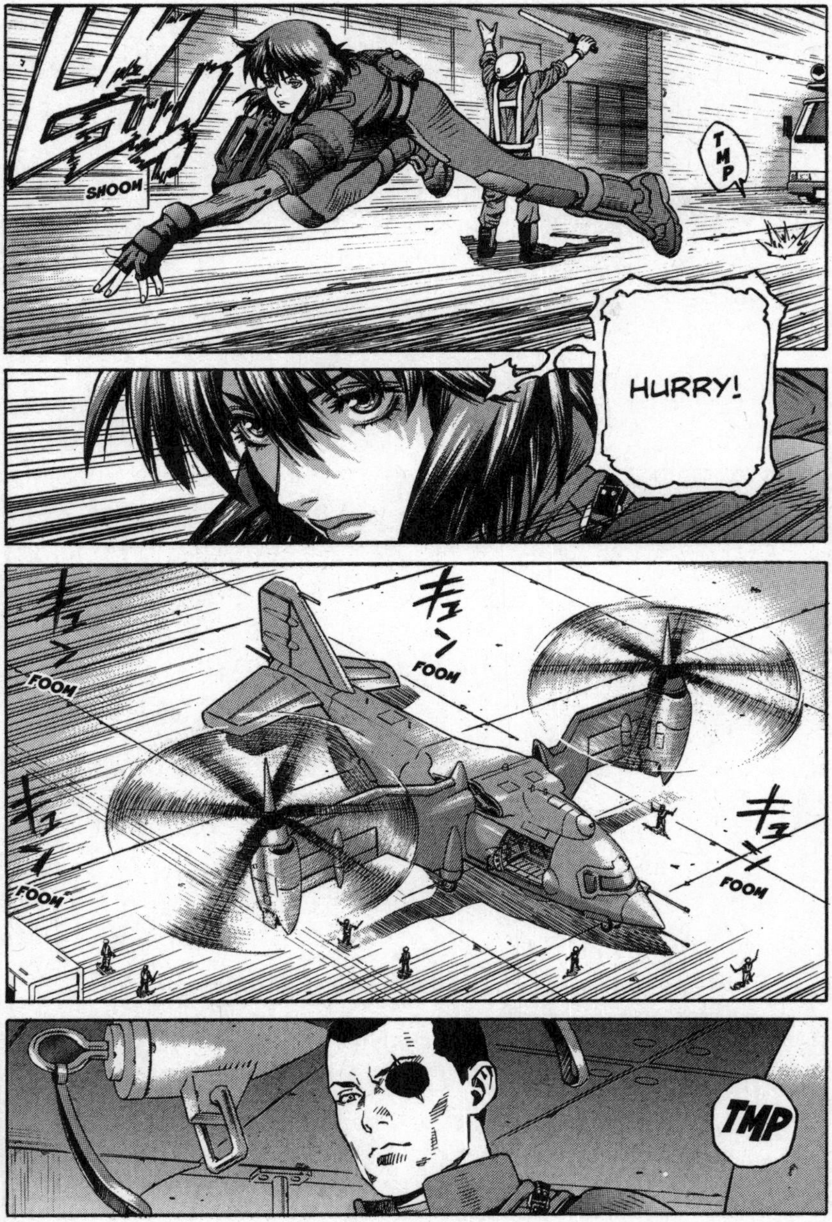
TMP
SHOOM
HURRY!
FOOM
FOOM
FOOM
FOOM
TMP

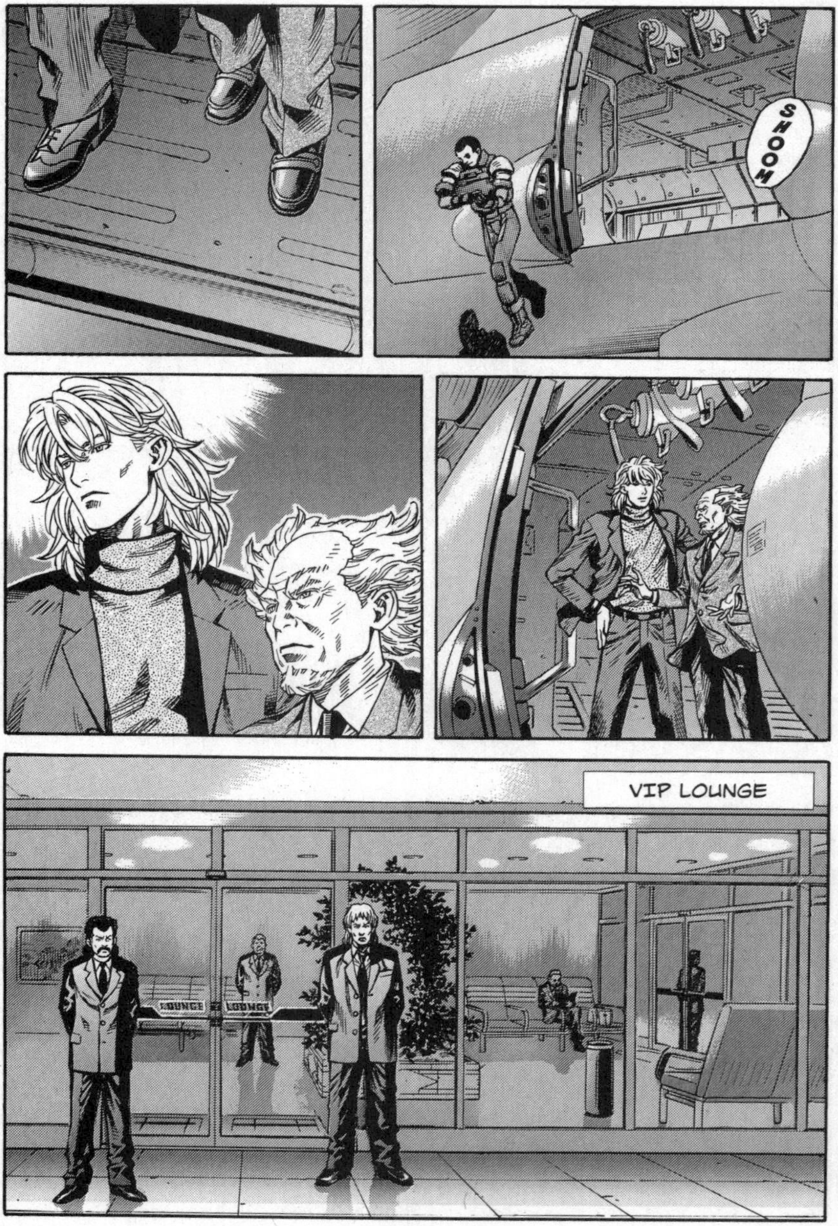
SHOOM
VIP LOUNGE

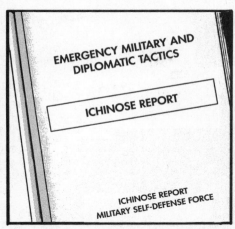

EMERGENCY MILITARY AND
DIPLOMATIC TACTICS

ICHINOSE REPORT

ICHINOSE REPORT
MILITARY SELF-DEFENSE FORCE

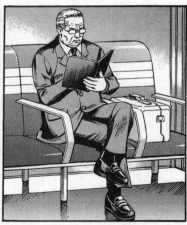

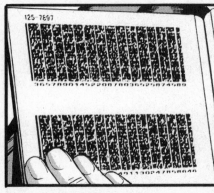

125-7897

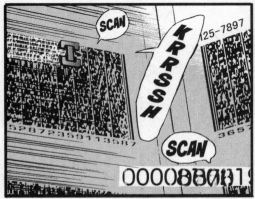

SCAN

KRRSSH

125-7897

SCAN

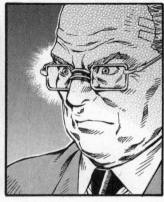

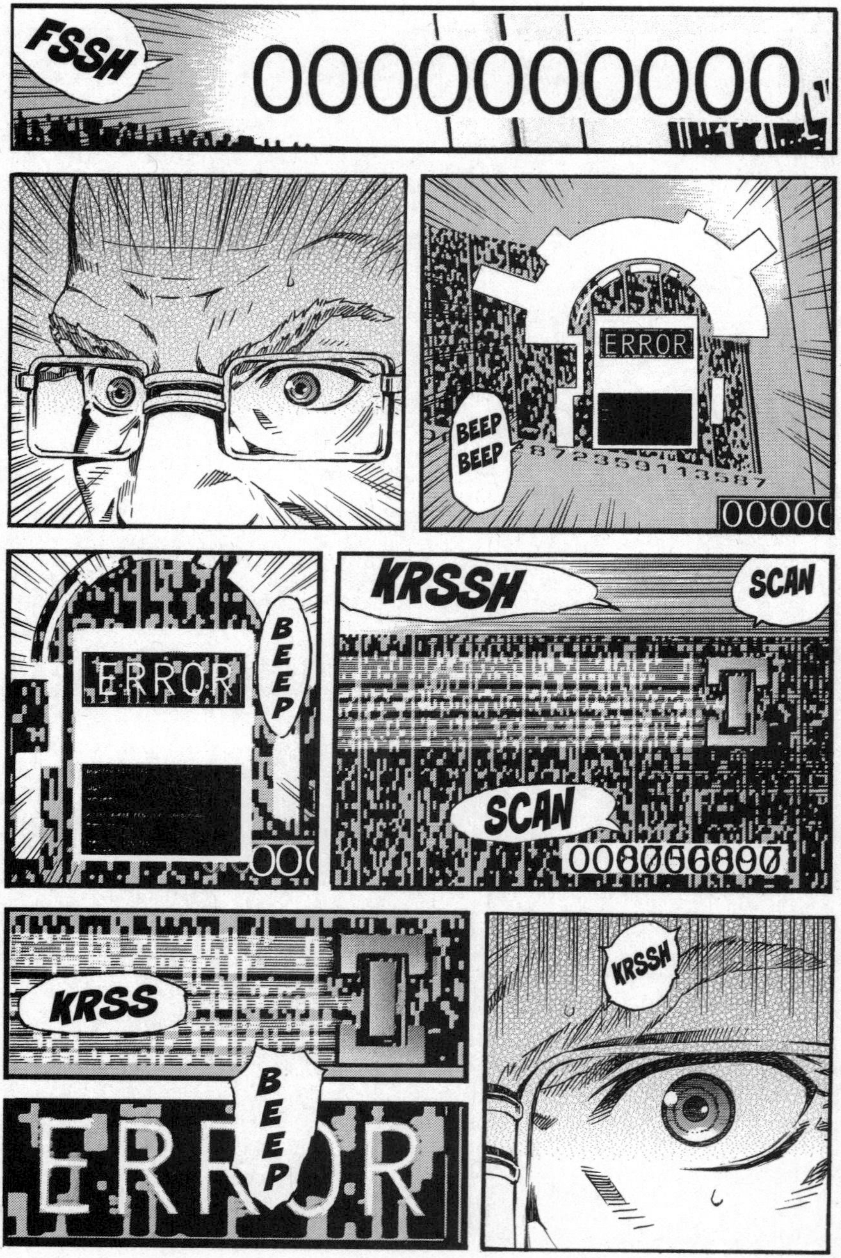
FSSH
00000000000
ERROR
BEEP BEEP
00000
KRSSH
SCAN
SCAN
0080066890
ERROR
BEEP
KRSSH
KRSS
ERROR
BEEP

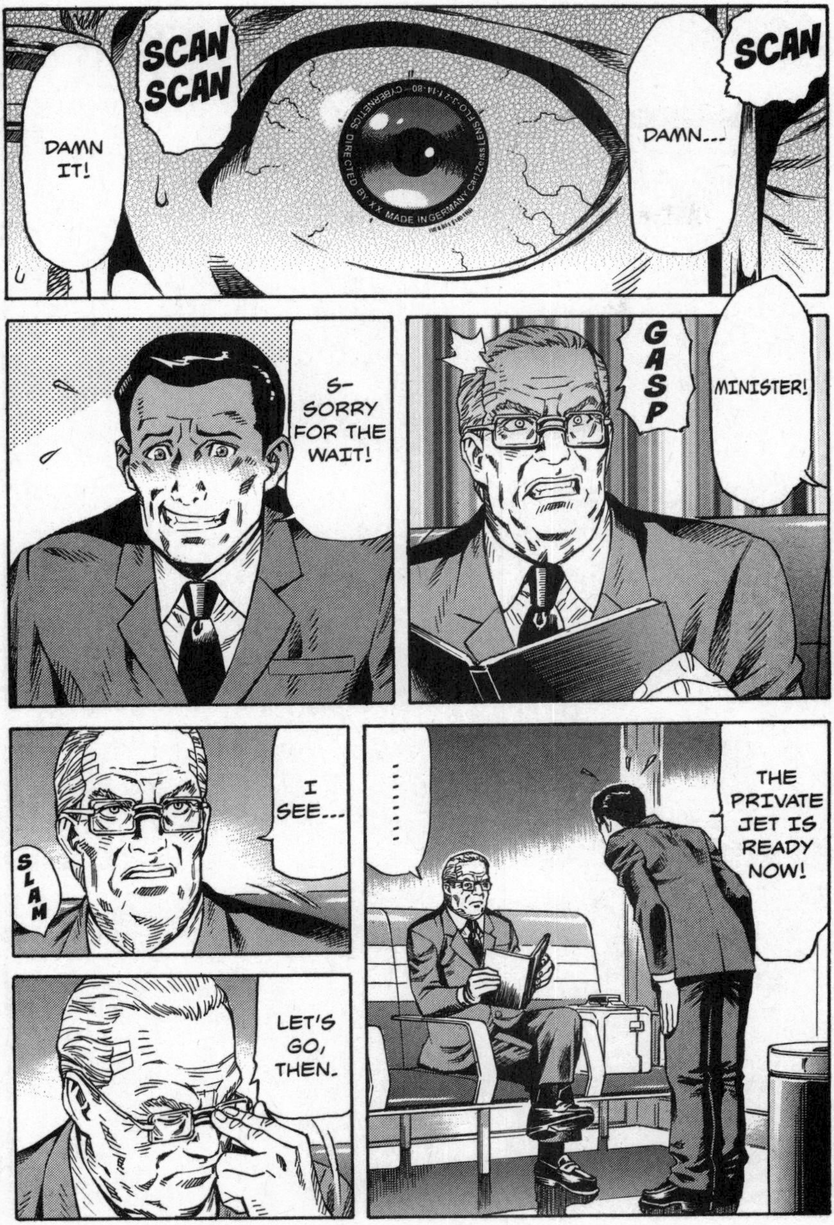
SCAN
DAMN...
SCAN SCAN
DAMN IT!
CYBERNETICS DIRECTED BY XX MADE IN GERMANY Carl Zeiss LENS
MINISTER!
GASP
S-SORRY FOR THE WAIT!
THE PRIVATE JET IS READY NOW!
......
I SEE...
SLAM
LET'S GO, THEN.

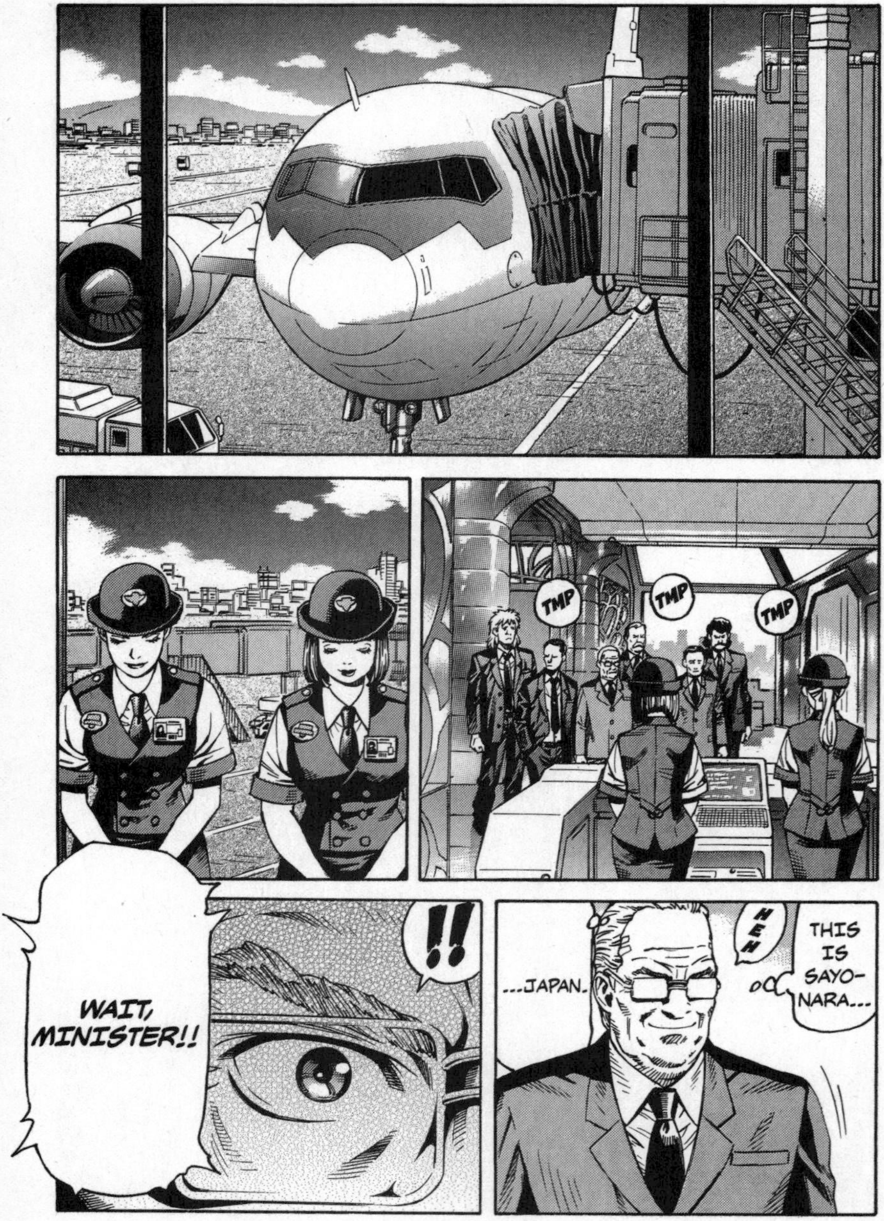
TMP
TMP
TMP
THIS IS SAYO-NARA...
HEH
...JAPAN.
!!
WAIT, MINISTER!!

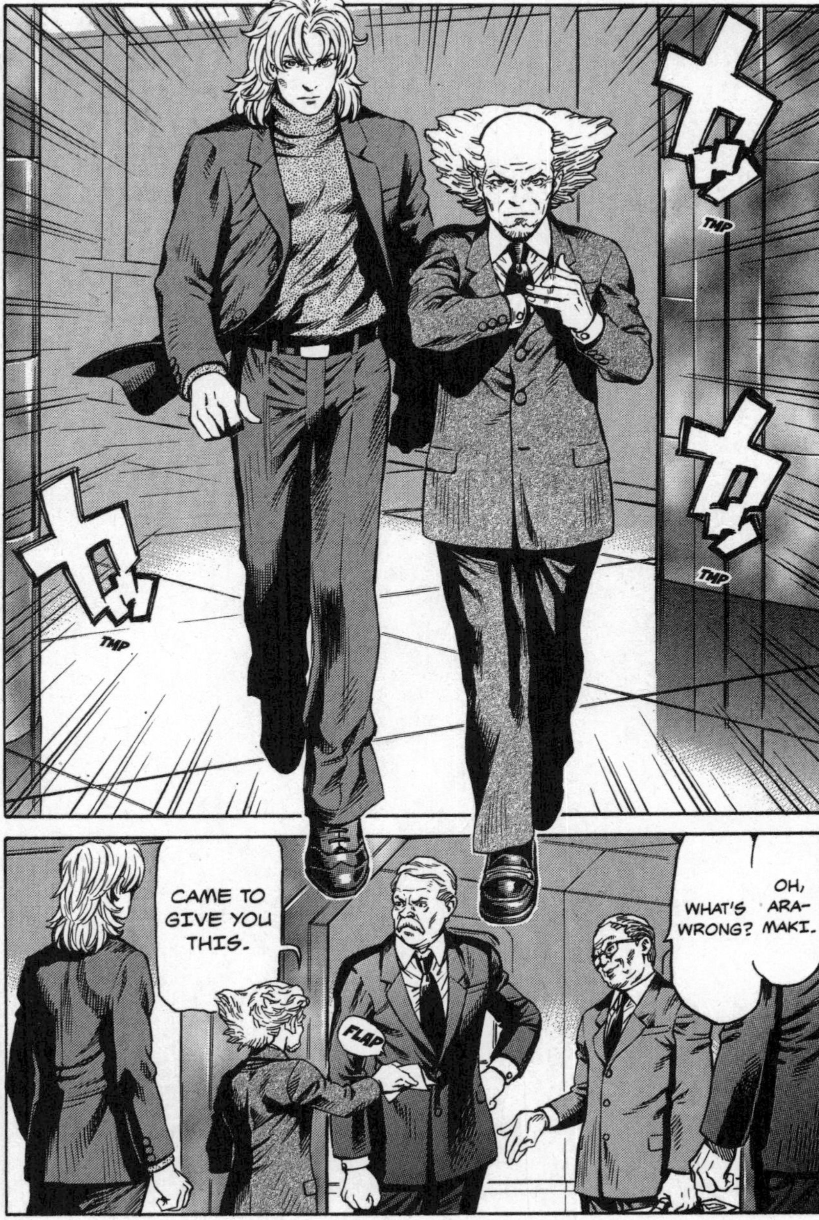
カッ
TMP
カッ
TMP
カッ
TMP
OH, ARA-MAKI. WHAT'S WRONG?
CAME TO GIVE YOU THIS.
FLAP

THUNK
RUSTLE
WHAT'S THIS?
"ORDERS FOR REMOVAL FROM OFFICE DUE TO MEDICAL TREATMENT"?
WHAT IS THIS ALL ABOUT?!
NOW THAT YOU'VE READ THAT, YOU ARE NO LONGER THE MINISTER OF FOREIGN AFFAIRS.
WHAT? BY WHOSE AUTHORITY?!

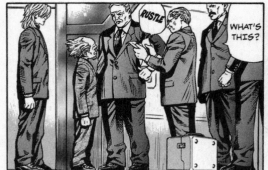

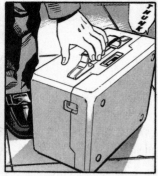

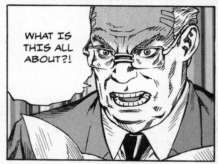

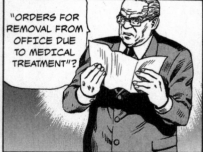

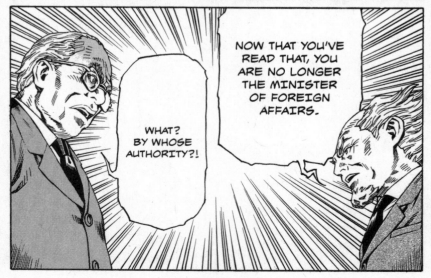

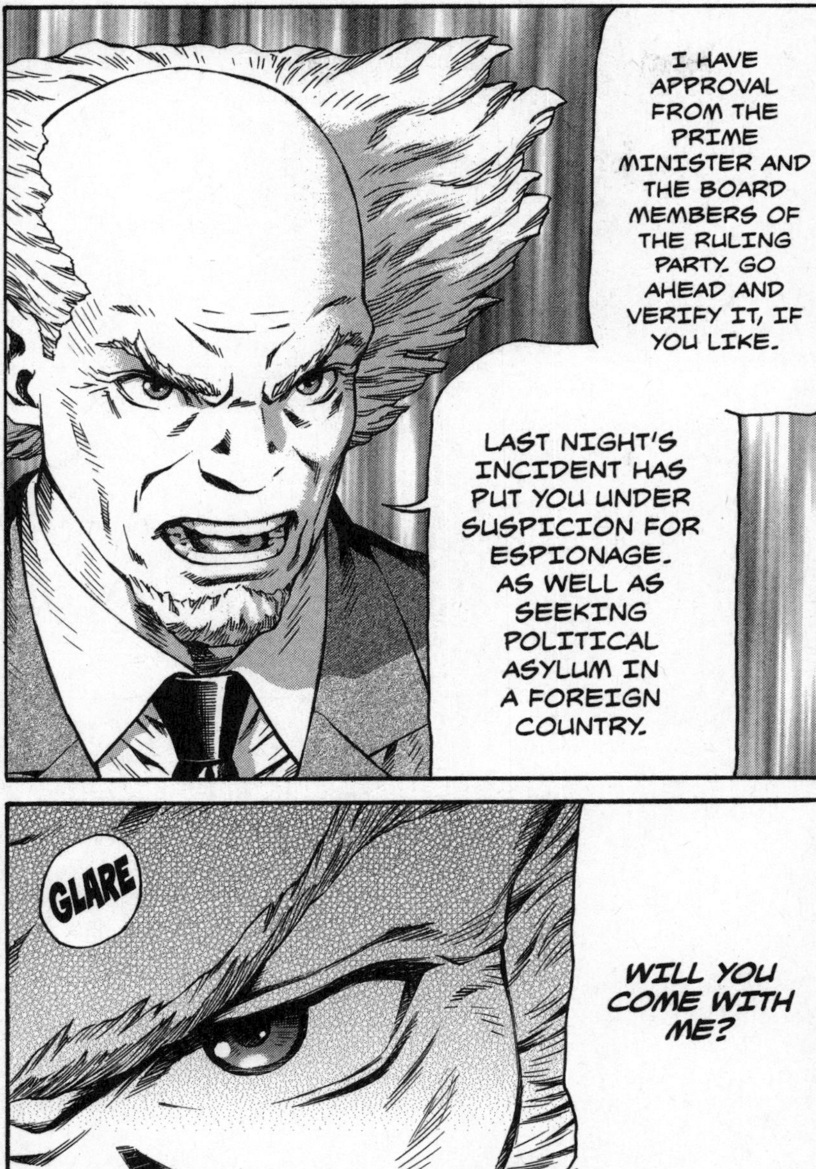
I HAVE APPROVAL FROM THE PRIME MINISTER AND THE BOARD MEMBERS OF THE RULING PARTY. GO AHEAD AND VERIFY IT, IF YOU LIKE.
LAST NIGHT'S INCIDENT HAS PUT YOU UNDER SUSPICION FOR ESPIONAGE. AS WELL AS SEEKING POLITICAL ASYLUM IN A FOREIGN COUNTRY.
WILL YOU COME WITH ME?
GLARE

#009 / End

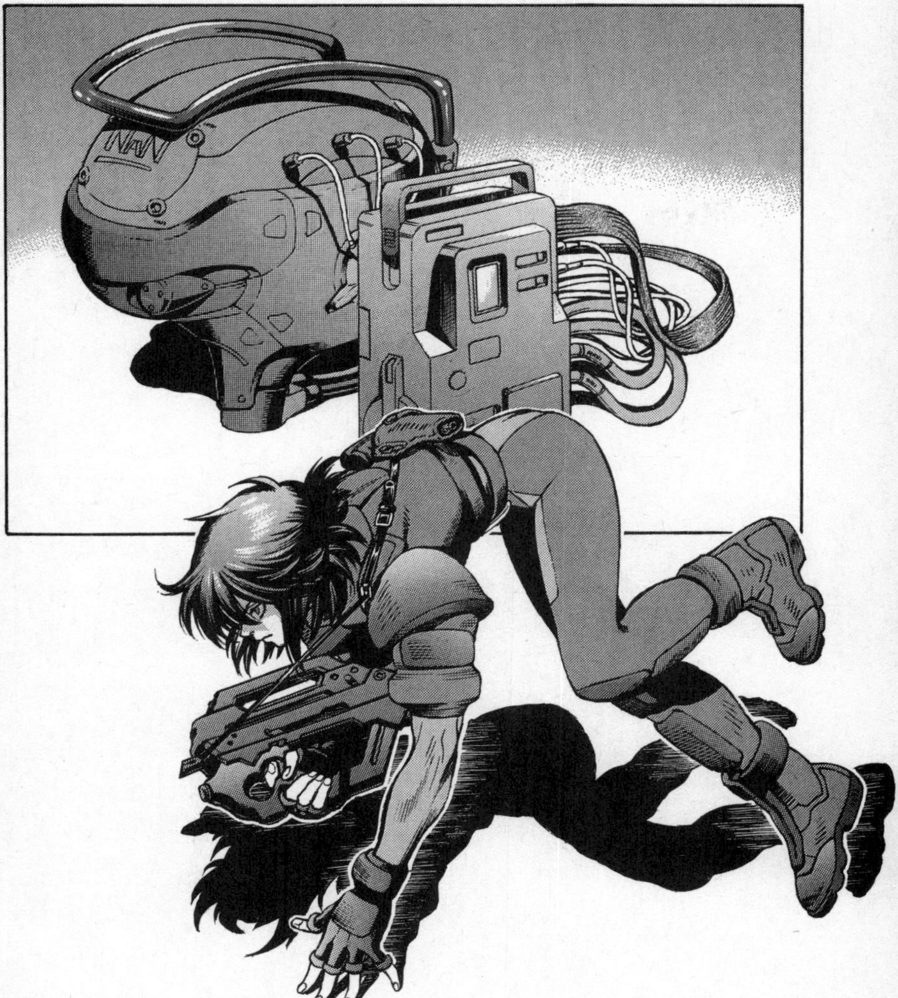
NAW

#010: Impostor

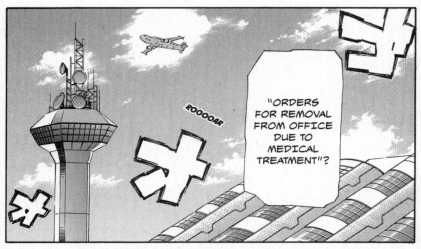

ROOOOAR

"ORDERS FOR REMOVAL FROM OFFICE DUE TO MEDICAL TREATMENT"?

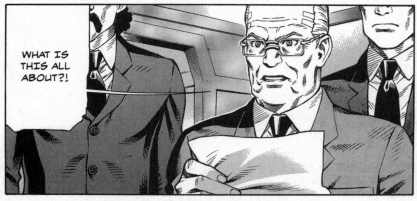

WHAT IS THIS ALL ABOUT?!

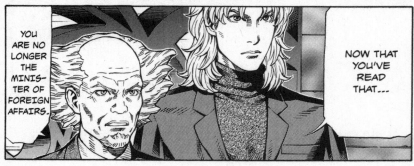

YOU ARE NO LONGER THE MINISTER OF FOREIGN AFFAIRS.

NOW THAT YOU'VE READ THAT...

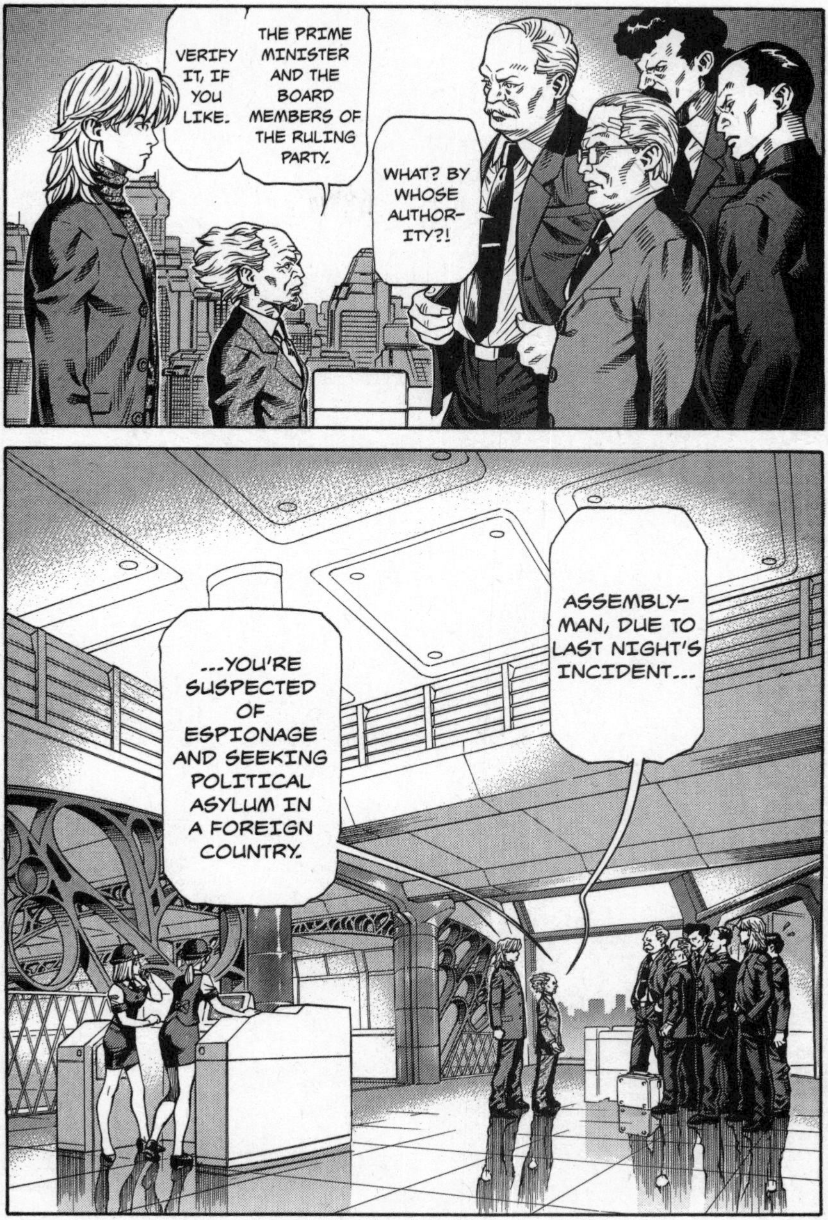
WHAT? BY WHOSE AUTHORITY?!
THE PRIME MINISTER AND THE BOARD MEMBERS OF THE RULING PARTY.
VERIFY IT, IF YOU LIKE.
ASSEMBLYMAN, DUE TO LAST NIGHT'S INCIDENT...
...YOU'RE SUSPECTED OF ESPIONAGE AND SEEKING POLITICAL ASYLUM IN A FOREIGN COUNTRY.

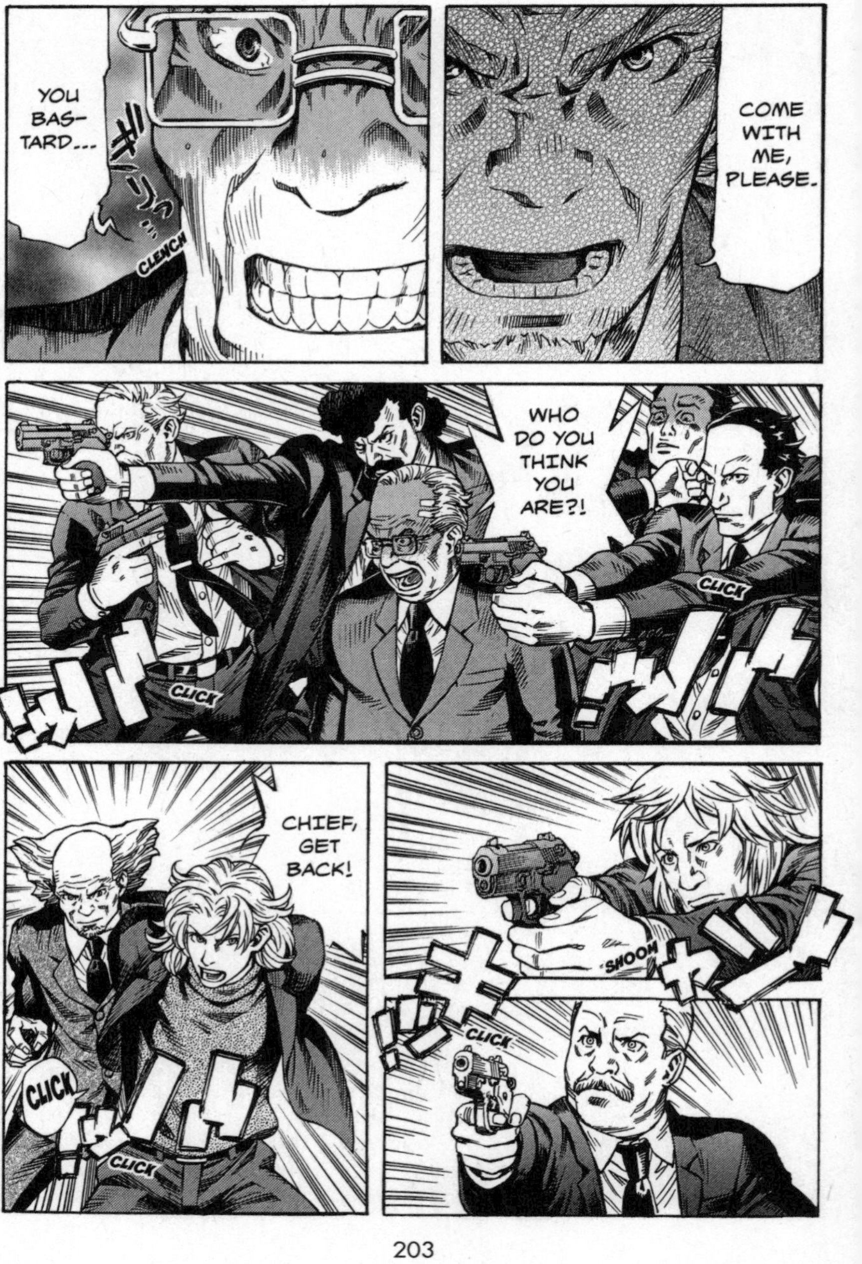
COME WITH ME, PLEASE.
YOU BAS-TARD...
CLENCH
WHO DO YOU THINK YOU ARE?!
CLICK
CLICK
SHOOM
CLICK
CHIEF, GET BACK!
CLICK
CLICK

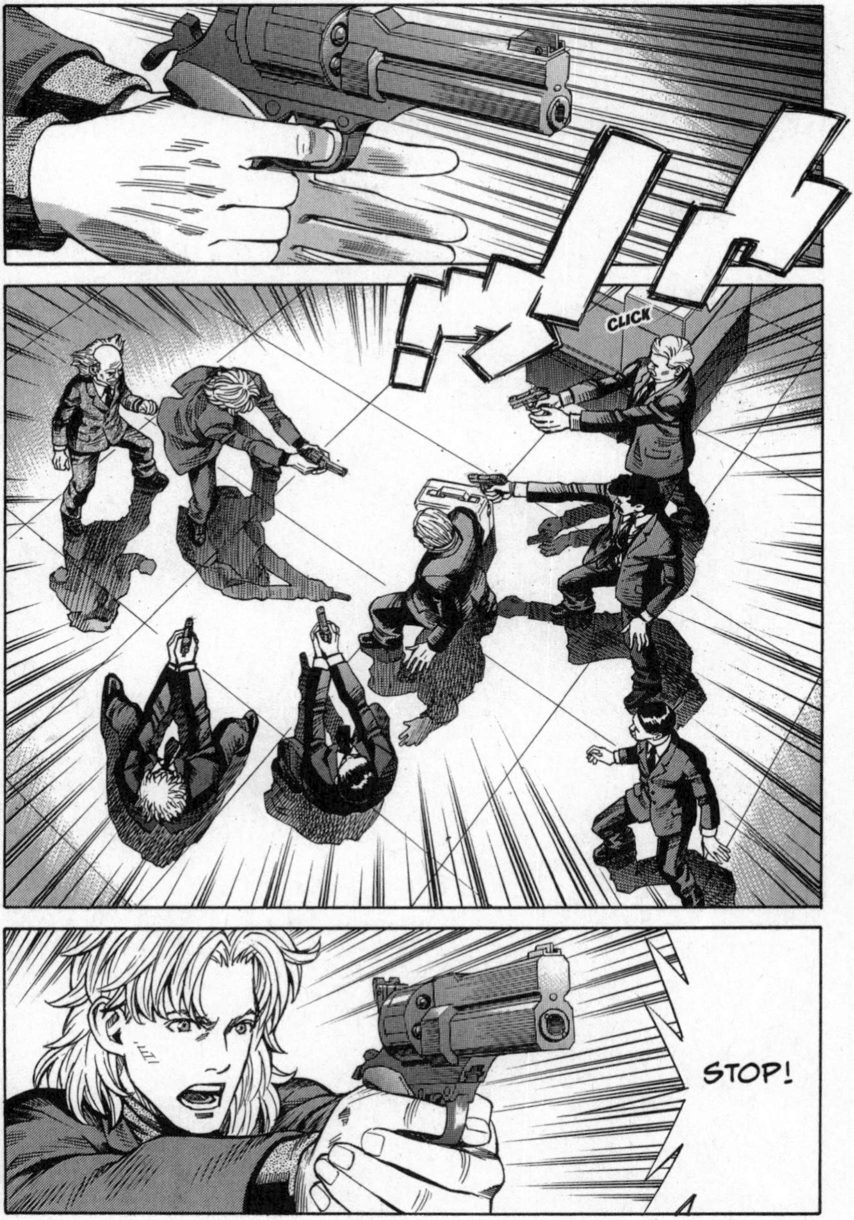
CLICK
STOP!

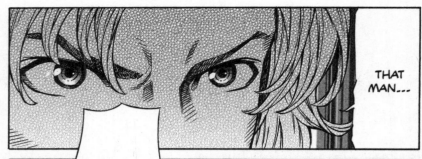

THAT MAN...

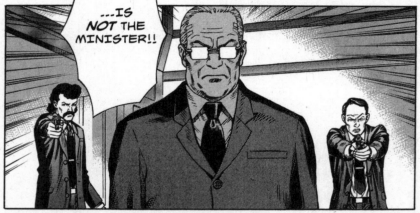

...IS *NOT* THE MINISTER!!

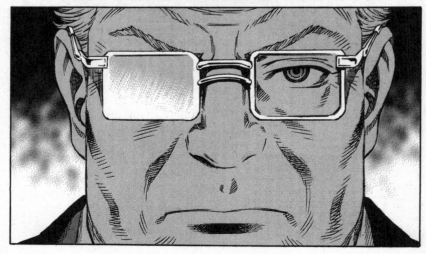

205

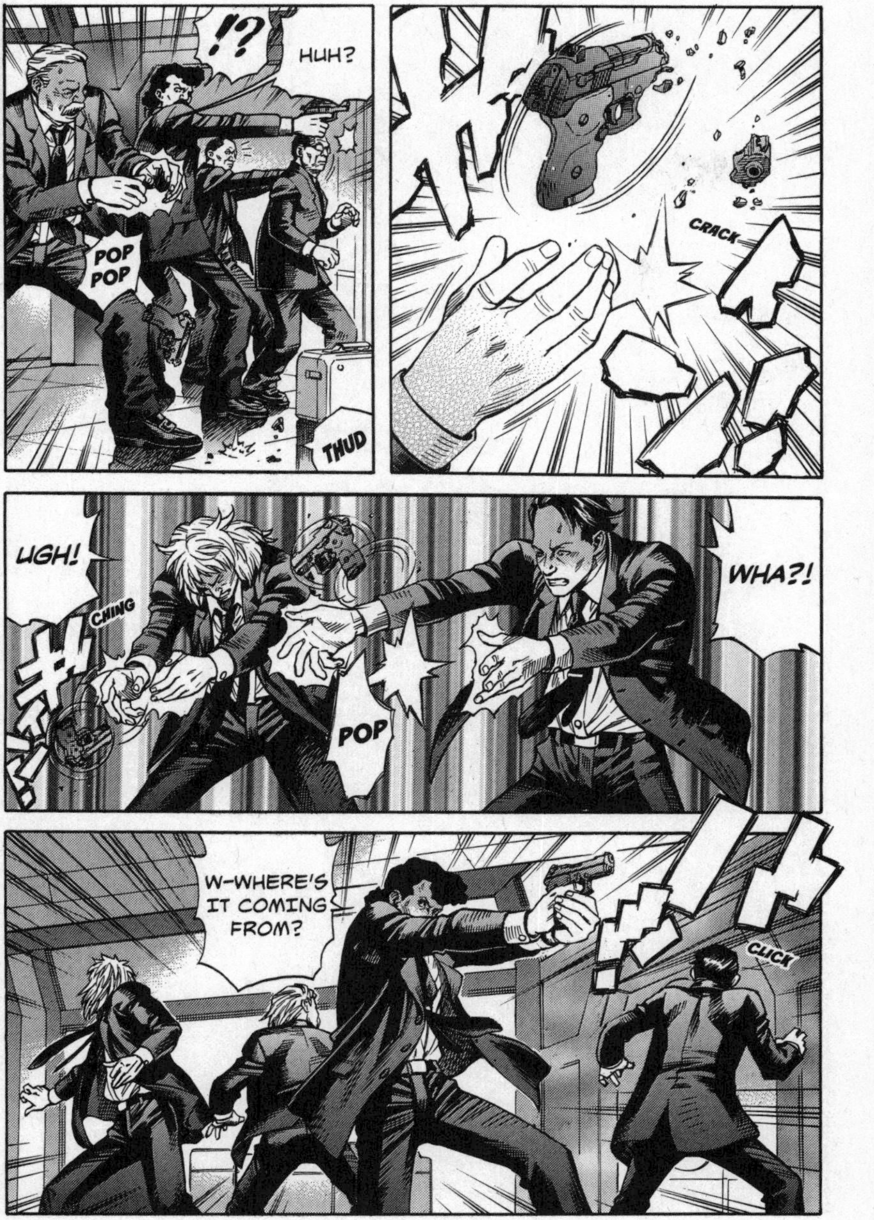
CRACK
HUH?
!?
POP POP
THUD
WHA?!
UGH!
CHING
POP
W-WHERE'S IT COMING FROM?
CLICK

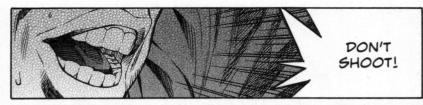

DON'T
SHOOT!

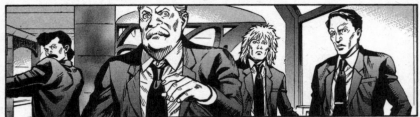

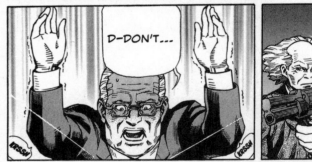

D–DON'T...

KRSSH

KRSSH

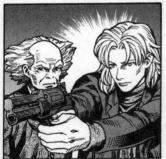

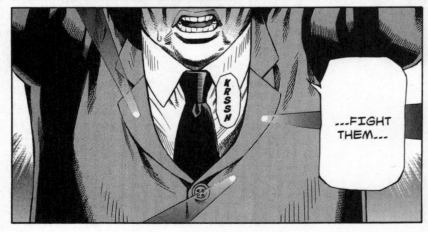

KRSSH

...FIGHT
THEM...

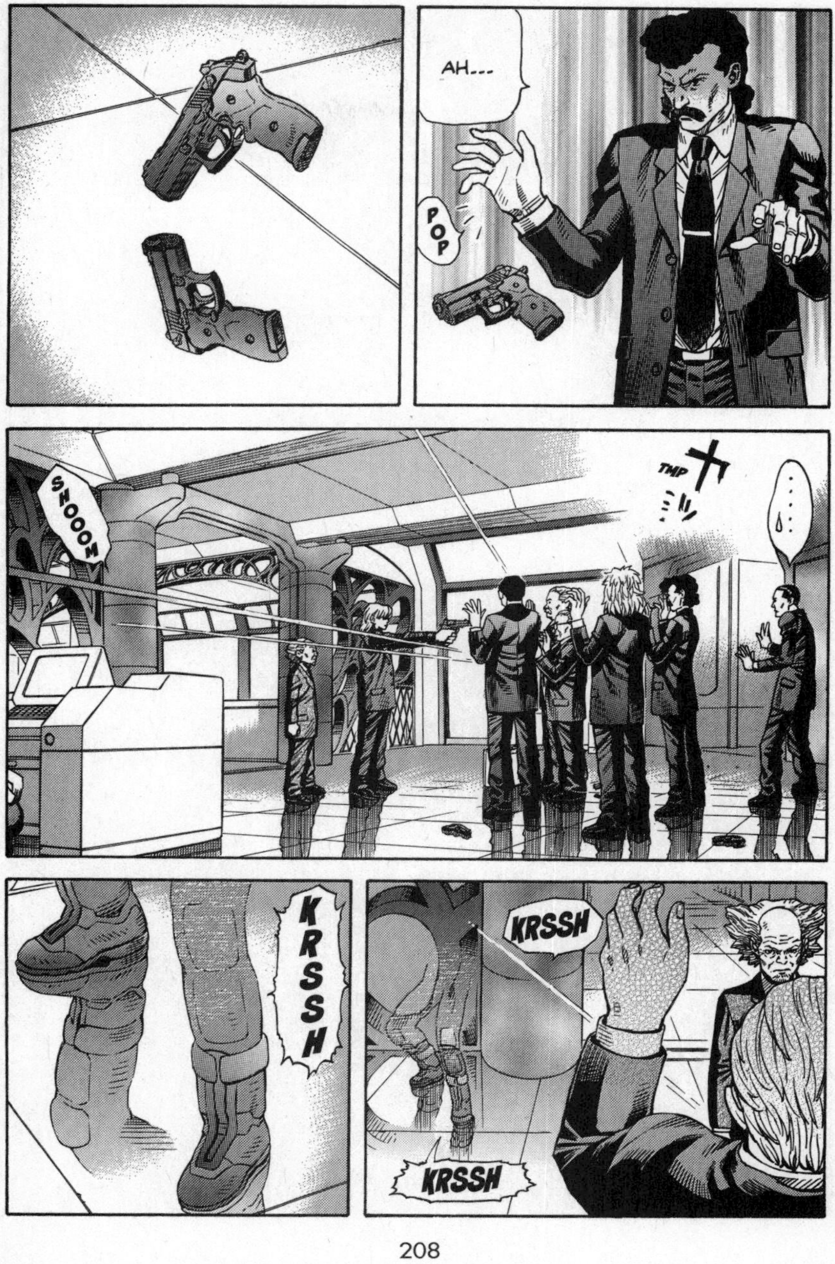
AH...
POP
...
TMP
SHOOOM
KRSSH
KRSSH
KRSSH

KRSSH
KRSSH
KYAAAH!
HUH?
KRSSH

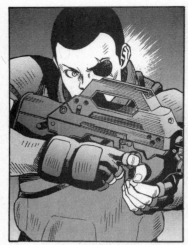

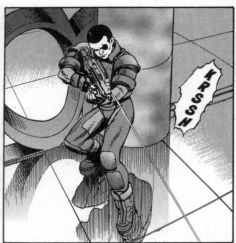

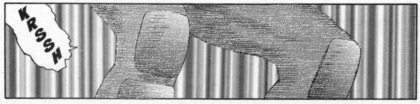

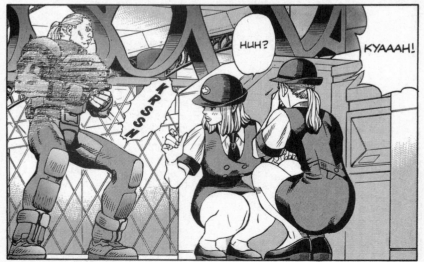

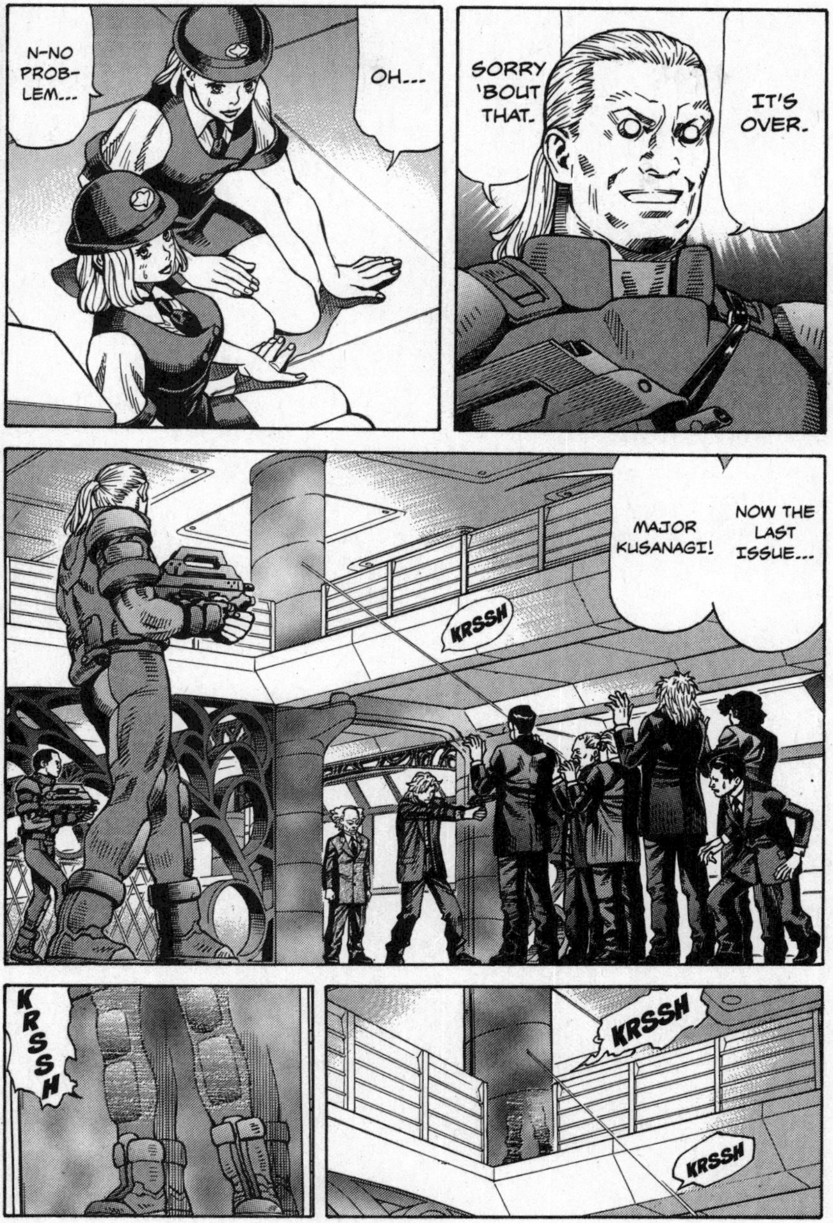
IT'S OVER.
SORRY 'BOUT THAT.
OH...
N-NO PROBLEM...
NOW THE LAST ISSUE...
MAJOR KUSANAGI!
KRSSH
KRSSH
KRSSH
KRSSH

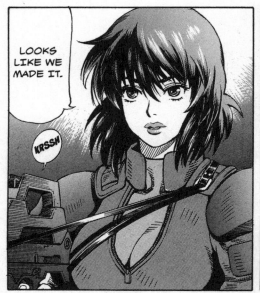

LOOKS LIKE WE MADE IT.

KRSSH

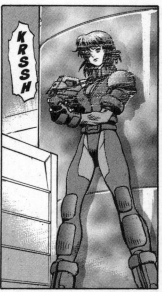

KRSSH

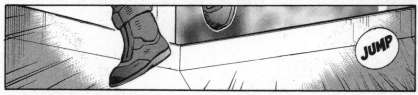

JUMP

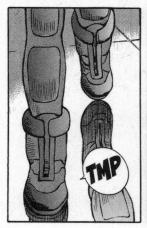

TMP

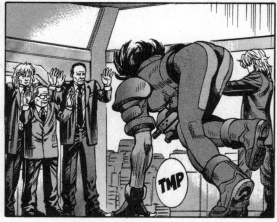

TMP

211

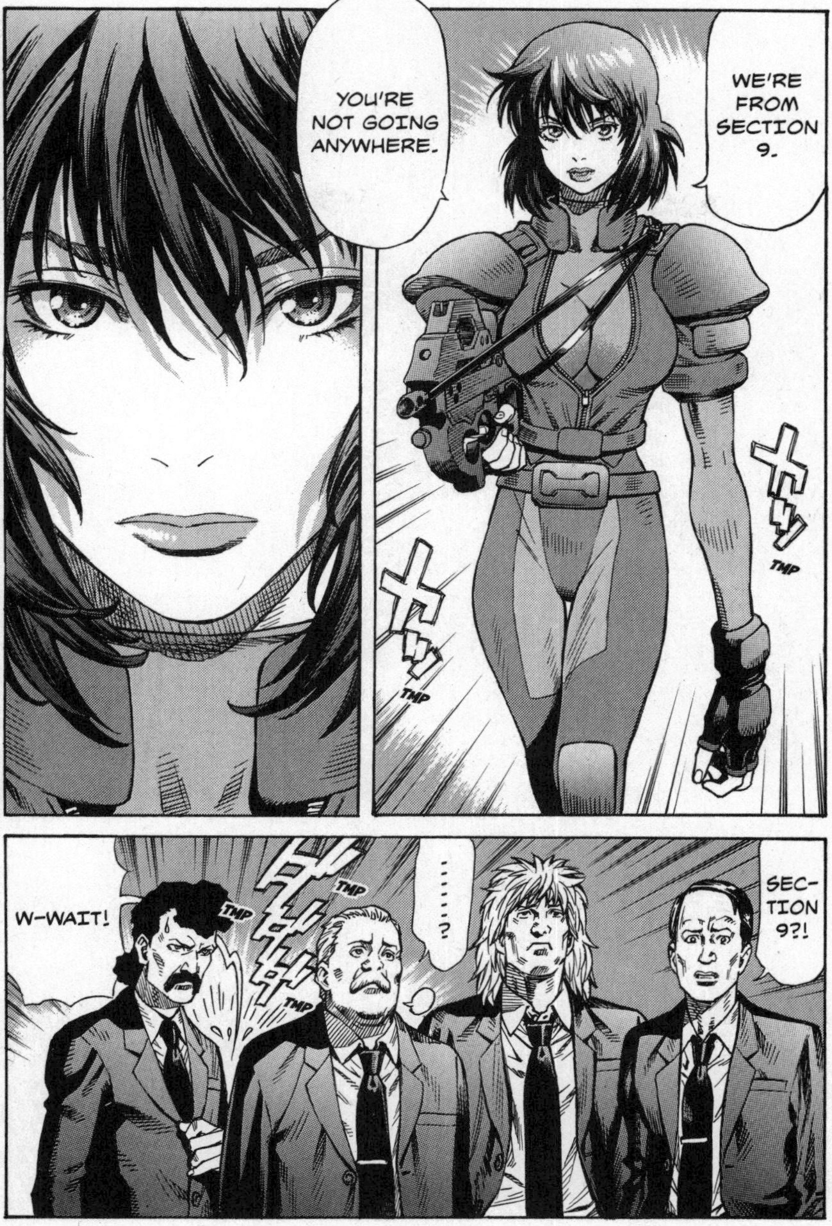
WE'RE FROM SECTION 9.
TMP
TMP
YOU'RE NOT GOING ANYWHERE.
SEC-TION 9?!
......?
TMP
TMP
TMP
W-WAIT!

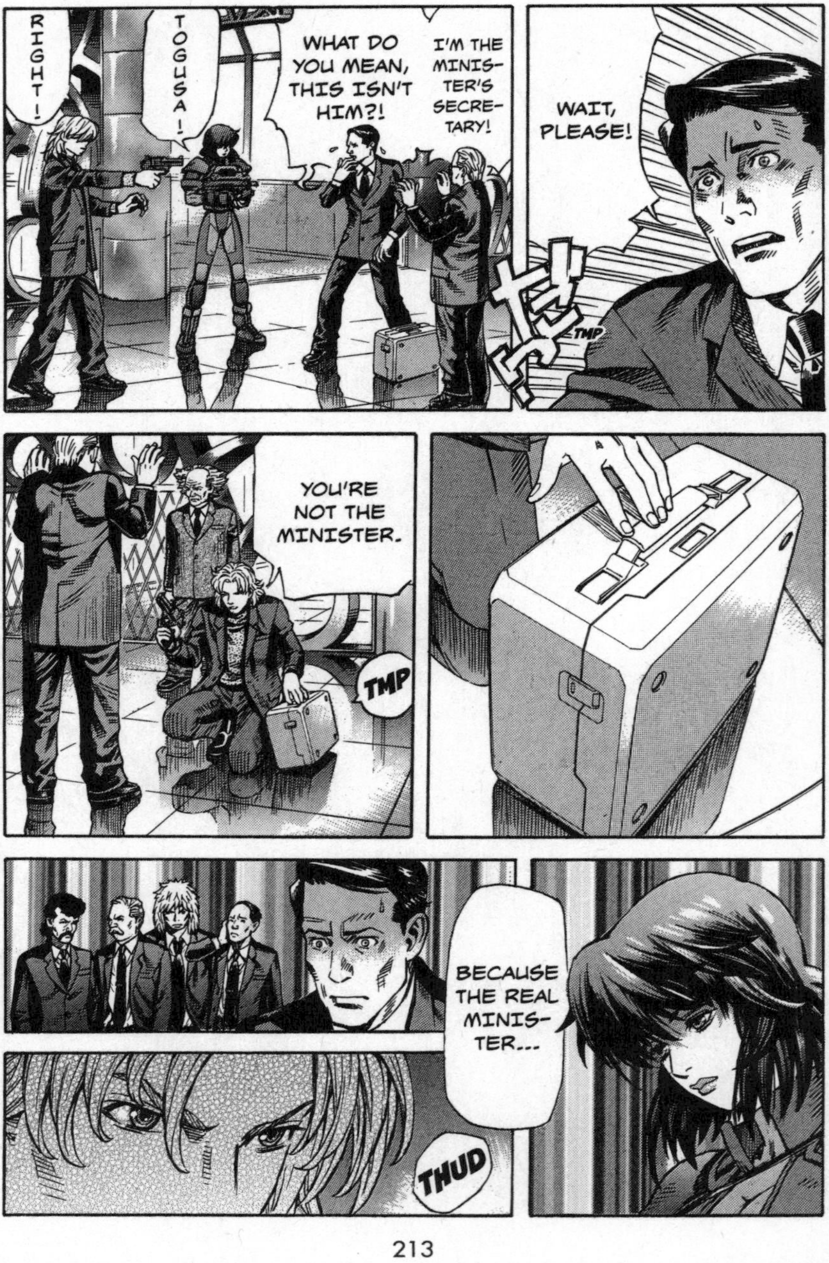
WAIT, PLEASE!
TMP
I'M THE MINISTER'S SECRETARY!
WHAT DO YOU MEAN, THIS ISN'T HIM?!
TOGUSA!
RIGHT!
YOU'RE NOT THE MINISTER.
TMP
BECAUSE THE REAL MINISTER...
THUD

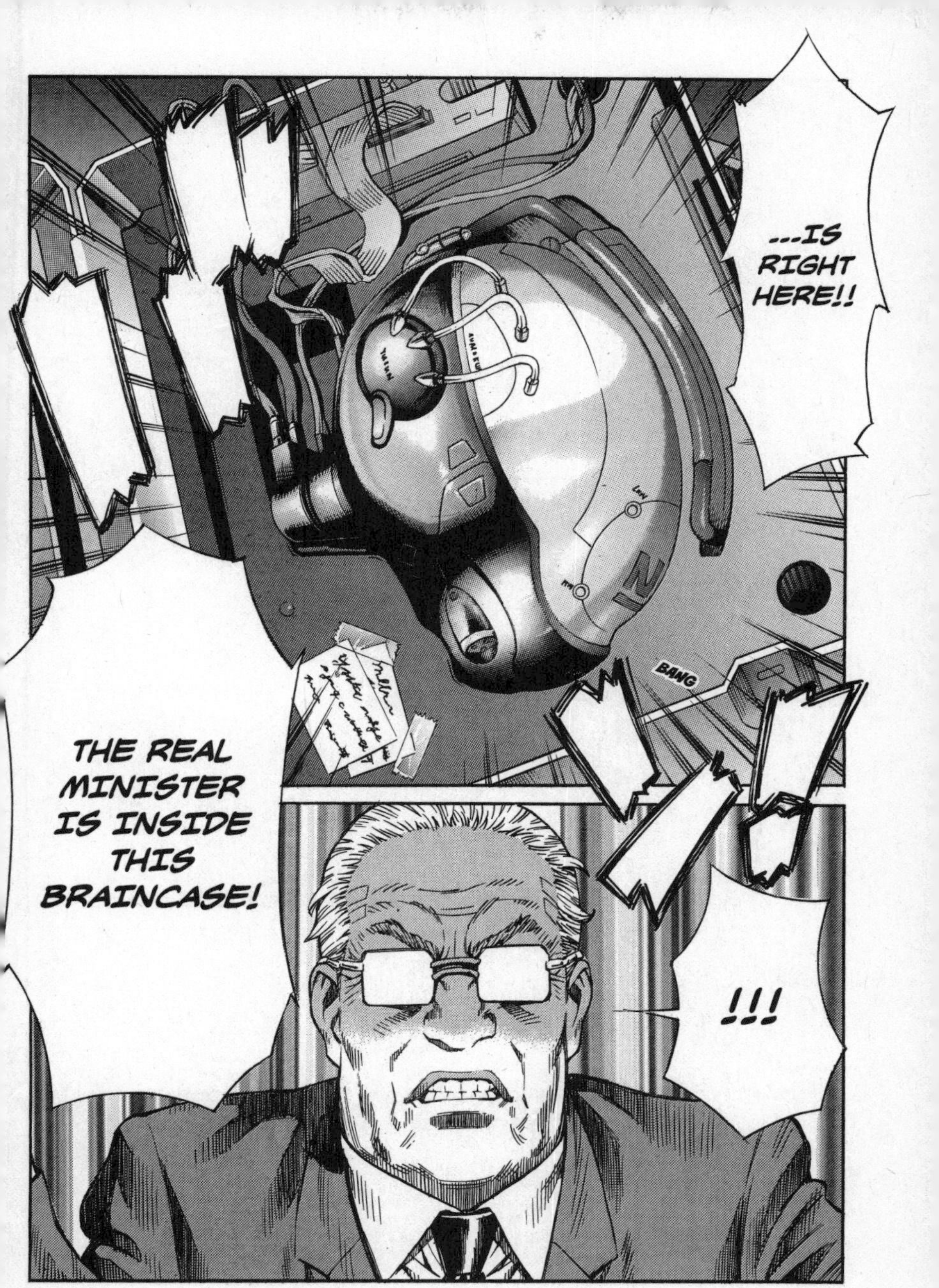
---IS RIGHT HERE!!
BANG
THE REAL MINISTER IS INSIDE THIS BRAINCASE!
!!!

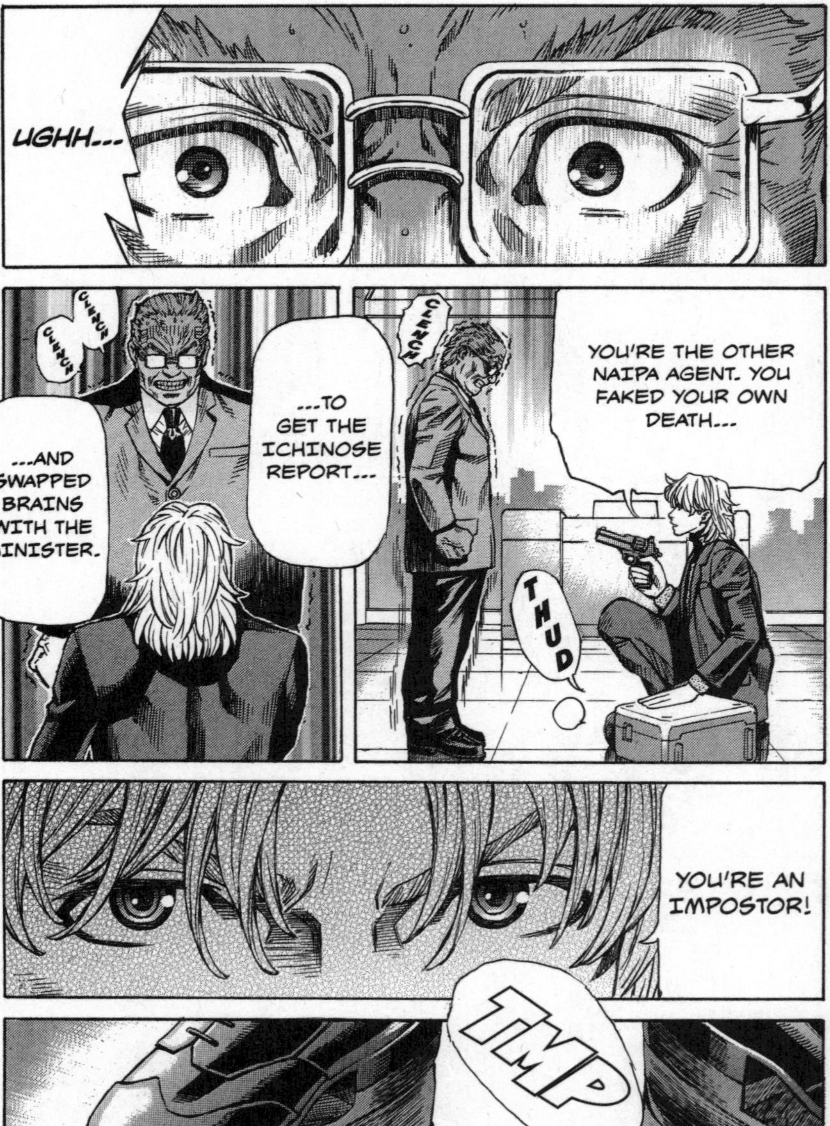
UGHH...
YOU'RE THE OTHER NAIPA AGENT. YOU FAKED YOUR OWN DEATH...
CLENCH
THUD
...TO GET THE ICHINOSE REPORT...
CLENCH
CLENCH
...AND SWAPPED BRAINS WITH THE MINISTER.
YOU'RE AN IMPOSTOR!
TMP

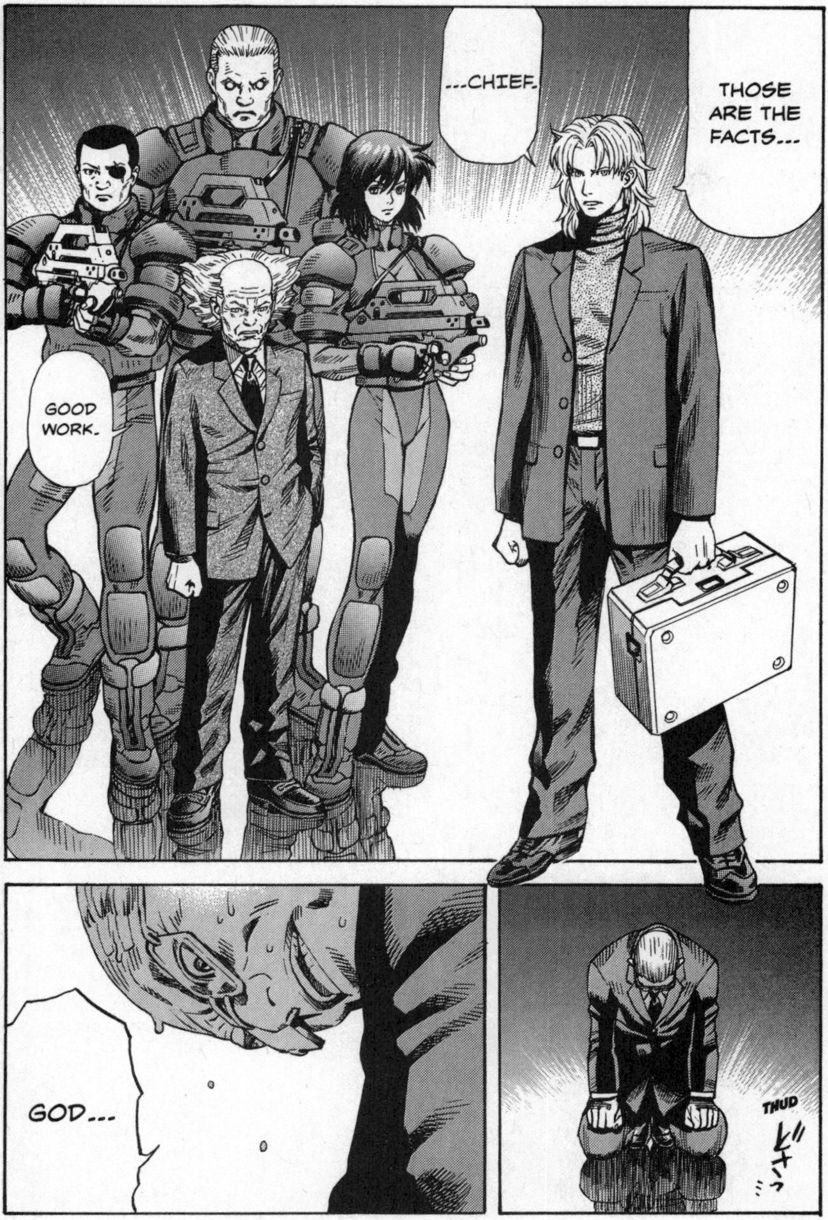
THOSE ARE THE FACTS...
...CHIEF.
GOOD WORK.
THUD
GOD...

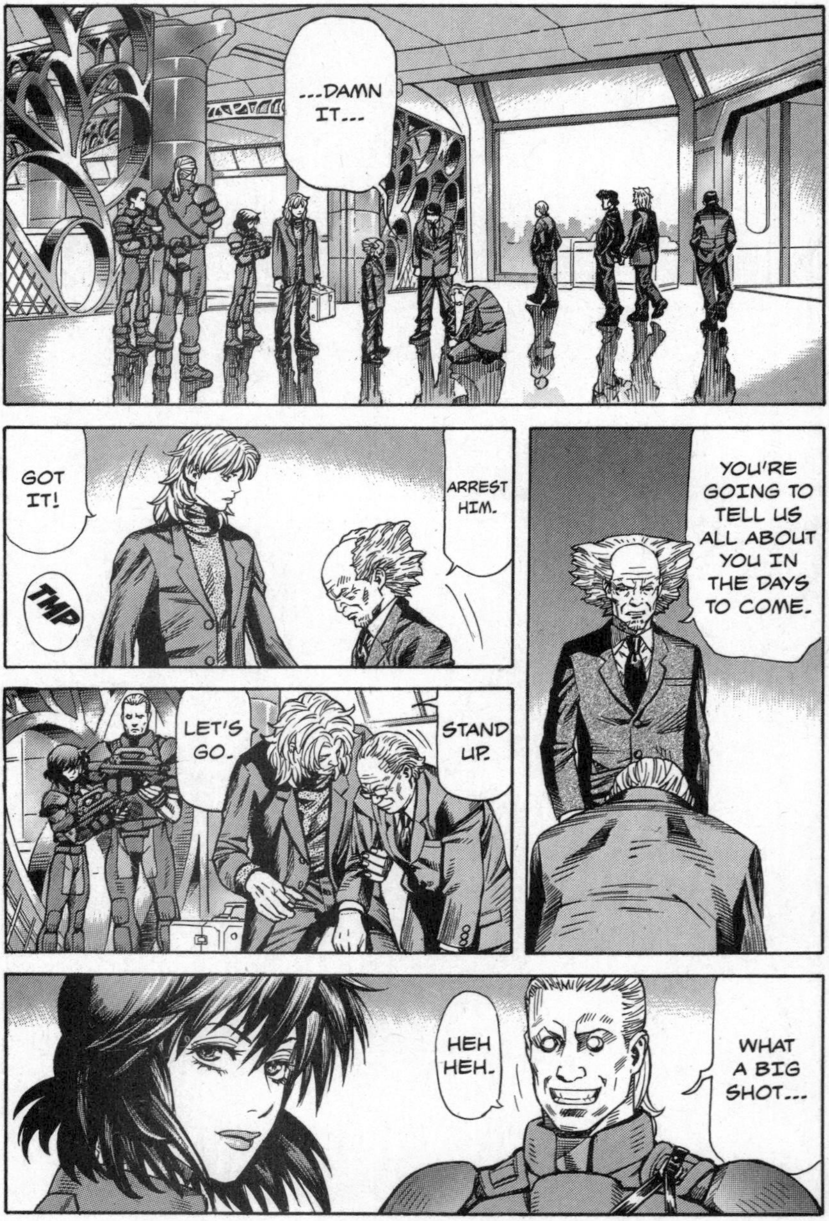
---DAMN IT---
YOU'RE GOING TO TELL US ALL ABOUT YOU IN THE DAYS TO COME.
ARREST HIM.
GOT IT!
TMP
STAND UP.
LET'S GO.
WHAT A BIG SHOT---
HEH HEH.

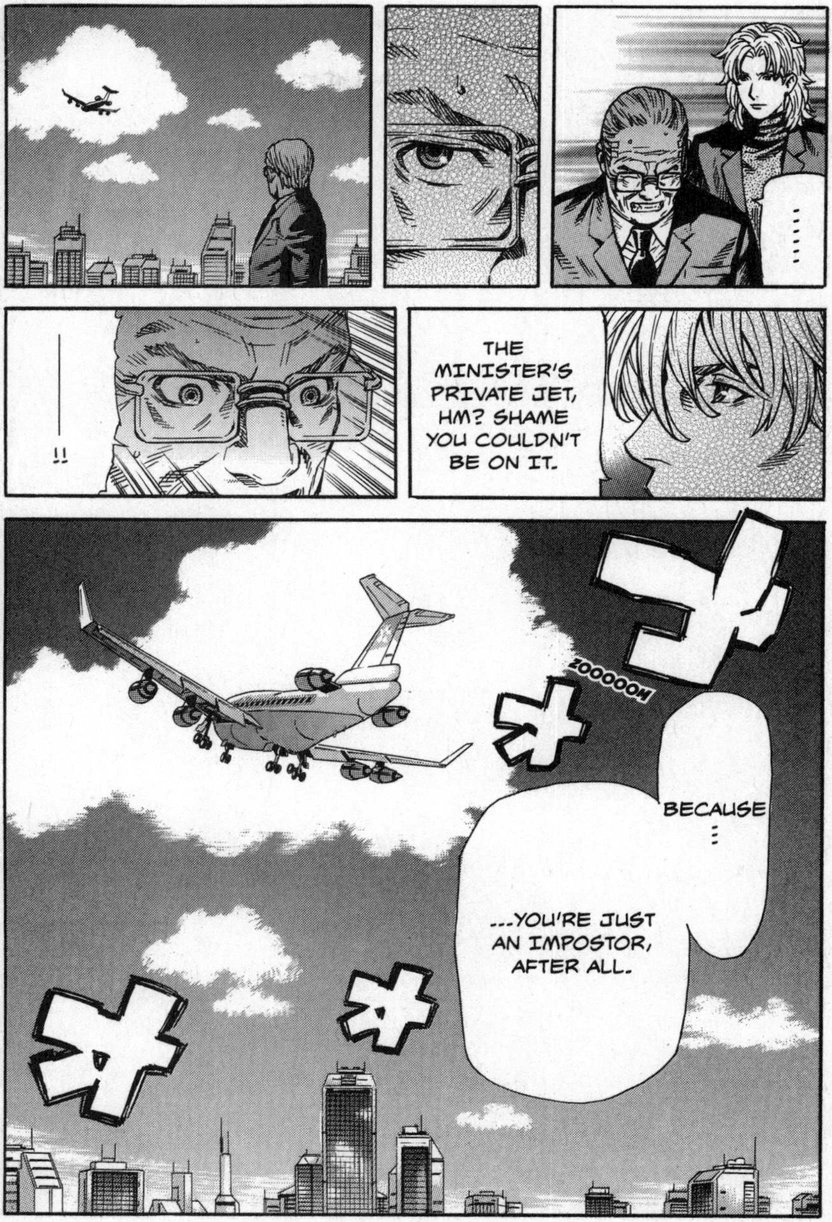
......
THE MINISTER'S PRIVATE JET, HM? SHAME YOU COULDN'T BE ON IT.
——!!
ZOOOOOOM
BECAUSE...
...YOU'RE JUST AN IMPOSTOR, AFTER ALL.

#010 / End

#011: The Truth

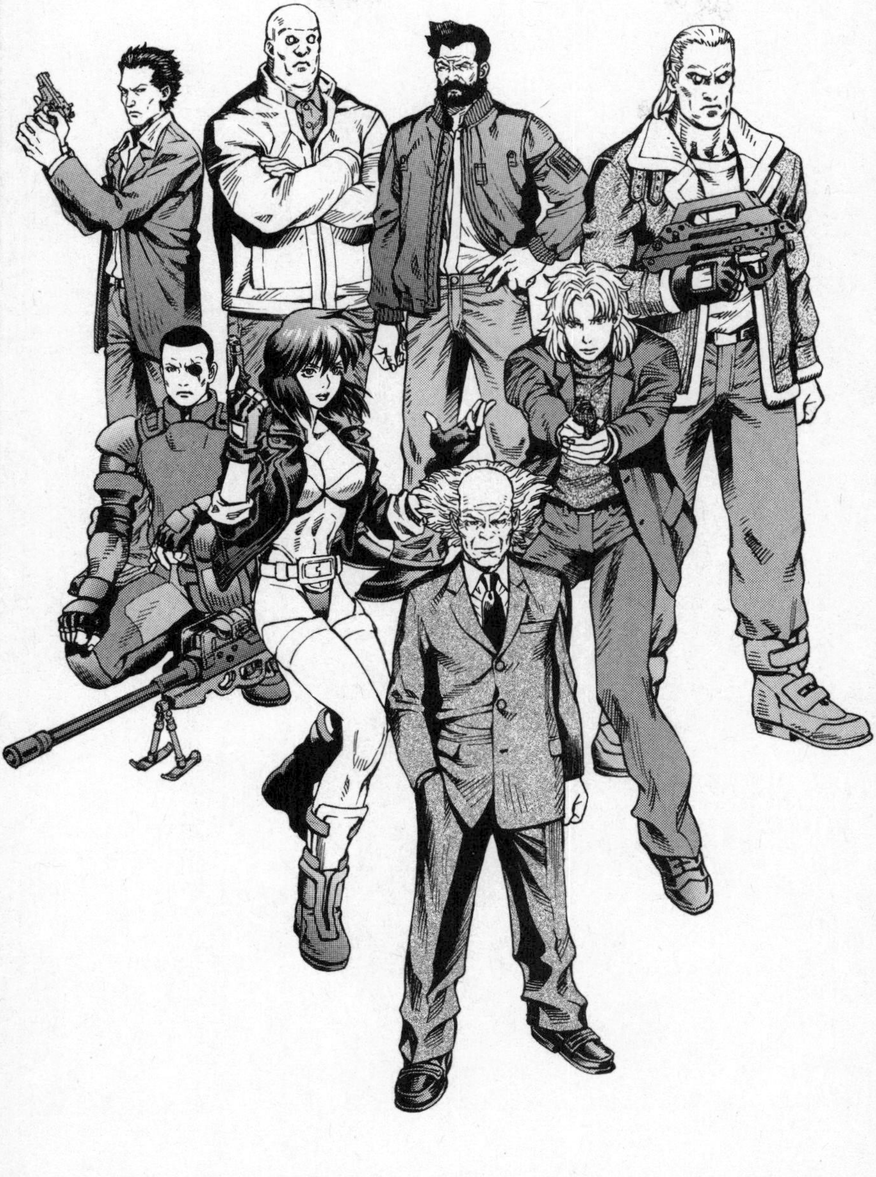

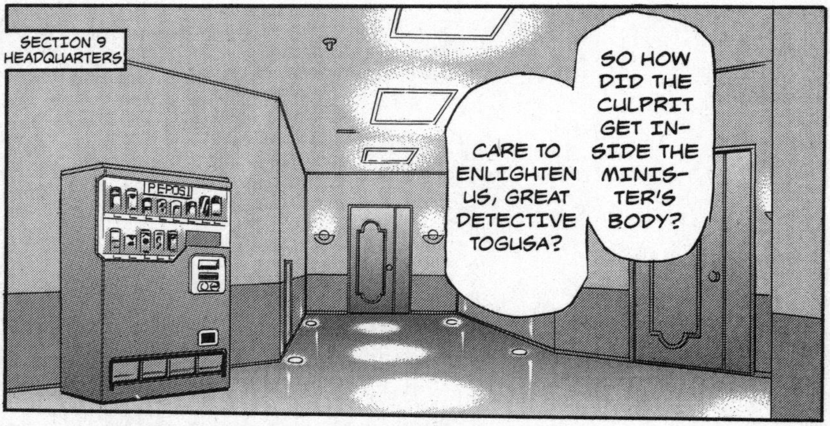
SO HOW DID THE CULPRIT GET INSIDE THE MINISTER'S BODY?
CARE TO ENLIGHTEN US, GREAT DETECTIVE TOGUSA?
SECTION 9 HEADQUARTERS

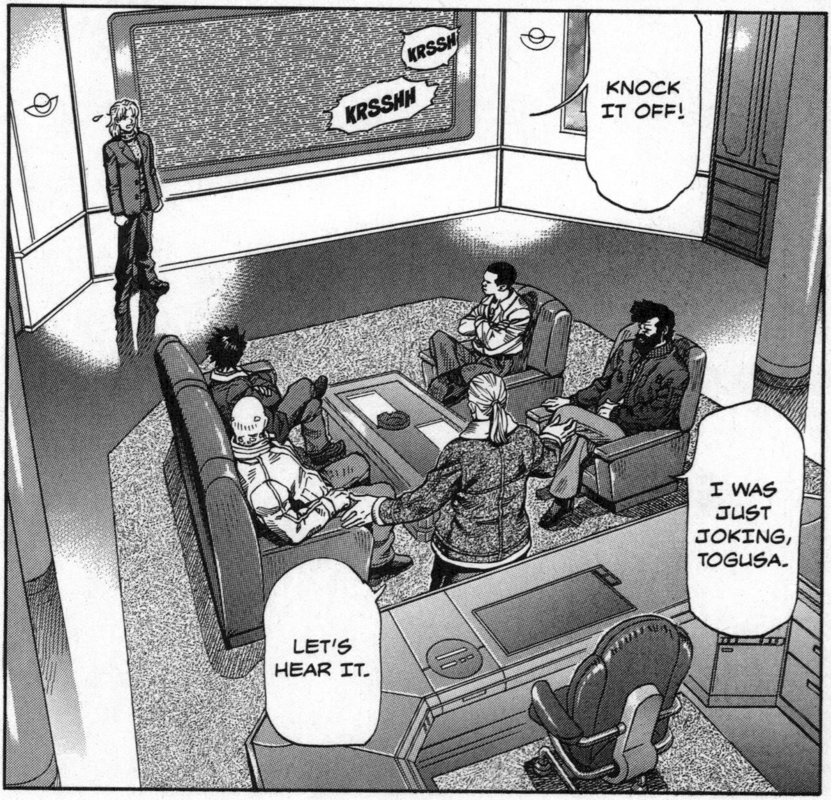
KNOCK IT OFF!
KRSSH
KRSSHH
I WAS JUST JOKING, TOGUSA.
LET'S HEAR IT.

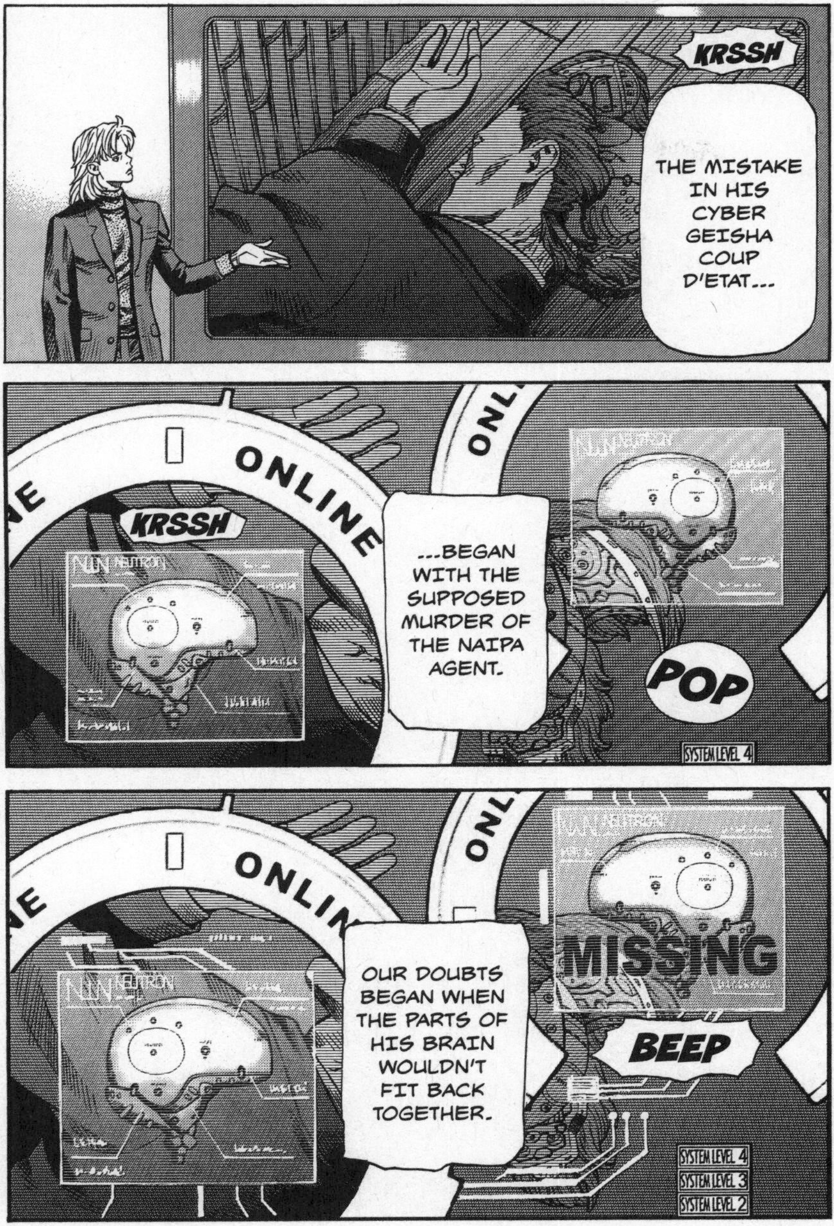
KRSSH
THE MISTAKE IN HIS CYBER GEISHA COUP D'ETAT...
ONLINE
...BEGAN WITH THE SUPPOSED MURDER OF THE NAIPA AGENT.
POP
ONLINE
KRSSH
SYSTEM LEVEL 4
ONLINE
MISSING
BEEP
OUR DOUBTS BEGAN WHEN THE PARTS OF HIS BRAIN WOULDN'T FIT BACK TOGETHER.
ONLINE
SYSTEM LEVEL 4
SYSTEM LEVEL 3
SYSTEM LEVEL 2

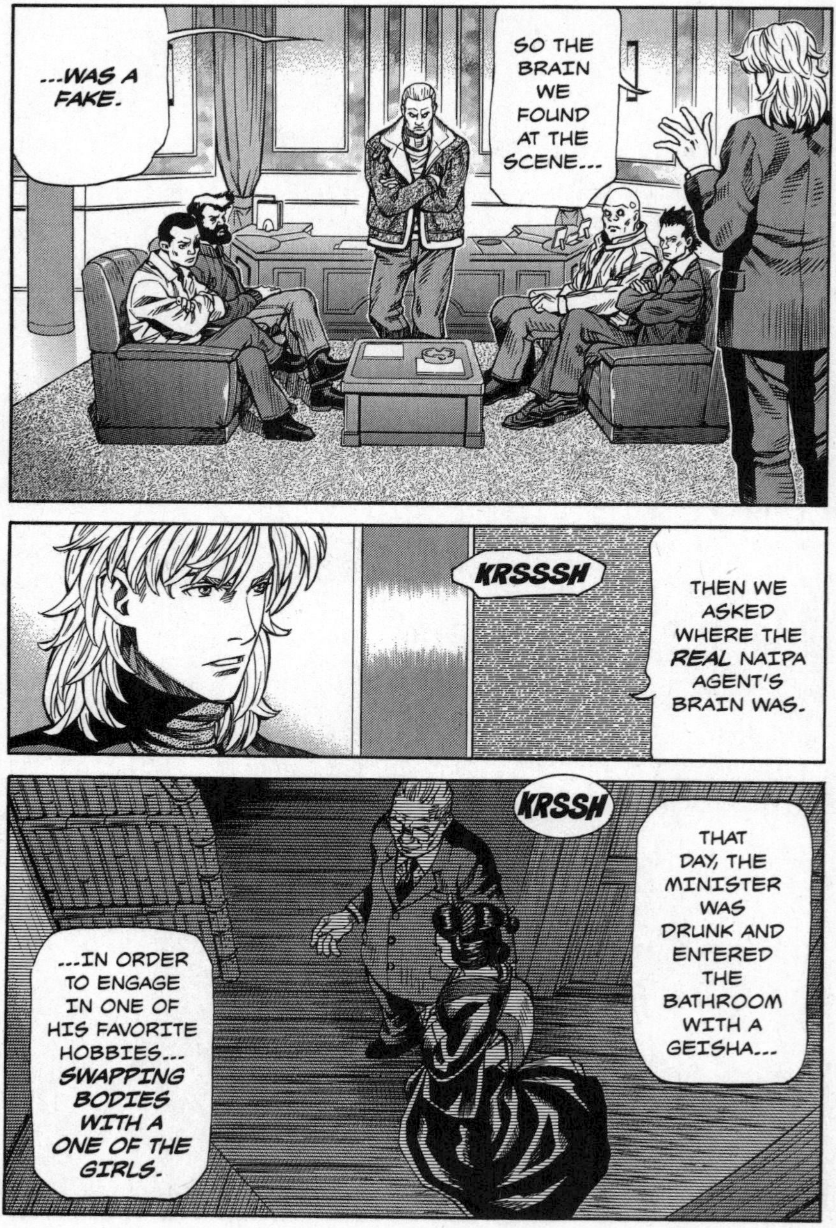
SO THE BRAIN WE FOUND AT THE SCENE...
...WAS A FAKE.
THEN WE ASKED WHERE THE *REAL* NAIPA AGENT'S BRAIN WAS.
KRSSSH
KRSSH
THAT DAY, THE MINISTER WAS DRUNK AND ENTERED THE BATHROOM WITH A GEISHA...
...IN ORDER TO ENGAGE IN ONE OF HIS FAVORITE HOBBIES... *SWAPPING BODIES WITH A ONE OF THE GIRLS.*

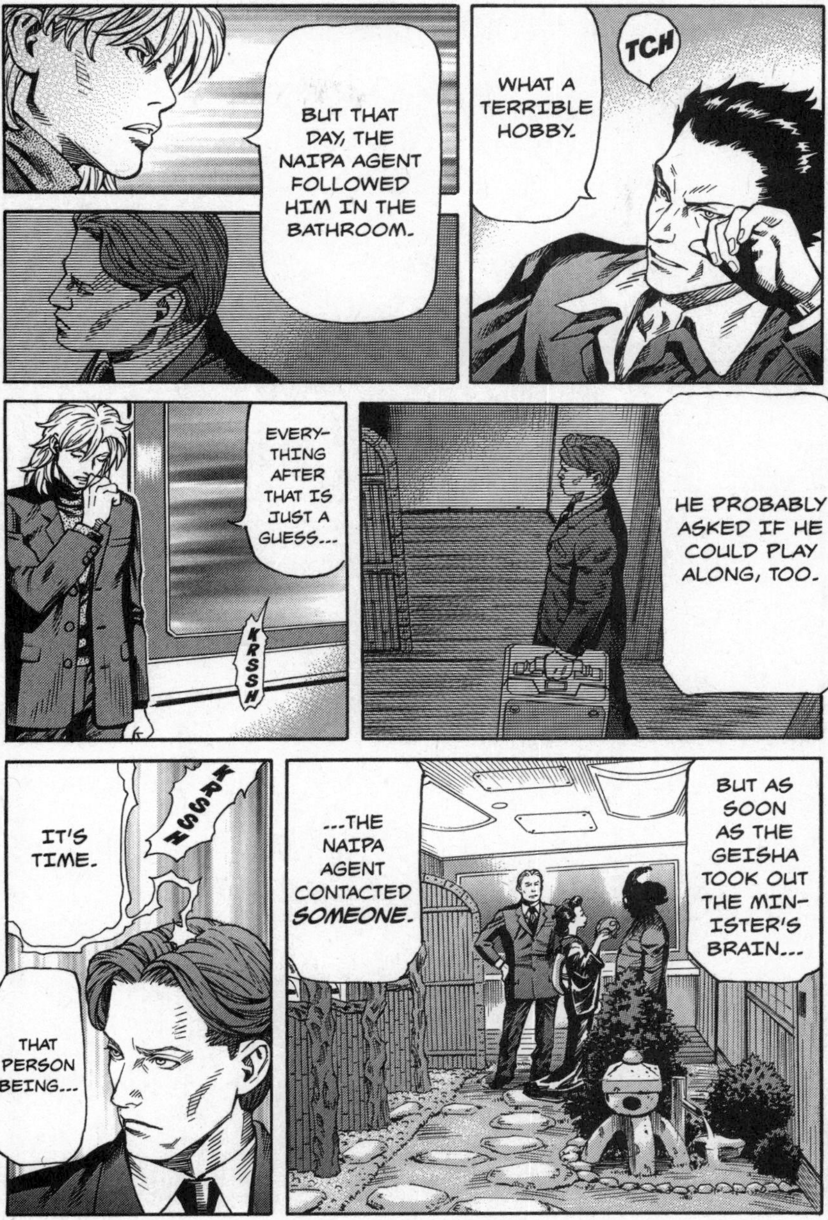
TCH
WHAT A TERRIBLE HOBBY.
BUT THAT DAY, THE NAIPA AGENT FOLLOWED HIM IN THE BATHROOM.
HE PROBABLY ASKED IF HE COULD PLAY ALONG, TOO.
EVERYTHING AFTER THAT IS JUST A GUESS...
KRSSH
BUT AS SOON AS THE GEISHA TOOK OUT THE MINISTER'S BRAIN...
...THE NAIPA AGENT CONTACTED SOMEONE.
KRSSH
IT'S TIME.
THAT PERSON BEING...

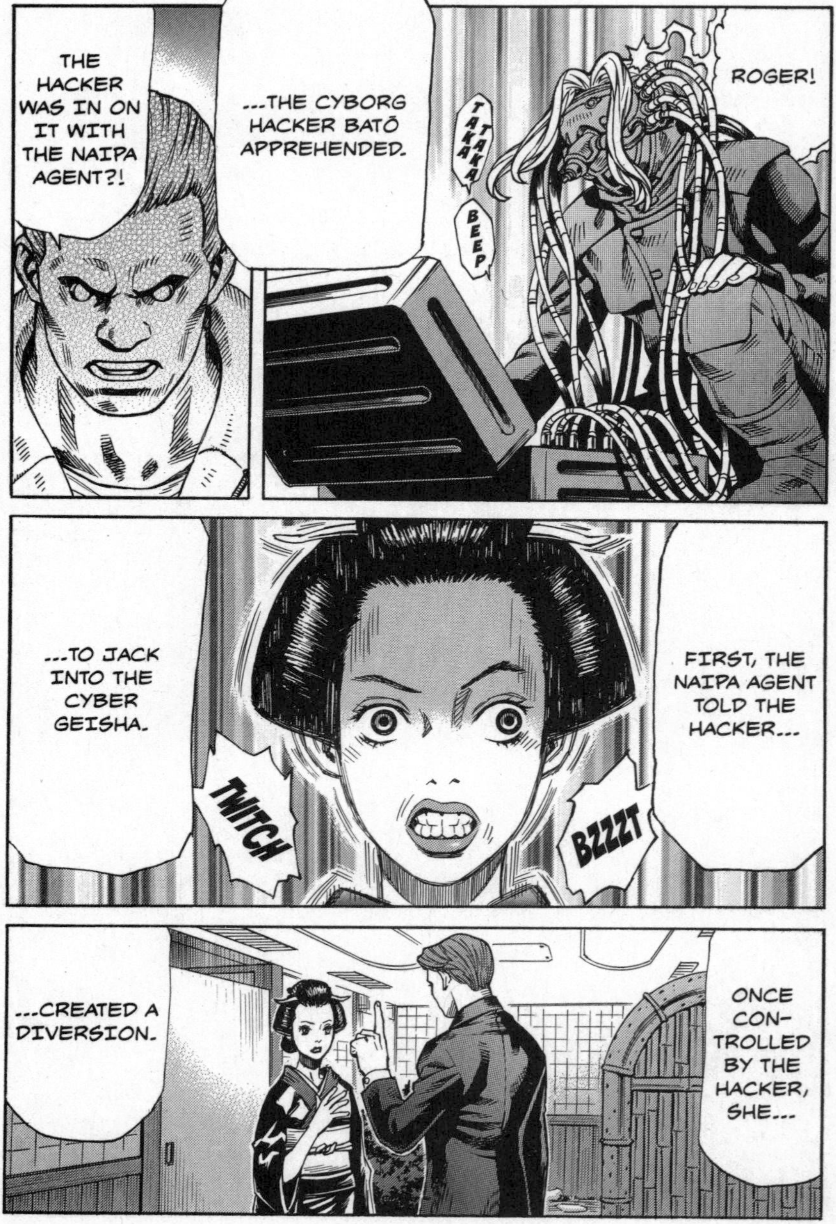
ROGER!
TAKA TAKA
BEEP
...THE CYBORG HACKER BATŌ APPREHENDED.
THE HACKER WAS IN ON IT WITH THE NAIPA AGENT?!
FIRST, THE NAIPA AGENT TOLD THE HACKER...
BZZZT
TWITCH
...TO JACK INTO THE CYBER GEISHA.
ONCE CON-TROLLED BY THE HACKER, SHE...
...CREATED A DIVERSION.

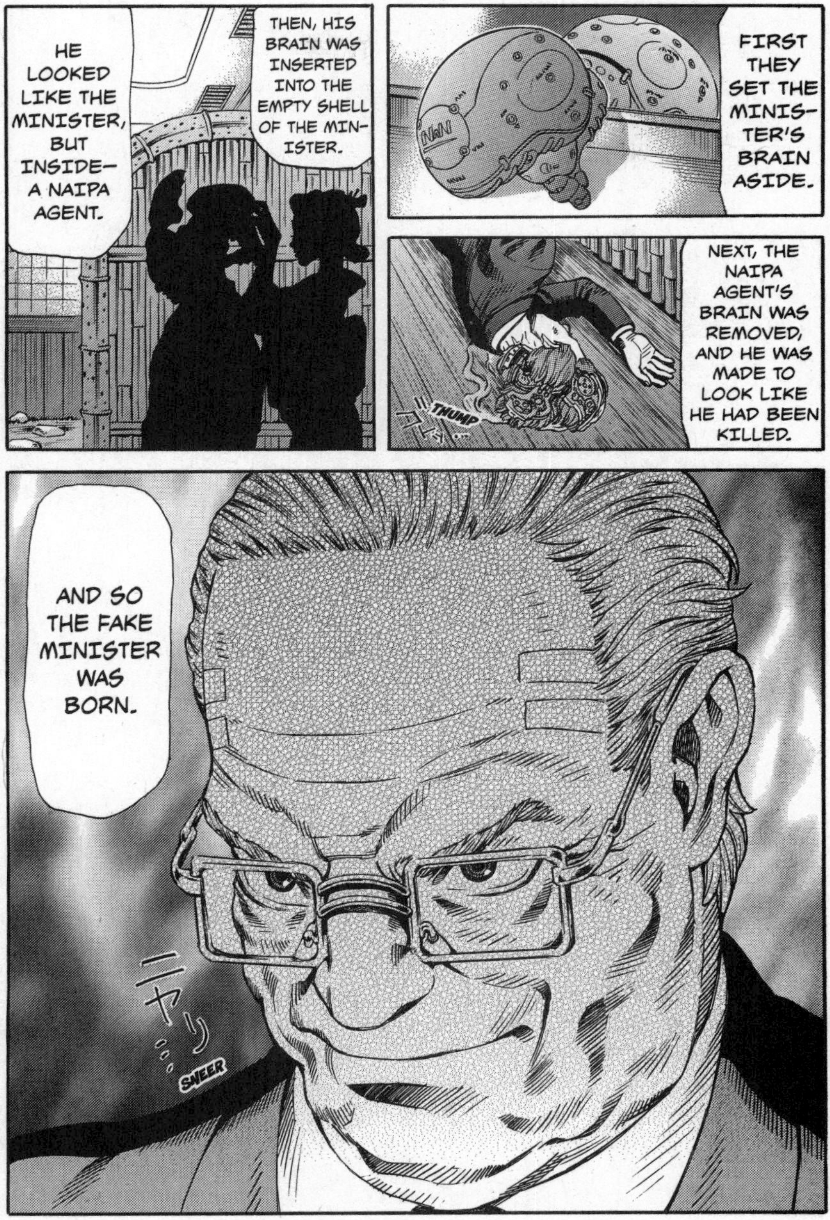
FIRST THEY SET THE MINISTER'S BRAIN ASIDE.
NEXT, THE NAIPA AGENT'S BRAIN WAS REMOVED, AND HE WAS MADE TO LOOK LIKE HE HAD BEEN KILLED.
THUMP
THEN, HIS BRAIN WAS INSERTED INTO THE EMPTY SHELL OF THE MINISTER.
HE LOOKED LIKE THE MINISTER, BUT INSIDE— A NAIPA AGENT.
AND SO THE FAKE MINISTER WAS BORN.
ニヤリ
SNEER

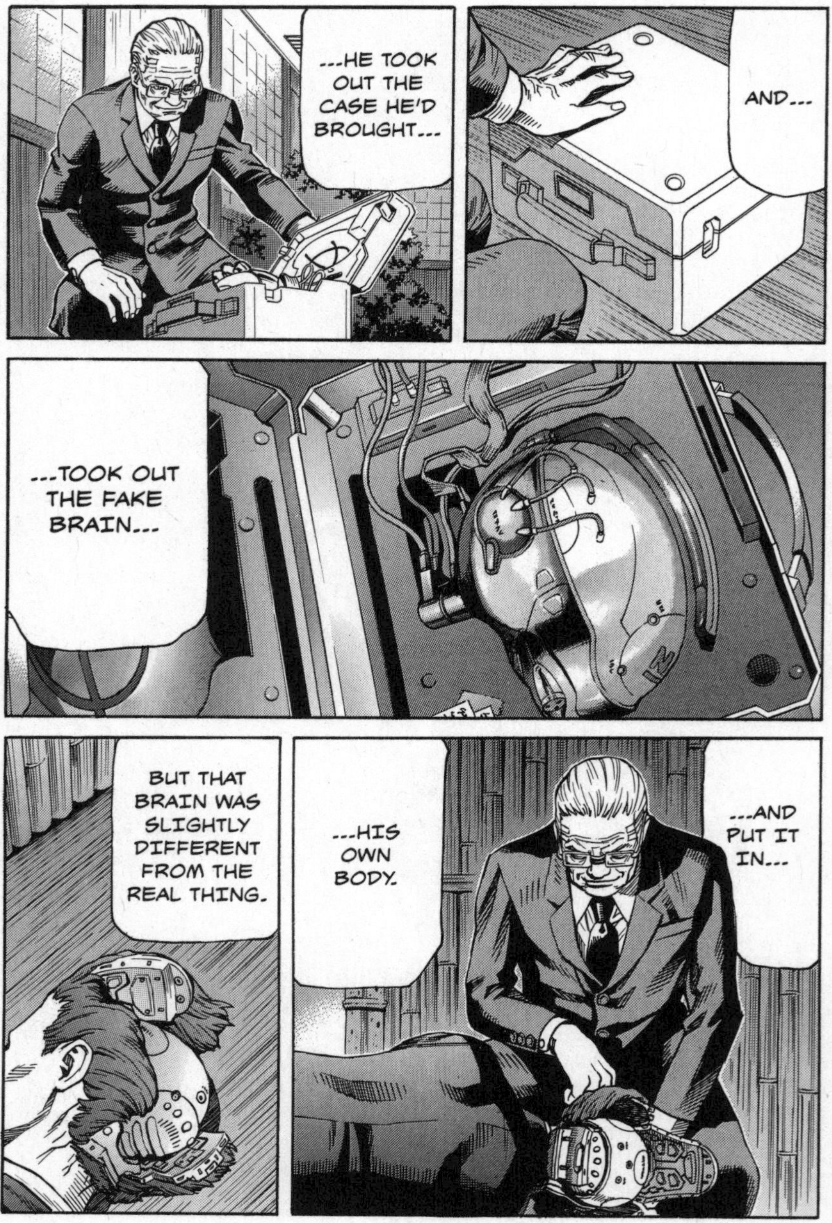
AND...
...HE TOOK OUT THE CASE HE'D BROUGHT...
...TOOK OUT THE FAKE BRAIN...
...AND PUT IT IN...
...HIS OWN BODY.
BUT THAT BRAIN WAS SLIGHTLY DIFFERENT FROM THE REAL THING.

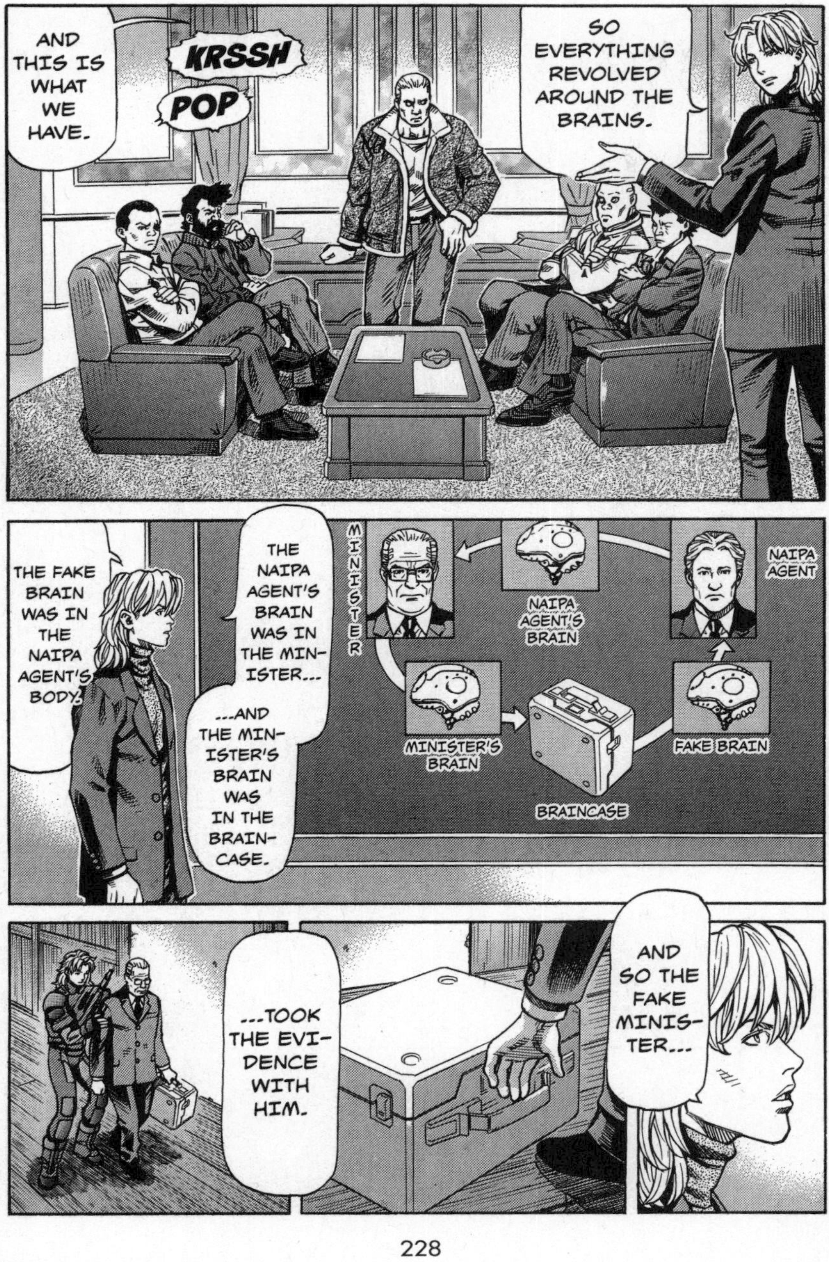
SO EVERYTHING REVOLVED AROUND THE BRAINS.
KRSSH
POP
AND THIS IS WHAT WE HAVE.
NAIPA AGENT
NAIPA AGENT'S BRAIN
MINISTER
FAKE BRAIN
BRAINCASE
MINISTER'S BRAIN
THE NAIPA AGENT'S BRAIN WAS IN THE MINISTER...
...AND THE MINISTER'S BRAIN WAS IN THE BRAINCASE.
THE FAKE BRAIN WAS IN THE NAIPA AGENT'S BODY.
AND SO THE FAKE MINISTER...
...TOOK THE EVIDENCE WITH HIM.

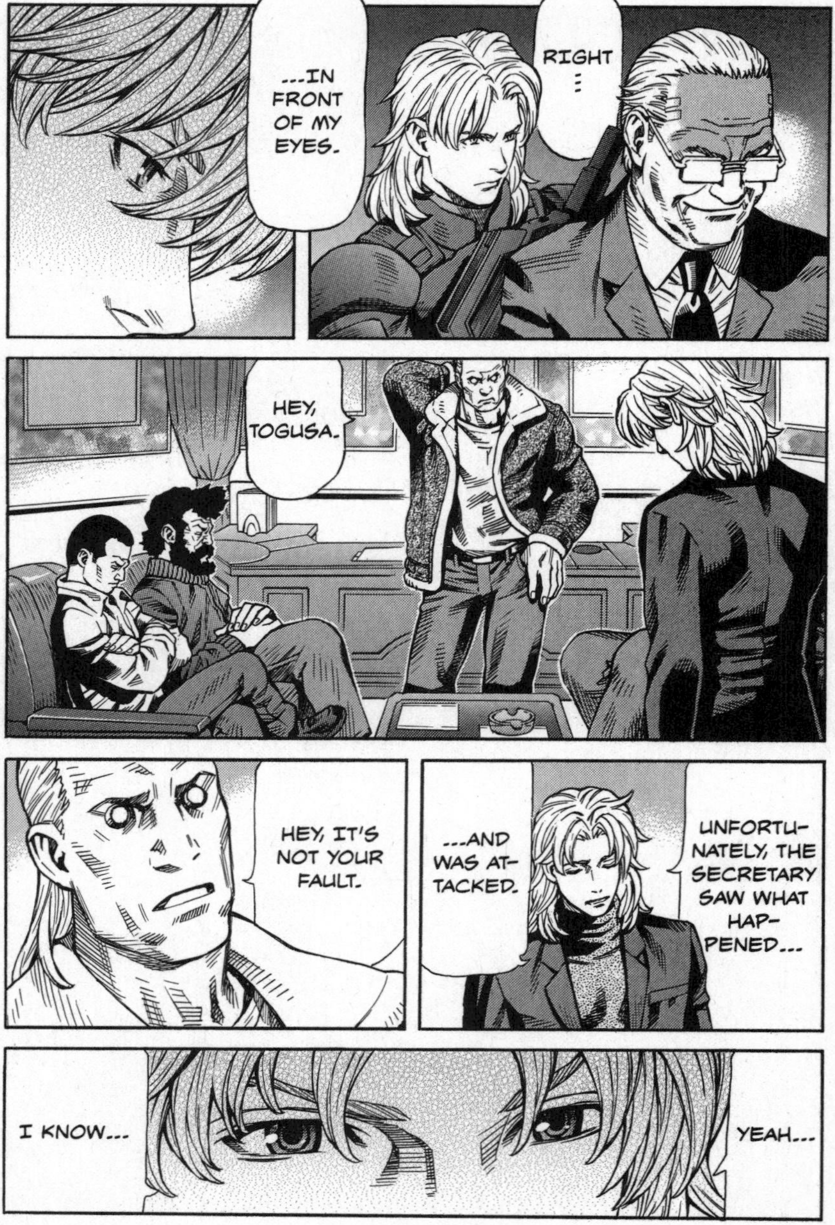

RIGHT...
...IN FRONT OF MY EYES.
HEY, TOGUSA.
UNFORTUNATELY, THE SECRETARY SAW WHAT HAPPENED...
...AND WAS ATTACKED.
HEY, IT'S NOT YOUR FAULT.
YEAH...
I KNOW...

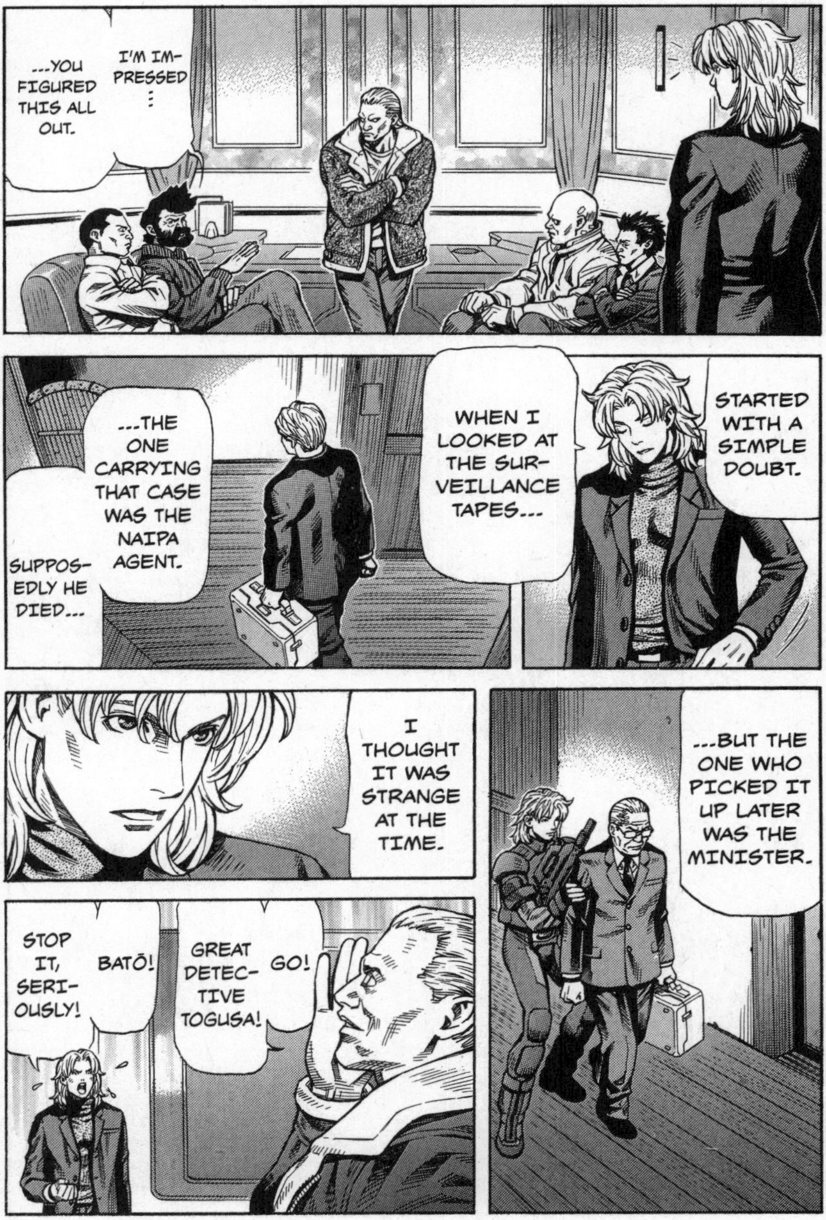
I'M IM-PRESSED ⋮
...YOU FIGURED THIS ALL OUT.
STARTED WITH A SIMPLE DOUBT.
WHEN I LOOKED AT THE SUR-VEILLANCE TAPES...
...THE ONE CARRYING THAT CASE WAS THE NAIPA AGENT.
SUPPOS-EDLY HE DIED...
...BUT THE ONE WHO PICKED IT UP LATER WAS THE MINISTER.
I THOUGHT IT WAS STRANGE AT THE TIME.
GO!
GREAT DETEC-TIVE TOGUSA!
BATŌ!
STOP IT, SERI-OUSLY!

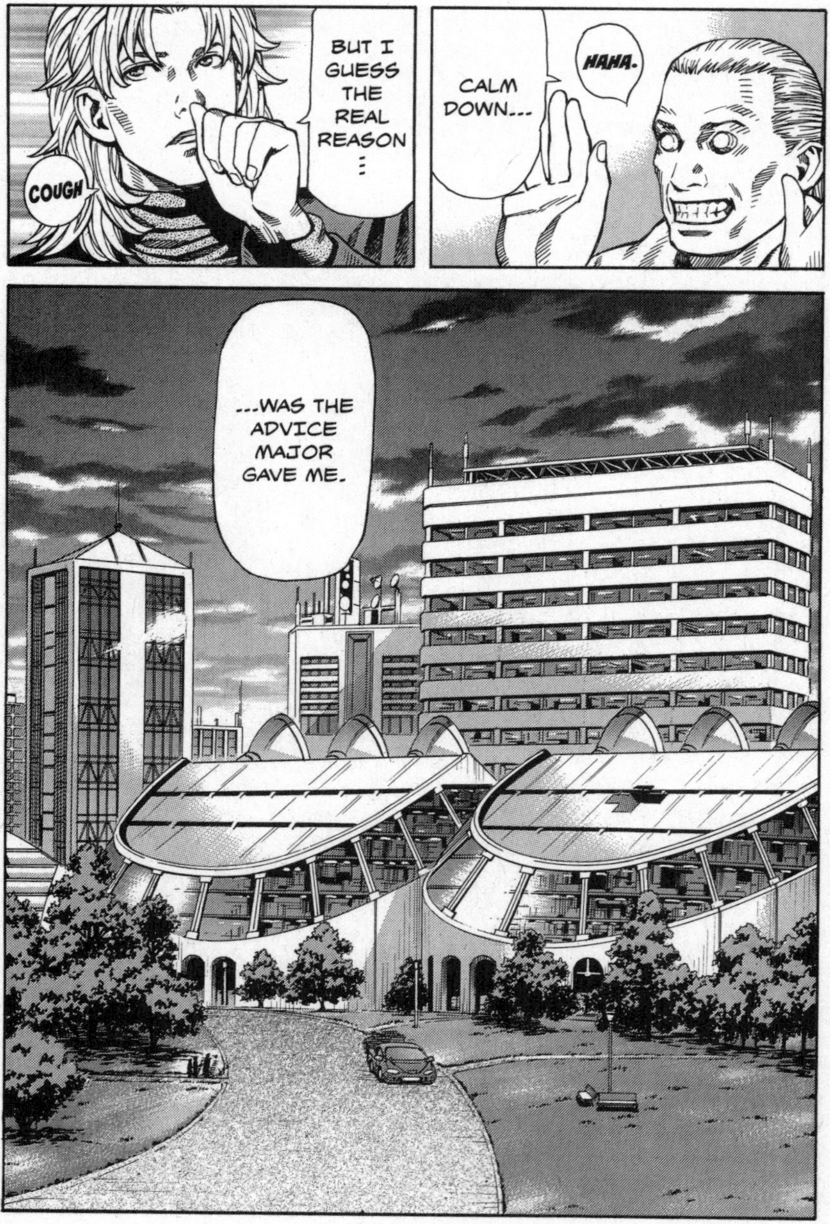
HAHA.
CALM DOWN...
BUT I GUESS THE REAL REASON ...
COUGH
...WAS THE ADVICE MAJOR GAVE ME.

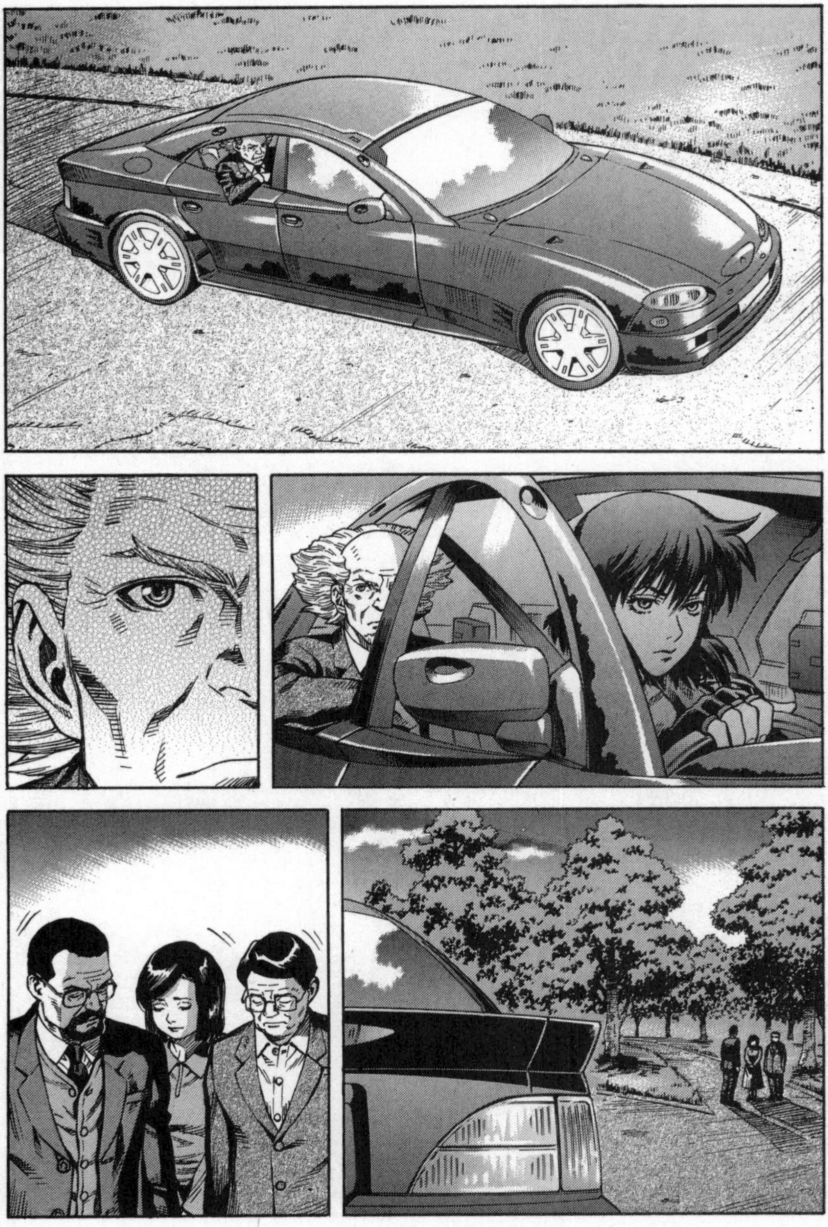

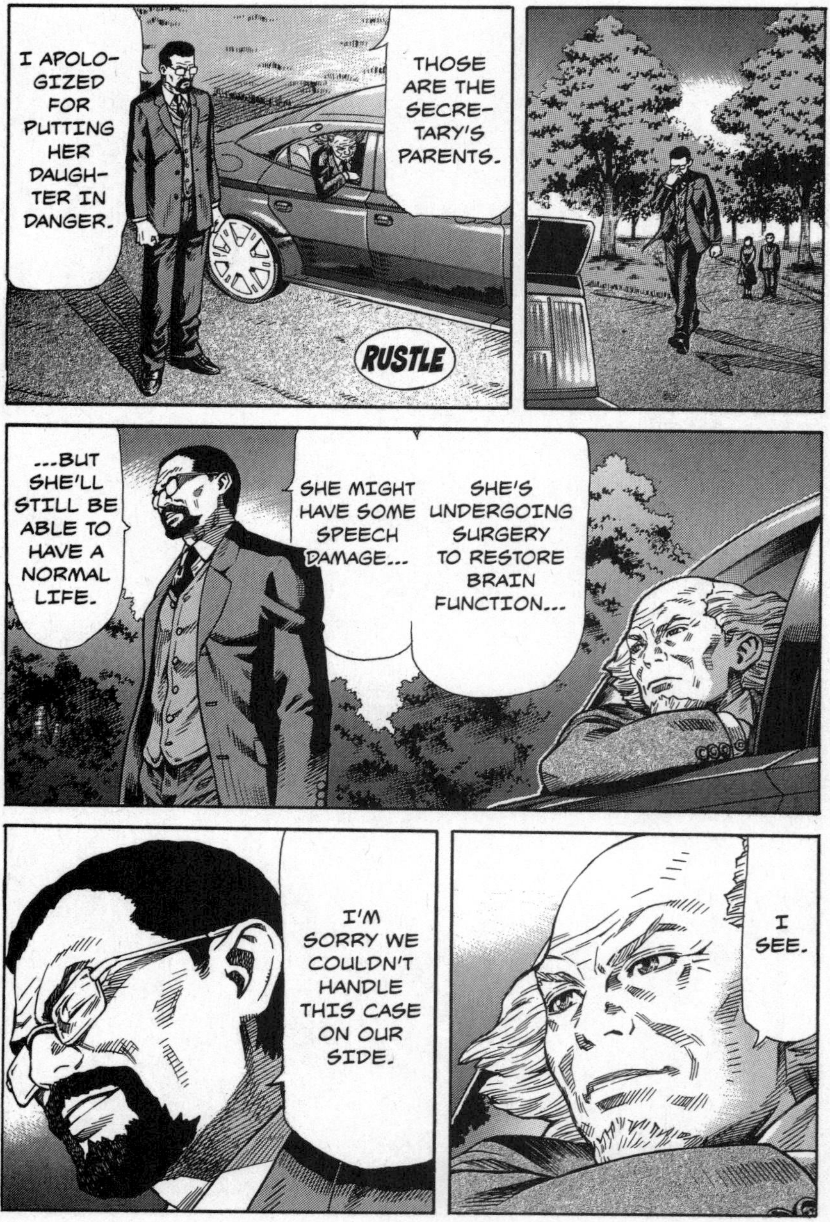
THOSE ARE THE SECRETARY'S PARENTS.
I APOLOGIZED FOR PUTTING HER DAUGHTER IN DANGER.
RUSTLE
SHE'S UNDERGOING SURGERY TO RESTORE BRAIN FUNCTION...
SHE MIGHT HAVE SOME SPEECH DAMAGE...
...BUT SHE'LL STILL BE ABLE TO HAVE A NORMAL LIFE.
I SEE.
I'M SORRY WE COULDN'T HANDLE THIS CASE ON OUR SIDE.

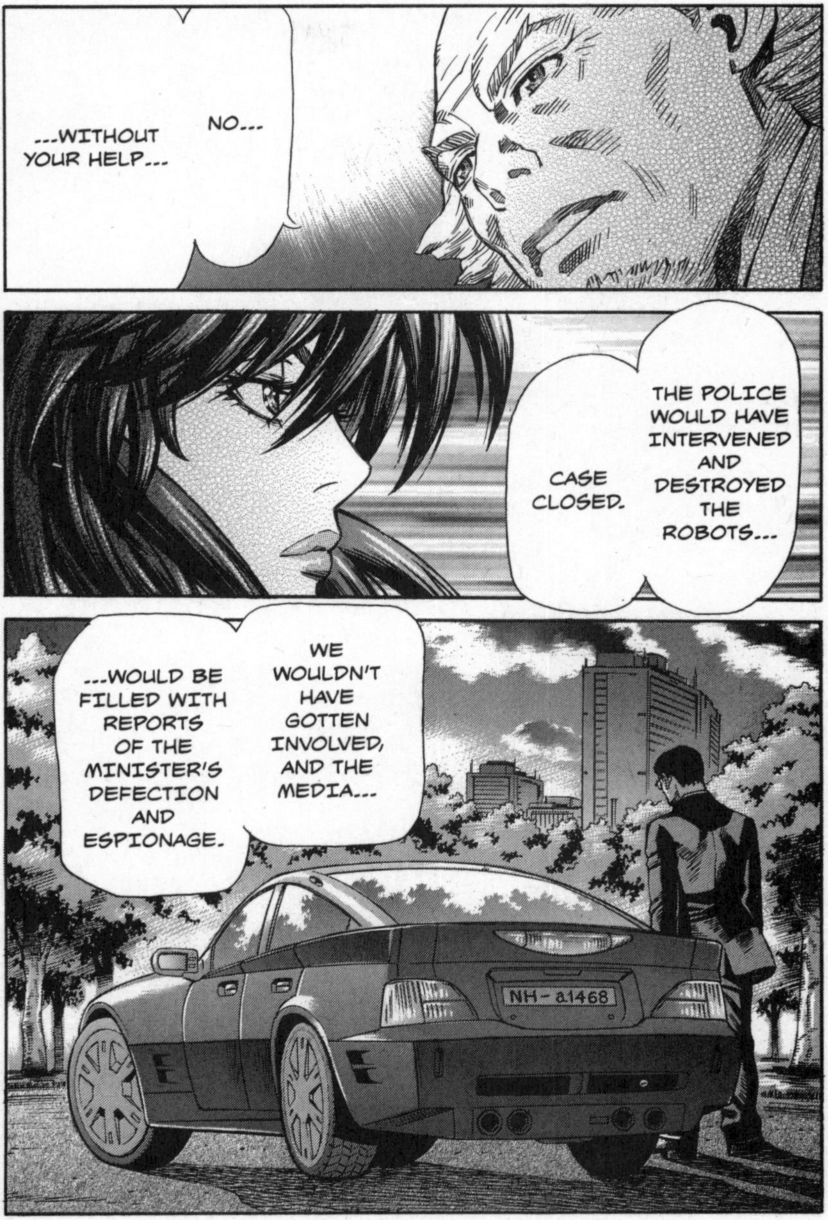
NO...
...WITHOUT YOUR HELP...
THE POLICE WOULD HAVE INTERVENED AND DESTROYED THE ROBOTS...
CASE CLOSED.
WE WOULDN'T HAVE GOTTEN INVOLVED, AND THE MEDIA...
...WOULD BE FILLED WITH REPORTS OF THE MINISTER'S DEFECTION AND ESPIONAGE.
NH-a1468

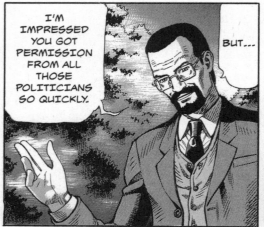
I'M IMPRESSED YOU GOT PERMISSION FROM ALL THOSE POLITICIANS SO QUICKLY.

BUT...

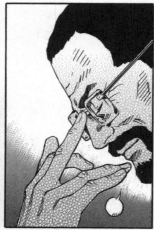

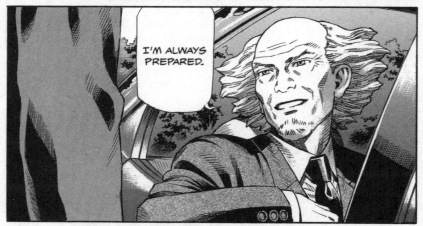
I'M ALWAYS PREPARED.

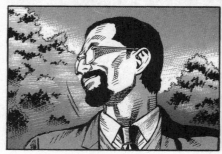

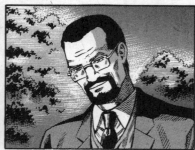

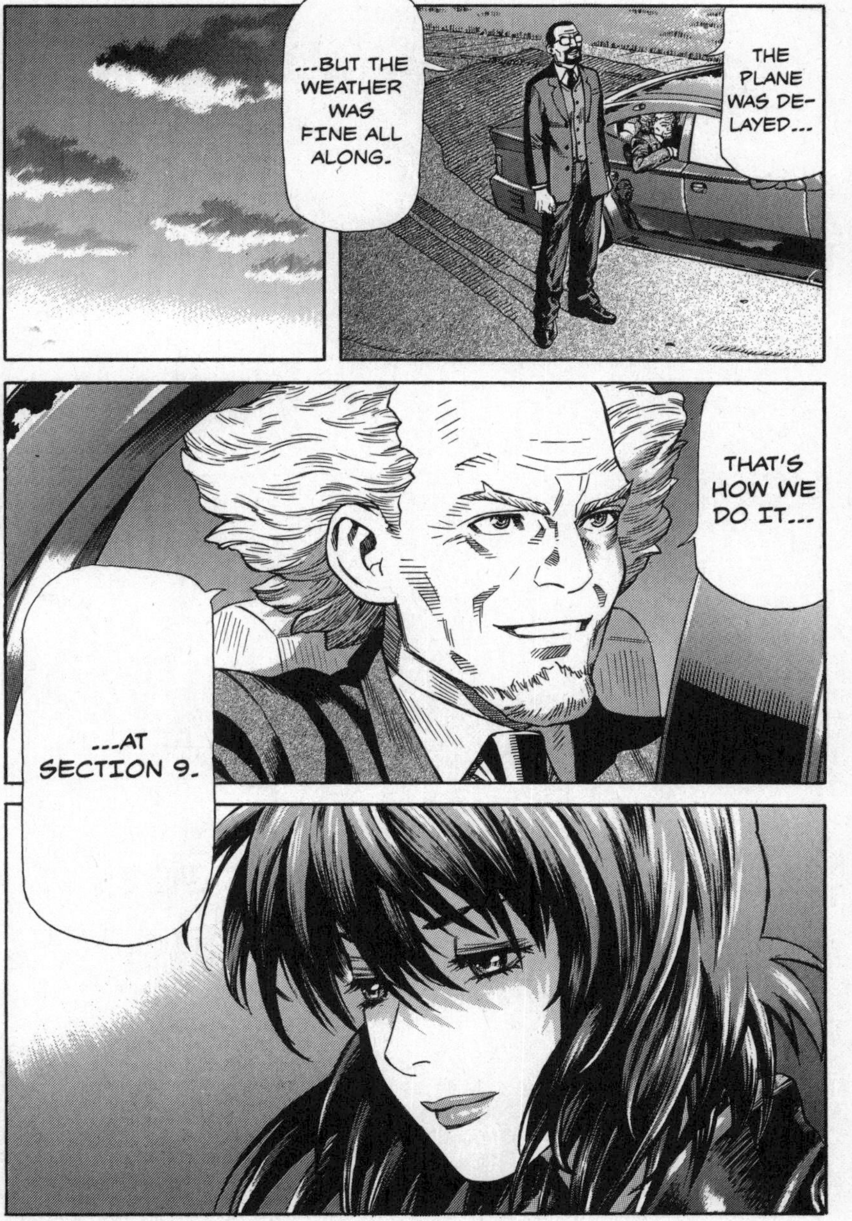
THE PLANE WAS DE-LAYED...
...BUT THE WEATHER WAS FINE ALL ALONG.
THAT'S HOW WE DO IT...
...AT SECTION 9.

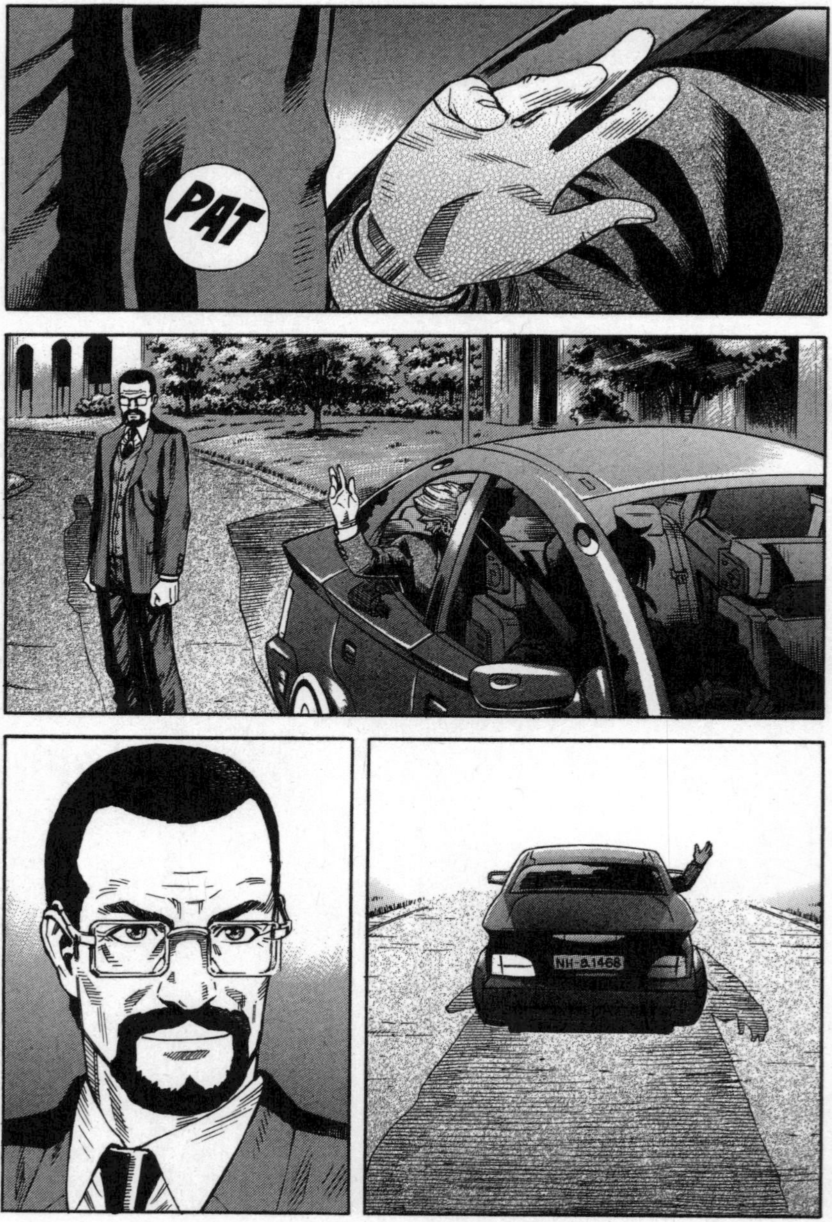
PAT

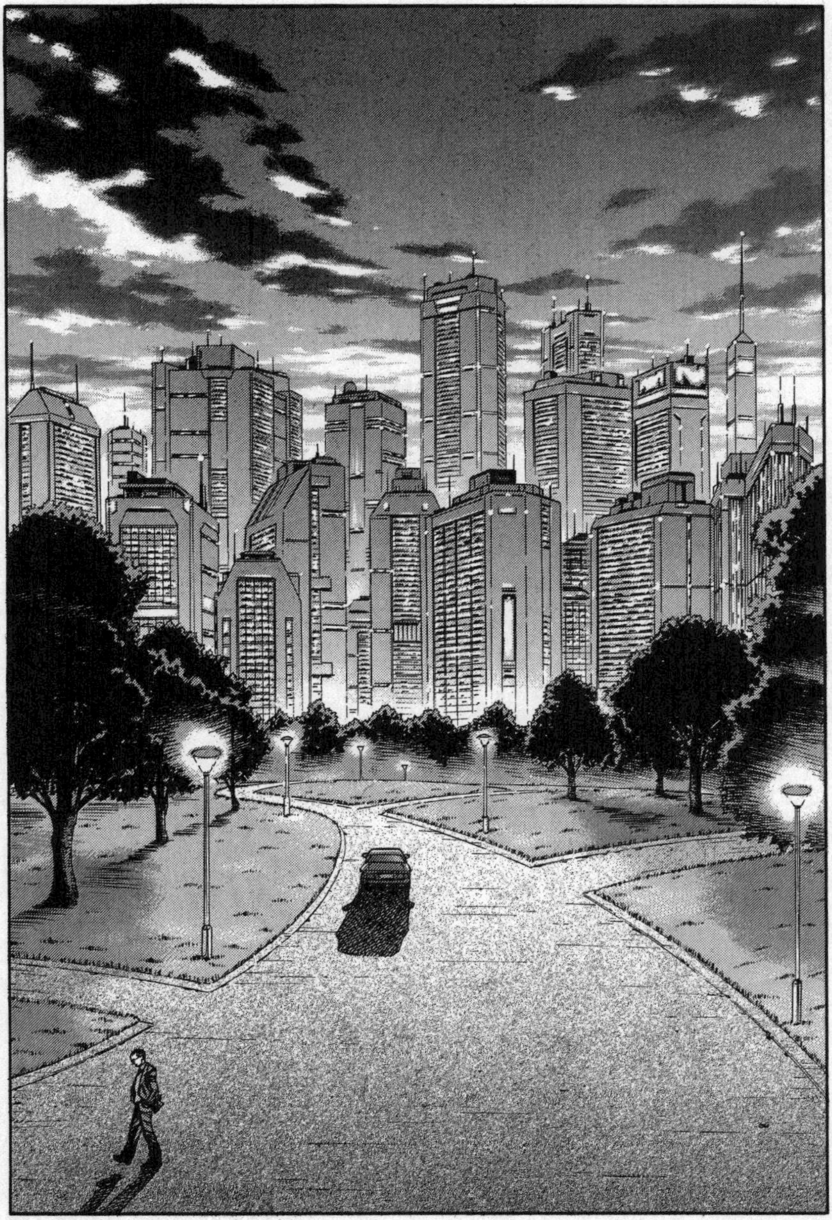

#011 END

Episode 1:Section 9 END

Bonus Manga

Ghost in the Shell S.A.C. Tachikoma Days

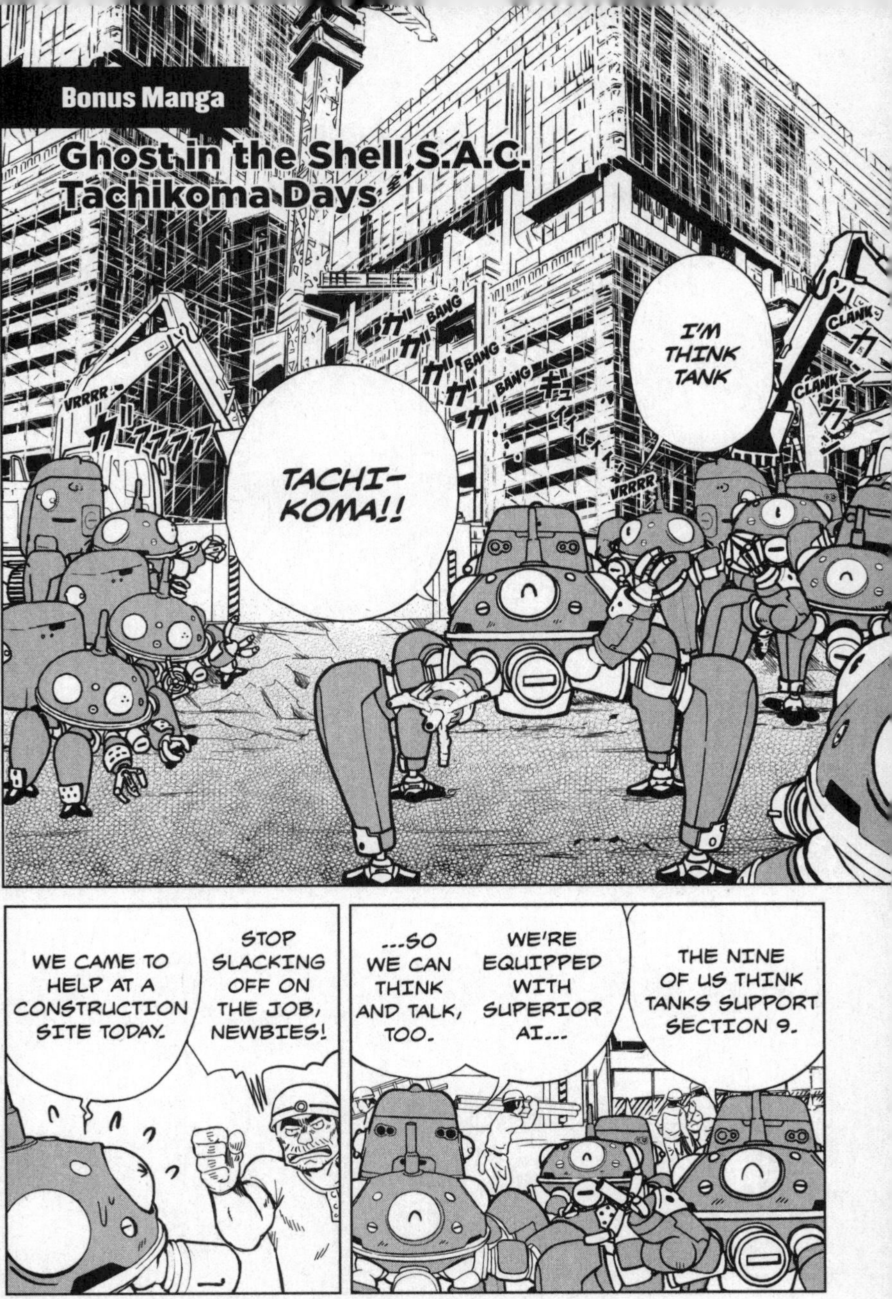

CLANK
CLANK
I'M THINK TANK
VRRRR
BANG
BANG
BANG
TACHI-KOMA!!
VRRRR
THE NINE OF US THINK TANKS SUPPORT SECTION 9.
WE'RE EQUIPPED WITH SUPERIOR AI...
...SO WE CAN THINK AND TALK, TOO.
STOP SLACKING OFF ON THE JOB, NEWBIES!
WE CAME TO HELP AT A CONSTRUCTION SITE TODAY.

Masayuki Yamamoto

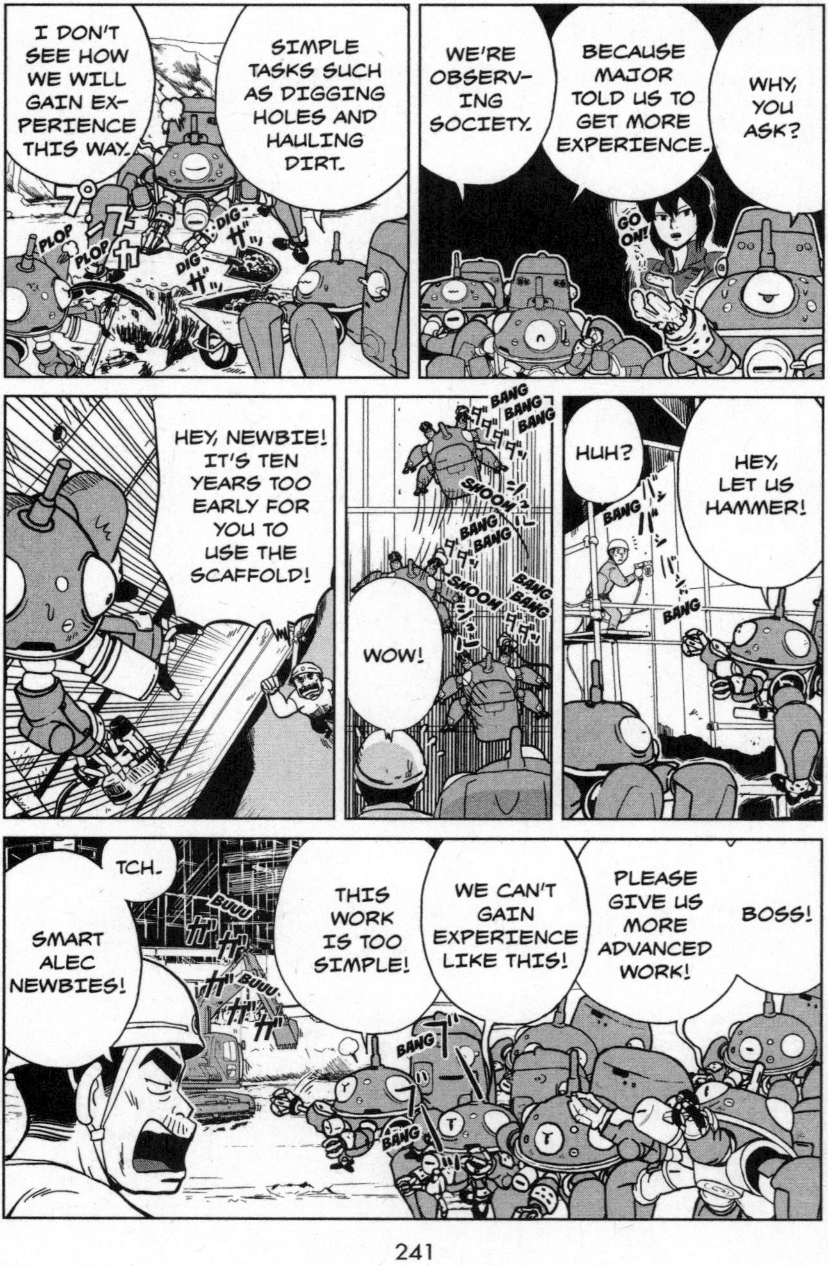
WHY, YOU ASK?
BECAUSE MAJOR TOLD US TO GET MORE EXPERIENCE.
WE'RE OBSERVING SOCIETY.
GO ON!
SIMPLE TASKS SUCH AS DIGGING HOLES AND HAULING DIRT.
I DON'T SEE HOW WE WILL GAIN EXPERIENCE THIS WAY.
DIG
DIG
PLOP
PLOP
HEY, LET US HAMMER!
HUH?
BANG
BANG
BANG BANG BANG
SHOOM
BANG BANG
SHOOM
BANG BANG
WOW!
HEY, NEWBIE! IT'S TEN YEARS TOO EARLY FOR YOU TO USE THE SCAFFOLD!
BOSS!
PLEASE GIVE US MORE ADVANCED WORK!
WE CAN'T GAIN EXPERIENCE LIKE THIS!
THIS WORK IS TOO SIMPLE!
BANG
BANG
TCH.
SMART ALEC NEWBIES!
BUUU
BUUU

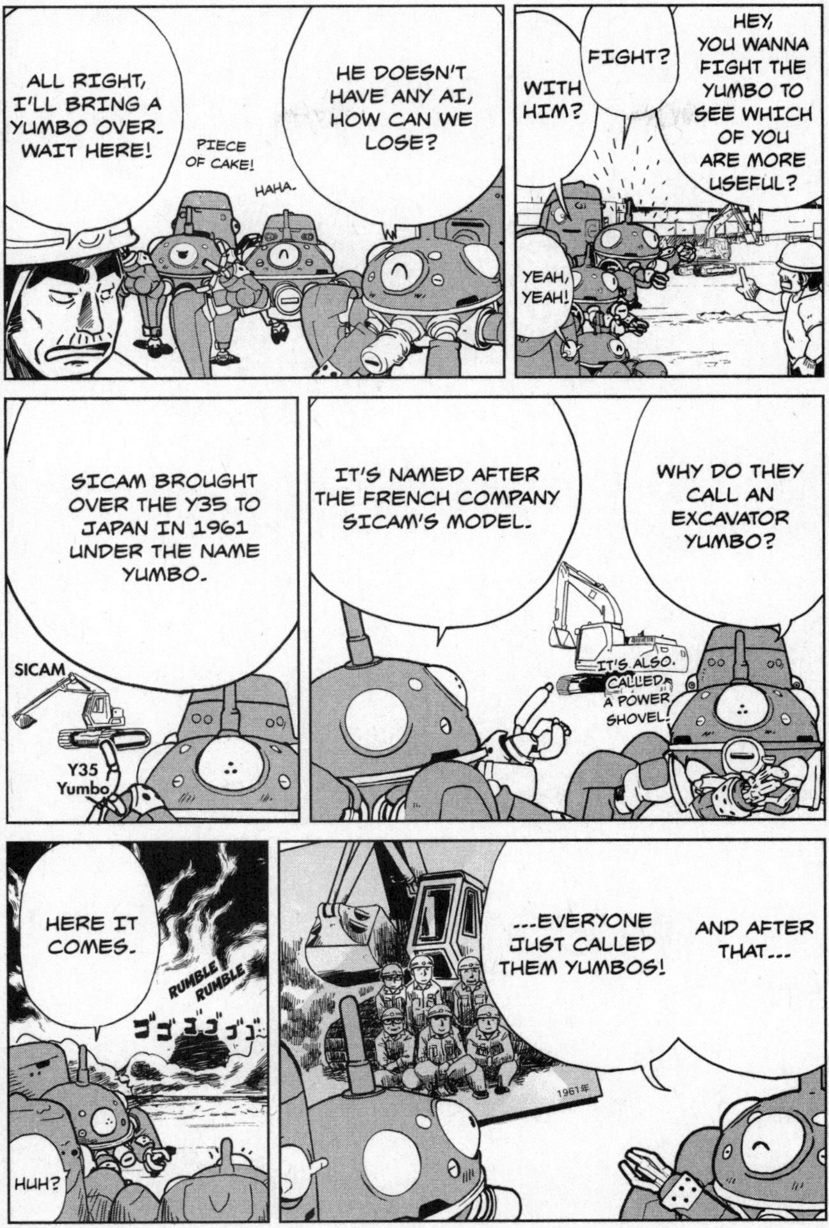
HEY, YOU WANNA FIGHT THE YUMBO TO SEE WHICH OF YOU ARE MORE USEFUL?
FIGHT?
WITH HIM?
YEAH, YEAH!
HE DOESN'T HAVE ANY AI, HOW CAN WE LOSE?
HAHA.
PIECE OF CAKE!
ALL RIGHT, I'LL BRING A YUMBO OVER. WAIT HERE!
WHY DO THEY CALL AN EXCAVATOR YUMBO?
IT'S NAMED AFTER THE FRENCH COMPANY SICAM'S MODEL.
IT'S ALSO CALLED A POWER SHOVEL.
SICAM BROUGHT OVER THE Y35 TO JAPAN IN 1961 UNDER THE NAME YUMBO.
SICAM
Y35 Yumbo
AND AFTER THAT...
...EVERYONE JUST CALLED THEM YUMBOS!
1961年
HERE IT COMES.
RUMBLE RUMBLE
HUH?

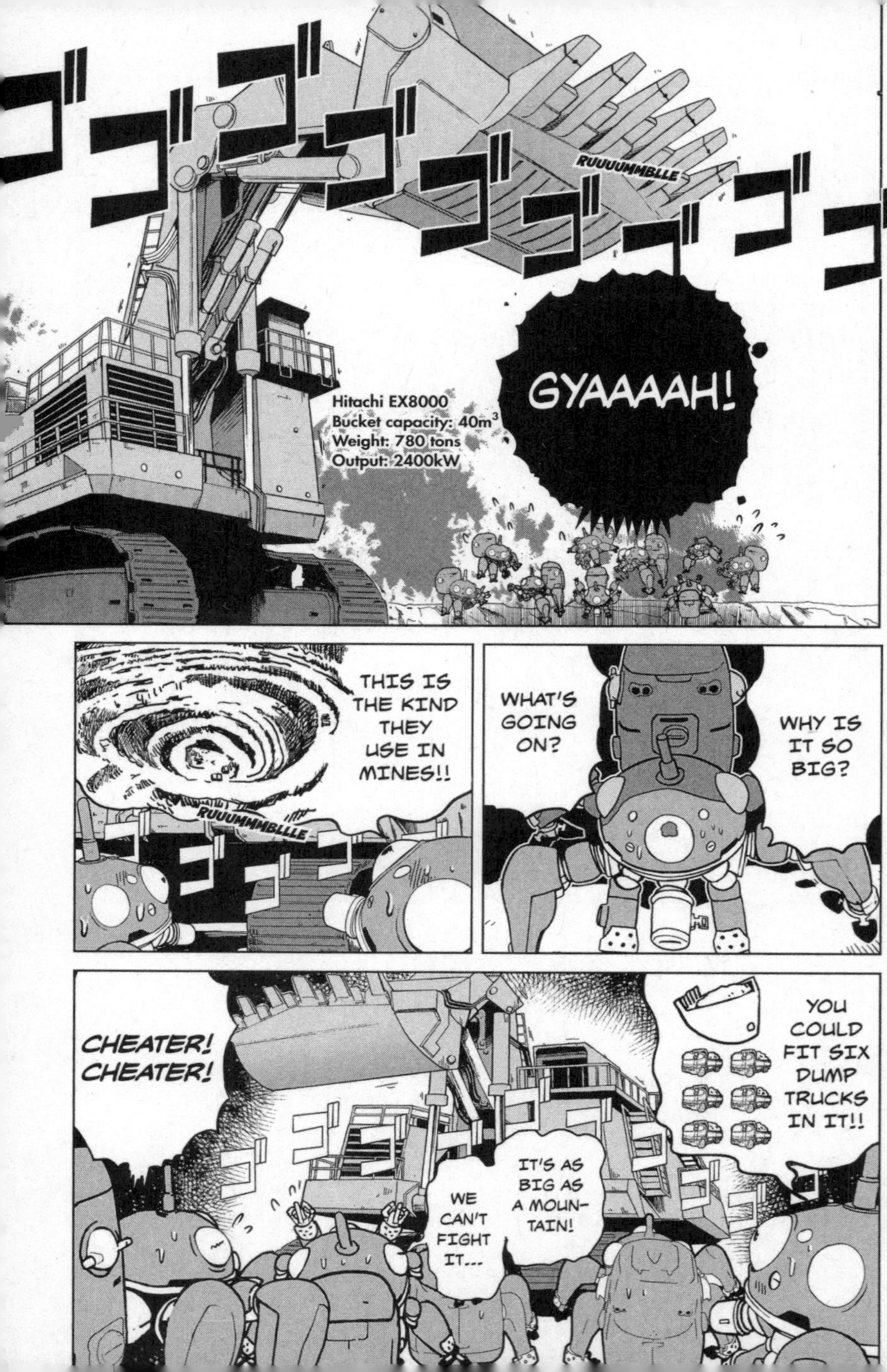
ゴゴゴゴゴゴゴゴ
RUUUUMMBLLE
GYAAAAH!
Hitachi EX8000
Bucket capacity: 40m³
Weight: 780 tons
Output: 2400kW
WHY IS IT SO BIG?
WHAT'S GOING ON?
THIS IS THE KIND THEY USE IN MINES!!
RUUUMMBLLLE
YOU COULD FIT SIX DUMP TRUCKS IN IT!!
CHEATER! CHEATER!
IT'S AS BIG AS A MOUN-TAIN!
WE CAN'T FIGHT IT...

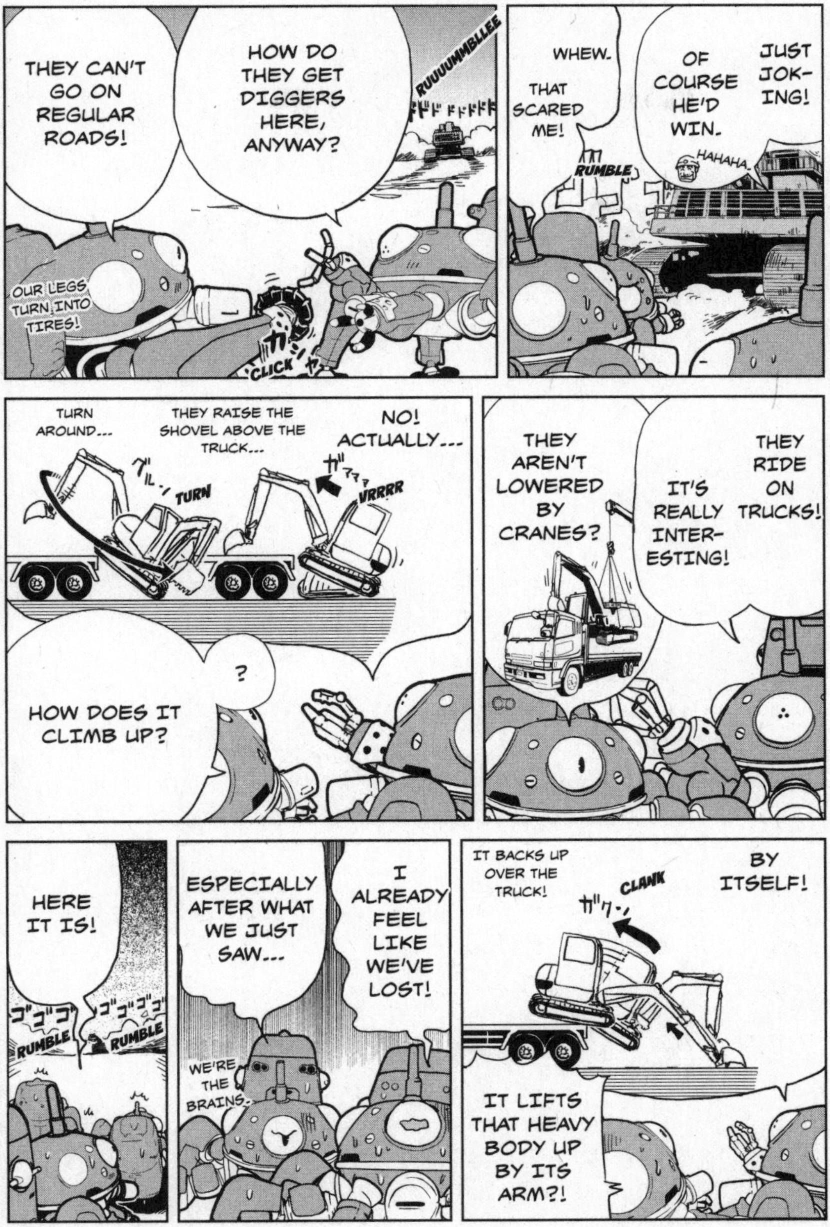
JUST JOK-ING!
OF COURSE HE'D WIN.
WHEW.
THAT SCARED ME!
HAHAHA.
RUMBLE
RUUUUMMBLLEE
HOW DO THEY GET DIGGERS HERE, ANYWAY?
THEY CAN'T GO ON REGULAR ROADS!
OUR LEGS TURN INTO TIRES!
CLICK
THEY RIDE ON TRUCKS!
IT'S REALLY INTER-ESTING!
THEY AREN'T LOWERED BY CRANES?
NO! ACTUALLY...
VRRRR
THEY RAISE THE SHOVEL ABOVE THE TRUCK...
TURN AROUND...
TURN
?
HOW DOES IT CLIMB UP?
BY ITSELF!
IT BACKS UP OVER THE TRUCK!
CLANK
IT LIFTS THAT HEAVY BODY UP BY ITS ARM?!
I ALREADY FEEL LIKE WE'VE LOST!
ESPECIALLY AFTER WHAT WE JUST SAW...
WE'RE THE BRAINS.
HERE IT IS!
RUMBLE
RUMBLE

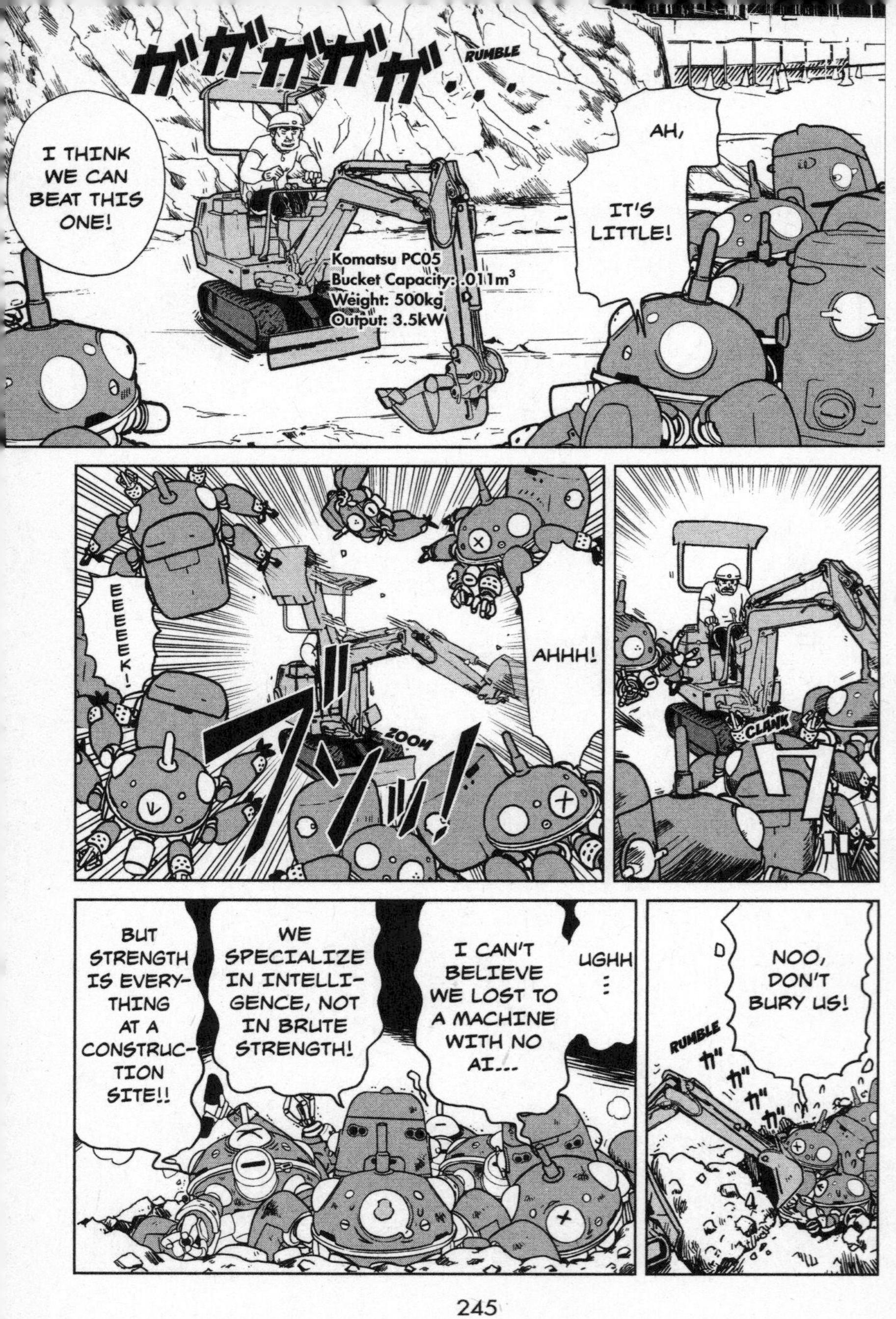
ガガガガガ
RUMBLE
AH,
IT'S LITTLE!
I THINK WE CAN BEAT THIS ONE!
Komatsu PC05
Bucket Capacity: .011m³
Weight: 500kg
Output: 3.5kW
CLANK
AHHH!
EEEEEK!
ブンッ!
ZOOM
NOO, DON'T BURY US!
RUMBLE
ガガガガ
UGHH...
I CAN'T BELIEVE WE LOST TO A MACHINE WITH NO AI...
WE SPECIALIZE IN INTELLIGENCE, NOT IN BRUTE STRENGTH!
BUT STRENGTH IS EVERYTHING AT A CONSTRUCTION SITE!!

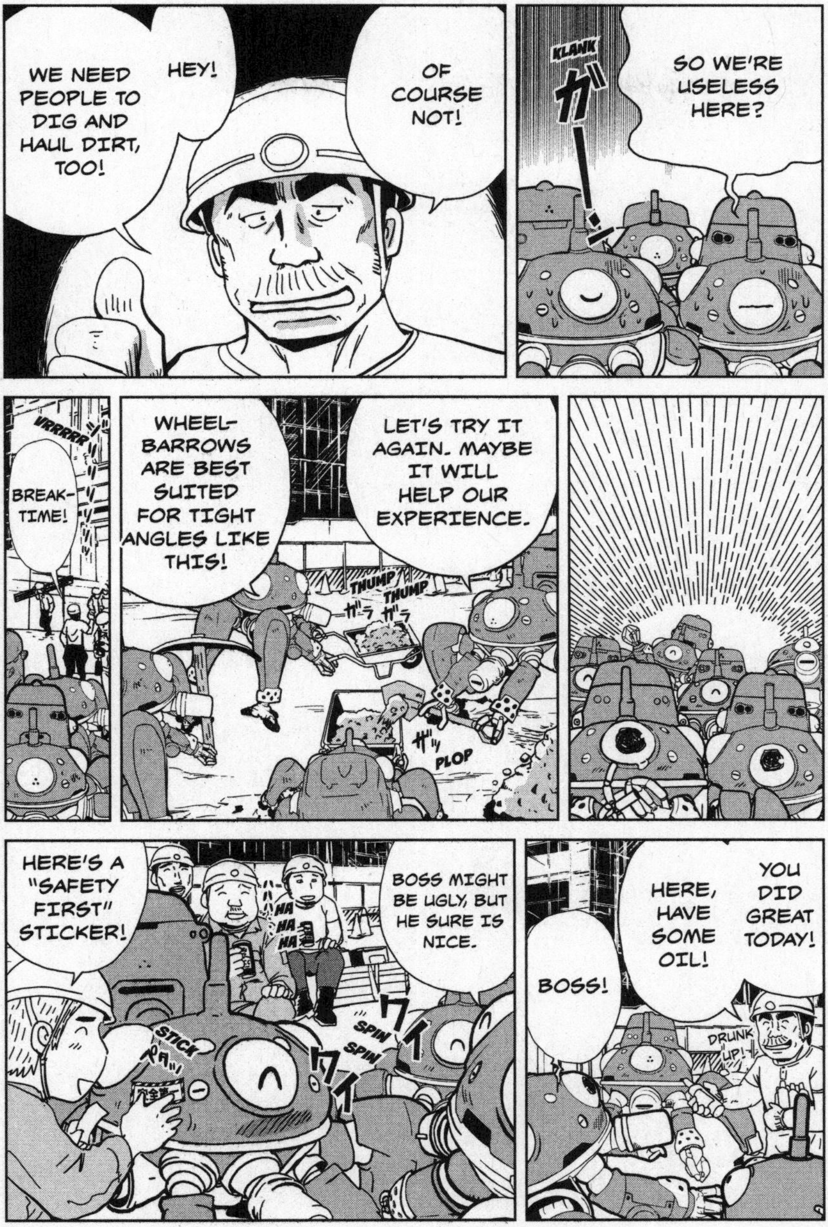
KLANK
SO WE'RE USELESS HERE?
OF COURSE NOT!
HEY!
WE NEED PEOPLE TO DIG AND HAUL DIRT, TOO!
LET'S TRY IT AGAIN. MAYBE IT WILL HELP OUR EXPERIENCE.
WHEEL-BARROWS ARE BEST SUITED FOR TIGHT ANGLES LIKE THIS!
THUMP THUMP
PLOP
VRRRRR
BREAK-TIME!
YOU DID GREAT TODAY!
HERE, HAVE SOME OIL!
BOSS!
DRUNK UP!
BOSS MIGHT BE UGLY, BUT HE SURE IS NICE.
HA HA HA
HERE'S A "SAFETY FIRST" STICKER!
STICK
SPIN SPIN

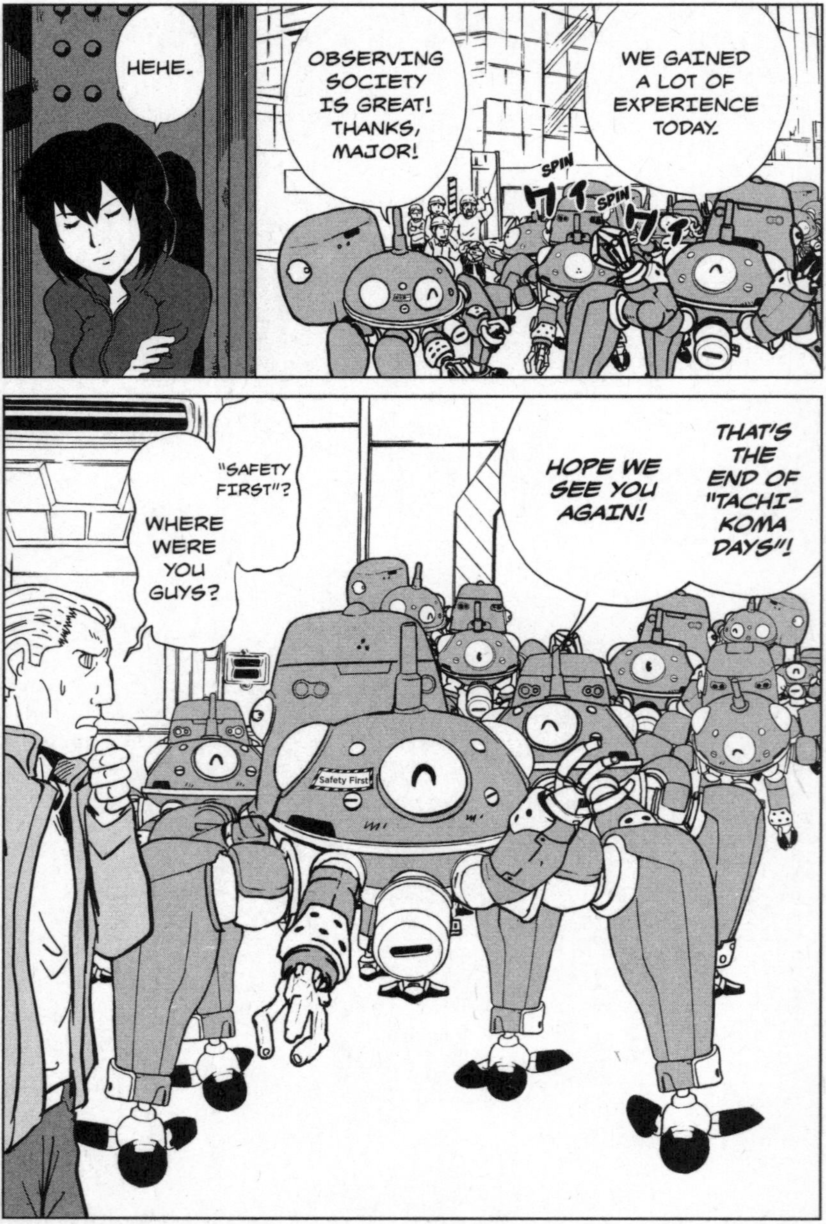
WE GAINED A LOT OF EXPERIENCE TODAY.
OBSERVING SOCIETY IS GREAT! THANKS, MAJOR!
SPIN
SPIN
HEHE.
THAT'S THE END OF "TACHI-KOMA DAYS"!
HOPE WE SEE YOU AGAIN!
"SAFETY FIRST"?
WHERE WERE YOU GUYS?
Safety First

BONUS MANGA / END

TRANSLATION NOTES

Japanese is a tricky language for most Westerners, and translation is often more art than science. For your edification and reading pleasure, here are notes on some of the places where we could have gone in a different direction with our translation of the work, or where a Japanese cultural reference is used.

ASSEMBLE THE TEAM WITH A2 LOADOUT!
CHAKK
CHAKK
CHAKK
LOCATION 82-D3!
CHAKK

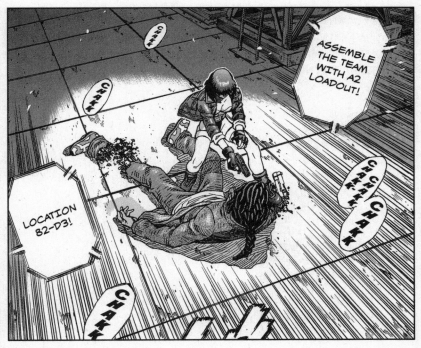

Loadout, p 23

A military term describing specific equipment, ammunition, tools, and clothing to be used during an operation.

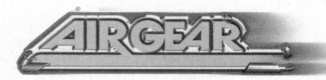

AIR GEAR

BY OH!GREAT

AIRGEAR
1
Oh!great

Itsuki Minami needs no introduction—everybody's heard of the "Babyface" of the Eastside. He's the strongest kid at Higashi Junior High School, easy on the eyes but dangerously tough when he needs to be. Plus, Itsuki lives with the mysterious and sexy Noyamano sisters. Life's never dull, but it becomes downright dangerous when Itsuki leads his school to victory over vindictive Westside punks with gangster connections. Now he stands to lose his school, his friends, and everything he cares about. But in his darkest hour, the Noyamano girls give him an amazing gift, one that just might help him save his school: a pair of Air Trecks. These high-tech skates are more than just supercool. They'll enable Itsuki to execute the wildest, most aggressive moves ever seen—and introduce him to a thrilling and terrifying new world.

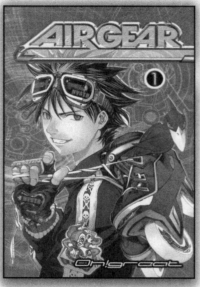

Ages: 16+

Special extras in each volume! Read them all!

KC KODANSHA COMICS

VISIT WWW.KODANSHACOMICS.COM TO:

- View release date calendars for upcoming volumes
- Find out the latest about new Kodansha Comics series

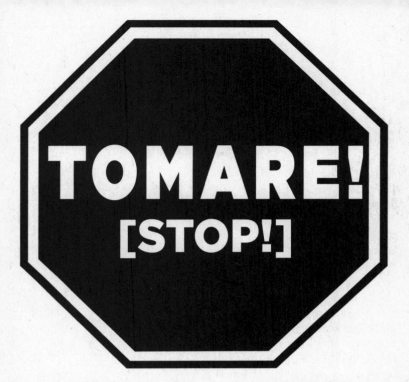

TOMARE!
[STOP!]

You are going the wrong way!

Manga is a completely different type of reading experience.

To start at the *beginning*, go to the *end*!

That's right! Authentic manga is read the traditional Japanese way—from right to left, exactly the *opposite* of how American books are read. It's easy to follow: Just go to the other end of the book, and read each page—and each panel—from right side to left side, starting at the top right. Now you're experiencing manga as it was meant to be.